THE LIAR'S TALE

A HISTORY OF FALSEHOOD

The Liar's Tale

JEREMY CAMPBELL

W. W. Norton & Company

New York · London

Excerpt on pages 54–55: Reprinted by permission of the publishers and the Trustees of the
Loeb Classical Library from *Plato: Volume II*, Loeb Classical Library Volume L165, translated by
W. R. Lamb, Cambridge, Mass.: Harvard University Press, 1924. The Loeb Classical Library ®
is a registered trademark of the President and Fellows of Harvard College.

For information about permission to reproduce selections from this book, write to Permis-
sions, W. W. Norton & Company, Inc., 500 Fifth Avenue, New York, NY 10110

The text of this book is composed in Legacy Serif,
with the display set in Goudy Text and Avenir Black.
Composition by Sue Carlson
Manufacturing by Quebecor Fairfield
Book design by Charlotte Staub
Production manager: Julia Druskin

Library of Congress Cataloging-in-Publication Data

Campbell, Jeremy, 1931–
    The liar's tale : a history of falsehood / by Jeremy Campbell.
        p. cm.
    Includes bibliographical references and index.
    ISBN 0-393-02559-4
1. Truthfulness and falsehood—History. I. Title.
BJ1421 .C35 2001
177'.3—dc21   2001030286

ISBN 0-393-32361-7 pbk.

W. W. Norton & Company, Inc., 500 Fifth Avenue, New York, N.Y. 10110
www.wwnorton.com

W. W. Norton & Company Ltd., Castle House, 75/76 Wells Street, London W1T 3QT

1 2 3 4 5 6 7 8 9 0

For Judith and Robert Martin.
Good companions and good times,
in magical places.

Contents

Introduction   11

1 The Horrid Doubt   17

2 The Evolution of Cunning   31

3 Enter the Logos   43

4 The Absolute Talker   58

5 The Double Truth   74

6 The Imp of Falsehood   89

7 The Suicidal Tendencies of Reason   102

8 Interlude: The Simple Truth   112

9 The Inner Light   127

10 Truth at Arm's Length   141

11 The Pleasures of Falsehood   157

12 A Cloak for Quite Different Impulses   173

13 Curing by Fiction   186

14 Pretty, Shining Lies   203

15 A Life of Its Own   220

16 Playing the Truth Game   235

17 Giving Truth a Bad Name   252

18 Language Made Me Do It   266

19 A Certain Kind of Madness   285

20 Good at Being Human   302

Notes   315

Index   345

THE LIAR'S TALE

Introduction

*The Kaiser Family Foundation reported that physicians routinely give mislead-
ing statements to insurance companies in order to secure patient reimbursement
for treatments the physicians believe to be necessary. And most physicians
believe that, if such lying did not occur, substandard care would be routine,
because insurance companies are so loath to approve expensive treatments.*
　　　—The New Republic

*Many categories of responses which are misleading, evasive, nonresponsive or
frustrating are nevertheless not legally "false" [including] literally truthful
answers that imply facts that are not true.*
　　　—Legal brief filed by President Clinton's lawyers to a committee
　　　of the Arkansas Supreme Court which recommended that he
　　　be disbarred for "serious misconduct"

 PAIR OF UNIVERSITY STUDENTS FAKE AN
ugly demonstration of hate, hanging a black doll from a
noose in a tree. The students are black. Their fabrication
is exposed; nevertheless, it is thought worthwhile as a
means of highlighting the issue of race relations on campus. One
way of looking at the incident is to call it a piece of theater, a drama-
tization of something that might have happened; and, as in all forms
of art, the fiction seems more significant, more important, even more
loyal to life, than mere fact. The fraudulence of the hoax is a petty
consideration alongside its larger intent to highlight a piece of social
injustice.

Alternatively, one could call it a barefaced lie.

College authorities tend to take the view that fictitious dramati-
zations masquerading as plain fact are more effective than truth in
jolting the university body into facing up to malignancies in their
midst. Falsehood in a good cause has a value that reality lacks.

"There are things much more important than civility." A political
journalist quotes this statement with approval, lamenting the fact
that a revival of politeness undermines radical forms of anti-
establishment dissent. Good manners, he thinks, are a kind of men-

dacity, a vehicle of falsehood, a "theater of operations" to conceal the wrongdoing of those in power. Similarly, it is a creeping assumption at the start of a new millennium that there are things more important than truth.

In itself, this is nothing new. Socrates was told as much twenty-five centuries ago by a man of the theater. But the idea that truth is a pigmy, a midget, a dullard, and a bore in contrast to the scintillating and extraordinary inventions of falsehood is more fashionable now than it has ever been.

David Stoll, a professor at Middleburg College, examined an autobiographical account of the civil war in Guatemala by Rigoberta Menchu, who won the Nobel Peace Prize in 1992. A social democrat with no particular ax to grind, Stoll listed an impressive number of exaggerations and falsehoods in the book. A brother the author said she saw starve to death is actually alive and well in Guatemala. Her depiction of childhood poverty and illiteracy comports poorly with the fact that she attended two private boarding schools. Yet academics of high repute were furious with Stoll for putting obstacles in the path of justice for the oppressed and assisting the case of U.S. imperialism. "Whether her book is true or not, I don't care," wrote Wellesley College professor Marjorie Agosin. "We should teach our students about the brutality of the Guatemalan army and the U.S. financing of it." The Nobel Prize Committee also came to the rescue: "All autobiographies embellish to a greater or lesser extent." The author of a biography of Ronald Reagan, baffled by the opaque surface of his elusive subject, reeling under the banal and trite materials of the presidential diaries, invents a fictional narrator as a way of providing the human drama, the prodigality of meanings, that bare facts are unable to supply

To refuse to embellish is to rule out possibilities, which are the source of new meanings. Four centuries ago Montaigne wrote that, while there are an infinite number of falsehoods, there is only one Truth. When art takes hold of history, it may rearrange it in order to liberate ideas more illuminating than those life grudgingly dispenses. A new dramatic genre, "theater as metabiography," puts Freud in a room with Salvador Dali and has Orson Welles converse with

Vivien Leigh. Though these encounters may have taken place under other circumstances, facts can always do with a little improving. In metabiography, we are told, "lives are transformed, abstracted and mythologised in pursuit of more essential truths."

Psychoanalysis was based on the idea that falsehood and illusion are useful clues to understanding the mystery of human personality. Freud took with many a pinch of salt what his patients told him under the heading of unvarnished fact, but he held the view that lies are often more informative than literal truths. In an odd way, they are privileged information.

The emergence of modernism, a movement that lasted for more than half a century, coincided with a time of widespread disillusion with political action. Modernism tended to prize the arts as superior to the sciences; what is more, the arts aspired to be at least the equal of the Philistine world of politics and commerce in their power to remake society. Modernism was a lineal descendant of the art for art's sake cult of the late Victorian era, one of whose practitioners, Walter Pater, talked about "aesthetic truth," a new sort of veracity fit for a world of civilized artifice, a world where the given truths of nature recede and the inventions of culture require us to search for truth by an entirely different route. Picasso wrapped this thought in a famous paradox: "Art is the lie that makes us realize the truth."

In the modernist novel, lies and liars proliferate, reflecting a deep suspicion of the value of truth in its literal, public form. Obscurity becomes a trademark of modernist writing, a device that obliterates the easy attunement between the mind of the author and that of the reader and renders suspect the notion that truth is single or simple, that it can be communicated at all through the suspect vehicle of language, or even that it is desirable to do so.

Late twentieth-century intellectual fashion carries these tendencies to egregious extremes. A shift of emphasis from truth to meaning, in play since the eighteenth century, acquires fantastic new dimensions. Art for art's sake becomes language for the sake of language, which is now the chief focus, even the obsession of philosophy. Language becomes a centrifuge, throwing out untethered meanings. It loses its connection with logic, where a proposition is either true or false. Words do not refer to things, or to specific concepts, but only to other words. The idea takes hold that language is not primarily communication, that it is treacherous to the intentions of the author, so that its role as a vehicle of sincerity and truth is fatally compromised. Deconstruction, the literary cult of postmodernism, is a form of close reading which sees language as unstable to the core, riven by internal conflicts, breaking up into layers of meaning that never terminate; meaning is something that leaks, spills, overflows, seeps, from one text into a profusion of others.

One author, one interpretation, is not enough to satisfy our era's appetite for possibilities, its preference for the new and surprising over the familiar and obvious. Roger Shattuck argues that what he calls the "Demon of Originality" demands insatiably an endless supply of interesting fictions. In the Middle Ages the word "original" meant that something had existed from the beginning, but in the eighteenth century it took on the sense of coming into existence for the first time, of being entirely different from anything that went before. An original person was bizarre, extravagant. Today, the need for the new is so intense as to foster a desire to annihilate everything that is not new. Philosophers call for an end to philosophy. Consciousness, the instrument René Descartes trusted to deliver truth by subtracting possibilities, is now an obstruction, an impediment. The postmodern thinker Roland Barthes said that only "absolute newness" gives him full satisfaction, because it weakens consciousness.

Literal truth-telling may even be a symptom of mental inadequacy, a clinical defect, a manifestation of the abnormal. Autistic children, it turns out, are handicapped by an inability to lie, to pretend and conceal. An autistic child lacks a "theory of mind" by means of which healthy children are able to attribute certain beliefs and desires to other people, and thus trick them into false beliefs. There is a preference for sameness, an aversion to novelty, an avoidance of differences. Parents sometimes feel a distinct sense of relief when their autistic child, competent in other respects, tells his first clumsy lie in his teens.

The theme of this book is that, for better or worse, lying, untruth, is not an artificial, deviant, or dispensable feature of life. Nature engages in it, sometimes with remarkable ingenuity. Art, with its "telling of beautiful, untrue things," has at times so dominated the mind of a period thinkers could seriously argue that life may be understood truthfully only in aesthetic terms. The impulse to transcend mere literal fact occurs throughout nature. Quite humble biological organisms evolve as a semblance, an alias; a pictorial rendering of some other, less vulnerable organism. Might we not say, for example, that species of *Cycloptera*, insects that resemble leaves, trompe d'oeil masterpieces which might have been painted by a seventeenth-century Dutch master, perfect in color, shape, and size, even complete with imitation veins and fungus spots, are works of art?

It is a seductive hypothesis that falsehood is "on the side of life," is the lubricant that makes society run, while truth can be harsh, dangerous, and destructive; too simple, too naked, for the complexities of twenty-first-century society, inheritor of one of the most brutal hundred years in the history of mankind. To survive in such a society, human beings have evolved, in Nicholas Humphrey's phrase, as "born psychologists," natural mind-readers, whose insights into the thoughts of others enable them both to ease their fears and to manipulate those other minds with the subtlest kinds of deception. The rise of evolutionary psychology, the belief in the curative powers of fiction, the need to accept what ought to be true as if it were true, have all contributed to an almost unprecedented tolerance of falsehood.

Friedrich Nietzsche called the world cruel, contradictory, misleading, and senseless, and concluded that we *need* lies in order to live with such an abhorrent reality. That lying is a necessity of life is part of the terrifying and problematic character of existence. We have come full circle from the ancient thesis that truth and goodness are inseparable twins. The notion embedded in our cultural attitudes is that humanity would never have stayed the grueling course to its present high place on the evolutionary ladder on a diet as thin and meager as the truth. "We secrete from within ourselves," wrote George Steiner, "the grammar, the mythologies of hope, of fantasy, of self-deception without which we would have been arrested at some rung of primate behavior or would, long since, have destroyed ourselves."

The irony, of course, is that lying cannot hope to succeed in its aim unless truth is the normal practice of a society. In the nineteenth century there was a sense that democracy, more than other forms of government, needed truthfulness if it was to increase and flourish, that mendacity in a politician was more to be deplored than any other category of offense. The converse of that view is that in a system which draws much of its strength from candor, lies are all the more effective, all the more insidious. For that reason, so this argument goes, they will never be removed from our type of democratic community. But if lying becomes the norm, on the thesis that it softens the "cruelty" of life, it defeats its own purpose. Truth might then become more powerful than untruth, as in George Orwell's bureaucratic nightmare, *1984*, where a person who dared to speak the truth was so dangerous to the state as to be in urgent need of liquidation.

CHAPTER ONE

The Horrid Doubt

If, as Western ethics and theology purport, the existence of some creatures serves solely to benefit others, and honesty and altruism are always the best policy, how are we to explain the occurrence and ubiquitousness of selfishness and deception? —Emil Wenzel

S NATURE A LIAR? A DELIBERATELY PROVOCA-tive opening. Yet Charles Darwin, decidedly not a provocative person by temperament or inclination, suggested it might be helpful when trying to understand how nature keeps the enterprise of life in business and engineers her new and wonderful productions, to think of her, not as the embodiment of a Creator's truth, but as partly insincere, as harboring a propensity for cheating.

Evolution theory can accommodate the idea of cooperation, in which like tells the truth to like, but it must also face up to the harsher facts of competition, where rules of fair play and honesty need not apply, or of actual war, in which fraud is a positive asset. The spider is not obliged to warn its insect victims of possible health hazards if they make contact with its web, nor need the fox feel badly about shamming dead when it is really very much alive, and hungry. When winning is the important factor, deceitfulness is a kind of ethic, small lies serving nature's larger truth, the "grandeur" that Darwin saw when "from the war of nature, from famine and death, the most exalted object which we are capable of conceiving, namely the production of the higher animals, directly follows."

In the world of life, even fairly primitive life, Darwin recognized that falsehoods and chicanery are part of the game of survival. Writing in the *Descent of Man*, he commended as "admirable" a paper by the entomologist Henry Walter Bates on mimicry in nature, published in 1862. Bates had accompanied Alfred Wallace, the co-discoverer of evolution, on his first trip to South America, making a special study of the brightly colored insects of the Amazon forests. The paper, Darwin said, threw "a flood of light on many obscure problems," giving new support to his theory of natural selection. Mimicry in effect was a pretense, a form of lying, a means of gaining an edge on survival by deceiving predators as to the "real" character of their potential victims, though of course no intelligence would be involved. Darwin was struck by the "marvelously deceptive appearance" of certain butterflies observed by Bates, which imitate the markings of the *Helicondae*, a species which protects itself by secreting a noxious substance, disgusting to predators. The stripes and shades of color on the wings of the impersonators are amazingly realistic forgeries, resembling those of the *Helicondae* so closely that only an experienced entomologist like Bates could tell them apart. Though perfectly edible, they dupe birds into avoiding them under the misconception that they are thoroughly unappetizing.

Cheating, seen as an evolutionary strategy, helped Darwin to solve the puzzle of why some male butterflies of the order of the *Leptalides* have wings of which the upper half is a pure white, while the rest is barred with black, red, and yellow, in imitation of another species. The answer is that this butterfly usually hides the white patch by covering it with the upper wing, except when it is courting a female, who finds the "genuine" markings of her order more alluring than the spurious ones proclaiming the male to be something he is not.

Adaptation to the conditions of life, which Darwin's theoretician-philosopher colleague Herbert Spencer considered basic to all ethical progress, can and does involve deception. That is a major theme of evolutionary studies today. Certain species flourishing now might be extinct if they had depended on truthfulness to increase and multiply. Mock shows are part of evolution's stock in trade. Orchids mimic the look of female insects, and thus invite pollination by males. Pied flycatchers masquerade as bachelors by keeping a mate in a secret place, thereby seducing unsuspecting females into supposing them single, and therefore mate material. There is a tropical fish called a blenny, a confidence trickster which impersonates fish known as cleaners; these perform a service to larger fish by removing parasites from their bodies. The true cleaner and the host fish are attuned to each other as part of natural selection. The impostor adopts vivid stripes on the lateral surfaces of its body, resembling the cleaner. Lurking in the crevices of rocks, it does not clean passing fish, but instead rips off pieces of their flesh.

Cuckoos lay eggs that mimic those of the bird into whose nest they gatecrash. A reed warbler will accept and nurture a green egg planted there by a cuckoo, which specializes in fooling such a host into providing free accommodation and mothering; a meadow pipit is taken in by brown and spotted ones. Ingrates all, the chicks that hatch from these "counterfeit" eggs promptly throw the genuine eggs out of the nest. When fully fledged, they make off without so much as a thank you to join members of their own species; they have nothing further to do with the host parents, who never tumble to the fact that they have been duped.

Quite recently, it has been found that a certain genus of beetle, *Phyllobaenus*, has found a way to trick a plant into feeding it, a privilege previously thought by biologists to be reserved exclusively for a single species of ant, *Pheidole bicornis*. The ants reside inside the small tropical tree of the genus *Piper*, which provides them with food and shelter. The inside surface of the tree produces food which ants take and give to their larvae. The food appears only when *Pheidole* ants are in residence, and disappears when they are absent. It is as if these preferred guests possess a code, a sort of membership number, which unlocks the source of nourishment. There is a good reason why they are *persona grata*. They provide their host with food in the form of dead ants and improve the health of the plant by stepping up the amount of carbon dioxide. Somehow, no one knows exactly how, the trickster beetles have found a way to break the code that admits ants to the feast. They have stolen the membership number and may freeload at will. If an ant objects, they simply crush its head. Such appreciation! And they do nothing to return hospitality to the plant they have inveigled.

Fraud may be the reason why some animal behavior is more complex than it would otherwise be. The evolution of surprisingly intricate communications among American fireflies seems to be the result of chronic deception. Fireflies flash in distinct patterns to attract a suitable mate. Each species has its own unique code. Certain fireflies have become specialists in imitating the signals of others, so as to prey on them. The typical sexual communication sequence is an exchange of flashes between a flying male and a perched female and is so simple it can be copied by a human carrying a flashlight. Others are highly complex. Most intricate of all is the flashing of the firefly *Photuris*, whose females imitate the mating signals of females of other firefly species, lure males, and promptly eat them. These scheming and wily impostors will sometimes hide in tall grass, dim their flashes, and answer a signal only some of the time, so the occasional unsophisticated male cannot easily detect the trick. His fate is to be eaten.

Some male fireflies are just as devious. They mimic a mimic, disguising themselves as a predator, thus frightening off rivals for the favors of a contested female. Some ingenious fakers will pretend to be both an available female and a nearby rival male, thereby enticing a competitive male to close in, making a meal of him. These deplorable ruses probably explain why the message system of fireflies is so elaborate in some species. The biologist James Lloyd thinks so. "I suspect that most of the coding and complexity that we read today in firefly signals has come about not because of selection in the context of reproductive isolation or even sexual selection, but because of selection by signal-tracking predators that culled out simpler, straightforward signalers," Lloyd says. "In fact, complexity, including red tape, may be a universal countermeasure for, or consequence of, dealing with deceivers in all sorts of biological systems. This idea, after 'evolution by means of natural selection,' may be one of the most important generalizations that can be made about communication."

Hugely ingenious too are the high-tech spinning skills of spiders, those master engineers and subtle predators. Some of them weave

subtle intricate special effects, optical illusions that act as deathtraps
for their unsuspecting victims. The cunning silver Argiope spider
uses silks that are almost invisible and spins its webs in bright, sun-
lit places where they are more easily seen. All spiders produce silk,
but this one uses highly evolved kinds of silk that are translucent.
Devious as they come, the Argiope embroiders the web with striking,
zigzag patterns that strongly reflect ultraviolet light. An insect is
hoodwinked into mistaking them for the stripes and chevrons on
the petals of flowers, their intended destination. The design is
changed every night, like the key to a military cipher, to further confuse the insect prey. It may be that the silk tufts reflecting ultraviolet
light that the Argiope weaves in its webs are a device to fool insects
into "thinking" they are sailing into open space, since the sky is the
only natural source of such light.

Darwin appreciated the paradox that the very mechanisms of
deception that one species uses to defraud another actually help the
scientist to arrive at the immense hypothesis of natural selection.
The small untruths of insects were a guide to the vast new truth of
human origins. Often personifying nature with a feminine pronoun,
Darwin regarded her, not as a moral agency, certainly, but as a sort
of tricky text, more like a detective story or the *Times* crossword puzzle, in which certain clues were planted that should have tipped off
alert investigators to the correct solution much earlier, if only they
had been smart enough to spot them. One such clue was the existence of life forms that dissembled and bluffed their way to survival,
in rivalry with others who were apt to bluff back.

Nature, Darwin said, "may be said to have taken pains to reveal her
scheme." Far from being a deliberate liar, the old girl actually went
to some trouble to give away her secrets. How, for example, could
naturalists have been so obtuse, so dense, as not to have drawn the
momentous conclusion from the presence of archaic, now useless
organs in certain species, such as embryonic teeth in the upper jaw
of the unborn calf, that never cut through the gums, showing a close
evolutionary link between ruminants and pachyderms? Or from the
shriveled wings of beetles, clear evidence that they evolved from earlier creatures?

Useless organs are so common throughout nature, said Darwin, it would be impossible to find one of the higher animals lacking a rudimentary or atrophied part of its anatomy. Male mammals, for example, possess worthless nipples. In snakes, one lobe of the lungs serves no purpose whatever. Birds have a "bastard" wing that is a rudimentary digit; in some species the entire wing is so underdeveloped it cannot be used for flight.

These futile organs, Darwin speculated, are like superfluous letters in the words of a language which are nevertheless retained in the spelling. Such remnants serve no purpose; they are even misleading for the purpose of pronunciation, but they give a clue to the derivation of a word. Obsolete letters do not correspond to anything "real" in terms of sound or meaning, but suggest the way in which a word has altered over the course of time. They are informative as to history.

That is the case, too, with obsolete anatomical features. They give the evolutionary game away. Darwin gently mocked Creation-minded historians who thought useless organs were there "for the sake of symmetry," or to "complete the scheme of nature," for that would involve some kind of deception or artifice on the part of the Creator. He refused to entertain such a hypothesis.

Public opinion was in Darwin's corner on this matter, as became evident in the strange affair of Philip Gosse, who was in late middle age when the *Origin of Species* burst upon the scene. Gosse, a respected zoologist and member of the fundamentalist religious sect of Plymouth Brethren, was disconcerted, as were many of his peers, to notice that the new geological evidence showing the Earth to be millions of years old was in violent contradiction to the vastly briefer timetable given in the Bible, which Archbishop Ussher calculated to be a hair longer than four thousand years, the world having got underway on October 23, 4004 B.C. In an attempt to reconcile the two versions, Gosse advanced the thesis that the seemingly gradual evolution of organic life, an index of the Earth's much more venerable age, was actually an illusion, a fraud perpetrated by the Author of the World, who deceptively placed fossils in the rocks at the moment of creation to mimic the appearance of slow, eon-by-eon evolution. The intention was to test the faith of mortals weak-minded enough to entertain the heresy of a creationless cosmos. This did not sit well with Victorian readers, who expected God to play with a straight bat. "Lying," joked Thomas Carlyle, "is not permitted in this universe."

The paradox was that nature's truthfulness about the origin of species revealed widespread fakery on the part of the products of that evolutionary process. The notion that guile, and its inseparable partner, suspicion, might be part of the normal order of things, became apparent as soon as nature was interpreted, not as reflecting the mind of a Creator, but as competition among species for the necessities of existence.

Some scientists question whether truth is a basic instinct among living things. Is fraud merely parasitical on truth? Or can we say that untruth is the more fundamental of the two? It certainly seems to have a life of its own in the long story of evolution. In many cases, deception may be more the rule than the exception. Fireflies are more apt to be signaled mendaciously than truthfully and some species of birds send out false alarm calls more often than genuine ones. There is a definite, built-in escalation of deceit even among lowly species. What happens is that the more often a swindle is practiced, the more intense is the selection for its detection, which in turn increases selection for more plausible kinds of deceit. Ultimately, a new sort of falsehood emerges by natural selection: self-deception, which, by concealing from the pretender the fact that it is pretending, makes the pretense seem all the more authentic to the individual being deceived.

An argument has been made for the existence of an instinct for truth in the depths of human biology, based on the technology of the lie detector. According to this thesis, the brain may be a fluent perjurer, but the body gives the brain away. The medical scientist Lewis Thomas claims the polygraph shows that "a human being cannot tell a lie, even a small one, without setting off a kind of smoke alarm somewhere in a dark lobule of the brain, resulting in the sudden discharge of nerve impulses, or the sudden outpouring of neurohormones, or both." That means lying is stressful for us humans, whatever our motives, setting off warning alarms that something has gone wrong.

It makes a kind of biological sense, Thomas thinks, to say that truth-telling is a genetic endowment, a birthright, as natural to human beings as feathers are to birds or scales to fish. The lie detector works because "we cannot even tell a plain untruth, betray a trust, without scaring some part of our own brains." After all, if truthfulness is merely a habit of upbringing and the rules of our culture, where is there a culture in which lying is practiced by all its members as a matter of course? Who has ever heard of such a community, except perhaps in the nightmare fantasy of an Orwell?

The phrase "Machiavellian intelligence" has been used by scientists to describe the deceptive tactics of animals in the wild and in captivity. There may be more to this metaphor than meets the eye. Niccolo Machiavelli, the sixteenth-century Italian statesman and philosopher, founder of realpolitik, took a radically naturalistic view of human nature and society, cutting politics loose completely from the church and exploding the belief that the institutions that keep society in business are made in the image of and mirror the cosmic order established by God. Part of the shock effect of his magnum opus *The Prince* is due to the fact that in that work he highlights the animal character of human beings. Machiavelli looked at political bodies much as Darwin regarded species, not as timeless manifestations of mind, but as natural occurrences that evolve, flourish, and decay at the mercy of happenstance or "Fortune," in the Renaissance sense of an agency cunning, whimsical, unpredictable, and deserving of a feminine pronoun.

In Machiavelli, as in Darwin, nature is set against nature. *Fortuna*, impersonal blind chance, the agency of floods, havoc-wreaking storms and plagues, confronts *virtù*, the power of mind to outwit the entropic, leveling tendencies of physical forces. The essence of *virtù* is to be clever and strong, and it is ethically neutral. A statesman must combine the qualities of lion and fox: the lion for brute force and the fox for guile, slyness, and double-dealing in the art of evading traps. A Prince must be "a great feigner and fraud." Neither *Fortuna* nor *virtù* is on the side of the angels. Opportunism rules, in Machiavelli as in Darwin, because all is unstable and impermanent.

The state is not the handiwork of God and cannot be understood in terms of goals and ultimate reasons. Even the best constructed society, even Rome, could not escape decline and death. Likewise, species that once lorded it over the earth became extinct. *Fortuna* extinguished them.

Machiavelli and Darwin had this in common: they both distrusted unworldly attitudes, all a priori principles aloof from actual observation. Machiavelli saw history as "an endless process of cut-throat competition" in which the only imperative is to succeed. Mankind does not possess an instinct for truth. Truth is what works in practice, *verita effettuale*, and Machiavelli blamed well-intentioned statesmen such as Savonarola for causing misery to his compatriots by trying to replace a successful falsehood with an ineffectual truth. Machiavelli talks about the "truth" of Christianity, but sees it as debilitating to the health and strength of the world. There is a truth that is "truer than every other truth," and that is worldly honor: men must be strong, armed and ready to defend their state. Error arises from weakness. The inference is that if Christianity has weakened humanity, it cannot be perfectly true.

Like Machiavelli, Darwin is a pivotal figure in the treatment of falsehood as an aspect of the world to be taken seriously. The focus of the eighteenth-century Enlightenment, of which Darwin was in many respects an inheritor, had been on truth and reason, the two being virtually interchangeable, and on Nature as a source of truth. Reason had a natural affinity with veracity, with clarity, with the transparency of a mind lacking murky depths and obscure nether regions. Darwin recognized that there is an immense difference between evolution and decency—and he was an eminently decent person. He did not believe that human beings have an instinct to be truthful, any more than they have an inborn belief in God. "Many instances," he writes, "could be given of the noble fidelity of savages towards each other, but not to strangers; common experience justifies the maxim of the Spaniard, 'Never, never trust an Indian.' " The love of truth, he noted, is not uniform across humanity. Certain "savage tribes" adhere to it more than do others, and it has rarely been thought a sin to lie to strangers. In a corrosive aside, reminiscent of

Machiavelli's comments on the ruthless and suspicious character of the diplomacy of his times, Darwin notes the useful role played by lying, adding: "as the history of modern diplomacy too plainly shows."

In his writings, reason seems to merge with instinct, the engine of evolution. Darwin spent considerably more ink on instinct than on reason, and wrote expansively on the connection between instinct and truth. Both he and the eighteenth-century proto-Darwinist Jean-Baptiste Lamarck thought the existence of instincts made a theory of the origin of species more difficult to defend, since they seem to entail an intelligence in nature that plans ahead, that calculates. Yet it is the very essence of an instinct that a creature follows it regardless of reason. Lamarck's answer was that habits acquired in the lifetime of individuals become heritable in the form of an innate disposition. That was so commonsensical it was bound to be wrong. Lamarck made a point of saying that instinct, unlike intelligence, cannot deceive and is adapted directly to a goal. He made a clean separation between instinct, as inherently aboveboard and honest in its operations, not a liar or a cheat, and intelligence, reason, which is capable of all kinds of sham and artifice.

In the 1830s, Darwin was a Lamarckian. He suggested that accidental alterations in the environment could produce new habits in animals, reorganizing their biological structure, and that the modifications were inherited by the next generations. In time, such structural innovations would result in a new species. As Darwin's thinking progressed, he came to regard instincts, not as paragons of nondeceitfulness, as Lamarck had believed, nor as instruments of truth in the sense that they enabled animals to harmonize perfectly with their surroundings, but more as analogues to parts of anatomy, which evolve to fit the organism to its habitat. When he came to write the *Origin*, he had given up the idea that species are completely adapted, with a sort of engineering precision. In that respect he had become a relativist. The fit between an individual and its milieu does not have to be exact for the creature to flourish. It only needs to be better adapted than its competitors. Natural selection was not a preserver of the status quo, a cybernetic force pushing and pulling species to keep them constant and stable, but a vehicle of novelty, sometimes producing life forms of startling, even bizarre originality.

Abandoning his belief in a perfect match between biology and environment, Darwin grew increasingly intrigued by misfits, oddities, deviations, and incongruities. Where Lamarck had made much of the reasonableness and truthfulness of nature, Darwin savoured its eccentricities and quirks, even occasionally its silliness. He looked for the marginal, the out-of-kilter, to bolster his argument for natural selection.

William Paley, the leading natural theologian of the day, conceded that some of the mechanisms of adaptation were extraordinarily ungainly and needlessly cumbersome. Why, for instance, is the eye such an intricate, rigged-up contrivance? Surely an all-powerful, all-wise God could have given his creatures the gift of sight at one stroke, by divine command. The explanation, said Paley, must be that intricacy in anatomy is a deliberate ruse on the part of the Creator to set up an analogy between reason in the workings of biology and reason in the thought processes of the human mind. We find nature intelligible because it is designed in ways that mimic our own clever machines.

Darwin, who as a young man had been impressed with Paley's arguments, drew the opposite conclusion. The eye is ingenious, certainly, but it is not a perfect piece of engineering, let alone a work of which the Ultimate Mind could be proud. Darwin quotes with evident relish from the German physiologist Hermann von Helmholtz, well known for his hostility to metaphysical speculation: "One might say that nature has taken delight in accumulating contradictions in order to remove all foundation from the theory of a pre-existing harmony between the external and internal worlds." Here we have the quintessence of Darwinism. No special creation, no perfect adaptation, no given attunement of mind to world. It was precisely the disharmonies that caught Darwin's fancy.

Just as anatomical features vary, enabling selection to sift the fit from the unfit, so instincts too ought to vary from one individual to another. Naturalists of Darwin's time pointed out that instincts do vary, sometimes to a remarkable degree. The honeybee, for example,

has about thirty different wired-in behaviors, each one tightly constrained. In that case there must surely be superannuated instincts,
analogous to the archaic relics of obsolete bodily organs, useless and
so in violation of the Lamarckian criterion for truthfulness: a biology that harmonizes a creature with its world.

Can the instinct of a bee to sting be called "truthful"? Once, the
sting was an instrument for boring, serrated like the edge of a steak
knife. Now used to poison enemies, the device, once inserted, cannot
be easily withdrawn and often kills its owner by tearing out its vis-
cera. A dog turns around several times before lying down to sleep,
evidently because, far back in the mists of the evolutionary past, its
ancestors made their bed by tamping down high grass. Today, that is
a futile gesture. Instincts can become false in their fit with the world,
and since Darwin decided that intelligence and instinct have a common base, there must be thoughts that are also false in the same way,
but held with equal strength. Instincts are every bit as able to dis-
semble and defraud as the most devious intellect. If the mind is an
organ that varies over generations, some of its variations preserved
and others discarded, we are surely mistaken in supposing it to be a
unique instrument, independent of nature, arriving at "truth" by a
privileged route.

Some of the mind's ideas may be suicidally wrong, the mental
equivalent of the sting of a bee. In a letter of July 3, 1881, Darwin
wrote: "with me the horrid doubt always arises whether the convictions of man's mind, which has been developed from the mind of the
lower animals, are of any value or at all trustworthy." After all, he
could not rely on his eyes when deceived by an optical illusion. How,
then, can we depend on the mind to know the world as it "really" is
when it evolved haphazard from rudimentary origins, as a device for
edging out the competition in sometimes violent and desperate skir-
mishing for survival?

A recurring theme in Darwin's writings, not often emphasized in
the multitude of books about him, is the resistance of the mind to
new and more accurate ideas about reality. False beliefs may come to
seem "natural" because of the history of the mind, or brain, which he
regarded as the same thing. "Natural selection simply does not care

about giving us a meticulously true and comprehensive insight into the nature of things," says the Darwin scholar Michael Ruse. "If we benefit biologically by being deluded about the true nature of formal thought, then so be it."

"Masters of Suspicion" is the phrase Paul Ricoeur applied to three thinkers who left to our time a legacy of mistrust of the human intellect: Karl Marx, Friedrich Nietzsche, and Sigmund Freud. Each in his own way looked askance at consciousness and called it false. Henceforth, "to seek meaning is no longer to spell out consciousness of meaning, but to decipher its expressions. What must be faced, therefore, is not only a threefold suspicion, but a threefold guile."

I suggest Darwin's name should be added to Ricoeur's list of the untrusting moderns. As one of these suspicious intellects, he was exceptional in his transparent openness of manner, a guilelessness almost amounting to naïveté. Yet he is undeniably a hinge figure in the transition to the mistrust of consciousness which has culminated at the turn of the millennium in the postmodern suspicion of language as a deceitful and self-serving vehicle, with no anchor in truthful meanings lodged in the mind.

Thomas Huxley, in an obituary of his hero published in *Nature* in April 1881, compared Darwin with Socrates. Socrates had been a pupil of Archelaus, who could, in a limited sense, be called an evolutionist. In youth, Socrates was strongly drawn to fashionable theories of the universe, what it is made of, how it began. Later, he became disenchanted with all such speculations and lost interest in physics. Instead, he set his mind to the question of civilization, of how human beings should live together in a society. Politics and language intrigued him, as well as decent conduct and valid reasoning. As Cicero said: "Socrates was the first person who summoned philosophy away from mysteries veiled in concealment by nature herself."

Darwin's case was somewhat different. He was confident that the secrets of the material world eventually could be unlocked by science, and he shared Huxley's reverence for scientific truth. But he harbored no such optimism as to what have been called "the great rolling themes" of traditional philosophy, questions of determinism versus free will, the origin of evil, the existence of God. "A dog might as well speculate on the mind of Newton," he once said. Darwin was the reluctant assassin of the doctrine of divine creation, already sickly and fragile in the clouded afternoon of high Victorianism. Ultimately he may also have been a conspirator in the murder of another tottering Victorian precept: the idea of an assured correspondence between the human mind and the ultimate truth of things.

CHAPTER TWO

The Evolution of Cunning

One of the most important things to realize about systems of animal communication is that they are not systems for the dissemination of the truth.
—Robert Trivers

HE EXISTENCE OF DECEPTION ON SUCH A grand scale in flora and fauna is an incitement to think of "nature" as possessing a devious kind of intelligence, and from there to leap to the obvious conjecture that human chicanery is somehow inevitable, a basic component of biology.

Sir Francis Bacon, polymath, prophet, founder of modern science in England, had found it necessary to impress on his readers that nature is sincere; she is not out to make a fool of the inquiring mind. We get nature wrong because of the "false mirrors" of our senses and our ingrained tendency to believe what we wish to believe. Two centuries later it was still possible to talk in metaphor about whether or not the universe is a cheat. In one of his most minutely parsed epigrams, Albert Einstein once said: "God is sophisticated but he is not malicious," by which he meant that physical nature, the world that Newton rather than Darwin made intelligible in an entirely new way, is not cunning or duplicitous, does not engage in bluff. The universe may conceal its mysteries by reason of its inherent loftiness and grandeur, but it will not do so out of mean-spirited guile, not out of sheer perversity.

But if cunning is the rule in so many species that are simple and ancient, how can we resist the temptation to say that nature herself is crafty, which opens the door to the heresy that she has a mind, that she knows where she is going? Some thinkers who commanded a respectful audience in the late Victorian era did succumb to that lure.

When Darwinism went into temporary eclipse around the end of the nineteenth century, awaiting rescue by the new science of genetics, "Fortress Darwin," manned by embattled defenders of the great naturalist, used the known facts about the deceitfulness of species to bolster the case for the temporarily unfashionable theory of natural selection. There had been a good deal of premature dancing on the grave of the selection hypothesis, even though the concept of evolution itself was alive and well.

Lamarck had died in piteous circumstances two-thirds of a century earlier, blind, belittled, and impecunious, the butt of a mortifying snub at the hands of Napoleon, who made it clear in the most public fashion that he considered Lamarck's work on weather forecasting a lot of nonsense. Now, however, in the vacuum created by the unpopularity of natural selection, certain aspects of Lamarck's account of evolution began to look quite tempting. Darwin himself had not closed off the possibility that selection might not be the one and only mechanism, becoming increasingly open to the possibility that it was augmented by others, such as the inheritance of habit, a Lamarckian idea.

Lamarck proposed that an animal develops new or modified parts of its anatomy according to what it needs to flourish in a particular habitat. A sort of subtle fluid, always in motion, acts to produce new organs or improve existing ones as a means of satisfying those needs. It is not a question of simply willing such innovations to come into existence. Needs are created by the environment, and these determine how a given animal will use its body; if it makes special use of an organ, that organ will draw more fluid, and more fluid means there will be useful changes in the organ. The animal's offspring inherit the changes and in the course of many generations an entirely novel organ can emerge. Giraffes, by Lamarck's lights, wanted to eat leaves on the upper branches of trees, and the weight of generations of wanting produced the requisite longer necks.

There was precious little in the way of evidence to support this theory, but it gave some comfort to those who found the doctrine of the survival of the fittest too harsh for their taste. It has been suggested that the revival of Lamarckism at the turn of the century, at least in America, was partly due to a quasi-religious preference for a story showing nature as "purposeful and creative" rather than blindly stumbling onto successful forms of life by accident. According to a popular interpretation of Lamarck, species are in the driver's seat, guiding evolution by a sort of private enterprise, though always indebted to the benevolent wisdom of the Creator.

The incidence of trickery and disguise in the animal world, with species "pretending" to be other and different species for their own advantage, provided some ammunition against the enemies of natural selection. Naturalists working in the field, often getting wet and cold, as opposed to scientists sitting warm and dry at laboratory benches, were aware of what animals actually got up to in the competitive arena of the wild, and some of it was quite underhand. These observers attached high importance to aspects of nature the indoor experimenters tended to ignore. One such feature was geographic isolation as a factor in the origin of species. Another was fraudulent display and deception.

Lamarck had spoken of complex life forms as having *besoins*, "needs," and new kinds of needs might arise if the environment altered. A need alerted what he called an "internal feeling," or *sentiment intérieur*, which in turn set off the action of the subtle fluids. Such a need was "pressing," in Lamarck's term. The word *sentiment* has been translated as "consciousness," or more vaguely "life force." Language of this sort, coupled with Lamarck's loosely organized method of presenting his views, invited readers to conclude that transformations of anatomy during evolution were instigated by a kind of mental operation, smacking of purposeful intelligence and deliberate choice.

Samuel Butler, an amateur, passionately motivated anti-Darwinist with a private income, an ex-sheep farmer turned novelist and critic, developed his own version of Lamarckism, drawing also on the ideas of Darwin's polymath grandfather Erasmus. Butler spent nearly a decade quarreling with Darwin. He had read the *Origin of Species* avidly while surrounded by New Zealand sheep. Back in England in the 1870s, Butler found he was "simply driven into" defending Lamarck willy-nilly. He dismissed Darwin's theory of natural selection as "a rope of sand." Elsewhere he called it an esoteric doctrine, and if that irritated Darwin, so much the better.

Butler used the word "cunning" to describe the strategies of Lamarckian organisms in adapting to the environment, cunning as opposed to "strokes of luck." It carried the suggestion of something devious and not quite aboveboard.

The unscientific term was to resonate beyond the anti-Darwin period. The twentieth-century philosopher Karl Popper acknowledged that cunning does exist in nature, though he attributed it to the result of selection rather than to a basic a priori force driving evolution. Butler, less cautiously, asserted the existence of a "mind and intelligence throughout the universe." In his *Unconscious Memory*, published in 1880, he recommended the reader "to see every atom in the universe as living and able to feel and to remember, but in a humble way." The inheritance of acquired characteristics by succeeding generations was effected by a kind of unconscious memory. It was asking too much of the reader, Butler conceded, to place himself on the "same moral platform as a stone." Sufficient just to agree that the stone has a moral platform of its own, perhaps involving little more than a profound respect for the laws of gravitation. With the supreme confidence of the nonexpert, bolstered by his considerable literary gifts, Butler decided that consciousness pervades the entire realm of life. In *Luck or Cunning?*, published in 1886, he wrote: "The theory that luck is the main means of organic modification is the most absolute denial of God which it is possible for the human mind to conceive."

One person strongly attracted to Butler's ideas was George Bernard Shaw, who devoured the pages of *Luck or Cunning?*, sitting up with it late at night and taking it with him on walks in Hyde Park. He reviewed it favorably, under the gleeful headline: "Darwin

Denounced!" The book suited Shaw's mystical view of evolution and resonated with his complaint that Darwin had banished mind from the universe. Shaw was uneasy with the idea that life was just a colossal accident. Such an account signified "a chaotic loss of control which filled him with dread." Early on, Shaw was an admirer of Marx, who argued that changes in social and economic conditions were not the result of chance, but of a universal principle. Shaw preferred the wilful and purposive picture of life drawn from Lamarck and espoused a philosophy of the Life Force, a cunning and creative agency that struggles to become conscious of itself, partly through ideas, art, and literature. Human beings are an experiment by the Life Force aimed at making mankind into God, a gigantic research project to produce individuals of higher and higher quality. From time to time, the Life Force is clever enough to bring forth a genius of the order of Shaw himself, as a sort of preview of coming attractions.

Part and parcel of being godlike is perfect knowledge, full comprehension, possession of the Truth. For Shaw, we are a society that operates under cover of a screen of lies, that is steeped in hypocrisy. It has been noted that Shaw's works are full of words like "humbug," "sham," "imposture," "pretense." By contrast with society, the Shavian Life Force is essentially honest, on the side of truth and adamantly opposed to fraud, especially when it is a fraud we perpetrate against ourselves. The person who is ruthlessly clear-sighted about himself can become something like a god. In *Man and Superman*, Don Juan insists that evolution works in the direction of "higher and higher individuals, the ideal individual being omnipotent, omniscient, infallible and withal completely, unilludedly self-conscious; in short, a god."

If Darwin had banished mind from the universe, the prevalence of pretense and dissembling in the animal world posed the question of how nature can be "cunning" and yet be explained without using a language of psychology. The debate was heated on both sides. Edward Poulton, professor of zoology at Oxford, made a strenuous case for "mindless" selection as the chief engine of evolution, and he used the observed facts about animal mimicry to bolster his argument. Poulton sided strongly with the field naturalists against the ivory tower theorists. Naturalists who watched at first hand the struggle for existence realized that the way a species looks is often connected with very grave issues of life and death. Poulton took the pigmentation of creatures seriously, not as an irrelevance, as many of the bench-bound scientists did. He wrote about the "meaning" of the colors of animals; the information, sometimes usefully misleading, they convey, as part of their effectiveness in the daily task of staying alive. At the same time he argued that it would be absurd to suppose creatures decide to tint themselves in a certain way, under the guidance of a Lamarckian interior sentiment. All such talk of mindfulness and purpose was so much nonsense. Would we want to attribute "cunning" or the deliberate satisfying of desire to insects who take on the appearance of wasps, nobody's favorite meal, thus avoiding being eaten by birds? Or regard as intelligent the grasshopper *Gryllacris*, which impersonates the bombadier beetle *Pherosphus agnathus*, a creature famous for its conspicuous orange legs and its nasty habit of squirting a caustic liquid when upset? Poulton could see no logic in that line of argument. The giraffe surely did not extend its neck out of a rational aspiration to obtain access to leaves so high as to be out of reach. That sounded almost as silly as the speculation of Shaw's friend Edward Carpenter, that the lark altered the shape of its wings "by the mere love of soaring and singing in the face of the sun." What happened was that giraffes which just happened to have longer necks than other giraffes tended to survive and reproduce in greater numbers.

Many biologists at the time disliked the notion that colors on animals "mean" something, preferring to see them as a coincidence or fluke. They put such ideas down to "overactive Darwinian imaginations." How, for instance, could the theory of fraudulent imitation as life insurance explain the colors on the *inside* of a snail's shell? Surely that would argue for coloration being an altogether internal affair. Others thought the similarity in appearance in different species too close, too perfect, to be the result of random selection.

In effect, scientists like Poulton made their case for the deceitfulness of nature by reminding their opponents: "It's a jungle out there." Laboratory types could pooh-pooh the theory of protective lying because they had no real understanding of the awful strains and pressures imposed on creatures in the feral world. Lamarck had taken a strangely offhand attitude toward the terrors of competition in the wild, regarding the attrition of less successful animals by more successful ones as a sort of prudent system of husbandry, nature's way of keeping numbers down to manageable size. One should not feel too sorry for the losers. Yet the study of mimicry did help to keep the flame of Darwinism alive until the arrival of a secure science of genetics, and it warred against the inclination to suppose that some benign form of mentalism, the operation of some mysterious intelligence, guided the operations by which species adapt to new circumstances.

Mentalism crept back into the study of deceit at a more sophisticated stage of neo-Darwinism, when the twentieth century was well advanced. The observable fact that creatures do not spend their whole time competing aggressively, one individual against another in endless rivalry, but are sometimes unselfish and cooperative, led to sociobiology, a discipline that made room for altruism and sacrifice alongside the existence of ruthless competition. Evolutionary success, in this view, is not just the result of a brute struggle to stay alive, but is sometimes a more subtle matter of passing one's genes on to the next generation. That can be achieved by assisting relatives to breed rather than breeding oneself. In colonies of ants and bees, there are certain workers unable to breed who spend all their time helping fertile brethren who can. The emphasis is on reproduction, not bare survival.

Sociobiologists talk about genes and for the most part eschew terms that suggest an animal has intentions and thoughts. It has been noted, however, that they can be quite free in using the language of economics when discussing reproductive strategies, including such words as "costs," "benefits," "investment," "budgets," "efficiency," "monopoly," and "advertising." All this conveys an impression of deliberate calculation, a sort of "cunning," although it is meant to eliminate any imputation of human attitudes. This is especially the case where deception is involved. Eileen Crist points out that while sociobiologists largely avoid mentalistic terms, faithful to the tenet that animals do not have minds, "an intermittent yet recurrent exception to this rule is a degree of willingness to attribute to animals either the intention to deceive and manipulate, or the shrewd ability to weigh advantages and disadvantages." The spirit of Machiavelli peeps through again.

Consider the case of the ten-spined stickleback *Pysgosteus pungitius*, recorded by Robert Trivers, a University of California biologist. Males of this species build nests shaped like small pipes into which females swim to lay their eggs. Sometimes, while one female is spawning in a male's nest, another female appears a short distance away. The male swims to her and invites her in, hoping to double his reproductive prowess. The female is supposed to lay her own clutch of eggs, whereupon the male moves in and fertilizes, as he fondly supposes, both clutches. Fooled you! On some occasions, the second "female" is actually a male, who sneaks in and fertilizes the first and only clutch of eggs. The trick is worked by the impostor altering its bright breeding coloration, which advertises its masculine gender, to the dingy, cryptic, nonbreeding coloration of the female. This dishonest behavior is known in the trade as "creeping." The intruder is so thorough in his chicanery that even while fertilizing the eggs, effectively cuckolding the other, unsuspecting male, he affects the posture of a female laying eggs.

Just where "mindless" Darwinian deception leaves off and intentional falsehood begins is a matter for debate. In some respects it resembles the inconclusive controversy over whether or not nonhuman primates have true language. Researchers who study deception tend to celebrate the *usefulness*, if not the accuracy, of treating animals as if they have minds. "Something priceless was lost," two scientists regretfully conclude, "when radical behaviorism triumphed over mentalism in animal psychology." Some observed forms of lying in the wild do suggest sophisticated intentions and an understanding of the mentality of the animal being deceived. Geoffrey Bateson called evolution a "mental process," while Robert Mitchell cautiously asserts that an animal posing as another sort of species involves natural selection "and/or some (other) mental process." That seems to cover all the bases. What is intriguing is that frauds, even misleading appearances, such as the butterfly with wings resembling its own head so that predators, programmed to go for the head, take a slice of wing instead, are so pertinent, so well fitted to the needs and perceptions of other animals in the environment. "Some formal similarity," Mitchell says, "exists between the products of natural selection and those of human action or mind."

Mitchell sees four levels of deception in nature. At the first, simplest level, a species deceives because it cannot do anything else but deceive. A viceroy butterfly with markings that mimic those of a monarch, noxious to blue jays, is a poseur all its life. At level two, the mendacious act occurs only when there is some other creature in the vicinity to be duped, as in the case of the firefly, whose fake signals need the response of other fireflies nearby to achieve their result. At level three, deception is not automatic but can be learned by trial and error. Lying behavior is modified according to whether it works or does not work. It is thought, for example, that some birds learn not one song but a repertoire of different ones to create the fiction of a densely crowded habitat, discouraging new birds from taking up residence nearby. Or, a dog may affect a sham limp, whereupon its human owners are apt to smother it with attention and sympathy. Such falsehoods are not perpetrated because the animal has insight into the minds of those who are deceived by its behavior. All the deceiver knows for sure is that the tricks work, and this can be learned by experiment and chance. Only at the fourth and highest level does an intention to deceive, not simply to manipulate, occur. Here, misleading actions are modified according to what they mean to others being misled. Humans excel at this type of fraud, but chimpanzees can also become quite good at it, especially after training with human caretakers. Frans de Waal has found among chimps "a pervasive distortion of information" in contrast to the simpler deceptive practices of macaques.

The American philosopher Daniel Dennett once thought that even the most advanced nonhuman animals, like chimps or dogs, were unable to entertain beliefs about the beliefs of others, or desires and fears about the desires and fears of others, abilities indispensable if one is to truly deceive. Dennett was convinced that only the unique human species, whose uniqueness resides in the fact that it can talk, is able to have beliefs about the beliefs of others. Animals without language are incapable of such sophisticated insights "for the same reason that they cannot have beliefs about Friday, or poetry." Later, Dennett was not so certain. He began asking around for stories about animals that seemed to have insights into what was going on inside the heads of others, including humans. Among the evidence he found, the most powerful dealt with animal deception. A friend wrote to him about the occasion when, one evening, he was sitting at home in the only chair on which his dog was allowed to sleep. The dog, deprived of that comfortable spot, lay whimpering at his feet. When that simple and honest form of coercion did not work, the dog stood up and walked to the door, where she could be easily seen by her master. She scratched at the door, a clear signal that she had given up trying to wheedle him out of the chair and had decided to go out. But that was a lie. The moment the unsuspecting owner went to the door to let her out, she scampered back across the room and leapt into the vacated chair, where possession was nine-tenths of the law.

"Here," says Dennett, "it seems we must ascribe to the dog the *intention* that her master *believe* she *wants* to go out." The canine animal is attempting to cause the human animal to do something he would never do if his beliefs about what was going on were accurate and true. Dennett speculates, however, that a dog might simply know she has conditioned her master to go to the door when she scratches it, in which case it is a case of simple behaviorism. If she had run to the window and looked out, growling suspiciously, a novel scheme not tried before, evidence of a true deception would have been stronger.

More striking is the case of Austin, a chimp in captivity studied by Sue Savage-Rambaugh and Kelly McDonald. Austin was the victim of rough treatment by another, larger chimp named Sherman, a common bully. Like many bullies, Sherman had a cowardly streak, in this case a very specific one: he was afraid of the dark. Austin, who had no such fears, used to slip outside after nightfall and make noises on the wall of the sleeping room which sounded like an intruder scraping or pounding on the metal, trying to break in. He would then surreptitiously sidle back in and start to peer out as if trying to see where the suspicious noises originated. The effect on Sherman was dramatic. Vague intimations of a menace lurking in the night were enough to bring out all his quaking reflexes, so much so that he actually turned to Austin, his browbeaten subordinate, for comfort and hugged him. This trick was not a sudden inspiration, however. Austin perfected it over several years.

Nonhumans, even the clever ones, seem to possess a restricted repertoire of falsehoods. The plover, for example, is a one-deception species. It can mislead a potential intruder by flying away from its nest of fledglings, and this seems to be an inborn disposition. But the plover does not similarly distract a rival away from a willing mate or a piece of material for building a nest. Apes and monkeys are more versatile in their range of frauds, but the animal psychologist David Premack suggests that the chimp can understand only rather simple states of mind: seeing, wanting, expecting. Belief, which is a highly complex mental condition, is more doubtful. An animal will not attribute to another a state of mind it cannot have or know it has. Language is simply an amplifier of such competencies, making them more powerful.

It has been noted that fraudulent behavior in primates other than humans tends to revolve around the extremely uninteresting business of getting, and preventing others from getting, food. In one of the most potent myths of human origins, the first man and woman made the precipitous descent from perfect innocence to guilt and shame by the act of eating an apple. That fateful lapse was the finale of a drama played out against a backdrop of misinformation. "Within little more than a week of the Creation," writes Nicholas Humphrey, "Eve had been beguiled by a subtle serpent, she had tempted Adam, and God himself had been caught telling lies. 'But of the tree of the knowledge of good and evil,' God had said, 'thou shalt not eat of it: for on the day that thou eatest thereof thou shalt surely die.' But the serpent had told the woman, 'Ye shall not surely die.' And Eve had eaten the apple—and she had not died, nor had Adam. Men, women and Gods too, it seems, were deceivers ever." God had said that "on the day" that they ate it, they would perish; but Adam lived to be 930 years old.

Where simpler species disguise themselves with borrowed plumage, we obfuscate with words, plant doubts in minds we are able to read; the subtlety of our minds and the complexity of human society make it all but inevitable that we should do so. "At every level," said the scholar of language George Steiner, "from brute camouflage to poetic vision, the lingustic capacity to conceal, misinform, leave ambiguous, hypothesize, invent, is indispensable to the equilibrium of human consciousness and to the development of man in society."

We are still carrying on Eve's, and the serpent's, work.

CHAPTER THREE

Enter the Logos

It is much easier to recognize error than to find truth; the former lies on the surface, this is quite manageable. The latter resides in the depth, and this quest is not everyone's business. —Goethe

HE SUSPICION THAT THE UNIVERSE IS MALIcious in Einstein's sense, and the many ingenious efforts to lay that suspicion to rest, are extremely ancient in the history of thought. A marked tendency is to interpret the universe as being in tune with the human mind, in some sense constructed along similar lines, so that if the mind is sincere and truthful, the universe will respond with honest answers instead of sly evasions. Going back many centuries in time, we can see how deeply attractive yet how prone to rebuttal is this idea of the mindful cosmos, and its corollary, that truth is part of the natural order of things.

Since its beginnings, philosophy has spilt much ink and spun many ingenious arguments in the search for answers to a pair of related questions: Is there a perfect fit between the mind and the world, guaranteeing truthful knowledge of it? And secondly, is such a correspondence part of the given order of things, or is it a human contrivance? Putting it another way: If human beings are by nature philosophical—in Aristotle's idiom, born with a desire to know—to what extent is the world they inhabit "philosophical," giving back answers that satisfy the inborn need to understand? Is the world inherently hospitable to the inquiries of human reason, and being hospitable, never leading us astray?

In the epic poems of Homer, there are suggestions that the world is anti-philosophical, actually resistant and obdurate to the efforts of humans to understand it. Homer does make his universe intelligible in the sense that his gods and goddesses behave very much like human beings, enabling his audience to feel at home in his world. In certain respects, Homer's divinities are no more otherworldly than characters in a daytime television soap opera. His "explanation" for natural happenings is therefore quite accessible, but it is far from satisfying to the philosophic mind. Homer's celestial personages are not fully in command of the forces of nature, and there are many competing gods and powers. Zeus, supreme among the gods, has designs and plans, exerts his will, and makes intelligent decisions like the CEO of a Fortune 500 company or a prime minister; but the Fates, the *morai*, seem to play an independent role as forces of necessity, scheduling this or that event, such as when a given individual is to die. The Fates are impersonal in a way that Zeus is not, and they are definitely not reasonable as the human mind is reasonable. They represent Necessity, but not a cosmic intelligence.

The important role of tricks and ruses in Homer's poems suggests a world so dominated by a ruthless necessity, and by semblance rather than plain dealing, that cheating and artifice may sometimes be the most rational way to deal with it. Odysseus in his wanderings evades the necessity of death at every turn, by swindles and shams. He is the "man of many turns," *polytropos*, the cunning escape artist who manipulates fate, reinvents himself, alters reality to his own advantage. He wears disguises even when there is no pressing need to do so. But his falsehoods are usually "ethical," in the archaic sense of defying fate, worsting one's enemies and protecting one's friends. Lying suggests the liar has a superior intelligence, is a practical and ingenious person, creating alternative versions of reality, as the poets do. When Odysseus cooks up a piece of fiction to hide his true identity from Athene, who is clad in the disguise of a shepherd's boy, Athene, seeing through the hoax immediately, says with obvious appreciation of his powers of invention:

> Whoever gets around you must be sharp
> and guileful as a snake; even a god
> might bow to you in ways of dissimulation.
>   You! You chameleon!
> Bottomless bag of tricks! Here in your own country
> would you not give your stratagems a rest
> or stop spellbinding for an instant?

Athene adds that she knows the art of misleading as well as Odysseus; among the gods she is famous for deceptions and plots. But Odysseus' wile is a Darwinian trait that brings him safely through the perils of his wanderings. It is embedded in his nature, as disguise is born into the chameleon, and for much the same reason. Most important, Odysseus is a master of tricky language, like Hermes, the trickster god linked to deceitful communication. He is an expert in the use of words to veil, inveigle, and test. His disguises are accomplished, not only with costume, but with language; he weaves fictional biographies of himself as a protective maneuver. "Were we to trace Odysseus's qualities to one common source," writes the scholar Paolo Vivante, "we would have to look for it in the sheer vitality of his nature—his instinct to survive, to live, to be free. Here is craftiness; but because it is a way to safety or recovery, it becomes skill, ingenuity, inventiveness."

When thinkers of antiquity did tackle what Homer left untouched, namely, a "Theory of Everything," accessible to human reason, at the turn of the sixth century B.C., making bold guesses as to what sort of stuff the world might be made of, the answer to the question of whether the world is intelligible to mind was a "Yes, but . . . " Some of the first theories were almost as childish as those of the mythmakers with their cast of gods and nymphs, but from the start the new *physikoi*, or students of the nature of things, veered away from ordinary common sense. Aristotle famously said philosophy begins in wonder, which means it cannot possibly be content with lame or obvious answers. That never ceased to be true. Some 2,500 years after the early Greek naturalists began to speculate about what the world "really" is, Bertrand Russell, in his *Problems of Philosophy*, wrote that "the truth about physical objects *must* be strange. It *may* be unattainable, but if any philosopher believes he has attained it, the fact that what he offers as the truth is strange ought not to be made a ground of objection to his opinion." The new breed of Greek *physikoi* wanted to construe the world, not in terms of a blind necessity but as something profoundly natural, attuned to its human inhabitants and understandable in human terms; we should not need to trick or lie to it in order to get by. According to the classical scholar G. S. Kirk, these thinkers "were not simply trying to explain the world as it is, but rather the world as man needs it to be—unified, comprehensible and ultimately sympathetic." This inclination to see the cosmos in terms of needs, Kirk goes on, "can never be entirely eradicated from human thinking; but it was stronger for the Greeks than for the new scientists of the Renaissance or their modern successors."

By tradition, the earliest of these investigators was Thales of Miletus, a man of Phoenician descent, in his prime around 585 B.C. Evidently, he was brilliant. Though not the first of the Greek natural philosophers, he was so far ahead of his predecessors that they faded into obscurity. Thales was by reputation a polymath, an astronomer who predicted with reasonable accuracy an eclipse of the Sun, using Babylonian tables of solar and lunar orbits. A practical man, he reputedly made a considerable amount of money by using his astronomical know-how to predict a bumper harvest of olives, taking care to corner the market in olive oil presses early in the year, and switched the course of a river, enabling the army of King Croesus to ford it.

Thales presented the startling hypothesis that the *arche*, the rock-bottom principle of the world, its basis or origin, is water. He said the world floats on water like a ship. When people say that it "quakes," that is actually due to the rocking motion of the water. Scholars think this preference may have something to do with the fact that water had a special significance in the ancient cosmogonies of the Hebrews, Egyptians, and Babylonians. Thales learned geometry from Egyptian priests and was probably *au fait* with Babylonian traditions. He turned geometry from a simple system of measurement into a deductive science. On the one hand, of course, his theory was deeply reductionist. Water is the simplest of the elements. It was also omnipresent in the lives of people in Thales' vicinity, especially the Ionian traders, who carried out their commercial activities on the sea. At the same time, the Thalean *arche* was not merely physical. It was thought to be animated and divine, which linked it to myth, with its gallery of gods and goddesses. According to Aristotle's hearsay account, Thales held that "all things are full of gods." That was compatible with the Greek propensity to treat the world as a living organism, reducing and familarizing its "otherness" with respect to human life. Mind and water are both fluid and quicksilverish, assuming an endless variety of forms. Thus the water hypothesis made the world intelligible, user-friendly, not apt to deceive us, since it explained it in terms of something utterly commonplace. The world does not play tricks on us, so we do not have to play tricks on it. Yet nobody could accuse Thales of explaining nature in terms of how it appears to the untutored eye, or the literal-minded brain. It would not occur to most people to liquify the universe.

With Thales, there is an unspoken premise that the mind is so constructed that it fits reality, and therefore has a built-in connection to truth, but not in the way the man in the street might expect. One of his pupils, Anaximander, the first to use the word *arche* as a philosophical term, went further and argued that even this was too optimistic a view of human knowledge; in particular, it overestimated the affinity between language and the world. Odysseus had shown how easily words can be made to misrepresent, to make fictional worlds, fake résumés, identities, and disguises.

In denying human access to ultimate truth, Anaximander seems to take the view that mystery can never be eliminated from life and nature. His name for the *arche* was "the indefinite," *to apeiron*, something which, though material, we cannot even talk about, let alone observe, suggesting not only that the world is unphilosophical to the core, but also that the whole enterprise of philosophy is absurd. It is pointless to discuss origins, though we can still go on with the superficial and second-rate work of describing appearances. Anaximander, one scholar speculates, really intended to say that the world is knowable, but only as a mystery, which hardly makes much of an advance on myth. The whole point of *to apeiron* is that it cannot be captured in words.

This sense of dislocation, of a difference between reality and what we can say about reality, simmered in pre-Socratic thought and burst into the open with a vengeance later on. Departing from common sense as they did, the first post-mythological natural philosophers could not simply state their theories of how the world was made in ordinary, flat, prosaic language. The ideas being bizarre and fanciful, their words could hardly be pedestrian. Anaximenes, a student of Anaximander, who was born about the time that Thales was in his prime, held that the *arche* is air, which when rarefied becomes fire, when condensed becomes wind, then cloud, then water, earth, and finally stones. Air formed the earth, and in its rarefied state made the heavenly bodies. Anaximenes suggested a sort of correspondence between human things and the vast cosmos by means of poetic analogies. The outer world was a metaphor for the inner life of man, and vice versa. The stars, he said "move around the earth, just as a turban winds around our head." And he described the sun as "flat like a leaf." Air is the breath of the world, immortal and divine, a source of gods. A broad, flat, shallow world rests on air, as that of Thales floated on water. Anaximenes said that as the human soul, being air, holds us together and controls us, so does wind and air enclose the whole world. The use of metaphor was just about the only way he could have put his message across that we and the universe are made of the same stuff and play by the same rules. Later, the idea that inferences can be made from the microcosm to the macrocosm became a settled doctrine; information about the one could be used to increase understanding of the more mysterious other.

The fit between thought, language, and reality becomes paramount in the work of Heraclitus, who lived in Ephesus, an Ionian city of Asia Minor, at least a generation later than Anaximenes, probably during the reign of Darius, 521 to 487 B.C. Most of the stories about Heraclitus, some of them quite piquant, seem to have been made up. But the flavor of his known writings is sarcastic, clever, enigmatic, prickly, riddling, aristocratic, introspective, not the work of a man who suffers fools or makes concessions to fashion or popular whim. Political correctness was not his style. More than Anaximenes, Heraclitus was a poet, with a poet's flair for keeping clear of the obvious. Ancient commentators tended to brand him a snob who kept the masses at arm's length by writing in a deliberately cryptic and difficult style. "He was fond of concealing his metaphysics in the language of the Mysteries," complained Clement of Alexandria. Socrates remarked that it would take a Delian diver to get to the bottom of his ideas. Admirers of Heraclitus argue that he wrote for grownups, and it takes an adult mind to appreciate him. "There comes a stage in one's intellectual development," says Philip Wheelwright, "when reality as actually encountered seems too dark, too riddling, ambiguous and irreducibly many-sided to be expressible in ordinary plain terms, and sometimes a well chosen paradox comes closer to representing our experienced view of the world than any logical tidiness can accomplish." If it is paradox you want, Heraclitus is your man.

Called "the dark one" for his obscure but highly suggestive aphorisms, shot through with an irony that seems almost late twentieth-century in its acidic power to deconstruct the familar, Heraclitus today enjoys a reputation almost as great, if less widely appreciated, as in classical times. What makes him a hinge figure is his use of the word "Logos," which conveys the idea that a kind of reason or mindfulness exists in nature and is on the same wavelength as human thought and understanding. That is exactly the conjecture Darwin refused to entertain. So potent has this doctrine proved, however, that as late as the second half of the twentieth century the movement known as deconstruction thought it worthwhile to aim much of its intellectual artillery at this ancient idea of a natural consonance, a guaranteed coming together, of the structure of the understanding and the structure of the world.

Originally a term of mathematics, "Logos," as Homer used it, has the sense of counting or reckoning, the kind of procedure in use before the arrival in Greece of fully abstract deductive reasoning. In Greek, the word came from the verb *lego*, which early on meant "to gather," and hence to collect together things that have some connection with one another. With the development of pure math, emphasizing structure and correspondence, and a one-world, unified order replacing the Homeric confusion of physical powers and agencies, Logos acquired another meaning, as a principle not only of order, but an intelligible order that exists throughout the universe and is accessible to the human mind, for the excellent reason that it is also in the human mind. Logos could also refer to connected, reasonable speech and thought. According to the scholar Granville Henry, Logos was first given metaphysical status by Heraclitus, as a principle of stability, measure, and order in a world that seems to be unstable and disorderly, forever fluctuating, and therefore unreliable, irrational, and misleading. Obviously, we cannot talk about the "truth" of nature unless it behaves in a consistent fashion. Logos, according to Heraclitus, is also the truth of religion, the one and only route to a moral existence. Even today, something of the same importance is given to the term by modern theologians. In the prologue to the Gospel of St. John, says the scholar C. H. Dodd, Logos, the "Word," is the command of God, but at the same time "the meaning, plan or purpose of the universe, conceived as transcendent as well as immanent."

In the writings of Heraclitus, the Logos is in the knower as much as it is in the known. He emphasizes the immaterial, thoughtlike aspects of the physical world, suggesting that the arrangement, the structure and relation of things is more important than the stuff they are made of. Heraclitus chose as his *arche* the element of fire, but a reader might be forgiven for supposing that it is the Logos itself, mindstuff, the Shakespearean element of mercurial thought and fancy, like fire always altering its shape, blazing and leaping, flickering, dancing, guttering, subsiding in smoky embers. More than water or air, Heraclitean fire is a form of intelligence that steers the world and has an affinity with the mental agility of men and women.

At first glance, Heraclitus seems to be saying that everything in the world is always in a state of flux, never settling down for an instant, subverting the integrity of language in such a way that it is impossible to say something definite about anything; the next moment it might have changed into its opposite. Later, Aristotle showed some impatience with the followers of Heraclitus, who became a literary classic after his death. The adherents of the great riddler carried this part of his doctrine to laughable extremes, especially Cratylus of Athens, who decided that the world was so unstable, words were more or less useless as fixed meanings, and recommended simply moving a finger instead of speaking. This was a violent affront to Aristotle's core belief in the reality of substance, the stuff that endures intact though its attributes might alter, and in the importance of the rule that to say "Everything both is and is not" makes all things true, and therefore all philosophy pointless. In fact, Aristotle suggests that Heraclitus might have been simply blowing hot air at his readers, talking for the sake of talking. "What a man says does not necessarily represent what he believes."

This of course was a travesty of what Heraclitus was actually trying to get across. What is quite arresting in his writings is not the ubiquity of flux, but the principle of order underlying the flux, the rational intelligence that directs the universe, ensuring that some things remain the same when all else is changing. For Heraclitus, the Logos supplies the harmony; it makes sense out of the apparent nonsense. But whereas the fluctuating nonsense is easy to be aware of, the hidden sense is much more difficult to fathom, and some people never do discover it. Truth is not handed up on a plate. Heraclitus presents the paradox that Logos is universal, "common to all," extending from the remotest reaches of the cosmos to the uttermost depths of the human psyche, and yet, immersed in it, sharing in it, the majority, even the famous and great, do not even realize it exists.

The idea that Truth is one thing, available only to a select elite, and that the world is ruled by a single principle of order, not by multiple gods, is in some respects an aristocratic point of view. Logos is perfectly trustworthy and truthful, but it is remote from the quotidian and the ordinary. It does not open itself to the literal-minded, because it does not wear meaning on its sleeve. It requires interpretation of a special kind, much more intricate than the relatively easy task of untangling the codes of Homer. One must decipher the signs, and that takes effort, brains, and culture. "Eyes and ears are bad witnesses to men having barbarian souls"—a handicap of language, since barbarians typically do not speak Greek.

Language for Heraclitus is a sign that only hints at meaning. It conceals as much as it discloses, like his own enigmatic fragments. He speaks in conundrums, sometimes shrouding meaning rather than illuminating it, perhaps to make the point that language is not transparent. His complex, abbreviated sentences express a paradox: Logos makes the world intelligible to mind, but there is not a tight fit between language and the truth he prods his audiences to seek. "Nature loves to hide," and so does Heraclitus, behind a literary manner that is purposefully abstruse. He put mind into the universe as firmly as Darwin long afterwards was to take it out, and for that very reason the universe needs to be interpreted, not merely observed. The same goes for language, because it does not match reality exactly, as a key turns in a lock. This has the effect of disengaging language from the deepest kinds of truth, making it independent, separate and self-sufficient, like the reclusive and snobbish Heraclitus himself.

Another aristocratic thinker, in his prime at about the same time as Heraclitus, was Parmenides of Elea. Like Heraclitus, Parmenides taught that reason is the road to truth, and he linked reason to language. In that sense, he was a believer in the power of the Logos. At the same time, he made more obtrusive the unsettling idea that there is a complete rupture between language and ordinary experience. Parmenides was not a pure contemplative; he did provide "admirable laws" for Elea. Yet with him, thinking became an absolute. It was his *arche*. He was a rationalist, believing that reason is more trustworthy than anything the senses tell us, because the senses can and do play tricks. Parmenides was known in antiquity as *Aphysikos*, the "Anti-naturalist," because he denied that anything can be known by studying the works of nature. He was the first to argue in a formal fashion, deducing strange conclusions from self-evident premises. Whereas other philosophers had started with something familiar—earth, water, fire—he began with thinking, and austerely logical thinking at that. For Parmenides, thought and Being are one and the same. Follow a chain of reasoning to its inevitable end, and you have the truth about reality. Since truth is defined as something that is thinkable, and only what is thinkable can be Being, it is impossible to know or speak about what does not exist. To say "Nothing exists" is a contradiction. It is nonsense. The world could not have been created out of nothing, because there is no nothing, and since Parmenides took it for granted that reality is one, it could not have been created out of something either, since there is no "something else," only what is. Any destruction of what exists is out of the question: destroying would mean converting matter into nothing, which is impossible. Therefore, change cannot occur. Diversity is a fiction and sameness rules the universe.

In the sharpest contrast to this passive, spectator's view of the world as a sort of art object is the Greek concept of *Metis*, the type of intelligence that is cunning and devious and shrewd, that is adapted to the perilous jockeying for success in a highly competitive society, using wiles and ruses when sheer brute force is on the other side. An entire book has been devoted to the subject by two scholars, Marcel Detienne and Jean-Pierre Vernant, who oppose this kind of intelligence—"Machiavellian intelligence," in the coinage of modern ethologists—to the philosophical brand that emerges from the work of Parmenides and others who look for unalterable core truths behind the surface ephemera of the world. "It is an intelligence," say these authors, "which, instead of contemplating unchanging essences, is directly involved in the difficulties of practical life with all its risks, confronted with a world of hostile forces which are disturbing because they are always changing and ambiguous." A truly Darwinian situation.

Metis connotes flair, wisdom, subtlety, deception, resourcefulness, opportunism. And it works best in situations that are "transient, shifting, disconcerting and ambiguous," hardly the Parmenidean universe. The point is to be effective, and untruth can be of great assistance in this task, as also can magic, hallucinogenics, frauds, feints, and illusions. Zeus, the king of the gods, had Metis in abundance because he literally digested it. Metis was the name of Zeus' first wife, mother of Athene, equal of Odysseus in cunning. If she had been spared, Metis would have produced a son more powerful than Zeus, strong enough to topple the old man from his throne. Zeus forestalled that scheme by actually swallowing Metis, making himself more Machiavellian than all his rivals, since all tricky designs wherever in the cosmos must first cross his Metis-impregnated mind. Thanks to the Metis within him, Zeus is now forewarned of everything, whether good or bad, that is in store for him.

The Trojan Horse is Metis. So are the disguises of Odysseus, who has been likened to an octopus, the creature of many coils that cloaks its presence by adopting the color and shape of the rock to which it clings. In the *Odyssey,* Menelaus can take by surprise Proteus, the god of many shapes, the oceanic divinity, "the ancient of the salt sea," recruiting him as a guide for his homeward voyage only by imposture, by draping himself and his companions in sealskins, for Proteus was very partial to seals: "a strong disguise; oh yes, terribly strong as I recall the stench of those damned seals. Would any man lie snug with a sea monster?" Thank goodness the daughter of Proteus took pity and dabbed ambrosia under each man's nose, "a perfume drowning out the bestial odor." When you are dealing with a kaleidoscopic god, being obvious and truthful will not get you very far. You need Metis, and plenty of it.

"The many-colored, shimmering nature of Metis is a mark of its kinship with the divided, shifting world of multiplicity in the midst of which it operates," Detienne and Vernant write. "Its suppleness and malleability give it the victory in domains where there are no ready-made rules for success, no established methods, but where each new trial demands the invention of new ploys, the discovery of a way out (*poros*) that is hidden. Conversely, the ambiguous, disparate, unstable realities with which men attempt to come to grips may, in myth, take on the appearance of polymorphic monsters, powers of metamorphosis which delight, in their cunning, to disappoint all expectations and constantly to baffle the minds of men."

The influence of Parmenides on later philosophers was immense, especially in logic and dialectics, but his bent for carrying logical arguments to bizarre extremes left a legacy of playfulness, a taste for non-serious trifling with the machinery of thought that was to prove deeply subversive. It is a short step from saying "thinking is Being" to taking the position that reality is anything we say it is, a treacherous leap toward anarchy. Language becomes more autonomous and sovereign than anything in the thought of Heraclitus. Felix Cleve, a commentator on the pre-Socratic philosophers, coins a word to describe Parmenides: a "glossomorph," someone who disengages language from thought: "it shows that language wields a frightful sway over man."

Here the Logos has evolved into something quite remote from the idea of a natural attunement, a preestablished harmony, between one kind of intelligence and another. Language, which in Heraclitus needed a special kind of interpretation if the truth is to emerge, has become an independent entity, able to make hay of our most confident assumptions about everyday reality. Parmenides says those assumptions, however useful, are lies. They are fictions, chimeras, fallacies. The ordinary person replies that if they are false, they are absolutely indispensable for normal functioning in the world. What seems to have happened is that after the explanations of the *physikoi*, who took a secular view of a world previously seen through the apparatus of myth and divinity, Heraclitus and Parmenides gave abundant consideration to its aesthetic character. Anaxamenes must have been thinking in the same terms when he used such powerful literary artillery. Parmenides was a poet, and Heraclitus wrote anything but prosaically. Listen to the musical quality of his diction: "Mortals are immortals, and immortals are mortals, the one living the other's death and dying the other's life." Heraclitus said God undergoes alteration "in the way that fire, when it is mixed with spices, is named according to the scent of each of them."

Myles Burnyeat, professor of ancient philosophy at the University of Cambridge, thinks Heraclitus, like many a modern bard, deliberately spoke in riddles so as to make us face up to the difficulty of grasping unfamiliar truths lurking behind ideas that we take as obvious. That may be why his writing, like poetry, is always straining against the limits of sense, never so diaphanous as to allow its content to be captured simply by paraphrasing it in different words. The epigrams of Heraclitus fly in the face of a centuries-old tradition in Western philosophy that there is a close affinity between literal meaning and truth. One scholar maintains that we must read them, not as insights into the one reality, but rather as wisdom, as "a search for common understanding. This view was to influence both Plato and Aristotle, and the idea that philosophers seek understanding as much as truth is one that remains attractive."

Other commentators are not so sure. They do not share the opinion that truth is incidental to and separate from understanding. Plato was no great champion of common sense, but he was unhappy with a tendency, in part a reaction against the way the doctrines of Parmenides hinged so crucially on a point of language, to assume that language can be made to do anything we want it to do, that reality is what we think or say it is. The message of Parmenides is that the only way we can know the structure of reality is via the structure of thought and language. But if a clever logician can play such games with language as to make one aspect of the world intelligible at the expense of making everything else look like nonsense, what has become of the Logos that guarantees, as a metaphysical principle, that our minds are in tune with the truth of the world?

Jonathan Barnes, professor of ancient philosophy at Oxford, agrees that some of Parmenides' arguments are patently false, for example, the apparently perverse statement: "If something does not exist, it cannot exist." He writes that the whole system rests on a "sandy" foundation. Still, Barnes moderates his criticism by saying we should not ignore the "seductive powers" that certain falsehoods may have when they are stated informally in ordinary English or in ordinary Greek. To seduce, of course, suggests an element of artifice and devious allure, of pleasures that have an undertone of the illicit, of Circe-like dissembling and the casting of spells over the rational mind. Summing up, Barnes asserts that Parmenides was wrong; we can and do talk and think of things that do not exist. When did you last mention the tooth fairy? But he goes on to commend the Eleatic philosopher just the same, for reasons that are candidly aesthetic, treating Parmenides as if he were an artist or a weaver of literary images. His ideas, says Barnes, "are not merely antique exhibits in the roomy museum of philosophical follies: the arguments he adduces, though unsound, are ingenious and admirable; their conclusion, though false, has a strange plausibility and attractiveness." Aristotle himself suggested that Parmenides could only be taken seriously if we approach him as the creator of alternative worlds differing drastically from the one we inhabit, if we see him as an artist or poet. Artists do not dwell in the land of the ordinary. To think in that way in real life, Aristotle said, verges on insanity.

Art, as we shall see, tends to throw the concept of truth into confusion. It sanctions possibilities, expands the store of meanings, uses untruth to deepen our understanding of what life is all about. Perhaps it is not stretching a point too far to say that this is one reason why Parmenides, though "wrong," cast such a looming shadow over future centuries. He was a logician, and logic, a modern philosopher has said, is "an exploration of the field of possibilities just as truly as astronomy is an exploration of the field of stellar motions." Logic, as the most nonspecific of the sciences, deals with the possible rather than with the merely plausible, or with what seems to make sense in a real world. One could say that logic is promiscuous, not wedded inexorably to the truth; it needs to investigate the consequences of statements that are false, not just the ones that are true.

Loosen the rules, however, and argument, like the modern definition of art as "anything you can get away with," becomes a species of Metis, a technique of cunning and chicanery. We shall meet some of its practitioners in the next chapter. They dealt, not with truth, but with the rhetorical art of pleasing and persuading, of making falsehood plausible. The seeds were already planted. If Parmenides could argue with "admirable" but profoundly erroneous logic, if his conclusions, though incorrect, are comely and pleasing to the poetic sensibility, then why bother with truth? Karl Jaspers considered that one result of the work of Parmenides was to give rise to "the aesthetic view of being and the world, the intellectual frivolity which traces an endless variety of figures of thought, none of them binding." That outlook never permanently went out of vogue. Aestheticism has been a potent influence on modernism and postmodernism in our time, movements that sanction the practice of philosophy as playful interpretation, with absolutely no commitment to ultimate truth.

CHAPTER FOUR

The Absolute Talker

We have to mix a little falsehood into truth to make it plausible.
—Iris Murdoch

ROUND THE MIDDLE OF THE FIFTH CENTURY B.C., there came into fashion itinerant teachers who offered lessons, not in the philosophy of Truth, but in the art of power. The worst of them taught that truth may at times be a nuisance, an impediment to gaining or using power, and they removed it by the simple expedient of making truth secondary to power, even if it was only the power of persuasion, of using words to make falsehood more attractive to an audience than what is actually the case.

Ancient philosophers were inclined to regard truth as the normal condition of a person's mind. Anything else was a quandary. How anyone could say or even think what is false was a puzzle that provoked ingenious speculations. An untruth refers to something that does not exist, which seemed decidedly queer. Falsehood was deviant, it was odd, it was altogether quite a riddle. For the Greeks, Plato in particular, who knew perfectly well that people do not always tell the truth, and that some people habitually lie their heads off, falsehood was something that needed explaining; it deserved to be argued about.

Plato's Dialogue the *Euthydemus*, outstanding for its comic word-fencing and ingenious mockery, takes a satirical look at the fashion for disputation, an important part of the education of a smart young Athenian man. Two mischievous professors, the brothers Euthydemus and Dionysodorus, are showing off their mettle as quibbling virtuosos of spurious "proofs," demonstrating that something blatantly wrong can, by means of certain verbal contortions, be presented as seemingly true. This plausible pair is out to bewitch an impressionable and good-looking young man. Plato's intent is to expose the specious fictions of trained debaters in order to set the stage for the creation of an honest and sound logic that will safeguard truth.

With his celebrated irony, Socrates describes the brothers as "absolutely omniscient." They are athletes of argument, ex-military men, now warriors with words, who take no prisoners in a verbal showdown. Give them a piece of nonsense or a flat lie to defend, and they can do so as skillfully as they can knock down truth. "Nobody dares stand up to them for a moment," exclaims Socrates in mock admiration. "Such a faculty they have acquired for wielding words as their weapons and confuting any argument as readily if it be true as if it be false." It goes without saying that this duo was greatly in demand as defense counsel in the law courts. What is more, they guarantee to teach anyone else to be just as clever—for a fee. Socrates encounters them in the gymnasium, together with some of their pupils. As a warm-up, he invites them to take in hand a young man named Cleinias, who needs to be set on the road to virtue and wisdom. One of the brothers, Euthydemus, begins by asking Cleinias: Which sort of men are learners, the wise or the foolish?

Smirking, Dionysodorus leans over and whispers in Socrates' ear: "Let me tell you beforehand, whichever way the lad answers, he will be refuted." Cleinias then replies that it is the wise who are the learners. Euthydemus at once closes the trap:

> *Are there persons whom you call teachers, or not?*
> Cleinias agrees that there are.
> *And the teachers of the learners are teachers in the same way*
> *as your lute master and your writing master, I suppose, were*

> *teachers of you and the other boys, while you were pupils?*
> Cleinias assents.
> *Now, of course, when you were learning, you did not yet*
> *know the things you were learning?*
> No.
> *So were you wise, when you did not know those things?*
> No, to be sure.
> *Then if not wise, foolish?*
> Certainly.
> *So when you learned what you did not know, you learned*
> *While being foolish.*
> Cleinias nods his head Yes.
> *Hence it is the foolish who learn, Cleinias, and not the*
> *wise, as you suppose.*

Immediately, the retinue of admirers of the two professors bursts into applause, laughing in chorus. Hardly had the noise died down than Dionysodorus chipped in.

> *Well now Cleinias, whenever your writing master dictated*
> *from memory, which of the boys learned the piece recited,*
> *the wise or the foolish?*
> The wise, Cleinias answers.
> *So it is the wise who learn, and not the foolish. Hence the*
> *answer you gave just now to Duthydemus was a bad one."*

At this slick reversal of a "truth" into a "falsehood," the claque around the professors waxes positively raucous with approval, to the quiet dismay of Socrates. The brothers gleefully proceed to pull off another coup, trapping their floundering young victim into agreeing, on the one hand, that learners learn what they know, and on the other, that they learn what they don't know. Dionysodorus puts his whispering mouth close to the ear of Socrates again: "All our questions are like that. They leave no escape."

Now Socrates steps in and decides to rescue Cleinias from further embarrassment. These smart-alec professors, he says, are just playing games, dancing around him and making merry like celebrants at the Corybantic rites, performing "sportive gambols," as part of his initiation. His chief mistake was to be duped by the false use of words.

"Learning" may mean acquiring knowledge starting from a state of complete ignorance, or using knowledge we already possess to investigate some specific matter, a process that could better be called understanding. That distinction should be kept in mind.

Such conjuring with the protean ambiguities of words, as Menelaus dissembled to trap the polymorphous sea god, is sport, not science, Socrates goes on. It is like slyly pulling a chair away just as someone is about to sit in it, howling with mirth to see the luckless victim sprawling on his back.

The same technique can be used to argue the impossibility of saying that anything is false, which means there is no such thing as a lie. If a person tells a lie, then he or she speaks of a certain subject matter, "a single one, distinct from all the others." The speaker refers to "that which is." Surely, anyone who tells what is, tells the truth. A liar does not speak of things as they are, but as they are not. It is silly to think you can have an effect on something that does not exist. Yet orators in the Athenian Assembly, famous for blarney and truth-twisting, certainly have an effect on votes, on policymaking, on history. They are makers, doers. A maker must make something, and Euthydemus has already tricked his opponent into conceding that it is impossible to make what is not. Consequently, nobody speaks what is false. And if that is the case, contradiction is also impossible. There is only one truth and anything that contradicts it must be untrue. Yet it has just been agreed that untruth, false opinion, cannot occur. Refutation is a fiction.

By the tenor of Socrates' remarks, it seems to have been well known in Athens that this kind of argument was suicidally self-destructive. Posing as a slow-witted, simple fellow, baffled by "these clever devices," Socrates eventually asks a devastating question: If there is no such thing as speaking false or thinking false, or of being stupid, and therefore no risk of ever making a mistake, what in heaven's name are these two professors doing charging inflated fees to teach young men not to make mistakes? The argument, Socrates says, "suffers from the old trouble of knocking others down and then falling itself."

We now call such counterfeit logic "sophistry," and we do so because its practitioners were known as Sophists, typified in its shallower form by the two shifty, profiteering educators of Plato's dialogue. At one point, Socrates singles out a man named Protagoras as the chief instigator of the curious notion that falsehood, and therefore contradiction, are impossible. Protagoras, perhaps the first and certainly one of the most formidable of the Sophists, was born about 500 B.C. at Abdera, far to the north of Athens. The famous doctrine of Protagoras was that "man is the measure of all things." That notorious epigram was the opening salvo in Protagoras' treatise *Truth*— known at a later time as the "Throws"—arguments calculated to floor an opponent in a debate as decisively as in a wrestling bout. Interpreted in a number of different ways, it seems to have meant that the properties of things have no independent existence apart from our perception of them. They are as we personally see, touch, and hear them. That put paid to the notion of an absolute truth, the same at all times for everyone, since my "measure" of the world may be radically different from yours, and who is to say which of us is correct?

Protagoras accumulated a large fortune, traveling throughout Greece giving tuition for a substantial fee. He was an agnostic; there is a story that he was banished from Athens for irreligion and his book *On the Gods* publicly burned in the marketplace after a herald had been sent to confiscate all copies in circulation. A tall tale says he was drowned while fleeing from pursuers in Athenian triremes, but that is exploded by Plato's report that Protagoras died at the age of seventy, still held in high esteem.

His temperament was down-to-earth, though if Plato is to be believed, he liked to be flattered and complimented; a bit of a snob, jealous of his reputation, a provincial anxious to make it in the big city. Protagoras had a well-developed practical streak in him, instructing the young and ambitious on how to advance their careers. According to Diogenes Laertius, a third-century profiler of Greek philosophers, a great plunderer of secondary sources with a taste for gossip, Protagoras invented the shoulder strap for porters of wood and was quite an innovator in the matter of compensation: he was the first to ask a fee of a hundred *minae* for his teaching services. That was an example of his knack, noted by Diogenes, of "seizing the opportune moment." Like Darwin, he was drawn to theories of the origins of the human faculties, mental, social, and moral, which enable people to deal with surfaces and appearances, with life as they meet and grapple with it. Abstractions beloved by mathematicians—dimensionless points, perfectly straight lines, and exactly circular circles—he dismissed as fictions which do not exist because we never come across them.

Protagoras was not a pragmatist in the modern sense of the word, someone who believes that "truth" is what works, what has useful and beneficial consequences. He simply shelved altogether the distinction between true and false as having no discernible bearing on human life. In that case, an argument, however firmly it seems to stand up, however watertight its logic, can always be demolished by a contrary argument, if made by a skilled debater, and Protagoras was in the lucrative business of training debaters. There is a well-known heads-I-win, tails-you-lose story about Protagoras. Euathlus, one of his students, agreed to pay his tuition only if and when he won his first case at law. Euathlus completed his studies, but never set foot in the courts. Protagoras threatened to sue him, arguing that however the case came out, Euathlus would have to pay up. If Protagoras won the suit, his student would have to comply with the court's judgment and pay the fee. If Euathlus won, he would still be liable for the tuition, since the original contract with Protagoras stipulated it. Euathlus had not graduated in the Sophistic technique for nothing, however. What Protagoras said was reasonable, but a little ingenuity could turn that thesis on its head. If I win, Euathlus could say, then by the ruling of the court, I need not pay you. If you win, I am free of all obligations, because our original agreement was that I would pay only if I won my first case.

Man is the measure of *all* things. That was the Protagoran thesis. It does not mean that each individual is the final arbiter. To a sick person a certain food may taste unpleasant, but to a healthy palate it is most appetizing. The sick man is not false in his judgment of the food, any more than the well person is speaking the absolute truth. Put simply, it is "better" to be healthy and nourished than sick and depleted. Life just works that way. "It is not possible to think what is false," Protagoras says. "A person can think only what he experiences, and what he experiences is true." Of course, that is twisting the meaning of the word "true," but such a device would cause a Sophist no particular qualms. Only the ignorant, Protagoras maintains, would suppose a Sophist actually corrects a person's judgment from false to true. It is just a question of transforming an unwholesome outlook into a salubrious one. "So, my dear Socrates," he crows, "instead of comparing us Sophists to jumping frogs as you did, you might have recognised us to be a kind of physician."

"A fiction, but a *fiction which is necessary to life*." That is how these practical men saw the idea of a "common world," which for Heraclitus had been made possible by the operations of the Logos. If the Logos is just a figment, a metaphysician's fancy, then something needs to be invented to take its place, as an artificial construct, as a social necessity in a democratic state. There is a distinctly Darwinian flavor to all this. The wise Sophist, doctoring the "reality" of the unhealthy citizen, is helping him to adapt to the environment of a societywide consensus. And the point of adaptation is to achieve dominance and mastery over the environment. In its more commercial and flaky incarnations, Sophism substituted winning and losing for truth and falsehood. Like Darwin, Protagoras threw out all concepts of truth that were in any way associated with the gods. He was an agnostic, and tended to parade the fact, unlike Darwin, who was more discreet about his religious views and was laid to rest in Westminster Abbey. The existence or nonexistence of the gods was a question Protagoras put at arm's length. Theology, he said, is so knotty a subject that life is too brief to even try to untangle it. The Persian Magi, perhaps his tutors, did invoke gods in their secret ceremonies, but they passed for agnostics by their avoidance of any public declaration of belief in divine beings. They were not anxious to give people the impression that their special powers required assistance from outside agencies.

Parmenides, in his great poem, had stressed that truth is reached by just one road, the "renowned way of the goddess." Survival, the healthy flourishing of an individual life or a state, on the other hand, can be achieved by many different routes. Aristotle regarded the *polis* as something that evolved quite naturally and inevitably out of the profoundly natural unit of the family: human beings were at home in the city, state, at home in the world. It was as if that were the only possible outcome. "Nature, we assert," said Aristotle, "does nothing in vain." That was clean contrary to Darwin, who believed that nature did plenty in vain. Her vanities even provided a clue to the theory of evolution. The Sophists would have agreed with him. They speculated that humankind had started in a state of primitive ignorance and squalor, pulling itself up by the bootstraps with painful effort, by means of technical prowess, trial and error, inventiveness, and language, the medium of unlimited possibilities, which can easily float up into the thin air of fantasy and fiction.

At the time of Protagoras, two words had particular resonance among educated Greeks: *physis* and *nomos*. *Physis* can be roughly translated as "nature." *Nomos* is an umbrella term for the traditions, constraints, rules implict and explicit, handed down from the past or created afresh. These terms had come to represent a crucial distinction between what is given to human beings and what humans make for themselves. If the state emerged by natural necessity, then it is physis. If, on the other hand, it depends on the intellectual effort of writing a constitution, of drafting laws which have the authority of the state behind them, it is created by nomos. When the Logos was intact, *physis* and *nomos* were not antithetical terms. Nomos was a given, part of the natural constitution and eternal order of the world, and it had a close affinity to physis. Justice, for example, was not an artifice, but something inherent in the cosmos.

There was a single, comprehensive law that included the macrocosmos of the universe and the microcosmos of the human individual. The Greeks talked about "unwritten laws" that were eternal and forever true. But when the gods lost their hold on the minds of practical get-aheads in the post-Logos age, the natural and the artificial went their separate ways. Nomos relinquished its intimate link with nature, in part because of a general disillusion with the speculations of the natural philosophers. It came to signify instead the artificial codes, prohibitions, and sanctions devised by men, which were sometimes at odds with nature. The given came unglued from the made. Nomos might signify a false but popular belief, and physis something that was evidently true, although the way things were going, you couldn't entirely trust the universe. Once nomos was denatured, almost anything could be called a mere fashion or transitory opinion, like saying honey is sweet for me, bitter for you. Plato's installation of the Forms, eternal truths that were not relative to anything, and were designed in part to counter vulgar Sophism, were quite distinct from and independent of the material world.

The conservative playwright Aristophanes, in his comedy *The Clouds*, notes this denaturing of nomos in a scene where an obnoxious young man, Pheideippides, threatens to whack his father hard with a stick. "But nowhere is it the custom for a father to suffer this," objects the parent, clearly a relic of a generation that believed in the permanence of decent standards of behavior and family honor. Whereupon the young whippersnapper, who had been sent to study at a Sophistic think tank and had learned his lessons all too well, argues that since such codes were made by men, they can be altered at will by other men: "Wasn't the person who first laid down this custom (*nomos*) a man, like you and me? And didn't he persuade the men of old by making a speech? Then is it any less possible for me now to lay down a custom for sons—to beat their fathers back?"

When filial piety, like justice, like truth, is no longer underwritten by a belief in the cosmic necessity of certain moral principles, fathers are apt to get treated like dirt. Partly due to dislocations caused by the war between Athens and Sparta, Greece lost the sense of being anchored to the natural order of things. In 429 B.C., Protagoras' mentor Pericles, who helped to reduce the powers of ancient institutions and usher in a radical democracy, died of the plague. Leaders who succeeded him were a new breed; small-minded, unscrupulous rabble-rousers, ridiculed and mocked in the comic theater. They lacked aristocratic lineage and their money came mostly, not from gentlemanly pursuits such as farming, but from working slaves for a pittance in sweatshops. *Arete*, the sort of human excellence which made its possessors leaders of men, was until the fifth century regarded as an inborn gift that came with high breeding, without explicit tutoring, as natural as breathing. Now, the new upstart commercial class, flush with recent wealth, better acquainted with foreign cultures and customs than were the old nobility, emerged to question the codes and ethics of the wellborn. They were well educated in such fields as finance and the navy, and in the art of speechifying. Basic institutions such as the city-state, once accepted for what they were, came up for critical scrutiny. Far from thinking of the state as *physis*, a living organism, in harmony with nature, newcomers like the Sophists saw it as something unnatural, an artifice cleverly put together, like a machine, by that most wonderful of creators, the human mind.

Downsizing the meaning of nomos in the fifth century was a significant turning point, a foretaste of modernity in the classical world. One scholar has called it "a spiritual revolution." Another thinks the breaking asunder of nomos from physis was "the beginning of a division between mind and world, where thought and reality no longer have a correlative fit." It coincided with the separation of Logos from Kosmos, and with the loss of myth's authority to make connections between culture and nature by interpreting nature in terms of sacred meanings. Rules of right and wrong and of proper conduct were no longer respected as part of the changeless order, but were subject to the whims of individuals powerful enough to say what was and what was not permissible. Of the Sophists, Albert Borgmann writes that they "started from the premise that the departed Logos had left behind a mass of unrelated, freely manageable fragments which the individual could use to his own liking."

The Sophists were not consistent or cohesive enough to be called a school or a movement. Some were admirable characters, others disreputable charlatans. Assessments vary wildly, as did the reputations of individual practitioners. Xenephon called them prostitutes who got rich peddling ersatz wisdom. Plato, in *The Sophist*, damned them as paid chasers after the young and wealthy, though he shows Protagoras a good deal of respect. Robert Brumbaugh likens Sophistic instruction to the English satirist Stephen Potter's notorious treatise *Lifemanship*, or "how to win in the game of life without actually cheating." Many Sophists were constantly on the move, working as touring lecturers and tutors to the rising class of young men eager to make their mark in politics, law, and business. A few came to Athens to talk about the theories of nature proposed by the *physikoi*, but that did not bring in much in the way of lecture fees. Youthful Athenians, intensely urban and practical in their outlook, were far more interested in the affairs of the *polis* and in competing for success in public life. They wanted tutoring in the mysterious art of "getting on." John Herman Randall compares this time in Greek history with that of the American colonies before the Revolution, or with the Victorian breed of energetic liberals dedicated to the idea that free discussion and debate could sort out most human problems; the kind who populate the Parliamentary novels of Anthony Trollope. Like the Victorians, the fifth-century Athenians were marathon, expansive, champion talkers. They talked, Randall says, not about deep imponderables, but "about the surface of human conflicts and relations, as intelligent governing classes do, in a time of assurance, of expanding social life, of untroubled confidence in fundamentals."

The Sophists made culture autonomous by splitting it away from nature. They did the same to language. Like Darwin again, they denied that there is a *natural* fit between mind, language, and reality. Culture is an artificial medium, making discoveries about itself rather than about the world. Since language is part of culture, not nature, subject to no irresistible constraints in the "real" world, one can manipulate and twist it to one's heart's content, using it to warp truth if that will benefit a ruling interest or a desirable state of civic affairs. Language can serve the principle that there is "something more important" than the truth.

In time, rhetoric replaced the old tradition of the Logos. Rhetoric is a medium of democracy, a vehicle of persuasion rather than of force. It does not flourish easily under tyranny, and it blossomed in Greece, was codified and given the academic primatur, in the first half of the fifth century B.C., at a time when personal liberty was a beacon on the horizon. In the late fifth and fourth centuries in Athens, the people ruled. Plato said they enjoyed acting like royalty. They had extraordinary power over the choice of their leaders. The Assembly, of which all male citizens over the age of eighteen were members, had ultimate authority over all key decisions on home and foreign affairs. It elected such important figures as army generals by a show of hands. Members of the Council of Five Hundred and the courts were selected by lot and served for only one year, so as to give the ordinary person maximum participation in the state. All citizens were able to challenge the performance of any official, present or past. In the courts, the judgment of the people was final, irrevocable.

Along with the freedom to serve in almost any government post and to decide matters of the utmost national importance went an extravagant freedom of speech. Gorgias, a founder of Sophism, traced its origin in part to debates in the Assembly and the law courts, where a speech could win over the crowd because it was clever, not because it told the truth. In spite of penalties for impiety and corrupting youth, the free and easy atmosphere of Athens was such that libel and slander were not prosecutable offenses. The eminent and exalted, high military officers and politicians, could be held up to ridicule and contempt just like anyone else.

Given such license, it was inevitable that language should be pushed to the limit of its potential, subjected to warp and stress like an experimental airplane in a wind tunnel. It was used to state bald fact and actuality, but also to inveigle, play the vamp, beguile, and turn reality inside out. The city-state made such extremes possible. Athens was a highly competitive society. A citizen needed all the persuasive powers he could muster at law, at a time when the legal system was often used for trumpery or malicious reasons. It was common for a typical man of business to be hauled into court once a year to face a suit for breach of contract, and to conduct his own defense. Prominent Athenians might be accused of impiety or disloyalty merely as a political dodge. "Not only success, but sometimes effective survival, made skill in law something to be desired," Robert Brumbaugh notes. "The Town Meeting was much the same: a man who could not talk persuasively was at a serious disadvantage; not only would he be unlikely to hold elective office, but he might end up with a special contribution to the navy or the theater assessed against him."

Talk was a near obsession in Athens of the fifth century. Benjamin Jowett, the high Victorian classical scholar and master of Balliol,

coined the term "the Absolute Talker," *autos ho dialektikos*, as embody-
ing the Platonic ideal of argument and disputation. This was not an
inherently upper-class trait, although aristocrats did dominate the
proceedings of the Assembly, due to their often superior skill at
speechmaking. Starting with Pericles, Greek statesmen saw the need
to woo and court the people, and that meant learning to be profi-
cient in rhetoric; a course of lessons could be expensive. A new word,
philodemos, "love of the people," appeared. The public tended to
choose, says Robert Hall, "the most persuasive orator, who was not
necessarily an able statesman by Athenian standards. Although such
a leader could persuade the people to select him, in turn he was led
by them to satisfy their desires and inclinations." Plato condemned
this as mere pandering to the crowd's itch for pleasures. The Greek
term for an orator was demagogos, which at first meant a leader of
the people, but later carried the sense of "flatterer of the people,"
with all the fakery and flimflam the term implies.

It was part of the intention of the Sophists to explode the theory
of Parmenides, that all appearances are mere illusion. Rhetoric could
hardly exist as a going enterprise if that were the case, since all its
tricks and devices depend on surfaces, not profundities and depths.
There was a strong aesthetic component in certain of the techniques
of the Sophists, and this had an important bearing on theories of
truth and falsehood. The word *sophistes* in itself had arty overtones.
It was used by Pindar of poets and by Aeschylus of musicians, acquiring the sense of professional teacher only at the end of the fifth century. Protagoras, who was famous for interpreting poems by
Simonides and others, named Homer and Hesiod as closet Sophists.
He himself was a literary critic as well as a grammarian, commended
for his structural analysis of a passage of the *Iliad,* which strikes
today's scholars as surprisingly modern. Gorgias held that deceit can
be admirable if used for aesthetic reasons. He called speech "that
great potentate," which can achieve the most results with the least
amount of physical exertion, and poetry a form of speech. It casts
such a spell that "upon those who hear it there comes a fearful shud-
dering and a tearful pity and a mournful yearning."

In his *Poetics*, Aristotle said Homer taught his successsors "the

proper way of telling lies." What is convincing though impossible in
the drama, Aristotle says, must always be preferred to what is possible but unconvincing. Reading or listening to a poem, one must sub-
mit to its particular kind of fraudulence or miss the entire point. It
is better in that case to tune in to the mendacity than to tune it out.
In an essay entitled "Aristotle on Detective Fiction," the mystery
writer Dorothy L. Sayers, with a curtsy in the direction of the great
philosopher of antiquity, laid down as an *arche* of her trade that "Any
fool can tell a lie, and any fool can believe it; but the right method is
to tell the *truth* in such a way that the *intelligent* reader is seduced into
telling the lie for himself. That the writer himself should tell a flat lie
is contrary to all the canons of detective art."

These pronouncements, of course, are always trembling on the
brink of justifying utter dishonesty under the pretext that it is in the
service of a higher purpose. If Sophists are physicians, their task is to
make us feel better, not to ram the truth down our throats. Gorgias
maintained that tragedy produces a deception in which the deceiver
is more honest than the nondeceiver and the deceived wiser than the
undeceived. "The power of speech over the disposition of the soul,"
said Gorgias, "is comparable with the effect of drugs on the disposition of the body. As drugs can expel certain humors from the body
and thereby make an end either of sickness or of life, so likewise various words can produce grief, pleasure or fear, which act like drugs
when they give rise to bad persuasions in the soul." Socrates said Protagoras spoke with the voice of Orpheus, the spellbinding poet and
musician who enchanted wild beasts and made even the trees and
rocks move to his songs. Aeschylus called rhetoric "the charmer to
whom nothing is denied." Helen of Troy may have been seduced by
the allure of rhetoric; if so, she must be counted utterly blameless for
her infidelity. She was as helpless under its spell as if she had been
snatched up by a god, or abducted forcefully by a barbarian. Words
and words alone are as potent as a supernatural visitation or a rape.

There is a suggestion in the sayings of the Sophists that sticking
to plain facts, shunning falsehood with the absolute detestation that
Plato demanded of the ideal ruler of his Republic, is the pedestrian
attitude of the inferior mind. This point of view smacks of the aes-

thete who regards ordinary, straightforward truth as too easy, too undemanding and tedious, a symptom of a weak imagination and a literal way of thinking. And the absence of a sense of fun. Gorgias advised his pupils "to destroy an opponent's seriousness by laughter and his laughter by seriousness." Once, when a swallow flew over and dropped some waste matter on his head, Gorgias sang out: "Shame on you, Philomena!"

A Sophist was a maker, an inventor, not a finder or an observer. In Plato's *Gorgias*, Callicles, a follower of the Sophists, regards Socrates, who aims to find truth by rational observance of the rules of argument, not by charm and clever persuasion, as a stifling influence on true talent, holding back the creative impulses of men whose ambition is to dominate the democratic process. Socrates dissipates this life force with his old-maidish taste for sitting around drawing out slender filaments of deductive reasoning, taking it for granted that truth is something objective, something real, attainable though difficult to reach, often arriving at no final answers. Because he shuns relativism, the doctrine that tends to favor brute force, whether in action or in talk, Socrates is not a "real man." He lacks the desire to crush his adversaries. He is weak, cowardly, afraid to assert himself, all because he believes in a chimera called universal truth. He is destined never to say anything "free and great and vigorous." Socrates is passive and contemplative in a world where truth is actively made, not happened upon in an armchair.

One of the most sustained and vehement polemics against rhetoric came with the rise of the modern scientific mentality in the seventeenth century. Francis Bacon, in his *Novum Organum*, is as fierce as Plato in his dismissal of "sophistical" philosophy, where words acquire a tyrannical authority over fact: "for while men believe their reason governs words, in fact, words turn back and reflect their power upon the understanding." They can, and often do, refer to things that do not exist. Common sense usually dictates how words cut up and organize the world, but "when then someone of sharper understanding or more diligence in observation wishes to shift those lines, so as to move them closer to Nature, words shout him down." In rhetoric, words beget words. And philosophies, being made of words, beget more philosophies, producing fictitious stories that are more like poetic drama than science. They make the world pretty and charming, present the truth as we would wish it to be, not as it is. "The true end, scope or office of knowledge," Bacon instructs us, "consists not in any plausible, delectable, reverend or admired discourse, or in any satisfactory arguments, but in effecting and working, and in discovery of particulars, not revealed before."

Plato and Bacon each had his own reason to blow a trumpet blast against the wordmakers and poet-orators who used language as an unscrupulous apothecary might prescribe a mind-altering infusion of potent chemicals. Bacon wanted to assert the principle of truth as a stubborn, perhaps inelegant and awkward fact that needs to throw off the hypnotic charm of words. For that reason, science has to disenchant itself, or it will never advance. Plato, more concerned with the proper governance of a decent city-state than with the laws of nature, waged a war of resistance against the influential doctrine, held for different reasons by such strange bedfellows as Parmenides and Protagoras, that nothing we say or think can be false. He did so because the idea that truth is easy, or that it takes a back seat to winning, in the Darwinian sense of beating out the competition, was anathema to him. Plato put poets on a par with "representatives of falsehood and feigning in all departments of life and knowledge, like the Sophists and rhetoricians, the false priests, false prophets, lying spirits, enchanters of the world."

The notion that we can only speak what is true makes truth too cheap, too much of a screaming bargain. Genuine knowledge, the kind Plato's ruler must possess, ought to come more expensive than that, have a higher price tag. That price, Nicholas Denyer says, is that it is possible for us to make mistakes. "A principle requiring all beliefs to be true would obliterate the distinction between truth and falsehood no less thoroughly than a principle requiring them all to be false." It is a tribute to the influence and ingenuity of the Sophists that anyone should consider such a statement even needs to be made.

CHAPTER FIVE

The Double Truth

Theories usually result from precipitate reasoning of an impatient mind which would like to be rid of phenomena and replaces them with images, concepts, indeed often with mere words. One senses, possibly also realizes, that this is a mere makeshift. But doesn't passion and partiality always fall in love with makeshifts? And rightly so, because they are so greatly needed. —Goethe

LATO'S ANTI-SOPHISTIC VIEW OF TRUTH and lies threw its imposing shadow across the span of time historians call the Middle Ages. He fiercely denied that the words we use to describe reality are mere counters that can be shuffled and tweaked to befuddle weak minds in a game of power. In its pure form, Plato's theory says words refer to the eternally true, absolutely real, and context-free Ideas. Consciousness is not an artifact built up in a person by years of observing the world, accumulating and memorizing facts. It is something we are born possessing, and it is somehow in communication with the super-world of the Ideas.

This doctrine, that truth is not to be found in differences but in identity, was strong in medieval times, from the third century on. There was a bias against originality and a belief that every singular thing in the world, including every person, should be as like as possible to its ideal type.

Then, toward the end of the eleventh century, a reaction against this sovereignty of the abstract absolute set in. The particular began to stake its claim in opposition to the universal, and to a marked extent subvert the strenuous efforts Plato had made to keep language honest. As long as Truth was external to minds, external to sentences and even to individual "true" things, it was safe. Language could not trivialize or belittle it. Plato said we know what truth is because Truth is an independent entity in a separate domain, and the Sophists should keep their greedy hands off it.

Danger beckoned once the reality of universals was under question, since Christianity itself was based on such otherworldly absolutes as God and the Trinity. What if these eternal entities were not real at all, not outside time and space and even human thoughts, but simply words, names, that human beings had invented? That unsettling thesis came to be known as "nominalism," originating in the teachings of the eleventh-century scholastic philosopher Roscellinus, whose Latin formula was *universalis sunt nomina*, "universals are (only) names." Nominalism was destined to cast its influence over most of Europe. It was known as the *via moderna*, or modern way, and eventually it was to spell the collapse of the whole grand synthesis of medieval thought. By arguing that there is no reality apart from the single individual, that the world can be understood only one thing, one fact, at a time, nominalism made all human knowledge suspect. It also threw into question the entire relationship between language and thought. Loosely speaking, nominalism was a latter-day revival of the Sophistic distinction between *physis* and *nomos*, the natural and the artificial, between what is given and what is made. A Sophist, holding the view that there is a profusion of "truths"—perhaps as many as there are people to believe them—but no single, final Truth, and that language makes its own reality, would have been a nominalist in the fourteenth century A.D.

In fact, Antisthenes, a leading Sophist who was among the handful of close associates present in the room with Socrates when he drank hemlock, has been called "the first nominalist." Antisthenes denied the existence of the Platonic Forms as independent realities. There is a tale that he once said to Plato: "I see a horse, but I don't see horseness." Don't feel proud of yourself, was the gist of Plato's response. Regard it as a defect of intuition. "For you have the eye with which a horse is seen, but you have not yet acquired the eye to see horseness." Or treeness, or blueness, or chariotness, presumably. To a nominalist, each tree, each shade of blue, every chariot, is unique and different. Even if we could conceive horseness, the universal equine essence, it would exist only in our minds, and is just a fiction of reason. A thing has one and only one Logos; it cannot be spoken of except by its own proper description. Therefore—here we go again—it is impossible to speak falsely or to contradict. Aristotle, the philosopher of common sense, called Antisthenes foolish and his followers "crude thinkers."

At first, the rise of nominalism seemed to pose no deadly harm to church teaching and in fact tended to underscore the importance of revelation, since it also contested the Platonic idea that human reason can show that universals are real. You had to rely on faith. In the fourteenth century, however, nominalism, with its world-altering message that mankind can never know ultimate truth by the power of reason alone, burst onto the scene with renewed intensity and force.

On the night of May 26, 1328, William of Ockham, a young Franciscan friar accused of propagating ideas deeply subversive of church authority, together with a handful of like-minded colleagues, fled from his convent in Avignon, home of the popes in exile. Barely escaping arrest, they took ship secretly down the Rhone. At Aigues-Mortes, an imperial galley waited to take them to the emperor Louis of Bavaria. A year earlier, Louis had deposed the Avignon pope, John XXII, and set up an anti-pope in Rome. Ockham, a lecturer at Oxford, had been summoned to Avignon, where a committee of six theologians decided that fifty-one items in his commentaries were "heretical and pestilential." He refused to disown them, inviting more grief for himself by taking sides against the pope on the bitterly controversial question of poverty. Ockham championed the cause of the Spirituals, a group of Franciscans who believed in practicing absolute poverty, as did the early Christians. Property, after all, did not exist in the Garden of Eden. Two years later, he signed a protest against a papal bull which condemned the doctrine. His escape enabled him to carry on his polemical opposition from a secure distance. He and his companions finally reached Pisa, where he put himself under the protection of the emperor, campaigning for political democracy in church and state, and stressing the importance of the individual over society as a whole.

The nocturnal flight of Ockham has been called a decisive moment in the history of European thought, comparable to the secret journey of Lenin in 1917 from Switzerland to Petrograd in a sealed train, there to spread the virus of an untested ideology. In a phrase intended to emphasize that the force of ideas is not weaker than the might of armies, Ockham's first words to the emperor are reputed to have been: "Protect me with your sword, and I will defend you with my pen."

Was Ockham the Lenin of his day? An exaggeration, certainly. In fact, he has been likened to a nineteenth-century liberal, someone like John Stuart Mill, for his utilitarian theory of property, his advocacy of civil and, to a limited extent, religious liberty and freedom of debate, and his strong belief that exceptions to rules are one of the inescapable facts of life. Like Darwin, Ockham also held fast to the view that metaphysics must be separated absolutely from the task of understanding nature. His ideas ultimately helped to bring about a fundamental change in Western ways of thinking. Well into the twentieth century, one scholar notes, "Ockham's name continued to carry the faint odor of disreputability and scandal in certain quarters." His ideas have been compared to those of the twentieth-century theorist of "language games," Ludwig Wittgenstein.

Ockham became a household word, thanks to his celebrated razor, the ever sharp blade of logic that shaves away superfluous terms and finicky distinctions that Scholasticism had manufactured in bulk over centuries of medieval thought. He probably never used such a word, but the metaphor of the razor as an instrument of economy and parsimony runs through all his work. "To employ a number of principles when it is possible to use a few is a waste of time," is a typical Ockhamist statement of belief in the power of logical frugality.

Ockham was profoundly loyal to the church. He did not place under suspicion such theological untouchables as the Trinity. He merely shelved all aspirations to match up the inadequate instrument of the human mind with the enormous mystery of God's operations. Like Protagoras, though in very different terms, Ockham decided it was a waste of time even to attempt such an ambitious task. God must remain incomprehensible, a book closed to reason. His Logos and ours are just completely different, and that is that.

Putting the divine purpose off-limits to discussion in that way had a tremendously liberating effect on secular thought. One could do philosophy, study the natural world, uninhibited by the encumbrances of theological dogma, speculation, and authority. This implied a clean separation of the human mind from the superhuman, of history from theology, the political from the ecclesiastical, and to some extent the present from the past. Eventually, Ockham's nominalism would lead to the vast upheavals of the Reformation, to Martin Luther. Already, in the fourteenth century, John Wycliffe in England had sided with nominalism in his campaign to make the scriptures available to all and sundry.

The sense that language had lost its moorings can be noticed in the work of William Langland, a younger contemporary of Ockham. His *Piers Plowman*, an allegorical poem about the search for truth, is full of tricky wordplay, verbal ambiguity, mistaken meaning, puns, and warped syntax. The scholar Mary Carruthers sees as a basic concern of the poem the task of redeeming a language that has lost its metaphysical connection with truth. The biggest fool in *Piers Plowman* is a character named Will, who has a hugely inflated idea of his own ability to interpret what others say to him on important matters.

Chaucer, the greatest poet of the fourteenth century, was familiar with nominalist thinking and tinkered with the notion that no two people can communicate with each other in any meaningful way. John Gardner presents Chaucer to us moderns as a philosophical poet fascinated with nominalism, especially the idea that since my abstraction from the concrete individual thing is not "real," but just a thought-up name, it may be entirely different from yours. I see a tomato and classify it as a fruit, but you may call it a vegetable. In the extreme version, the unreality of universals means that all ideas are private and uncommunicable: judgment subsides into mere opinion. Gardner inserts the fateful word "relativism" into his discussion of late medieval nominalism. Our minds are just not up to the task of dealing with absolutes. Chaucer explored the idea of a mismatch between God's doings and mankind's frail intellect in *The House of Fame*, contrasting the immense and systematic plan of the universe with the lame-brain narrator, "Geffrey," a soulmate of Langland's cloddish Will, who hasn't a clue about the universe, its grandeur and meaning, but uses its goods for his own benefit just the same. Just as they invent fictions known as universals, human beings tend to project their own personalities onto the cosmos. In the *Knight's Tale*, part of the *Canterbury Tales*, three characters—one admirable, one drunk, one congenitally inclined to malice—give opinions on how the universe works that are wildly at odds with one another and cannot be reconciled.

"No fourteenth century nominalist used the word 'relativism,' but every nominalist understood at least something of the queasy feeling we get while we laugh at a play by Samuel Beckett," says Gardner. "For a devout Christian artist, the only absolutes, finally, are God's love and man's art, that is, the trustworthy emotion and perception of a man who carefully sets down what he sees. But nominalism teaches that all vision, even the artist's vision, is mere opinion. One *feels* there are truths that can be discovered, not just affirmed (as we affirm, on scant evidence, God's justice and love). But how can we defend them? All serious artists today, I think, face what nominalists face: the impossibility of saying anything, though one knows, or at certain times briefly imagines, that there is something profoundly true that, somehow, cannot be said."

Such a philosophy tends to engender a deep suspicion of consciousness and its ability to discover truth, a suspicion that was to expand to mammoth proportions in the nineteenth and twentieth centuries. "There is hardly a day," wrote the modern theologian Paul Tillich, "that I do not fight against nominalism." Nominalism also encouraged an attitude of distrust toward nature, a sense that the world can be tricky, unreliable, deceptive, and may not play by the rules. It knocks flat the ancient Greek idea that the universe is philosophical, hospitable to our desire to understand it.

Tillich emphasizes that for the medievals, universals and essences, including the essence of truth, are powers that determine what each separate thing—a tree, a horse, a warrior—will become as it fulfills its destiny. That simplifies life a little. We can talk about "human nature" as the universal character of mankind, what every person has in common. Nominalism posed a disquieting threat to that neat philosophy, and to such socially stabilizing universals as "family, state, friends, craftsmen," collectivities which are prior to the individual. At the same time, it tended to make society more complex. "Without it," Tillich said, "the estimation of personality in the modern world— the real basis of democracy—could not have developed." Nominalism preserved or emphasized the value of the unique human person, which saved Europe from becoming Asiatic.

Nominalism also helped to loosen the fit between words and things, already problematic in the twelfth century, and one of the most insidious enemies of the concept of absolute truth. There was a revival on vastly different premises of the Sophistic emphasis on the arbitrary nature of words, spoken or written. Jacques Derrida, the leading exponent of today's doctrine of deconstruction, so hostile to the theory of the single truth, has said that trust in the correspondence of words to reality was lost as soon as the link between language and the Logos was broken. He traced such a disconnect to the eighteenth-century Enlightenment. But that is an unadventurous dating. The essence of deconstruction is the detachment of the "sign," whether word or spoken sound, from the "signified," the mental concept to which the sign refers. Ockham, in his *Summa totius logicae*, written about 1323, makes a distinction between words and concepts, noting that a word is a mere sign, a conventional token, like the letters of the alphabet in algebra.

"The separation of the sign from the signified did not occur as a result of the secularism of the Enlightenment, as Derrida claims," writes the historian of ideas Louis Dupré. "Already, the nominalist crisis had severed the bond between human words and the divine Logos. If we can no longer take for granted that God's decrees follow an intelligible pattern, then we also cease to trust that the eternal Logos secures the basic veracity of human speech. Henceforth, words were to be used at man's risk and discretion without carrying the traditional guarantee that, if properly used, they touch the real as it is in itself."

A theological controversy had been raging for centuries over whether there is more than one kind of truth. Thomas Aquinas, in the thirteenth century, attempted a reconciliation between faith and reason by arguing that philosophy and theology both aim at the same thing: the one truth about God. But he had to contend with the doctrine of the double truth, held at that time with vigor by the school of Siger of Brabant, a thirteenth-century French Scholastic. Siger was hauled in front of the Inquisition for perpetrating such ideas as that God does not know the future. He may have been murdered in 1284 after escaping from France. Siger was an adherent of the ingenious Arabic philosopher Ibn Rushd, known as Averroës, who held that intelligence falls from God onto mankind in a sequence of downwardly trending spheres, so that a theologian can interpret Scripture as allegory, while at the same time presenting it as literal truth to the ordinary untutored person.

Critics of Averroës accused him of installing a doctrine of dualism, by which one could simultaneously judge as true a discovery in natural philosophy and also its direct converse in theology. This smacked of the program of the Sophists, who had pronounced contradiction to be impossible. There were official condemnations of such unorthodox ideas at the University of Paris in 1270 and 1277. Accusations of a "double truth" may have been exaggerated, since no philosopher in the thirteenth century seems to have espoused it so nakedly. Averroës himself wrote a treatise, *On the Harmony Between Religion and Philosophy*, which proposed the existence of a single Truth, but allowed for many different ways of accessing it: the rhetorical method of persuasion, beloved by the Sophists, the dialectical, and the philosophical, open only to those fully qualified to use its technical resources.

An avant-garde troupe of young professors who clustered around Siger were suspected of surreptitiously promoting the doctrine of the double truth. Aquinas, in a sermon at the University of Paris, charged them with using Aristotle as a camouflage for this heretical thesis. "Among those who labor in philosophy," Aquinas said, "some say things which are not true according to faith, they reply that it is the Philosopher (Aristotle) who says so. As for themselves, they do not affirm it, they are only repeating the Philosopher's words." A rupture of fearful proportions opened up between what a person can believe to be true and what he or she can know to be true, helping to secularize knowledge and presaging the end of the Middle Ages. It was possible to investigate the human world without openly subverting church authority.

Ockham's nominalism also tended to reinforce the doctrine of the double truth. As a young man in Paris, Ockham had arrived at a decision that it is futile to try to prove God's existence, or that he is one, single, a unity. Reason and faith occupy different spheres, and because they are so foreign to each other, they may well contradict. If that makes faith unreasonable, then so be it. Faith has priority over reason. Early in his career, Ockham had studied the writings of Duns Scotus, a late thirteenth-century Oxford philosopher, a Franciscan, who stressed the unknowability of God, and whose ideas about language, like those of Ockham, are strangely prophetic of those of Wittgenstein eight hundred years on. Duns Scotus took issue with the sunny optimism of Aquinas, that we can construct a limited knowledge of God just from the evidence of our senses. He denied that "any sure and pure truth can be known naturally by the understanding of the wayfarer without the special illumination of the uncreated light." We cannot pierce the enigma of God by the route of reason, due to our fallen state.

Aquinas regarded the "laws of nature," the regularities that make science possible, not as an effect of God's will, acting from outside, but as arising from the inherent reasonableness of creation. Everything God made, from orchids to oak trees to black beetles, was subject to the selfsame eternal law. That ensured a nice, tight connection between the divine intelligence and the knowable order of the universe. We can rest easy and go on doing science in the secure belief that there is a rational order. Aquinas had maintained the doctrine of an intelligible creation by placing the Platonic Ideas, which in Plato's cosmological treatise, the *Timaeus*, existed apart from and independently of the Creator, safely tucked away in the mind of God.

The one fly in this soothing theological ointment was that the Ideas, as part of the software in the divine computer, would actually restrict God's freedom by confining him to the absolute Platonic values. If the Form of Truth is in God's mind, then he is not at liberty to dabble in falsehood, nor to act unjustly if he is constrained by the Idea of Justice. The Ideas were seen as cramping the style of the Almighty, almost as biological needs curb human thought and action. A truly unfettered God would be free to make nature hypocritical and fraudulent. He could lie to his creatures, as Philip Gosse in the Victorian turbulence of weak beliefs speculated that the fossils in the rocks were an elaborate hoax. The God of the medieval "Voluntarists" could make nonexistent unicorns appear real to us, create triangles with four sides, or cause time to run backward, though to us it would seem to move in the usual direction. His will would take precedence over his reason, a textbook definition of Voluntarism.

In 1277, when Aquinas had been dead three years, the controversy over God's will versus his reason came to the boil. Bishop Etienne Tempier of Paris was ordered by the pope to inquire into the doctrines taught at the University of Paris, including a number which had been held by Aquinas himself. Tempier condemned 232 propositions of theology and natural philosophy. Among them was the statement that "the impossible cannot be performed by God"—*Quod impossibile simpliciter non potest fieri a Deo*. Tempier could not stomach the heresy that God was anything but utterly free to do whatever he willed. That condemnation was a hinge event in the history of ideas. It marked the formal beginning of a theological reaction that was to preserve the freedom and omnipotence of God, but make the hope of fully understanding the world a dubious one. By insisting on a wilful God, the reactionaries could not be sure that his universe would be in any way regular and predictable, and an irregular world is not amenable to human understanding. It is apt to be slippery and deceptive.

Voluntarism, the doctrine that the will has priority over reason, begins with the premise that human beings have needs, and those needs confer meaning on a world that would otherwise be meaningless. For Plato, reason comes first. It selects goals and aims which the will is then conscripted to push to completion. Thus nobody can choose to do an evil deed knowing it is evil. Giving the will free rein spells the ruin of a person's character and actually twists out of shape what human nature is meant to be. For the Voluntarist, however, goals do not even exist until the will marks them out as such. And in the realm of the will, truth and falsehood cease to have any clear significance. A desire cannot be described as fallacious or erroneous. There is no such thing as a rational or irrational will. Far from warping human nature, the supremacy of the will just *is* human nature. It is odd that a philosophy based on the idea that God is all-powerful should begin to sound so remarkably similar to the late twentieth-century theory of evolutionary psychology, where behavior that seems irrational or arbitrary may have hidden causes planted deep in the distant beginnings of the human species.

Ockham, supposedly but not intentionally the founder of the Nominalist movement, which was to rule at a number of universities in the fifteenth century, held that God can do anything except contradict himself. He can perform immediately and directly what in the view of science and common sense needs a mediating cause. As for us human beings, we have no way of knowing whether the effect is natural or supernatural. God's absolute power makes for tremendous uncertainty in our endeavors to understand ourselves, the world, and our relation to the Creator.

Duns Scotus had used the argument of God's supreme power in an affirmative way. Ockham recruited it to show the vast unpredictability of everything. We can *think* that universals really exist, but who is to say whether God deceives us into trusting our intuition by giving us a false intuition of something he has destroyed? He could obliterate Monte Cassino and make us see it as still standing intact. Ockham stressed the primacy of the will and the crucial importance of freedom in human beings as well as in God. Nominalism was a warning not to take mental artifacts for the real things, not to sup-

pose that God's will is knowable through any avenue other than revelation. Truth today could be falsehood tomorrow if God so willed
it. Murder and adultery are sins now, but could be virtues at his command. We could even hate God and still be in his good graces. The
whole system of divine rewards and punishments goes out of the
window, since God is at complete liberty to recompense or penalize
as he desires.

The heresy of the double truth was deeply uncongenial to that
warp of the medieval fabric that cherished unity, the oneness of the
whole Christian enterprise. The high attainment of the Middle Ages
was a single Christendom under the rule of a single church. Nominalism has been blamed, or credited, for contributing to the shift
from one to many, leading ultimately to Protestantism, democracy,
national politics, secularism, positivism, and empirical science. And
all this was the effect of what was essentially just a theory of language, and the connection between language and truth. It warns us
not to dismiss too offhandedly late twentieth-century philosophy,
obsessed with language as it is, as wholly trivial or ivory tower. It may
inflict untold destruction on values so fundamental we assume they
are anchored firmly in the fabric of existence, entirely immune from
such remote questions as the instability of sign and signifier.

Double truth had a long and checkered career down the centuries,
surfacing in unexpected places—in the realpolitik of Machiavelli, in
the Darwinian controversies that wracked Victorian England. Noel
Annan has shown that even in the mid-Victorian period there was a
strong inclination to maintain the unity of truth. The Romantic
revival had toppled unity as the ruling principle of the cosmos,
replacing it with differences, singularities, one-of-a-kinds. Even
untruth contributed to the treasured profusion of life: "though
some poet's dream might be an illusion, the world was that much
richer, the Creator more fully realised." There were those who
believed that the biblical refrain, "Oh Lord, how manifold are thy
works," was strengthened by Darwin's description of the spectacular
variousness of orchids.

Rationalists in Darwin's England for the most part did not attack
openly the tenets of religion. When an American scientist, J. W. Drap-

er, made a crude appeal for all-out war between science and religion at a meeting of the British Association, the speech fell flat. He was rated an inferior thinker. By contrast with the ferments on the Continent, where Marx and Nietzsche rattled the cages of the devout, English intellectuals tended to accept the Protestant ethic and to trust authority, including the authority of the Roman Catholic Church. The young radicals, deploring the hypocrisy and inertia of the older generation in the face of devastating contradictions between Scripture and the new discoveries of science, took refuge in the belief that had once nourished medieval churchmen—the Unity of Truth. If biblical authorities said the Earth is barely more than four thousand years old, and science shows it is vastly more ancient than that, both versions cannot be correct. And such intolerable tension cannot continue indefinitely, even in smug Victorian England. "Truth can never be opposed to truth," said Dean Buckland, the first professor of geology at Oxford.

It could be, of course—and was. In science, the "truth" of Euclidean geometry, thought to be eternal law, built into the mind at birth according to Immanuel Kant, was elbowed aside by new, exotic geometries that were as valid as the old ones for certain purposes, in spite of violating axioms believed to be inviolate. Cardinal Newman, thinking of the collision between Galileo and the church over the movement of the Earth around the Sun, said a proposition about motion could be untrue philosophically but true "for certain practical purposes." In 1878, a paper was read to the Metaphysical Society with the title "Double Truth." John Morley poured scorn on those too craven to dissent from the prevailing views, yet who also sneered at Roman Catholics for accepting teachings flagrantly at odds with the latest scientific findings, according to the doctrine of the separation of faith and reason.

The heresy of the double truth not only licensed science to be as anti-intuitive, as uncommonsensical, as agnostic as it pleased. It also propped up and sustained dogmas held by church authorities that were increasingly at odds with secular thought. It served the latter function more effectively than the doctrine of the single Truth was able to do. As late as 1968, after the Second Vatican Council, the

Swiss theologian Hans Küng could write that the "lack of truthfulness" in the church was due not so much to individual fear or cowardice, but rather to positions taken at certain moments in the history of theology. Truthfulness, Küng noted, is not one of the "theological" virtues, which are faith, hope, and love. Sins against the eighth commandment, which treats of truthfulness, were classified as venial. Lying as such is an excusable act, whereas violating the sixth commandment was a mortal sin. The curious approach to truth-telling by Aquinas, Küng said, had important consequences. Aquinas stipulated that the intention to deceive is necessary to the act of lying. The nature of falsehood resides in the readiness to say something objectively untrue. In that way, truth-telling became an aspect of justice: a lie is a default on a debt, a failure to render to the other person what is owed.

That set the stage of the sophistries of the Counter-Reformation, the cult of the "technical" truth, the art of parsing a statement so finely that the lie it contains can masquerade as veracity. Hair-splitting distinctions, mental reservations, slippery language, could accomplish this maneuver.

At the Second Vatican Council, Küng chatted to the theologian John Courtney Murray about a certain American archbishop. Said Murray with a smile: "He is an absolutely honest man. He would never lie except for the good of the Church."

That attitude, said Küng, is now as obsolete, or ought to be, as the theory of angels dancing on the head of a pin. In the Middle Ages, when the ideal society was envisaged as a harmony between the single person and the community, truthfulness was not the preeminent, the indispensable and overriding virtue it became when tension grew between the individual and the community, and a self-conscious subjectivity began to emerge. But precisely because truth-telling is a modern virtue, it would be suicidal for any institution that hopes to survive into the twenty-first century not to adopt it as a first and unconditional priority. The time when lies could be told for the greater good of some grand organization, whether religious or secular, is past. Truth-telling is no longer just one virtue among others, or even just a very important virtue. "Since truthfulness does not concern man's state in this world and his relation to it—as, for instance, do the civic virtues of order, thrift and cleanliness, but the relation of man to himself," Küng wrote, it becomes absolutely fundamental. "If the relation of man to himself and hence of the community to itself is disturbed, if this relation to oneself is no longer clear and transparent, then the moral existence of man or of the community is threatened all along the line. Without this inner truthfulness, the civic virtues, and the other virtues too, are endangered at their roots: they are no longer possible in an authentic fashion."

CHAPTER SIX

The Imp of Falsehood

The human world flourishes best when refreshed by falsehood. —Roger Scruton

If everything is possible, nothing is true.
    —Alexandre Koyre on Descartes's Philosophical Writings

E HAVE SEEN HOW THE MEDIEVAL VIEW of God as a Being so omnipotent as to be more power-ful than truth, able if he willed to cause us to accept as true the most egregious falsehoods, makes science a tricky enterprise, since it means that nothing is securely predictable. René Descartes, who helped to establish the modern scientific world-view, had to meet head-on this troubling theological dilemma before he could formulate a scientific method free of the uncertainties that plagued adherents of Voluntarism in the preceding centuries. God, he affirms, could have made another world, identical in every respect to the one we occupy, in which things true in one would be false in the other. A truth is true only because God wills it.

Descartes' answer is that God, being perfect, could never perpetu-ate something as imperfect as an act of deception. That would be a fault and a defect in Him. Descartes defines God as supremely intel-ligent and supremely powerful, an attribute that, contrary to the Vol-untarists, makes Him entirely dependable. And here is the clinching argument against the notion that God would dangle falsehood in front of us and trick us into mistaking it for truth: fraud and decep-tion may *seem* to be a mark of subtlety and power (some of the

Sophists thought so), but, says Descartes, that is entirely mistaken. Lying, the desire to cheat, is actually the epitome of "malice or feebleness," a puny and weak-kneed sort of device, and who could imagine the existence of a weak-kneed God?

Our modern Masters of Suspicion distrusted consciousness and placed interpretation at the top of the agenda. Descartes, taking quite a different view, was suspicious of everything but consciousness itself, and whatever is in consciousness that precedes interpretation. Even recollection is suspect; he talks about "my lying memory."

Enter the famous genius of deception, malicious to the core, a Cartesian creation, totally unlike the honest God so perfect no human mind could have invented him. Descartes was then a man in his forties living quietly in a house on the windswept coast of Holland, worrying about his hair turning gray, cultivating herbs, tricking his landlady into taking in his "niece" Francine—in reality his natural daughter—and trying to find a firm foundation for knowledge at a time when the whole edifice of medieval thought was tottering under the impact of new discoveries in science. "I will suppose, then," he wrote in his *Meditations*, "not that there is the optimum God, the fountain of truth, but that there is a certain malign spirit, supremely powerful and clever, and [who] does his utmost to deceive me. I will suppose that sky, air, earth, colors, shapes, sounds, and all external objects are mere delusive dreams, by means of which he lays snares for my credulity. I will consider myself as having no hands, no eyes, no blood, no senses, but just having a false belief that I have all these things."

This spiteful imp of chicanery was designed to introduce such overpowering doubt as to the reality of our most ordinary sensations and thoughts that whatever survived the onslaught must be truth, a rock-bottom foundation on which to build secure, genuine, and permanent knowledge. That mental terra firma is consciousness. I can doubt everything except the fact that I am doubting, which means I think, I exist. Real knowledge begins with the first-person confidence that the whole world might be a lie, except one's own mind.

Descartes worshipped at the shrine of the single Truth. He was an anti-nominalist in the sense that he believed in the authenticity of universals. In terms reminiscent of the mystical poem of Parmenides, he describes how, one winter night near Ulm, on St. Martin's Eve, in a rented room with a warm stove, a major crisis befell him in the form of three dreams. Illumination came, not from wise teachers, or the learning he had stored up since his schooldays, but from secluded reverie. After a long struggle with his thoughts, Descartes decided that there must be a single Method which could be used to arrive at a single Truth: that all objects of human knowledge are interdependent. He was then only twenty-three years old and saw himself in possession of "everything at once." Then the dreams began, so amazing and strange they could only have come straight from God. Not from the fumes of alcohol: Descartes had been teetotal for three months.

The first dream smacked of an evil genius. Apparitions hovered, a Pentecostal wind blew him about. Descartes felt a pain in his left side, making it difficult to go where he wanted. The ghostly phantoms terrified him so much he couldn't walk straight. He staggered in the direction of a church to pray, but was thrown off his path, perhaps because the wicked one, not God, was impelling him in that direction. In a second dream he heard a loud noise like a thunderclap: a sign that Truth was about to strike? Sparks crackled all around the room, frightening him. The third dream was more pregnant with helpful meaning. Two books appeared on his bedside table, a dictionary and a collection of poems. The first represented all the sciences put together; the second that type of mysterious inspiration, akin to divine revelation, which descends on the artist. Descartes thought it showed him that God had chosen him to reveal the unity of all truth, of all sciences, of all knowledge.

The important lesson Descartes drew from these nighttime parables was that while a person can be blown hither and thither by the imp of falsehood, there is a straight path to truth, and God guarantees it will take us there. Even so, the God of Descartes is distinct from the world he created, and his ways are deeply mysterious. We know what a "truth" does for us, but it is a waste of time even to hazard a guess as to what the identical truth might do for Him. Our mathematics might be utterly different from God's mathematics, which means for the later Descartes that math by itself cannot be used to legitimate knowledge. Here the Logos is in peril of collapsing altogether, due to the inscrutable opaqueness of the divine intellect. Descartes undertakes a kind of rescue, by saying that rock-bottom truths are installed in our minds at birth, in everyone's mind, distributed equally; we do not need to receive a special kind of grace to know them. The organ of truth is thus something like the organ of conscience: it is there, and it is up to us to listen to it.

Descartes's metaphor of the mendacious demon in the *Meditations* is the converse of the single Truth: It is the embodiment of the single Lie. The philosopher Roger Scruton thinks the demon is arguably a better, more economical explanation of our ordinary experience than the commonsense view that we live in an objective world which corresponds to our opinions. "Instead of supposing the existence of a complex world, with a multiplicity of objects, whose laws we barely understand," says Scruton, "the demon hypothesis proposes just one object (the demon) operating according to a principle (the desire and pursuit of deception) that we are intimately acquainted with. The hypothesis is both simpler, and more intelligible, than the doctrine of common sense. Maybe it *is* the best explanation!"

At a time when Descartes was writing his *Meditations*, ancient skepticism in the form of Pyrrhonism was enjoying a revival, thanks to the rediscovery of the works of Sextus Empiricus, the "methodical" philosopher who flourished in the second and third centuries A.D. Sextus was a champion of his master Pyrrho, a Greek skeptic much taken with the atomic theory of Democritus. Pyrrho taught an extreme form of relativism in which the senses cheat. Eyes and ears are quite capable of lying to us and people are inclined to tell you the first thing that pops into their heads. Faced with that day-in, day-out mendacity, you might as well keep quiet and preserve *aphasia*, a noncommittal silence, an imperturbable serenity. Pyrrho himself was an exemplary Pyrrhonist. According to Diogenes Laertius, he was apt to wander around in traffic, not looking where he was going, so that his friends had to rescue him from "carts, precipices, dogs and what-not."

Sextus touched a seventeenth-century nerve with his insistence on the idea that each person's constitution is so radically different from anyone else's we cannot even pretend there is a single, truthful account of ordinary experience. The mental is so intimately linked to the physical, it is impossible to separate body from soul. And since bodies vary wildly from person to person, souls, or minds, must vary to the same extent. "We differ," Sextus wrote, "in our constitutional peculiarities. For some people, beef is easier to digest than rock-fish, and some suffer diarrhoea from inferior Lesbian wine. There used to be an old woman of Attica, they say, who could drink thirty grams of hemlock with impunity, and Lysis used to take four grams of opium without harm."

Michel de Montaigne, one of the most widely read Pyrrhonists of the period, took almost the opposite view from that of Descartes on the role of mind and reason. He believed consciousness can be deceived and can also deceive itself. Montaigne, who died four years before Descartes was born, and whose influence on his times has been likened to that of Freud on ours, held that the senses lie to the mind and the mind lies back in return. The two compete in defrauding each other. What is more, Reason is one of the imps of falsehood leading us astray. As an inner presence, it also enables us to deceive ourselves.

A provocative theme in Montaigne's writings is that ignorance, untruth, just not caring whether or not the whole world is a lie, can be a source of happiness and contentment to the human species. We can be deceived, be a prey to falsehoods, and still enjoy our existence. A big mistake is to try to separate our "higher" faculties from our personhood, from the quotidian condition of being human. We are all members of the common herd. The acids of Reason, which for Descartes were an elixir of psychological health, would, if allowed free rein, eat away and destroy our natural instincts, Montaigne warned. The mind is always trying to improve on nature, aspiring to be something it was never intended to be; it is artificial and pretentious. It has ideas above its station. The imagination, in particular, is flighty and poor at making a distinction between truth and lies. Like one of today's critics of the postmodernists, Montaigne pokes fun at the mania of his contemporaries for interpretation, for commentaries on commentaries, never agreeing on a final version. There is more bustle, more ink spilt on more paper, to interpret interpretations, than to interpret things. Critics occupy more space than original writers: "every place swarms with commentaries; of authors there is great scarcity." The natural disease of the mind is that it "does nothing but ferret and inquire, and is eternally wheeling, juggling and perplexing itself like silkworms, and then suffocates in its work."

Whereas Descartes went to great lengths to lift human beings out of nature, out of the common opinions and habits of other people, the conventions of society, Montaigne let himself be "ignorantly and negligently led by the general law of the world." It would be folly, he said, to worry and fret about whether such a law is correct and true, since it is not private and personal, but public and general. In a strongly worded passage at the end of the *Essays*, he advises against "disassociating" the mind from the body. People who do so "would put themselves out of themselves, and escape from being men. 'Tis folly; instead of transforming themselves into angels, they transform themselves into beasts. Instead of elevating, they lay themselves lower. These transcendental humors affright me, like high and inaccessible cliffs and precipices." We escape out of ourselves because we do not know how to live within ourselves.

" 'Tis to much purpose to go upon stilts," Montaigne noted, "for, when upon stilts, we must yet walk with our legs; and when seated upon the most elevated throne in the world, we are but seated upon our rump."

There is evidence that Descartes read Montaigne before beginning to write the *Discourse*. Montaigne's *Essays* were popular, went through several reprintings and were taken up by such figures as Father Pierre Charron, a skeptical theologian very close to Montaigne. Charron's book *De la Sagesse* was a treatise on the correct method for avoiding error and discovering truth, quite similar to the drift of Descartes's own approach. He denied that human beings have any sufficient mental apparatus enabling them to tell truth from falsehood. We are apt to believe any old thing under the pressure of social conformity and coercion.

It is clear that Descartes recoiled from Montaigne's view that mind must not be regarded as distinct and separate from the body or from nature. Montaigne had taken an almost Darwinian approach to the continuity of humans and nonhuman species. To suppose there is a profound break between the two is sheer conceit. "Presumption is our natural and original disease," he said, cutting us all down to size. "The most wretched and frail of all creatures is man, and withal the proudest. He feels and sees himself lodged here in the dirt and filth of the world, nailed and riveted to the worst and deadest part of the universe, in the lowest story of the house, and most remote from the heavenly arch, with animals of the worst condition, and yet in his imagination will be placing himself above the circle of the moon, and bringing heaven under his feet." And what is there in human intelligence that is not present in some degree in other animals? Why does the spider make her web tighter in one place and looser in another, if she does not deliberate and think about it? Look at the intelligence of the fox, who tests the thickness of ice on a river by putting his ear on it, harkening to the sound of the water's current, how deep it is or how shallow.

Moreover, beasts are at least as cunning and duplicitous as we ourselves. We plot strategems to trap and snare them, but they are a match for us; they are capable of "subtleties and inventions" to thwart such tricks. Consider the case of the mule belonging to Thales, the early Greek natural philosopher. This animal, carrying heavy bags of salt, conceived the dodge of "by accident" stumbling into a river, wetting the sacks and thereby lightening its load somewhat. Thales, it is said, tumbled to the ruse and made the mule carry wool instead of salt, whereupon it ceased its ploy forthwith.

Montaigne goes on for pages and pages about the wonderful cleverness of beasts, to deflate our complacently lofty opinion of human reason, which he considered to be nothing special. As for truth, even the vaunted science of Aristotle was being undermined. Had not a

New World been discovered on the other side of the Atlantic Ocean, an entirely different culture with strange customs and beliefs, different absolutes? The kingdom of the intellect was tottering, the singleness of the Roman Catholic Church under threat from the breakaway movement of the Reformation. "By extending the implicit skeptical tendencies of the Reformation crisis, the humanistic crisis, and the scientific crisis into a total *crise pyrrhonienne,*" says the historian of skepticism Richard Popkin, Montaigne's work "became the *coup de grâce* to an entire intellectual world."

Descartes met the crisis head-on. Earlier he had put on a famous "Sophistical demonstration" at the home of the papal nuncio in Paris. He took some arguments of "incontestable" truths, and by the use of plausible reasoning showed they were false. Then he took what was obviously a glaring falsehood and dressed it up as a seeming truth.

It was more than a mere philosophical interest in stabilizing the centrifugal dispersion of once unimpeachable truths, however, that motivated Descartes. He had been "devastated" by the condemnation of Galileo by the Roman Catholic Church for heresy, so much so that he decided to suppress his own treatise, *Le Monde*, which confirmed the Copernican thesis of the Earth's orbit around the Sun, and was within days of going to press. In 1624, Galileo had been given permission to write on the Copernican system as long as he did not take sides. But his next book, *Dialogue Concerning the Two Chief World Systems*, so upset the church that he was called to Rome to be "interviewed" by the Inquisition. The book was banned and burned in 1633, and Galileo was tried and sentenced to life imprisonment, though he was allowed to live under house arrest. Later he was ordered to recite the seven penitential psalms every week for three years. He signed a formal abjuration of his belief in the Copernican doctrine.

Descartes showed signs of panic at the news. It was clear that the church was not interested in truth, but in its own supremacy, its own authority, and Descartes's priorities were the exact reverse of those. He "quasi" decided to burn all his papers. "I cannot imagine," he wrote to a friend, "that an Italian, and especially one well thought of by the Pope from what I have heard, could have been labelled a criminal for nothing other than wanting to establish the movement of the earth." He saw this turn of events as a threat to the whole basis of his system. If Copernicanism is false, he said, "so too are the entire foundations of my philosophy." It was around this time that Descartes took up the challenge of skepticism in earnest. His method of metaphysical, "hyperbolical" doubt, the doubt designed to end all doubts, and the confrontation with the demon of falsehood, seem to have been a response to the Galileo affair. "Skepticism was simply a means to an end, and that end had nothing to do with certainty about the existence of the material world, but rather with establishing the metaphysical credentials of a mechanist natural philosophy, one of whose central tenets—the Earth's motion around the Sun—had been condemned by the Inquisition," in the view of his biographer Stephen Gaukroger.

One of Descartes's chief aims was to justify his belief in a mechanistic world. He was opposed to naturalism, the doctrine that what we might suppose to be supernatural acts of God can be explained without reference to God. Nature on its own possessed occult powers, according to the naturalist view. It was active and infinitely more mysterious than we might think, but at the same time more mundane. There were heretical suggestions that such God-linked activities as prayer and the sacraments were really states of mind, psychological attitudes. One answer to this dangerous theory of an active nature which behaved like supernature was to insist that the world is a mechanism. Matter is inactive, the supernatural is the supernatural, and never the twain shall meet. Nature has no occult powers. Descartes was intent on showing that God transcends nature, and that the mind, being entirely different from the body, cannot be part of nature.

Truth is obtained at the cost of a sacrifice. That is the conclusion of Descartes. The search for Truth is a lonely enterprise, a solitary mission. It requires the exclusion of possibilities, because the more possibilities there are, the less truth there is. Falsehood, error, uncertainty, arise because the will is free. Reason is the curb that reins in the licentiousness of the will, when it roams beyond the confines of reason. Reason is unfreedom. It rules out more than it rules in. That is what prompted Ernest Gellner to aim a withering blast at Descartes for being "profoundly bourgeois," essentially middle class, "unromantic, uncommunal, unhistorical," the self-made meta-physician, starting with nothing, coming up from nothing, proceeding step by step, tidily, not acting on impulse, above all self-sufficient. "It is indeed in this spirit that the bourgeois entrepreneur deploys his resources and keeps his accounts and records in financial and legal order—slow, careful, judicious, deliberate, omitting naught, accounting for all." Gellner lets the master of rationalism have it full in the face. Possessed of "a yearning for freedom from any kind of indebtedness, he will not mortgage his convictions to some common bank of custom, whose management is outside his control, and which consequently is not really to be trusted."

The difference between Montaigne and Descartes comes down to this. For Montaigne, there was "something more important" than truth. For Descartes, there was nothing more important. Said Montaigne: " 'Tis the misery of our condition, that often that which presents itself to our imagination for the most true does not also appear the most useful to life." Descartes, by contrast, gives the impression that misery is the absence of truth, and life comes in second place to truth. "Descartes lived an unhappy and indeed, for some considerable periods, a rather disturbed life," writes one of his biographers. "This is something he made every effort to deny or disguise, and the means he chose were intellectual. His sources of pleasure were few, but intellectual achievements figure prominently amongst these, and these achievements were elevated into virtually the only form of worthwhile pursuit, in a way that goes well beyond a commitment to a 'life of the mind,' for example." In the *Discourse*, Descartes announces his core ambition: "I always had an excessive desire to learn to distinguish the true from the false."

For sure, Descartes was a notable separator and sifter. He detached God from the world, mind from nature, reason from culture. And he—the bachelor who prized his privacy so highly—privileged single-ness as the pot of gold at the end of the philosophical rainbow. His method was to strip down to bare bedrock by doubting everything he had ever been told, suspecting all doctrines and systems, all scholarly worldviews. Start from scratch, alone, with just the elementary, primitive, original apparatus of thought itself and the clear and distinct ideas provided by the "truth conscience" organ with which we are born.

The life of the mind can be a rather removed and isolated existence. It is not necessarily a team sport. In the *Discourse on Method*, published in 1637, Descartes states in no uncertain terms that something which has *evolved*, which has a history, which has been been altered over long periods of time by a variety of circumstances, is inferior to a work created all at one time by a single author working on his own. Buildings designed by just one architect are usually more beautiful and better proportioned than those several generations of experts have tried to renovate and improve. A city that has grown up over centuries with ad hoc augmentations and extensions contains much higgledy-piggledy, needlessly complex design, with recent constructions perched on top of ancient masonry, streets crooked and irregular, giving the impression that the city emerged by accident rather than by the careful blueprints of an architect. Similarly, Descartes piously adds, "the constitution of true Religion whose ordinances are of God alone, is incomparably better regulated than any other."

A mind created at a stroke, by one and only one divinity, like a city laid out all at once by a single designer, would be immune to deception and falsehood. No crooked streets in the second, no twisted sophistries in the first. It is the long process of unhurried, organic development of knowledge over time and in history that lets in the fiends of error, the imps of delusion and fraud. As long as the mind does not contain its own mental geology, residues of old forms of knowledge buried like fossils in its depths; as long as it is underwritten by a God who finds it impossible to lie, the mind may be trusted not to swindle us. Descartes intended to cheat history by demolishing it with the wrecking ball of his Method, reducing everything to such simple, basic units they could not be false, creating a new sci-

ence of thought as an architect would raze a whole town in order to
build one that is his and his alone. In place of a Rome or Paris there
would be a Washington, DC, a Brasilia.

That, of course, was exactly the sort of metaphor that led William
Paley, in his *Natural Theology* of 1802, to the categorical assertion that
the universe is like a watch, and a watch must have had a watch-
maker, a single designer who made it at a stroke as a finished instrument for a specific use. There are no useless parts, still present in the
watch just because they are remnants of the history of watchmaking.
At the hinge of the intellectual revolution of the nineteenth century,
that analogy was thrown back in Paley's face. It was the heart and
soul of Darwin's theory that life has a history, mind has a history,
and the evolution of species, like the partly haphazard structure of
an ancient city, often updates obsolete parts of the body, leaving the
residue of archaic, obsolete organs in place. In the concluding chapter of the *Origin*, Darwin introduces a profoundly personal manifesto: "When we no longer look at an organic being as a savage looks
at a ship, as something wholly beyond his comprehension, when we
regard every production of nature as one which has a long history;
when we contemplate every complex structure and instinct as the
summing up of many contrivances, each useful to the possessor, in
the same way as any great mechanical invention is the summing up
of the labor, the experience, the reason and even the blunders of
numerous workmen; when we thus view each organic being, how far
more interesting—I speak from experience—does the study of natural history become!"

In published "Objections" to the *Meditations*, Descartes, who disliked criticism, was brought down to earth and reprimanded for his
refusal to recognize the role that "life," the wisdom and learning of
centuries, has to play in the formation of ideas he held to be the gift
of a non-deceiving God to the single individual. How could he be
sure that the idea of a perfect, supreme Being would have come to
him if he "had not been nurtured among men of culture"? To dismiss as suspect, as a source of falsehood, all that civilization has to
offer is cavalier, rash, and ungrateful. Did Descartes ever consider the
possibility that these ideas came from books, from conversation

with his friends, rather than being messages hatched in his own mind in isolation, or arriving from a supreme Being? Is truth a community venture, or an individual operation, with just one demon in attendance? That question was to haunt philosophy for centuries to come, culminating in the provocative notion, as diametrically opposed to the Cartesian view as could possibly be imagined, that "truth" is just a social construct.

CHAPTER SEVEN

The Suicidal Tendencies of Reason

There is no a priori reason for thinking that, when we discover the truth, it will prove interesting. —C. I. Lewis

I have come to think that if I had the mind, I have not the brain and nerves for a life of pure philosophy. A continued search among the abstract roots of things, a perpetual questioning of all the things that plain men take for granted, a chewing the cud for fifty years over inevitable ignorance and a constant frontier watch on the little tidy lighted conventional world of science and daily life—is this the best life for temperaments such as ours?

—C. S. Lewis, in a letter to his father

HE DOCTRINE, PROMOTED BY DESCARTES, that untruth is a mark of inadequacy, of a feebleness completely out of character with what is manifestly a grand and sturdy world, came to be challenged by a contrary set of ideas. If the universe and everything in it is just a machine, then we can know it by the methodical use of rules that sift truth from falsehood. But life does not work that way. Its very strength, its robustness, depends on *not* being a stickler for always insisting on the truth. Descartes himself acknowledged that while he was in the process of demolishing, razing to the ground, all the false ideas he had accumulated over a lifetime, he was obliged for the time being to "carry on my life as happily as I could." A person whose house is being pulled down by a construction crew needs a place to hang his hat until the work is finished. To this end, Descartes decided to do what his philosophy tells us not to do, namely, follow if necessary "opinions most dubious" as if they were rock-bottom truths, and treat the merely probable as if it were certain. If you are lost in a forest, the best recourse is simply to choose any direction at random, and then walk absolutely straight along it, whether it is the "right" one or not. Since the "actions of life" do not usually permit shilly-shallying or procrastination, we cannot afford to be too fussy about cleansing ourselves utterly of the untrue.

And what if the house is demolished by the wrecking crew, but the rebuilding is never complete? The unfortunate householder must stay in his temporary digs indefinitely. This dilemma was famously confronted when, almost exactly a century after the publication of Descartes's *Discourse*, there appeared a book that took another view of reason, *A Treatise of Human Nature*, by the genius of the Scottish Enlightenment, David Hume. Hume experienced no bursts of revelation in the dream state, no vision of the unity of all knowledge. He was more gregarious than Descartes, had many women friends though he never married, was witty, generous, and good company. If Descartes disguised a nervous collapse as a paroxysm of illumination, Hume was quite frank about his own breakdown in the 1730s, brought on by the strain of seeking "a new medium of truth." Shunning all pleasures, neglecting every other kind of business, he toiled for five years and broke his health. He recuperated at La Flèche, in Anjou, where Descartes had attended a Jesuit school.

That crisis seems to have marked Hume for life. If striving after ultimate truth ruins your well-being and makes you mope, if it shuts out the rest of the world and warps your temperament, what sense is there in making such a Herculean effort, especially if, at the end of it all, truth slips out of your grasp? In writing about the pursuit of philosophy, Hume repeatedly uses such terms as "fatigue," "painful," "burdensome," "melancholy." It is as if philosophy were some excruciating chore that makes the joints ache and the head throb, a two-Excedrin occupation. Hume might have agreed with the suggestion in Plato's *Symposium* that, while the petty vices of the ordinary person, his lax intellectual discipline and indulgence in carnal pleasures, may prevent him from obtaining the sort of truth available to Socrates, it was Socrates' very single-mindedness that made him less than fully human. Descartes deliberately sought solitude, moving to a foreign country, not giving out his address to all and sundry, so as to focus his mind on the all-important Method. Today, he would have had an unlisted telephone number. Hume, on the other hand, was apt, when alone in his study, to feel shut in, antisocial, and a little silly. Puzzling over questions of ultimate truth and falsehood put him in a blue mood.

If reason saved Descartes from collapse, Nature did the same for Hume. The human constitution, our biology and psychology, "Human Nature," militates against a hermetic, solitary dedication to the truth, at least in most people, Hume suggests. In his own case it tended to estrange him from the rest of the human species, leaving him "affrighted and confounded." He imagined himself "some strange, uncouth monster, who, not able to mingle and unite in society, has been expell'd from all human commerce, and left utterly abandoned and disconsolate." From this unnatural state, only Nature, referred to by Hume as "she," a sort of commonsensical mother figure who does not like to see her charges going to intellectual extremes, making them look pasty-faced, atrophying their other faculties, can effect a rescue. Mother Nature likes to see roses in our cheeks and frets if we sit for hours in a frowsty, stove-heated room. Perhaps we should pursue truth on Mondays and Wednesdays, and spend the rest of the week doing something a little more outgoing. The most natural life for humans is a "mixed" one, according to Hume. Says Nature: "Indulge your passion for science, but let your science be human, and such as may have direct reference to action and society. Abstruse thought and profound researches I prohibit, and will severely punish by the pensive melancholy which they introduce, by the endless uncertainty in which they involve you, and by the cold reception which your pretended discoveries shall meet with when communicated. Be a philosopher; but, amidst all your philosophy, be still a man." Hume knew all about cold receptions. His first book, the *Treatise*, which had cost him the bloom of his youth, "fell deadborn from the press." It was a non-event, but the ebullient Hume soon bounced back.

The antidote for the metaphysical blues is to do something less hifalutin', less otherworldly, more down to earth. Socializing "cures me of this philosophical melancholy and delirium, either by relaxing this bent of mind, or by some avocation, and lively impression of my senses, which obliterates all these chimeras. I dine, I play a game of backgammon, I converse, and am merry with my friends; and when

after three or four hours' amusement, I would return to these speculations, they appear so cold, and strained, and ridiculous, that I
cannot find in my heart to enter into them any farther."

Hume did not share the Cartesian belief that the work of a solitary
designer, a lone craftsman, is more to be trusted than a collective
effort by many different artisans over long stretches of time. A historian as well as a philosopher, he did not dismiss history. A skeptical character in his posthumously published *Dialogues Concerning
Natural Religion* says flatly: "The world plainly resembles more an animal or a vegetable, than it does a watch or knitting-loom." In the *Dialogues*, there is a passage which previews Darwin's express belief in the
biology of species as the "summing up of many contrivances." "If we
survey a ship," declares the same character, "what an exalted idea
must we form of the ingenuity of the carpenter, who framed so complicated, useful and beautiful machine? And what surprise we must
feel, when we find him a stupid mechanic, who imitated others, and
copied an art, which, through a long succession of ages, after multi-
plied trials, mistakes, corrections, deliberations and controversies,
had been gradually improving? Many worlds might have been
botched and bungled throughout an eternity, ere this system was
struck out."

There are no guarantees of truthfulness in Hume. Therein lies the
morbid fascination of reading him. In place of the Cartesian God,
Hume puts a Nature, personified and feminized, definitely not a perfect Being and in some ways fit to be called a "stupid mechanic."
When the Oxford philosopher Bryan Magee underwent a midlife crisis of "cataclysmic force" in the 1960s, floored by a sense of the ultimate meaninglessness of life, he turned to Hume for help,
speculating that Hume's "terrifying psychological experiences" were
similar to his own. He found only that the Scottish sage's essential
and mortifying message is this: "It's worse than you think."

Descartes's prescription was to shun the inherited lore of one's
elders, ignore history, and make a fresh start with the lucid and bare
ideas God implanted in the mind. In that way you may construct a
version of the harmony between the mind and the world that had
fascinated thinkers in classical Greece. The Logos is intact, sort of.

Hume did not believe such a harmony was possible. We find the world we inhabit reliable for the most part; stable, "truthful" as far as our traffic with it goes, precisely because of custom, the beliefs and prejudices and useful biases by means of which we make sense of what is happening around us. Descartes wanted to banish illusions and false beliefs from his kingdom of truth. But what if those very illusions are what make an orderly existence possible? Hume held that reason on its own cannot make human beings securely at home in their world. Custom might accomplish that task, but at the price of removing the intellectual confidence of knowing we understand how the whole thing works. We are like the ignoramus who operates his personal computer without a shred of technical know-how as to the principles of computing.

Lurking in the background of Hume's philosophy is a demon at least as dangerous as the incubus of Descartes. Its name is common sense, habit, custom—human psychology. Like Montaigne, Hume is more interested in the human than in anything that transcends the human. In his work there is a prevailing flavor of biology and of how an individual fits into his or her natural habitat. No wonder Darwin was so impressed with Hume, reading him in the summer of 1838 when he was wrestling with the first drafts of his theory of natural selection, trying to give it philosophical weight. For his part, Hume considered philosophy, defined as a quest for the "really real," anti-life and anti-nature. Worse, Nature will have her revenge on those who presume to unravel the secrets of Being by reason alone. The wearisome, pointless enterprise will dry up their spirits and blight their lives. "The feelings of our heart, the agitation of our passions, the vehemence of our affections," dissipate all the conclusions of the abstract, speculative hunt for hidden truths, "and reduce the pro-found philosopher to a mere plebian." Ouch. Hume portrays the pure metaphysician as almost unfit for human society, as if he were anticipating the desiccated scholar Mr. Casaubon in George Eliot's *Middlemarch*, a miserable failure in marriage as in scholarship itself.

People may think they understand the world and can explain it in terms of cold, watertight logic, but that is a delusion. All they can do is describe what happens, and such a description is made in terms of our own psychology, of the expectations present in our minds by custom, and custom, like the Voluntarist's God, could have given us other and different kinds of expectations. Hume's core message is that the mind is finite; it is part of nature, not of some divinity. It cannot know everything, but is puffed up and conceited enough to suppose that it can. We might be frustrated and thwarted in the single-minded pursuit of truth, but we can obtain a sort of understanding, at least avoid rank falsehood, if we are modest enough to face up to the limitations of the intellect, rather than simply subscribing to the myth of its supernatural powers. We might have to be content with the "how" of the world rather than endlessly hankering after its "why."

It might seem glaringly obvious, for example, that one event is "caused" by another. Surely, when one billiard ball strikes another, the second ball will move away along a determined path. That is an inherent necessity, and has nothing to do with what we expect. Not in the least, Hume answers. In principle, the second ball could stay still, execute a pirouette, or change into a pumpkin. We have simply got into the habit of relying on it to cannon off in a predictable direction.

That is perfectly satisfactory for all quotidian purposes and one would have to be mad, or a philosopher, to bother about reasoning our way to certainty in such matters. The Humean imp of common sense deceives us into believing that whatever happens *must* happen, into supposing that imaginary connections between things are real, which makes life so much easier and simpler. We are so constituted as to take it for granted, automatically, that cause and effect are linked by necessity rather than being contingent. That is a result of "custom," but a custom that is universal, innate, part of human nature, part of biology. It is how we are made. Custom, Hume maintained, not only covers our natural ignorance, but even conceals itself from our awareness. It is "the great guide of human life," the sole factor that makes experience useful to us.

A temptation for adherents of the "organic" theory of the world, the view that the world resembles an animal more than it resembles a knitting loom, is to put Nature in the place of God. That suggests that Nature is reasonable, intelligible, mindlike. Quite possibly, Hume says, such a thesis is false, a lie. But Hume considered falsehood, or what he called "fictions," to be an irremovable element of life. A lie, say the "necessity" of cause and effect, may be a fabrication underwritten by a not particularly godlike Nature which helps to secure our well-being, our ability to function. Perhaps our deluded view that Nature is wise and rational arises out of a perfectly natural need to live in a stable world where purposes and plans are possible. There are a number of benign falsehoods in the "natural" mind. Hume helped to make them respectable, setting the stage for the psychiatric revolution of the twentieth century, whose practitioners, it has been said, are "professionally disinterested in the difference between truth and lies."

The downside of that thesis is that you cannot fully trust the convenient fictions of habit and custom that steer us through life, as the Logos of Heraclitus steered the universe. Our belief that we know the ultimate principles standing behind aspects of the world's behavior is one of the mind's illusions. The question is, how far should we surrender to those illusions? For Hume, that is a queasy predicament. To go along with all of them might make him the laughingstock of the intellectual community. At the other extreme is reason acting alone, and reason tends to feed on itself and lay waste not only philosophy but ordinary life as well. Hume is in a fix and he knows it. Should he continue to torture his brain with "subtleties and sophistries," knowing that reason cannot justify human beliefs or prove them true? Or should he indolently subscribe to the "general maxims of the world"—an echo of Montaigne—throw his books on the fire, order a high-cholesterol dinner, and have a hilarious evening with his chums?

Darwin thoroughly endorsed the Humean argument that useful deceptions are part of the natural equipment of the mind. Our deeply embedded "maxims of the world" are extremely robust, like the wellsprings of life itself. A certain "don't care" attitude to the nagging doubts of reason is part of our evolutionary baggage. "The mind is such," writes the Darwin scholar Michael Ruse, "that, even if abstract philosophy leads to skepticism, unreasoned optimism keeps us afloat. As human beings, we all believe in the reality of cause and effect, of the external world, whatever philosophy might prove. And that is what counts."

That falls in line with the tradition in Western thought we have repeatedly emphasized, that while truth is desirable, certainly, it may not be the most important thing. Socrates was caricatured by Aristophanes in *The Clouds* as a person who "loves the truth but has not given any thought to the possibility that others may love some things more than truth," which places a formidable barrier between him and them. John Danford sees the "immoderate" ambitions of early modern philosophers, who accepted reason as an all-conquering instrument of understanding, as running violently against that tradition.

The giant strides made by mathematics gave the early modern thinkers a haughtiness, a sense that they possessed the key to truth, denied to those not privy to its techniques. The upshot was a separation of philosophy from ordinary life, a neglect of topics which had wide appeal, such as the nature of good and the origin of evil, where mathematics is of scant assistance. Moderns like Descartes and Thomas Hobbes had stirred up an unhealthy optimism that truth was within the grasp of philosophers, an optimism which in our own epoch has led to the heresy that such "knowledge" is simply mythmaking, storytelling, linguistic artifacts floating in flimsy ether.

"I believe the disappearance of the notion of truth in our times is traceable precisely to these immoderate expectations," Danford writes. "By setting the standard for truth so high, Hobbes and others doomed those who followed them to disappointment and made inevitable, in later centuries, the reluctant abandonment of truth as a possibility. The loss of courage or commitment, so characteristic of our present crisis, has its roots in the forgetting of moderation at the time our modern situation was beginning to take shape." Another scholar, Robert Solomon, considers that after Hume, philosophers lost interest in the very concept of Truth with a capital T. It lost its godlike status. Scientists made impressive advances with false hypotheses; political demagogues not only rose to the heights of power but actually improved the condition of society by telling lies. "Philosophically," says Solomon, "the power of the word 'Truth' has always dwelled in its strong metaphysical linkage to the way the world really is. And having given up on that grandiose conception of Truth, many philosophers are sometimes inclined to give up the word 'truth' altogether."

Hume had a strong influence on two of the most original minds since Sir Isaac Newton. One was Darwin, a prophet of the limitations of reason. The other was Einstein, who was helped to come safely across his "strange seas of thought" to the theory of relativity by ruminating on Hume's assertion that exact laws of nature cannot be obtained by observation alone. Einstein read Hume with a group of friends who called themselves, with an ironic flourish, "The Olympian Academy," while he was living in Berne as a young man in his early twenties. He was impressed with Hume's statement that "habit may lead us to belief and expectation but not to knowledge, and still less to the understanding of lawful relations." In "common life," Einstein decided, we get by with convenient fictions, with instinct and habit, but that is not the case with theoretical physics, where good answers often come from flying in the face of common sense. His theory of relativity was built on the counterintuitive idea that there is no Universal Now of time, no master clock of the cosmos, no unique time sequence of before and after, an affront to ordinary experience. The "strange infirmities" of human understanding meant Einstein's genius could invent even stranger truths, whose chief virtue lay in the very fact that they contradicted mental habit and custom, which Hume said keep us anchored in sanity. Absolute time, so obvious it seems a little queer even to question it, turns out to be an arbitrary conjecture; the wildly implausible thesis of relativity is the more accurate view. It is an artifact of what Einstein called the "free creations" of thought. Of Hume's *Treatise*, Einstein said: "I studied it with fervor and admiration shortly before the discovery of the theory of relativity. It is very well possible that without these philosophical studies I would not have arrived at the solution."

Hume gradually came to recognize that free creations, running against the grain of habit and instinct, were a sort of "third force" of the mind, supplementing observation and reason. He cautions his readers that here we have a risky piece of mental equipment which needs gingerly handling. "Nothing is more dangerous to reason than flights of the imagination," he warns, "and nothing has been the occasion of more mistakes among philosophers." At the same time, imagination is part and parcel of understanding. It lures us into unreal fantasies, yet it is indispensable for any sort of knowledge. The same power that enables us to daydream about dragons and UFOs is recruited to work a more humdrum form of magic: converting the sense impressions that flit across the brain into perceptions of solid, enduring objects that make up the "real" world. A mythmaking faculty is also the source of such a down-to-earth feature of the mind as "knowing" that the room we fell asleep in last night is the same room we see on waking up in the morning.

By this thesis of the centrality of the imagination, which has been called "one of the most fascinating and disquieting" aspects of Hume's philosophy, Hume left a gap between what "seems" and what "is" that evolved into the now accepted convention that there is no hard and fast distinction between bare facts and theories, a doctrine that has done much to undermine the view of science as providing us exclusively with objective, mind-independent truths. We need imagination, the perilous vehicle that manufactures falsehoods as easily as it constructs a world we can trust. We need it even to recognize unadorned facts. Hume opens a space between what we call knowledge and the world itself. We cannot dispense with imagination, because reason by itself not only is unable to explain how or why we believe what we believe, but also tends to dissolve everything in an acid bath of skepticism. It has suicidal tendencies. There is a faint foretaste here of Gödel's celebrated Incompleteness Theorem, published some two hundred years after Hume's *Treatise*, which proved by logic that there will always be true statements that cannot be derived from a given set of axioms, putting ultimate truth out of reach.

CHAPTER EIGHT

Interlude: The Simple Truth

The truth is too simple: one must always get there by a complicated route.
　　　—George Sand

HEN TRUTH IS REPLACED BY "TRUTH," THE situation becomes a little trickier than it used to be. Sophistication, irony, a sense that sincerity on its own is not up to the task of dealing with the world, all signs of life's complexity, are apt to intrude. The feminist poet Adrienne Rich declared that there is nothing simple or easy about the idea of truth. "There is no 'the truth,' 'a truth'—truth is not one thing, or even a system. It is an increasing complexity. The pattern of the carpet is a surface. When we look closely, or when we become weavers, we learn of the tiny multiple threads unseen in the overall pattern, the knots on the underside of the carpet."

Maxim Gorky, in a moment of unintentional humor, once quoted a Soviet factory worker, Dmitri Pavlov, as blurting out in unaffected reverence for his leader, V. I. Lenin: "Simplicity! He's as simple as the truth." It can safely be said that neither Lenin nor Leninism was particularly simple. But is the truth simple? Early in the career of Russian communism there was an effort to bypass the extreme complexity of political theories, modern works of art and literature, avant-garde music, so as to reach the ordinary person for whom truth and simplicity are first cousins. This was pure sentimentality, of course, but Lenin himself made it one of his cultural aims.

Sometimes it happens, at moments of crisis, in the case of a doctrine that aspires to be a final explanation of mankind's predicament, that its defenders and champions are seized by an irresistible impulse to simplify. An epidemic of simplifying broke out in Victorian England when the bombshell of Darwin's *Origin of Species* burst, spelling trouble for all the elaborate theologies constructed around the thesis that God had created the world rather recently, with the human species as the point of the whole enterprise. Within little more than a decade after the book's publication, a spasm of anti-clerical writings put the intellectual life of the country on a secular path. One response to this development was the emergence of Evangelicalism. This movement, an offshoot of Wesleyanism, "scorned the value of evidences and proofs and wagered all on the conviction of faith." It made many converts. But by throwing off the intellectual difficulties of a theology that had occupied the subtlest minds for centuries, by reducing it to a bare, literal story of mankind's Fall, redemption, and expectation of an immortality either of pain or bliss, it could no longer come to terms with discoveries being made almost daily in the natural sciences and with the whole spirit of positivism. "By the very simplicity of its Christian message, Evangelicalism transformed practical religion and the nation's morality," Noel Annan has written. "But this same simplicity rendered it terribly vulnerable to the new weapons in the positivist armoury; and it is not, I think, an exaggeration to see Victorian theology in retrospect as a tireless, and at times almost desperate attempt to overcome the appalling weaknesses which this simple faith presented to positivist criticism."

The idea that truth is simple is often found lurking in the tradition that God is One Being, and not a profusion of glorious attributes. God is simple in the sense that he is single, a point on which the followers of Plato insisted. Aristotle, seeking singleness, wanted his God to be a unity, in part for reasons of philosophical economy. His deity amounted to thought thinking upon itself, and you can't get much simpler than that. The same economy applied to the world.

As we have seen, a maxim of the early Greek philosophers was "Nature does nothing in vain." That statement of the frugality of creation became linked to the belief that God, the Author of Nature, was not a frivolous or profligate craftsman adding needless complexity to his handiwork. In the Middle Ages, Thomas Aquinas made manly efforts to show that God is an absolutely simple Being, identical with his essence, his existence, his attributes, and all his internal parts. Perfections which are manifold and intricate in human beings are single and simple in God. Aquinas struggled with the task of reconciling that supreme simplicity with the "fact" of revealed theology, that God is also three persons in one nature, one of those persons being both human and divine.

The view today seems to be that a conception of divine simplicity is unworkable in its original strong form. Even in medieval times, doubts arose as to the accuracy of such a doctrine; it smacked of the presumptuous idea that human beings can tell God what he can and cannot do. Ockham, the most famous of the no-frills philosophers, did not say that the universe was simple, as the ancients seem to have believed. God could be deeply devious if he willed. He could create just for the pleasure of creating. "God does many things by means of more which He could have done by means of fewer simply because He wishes it," Ockham wrote. "No other cause of His action must be sought for and from the very fact that God wishes, He wishes in a suitable way and not vainly." So there. Ockham's razor was not for cutting the Author's options, but for ridding human thought of overruns to its intellectual budget, for simplifying ideas. The razor was not to be used on interpretations of Scripture or doctrine already decided by church authorities.

When philosophy entered firmly into partnership with science, when the medieval became the modern, the tradition of a simple God seemed congenial to thinkers trying to make the partnership work. The God of Descartes, who set the stage for the new science of the seventeenth century, and so for the modern world, was a philosophical divinity who did not go in for complexity for complexity's

sake. In Descartes's time, there arose a cult of the "Christian gentleman," which lasted in England until the Restoration. A distinguish-
ing trait of the Christian gentleman was that he could be relied upon
to tell the truth. He was a man of his word. He would not lie, because
his social position made him so secure he did not need to lie. That is
linked to the idea that God in his omniscience is too potent and self-
sufficient to resort to fraud. Plato, in the *Republic*, had said "a lie is
useless to the gods." Socrates agrees that "God is perfectly simple
and true both in word and deed; he changes not; he deceives not,
either by sign or word, by dream or waking vision." Earlier in the Dialogue, Socrates asks Cephalus, who inherited a fortune, to name the
greatest blessing of riches. Cephalus replies that, to a good man, the
possession of wealth means he has "no occasion to deceive or
defraud others, either intentionally or unintentionally." The rulers
of the ideal Republic, however, might have the privilege of being able
to lie if it is for the public good: "but nobody else should meddle with
anything of the kind."

Simplicity makes truth highly democratic, available to all and
sundry. In a letter to Marin Mersenne, Descartes wrote that truth
"seems a notion so transcendantly clear that no one could be ignorant of it." Descartes practiced what he preached, abandoning Latin,
the usual vehicle for scholarly treatises, and writing in the "vulgar
tongue" of French for readers he trusted to use "their natural reason." In that way the *Discourse* would be accessible "even to women."
He made do with just a bare four rules for his Method, deliberately
avoiding the elaborate terminology of the medieval schoolmen and
promising to begin with "the simplest objects, those most apt to be
known, ascending little by little, in steps as it were, to the knowledge
of the most complex."

Montaigne, who recommended plain, homespun virtues, resisting
the urge to unlock all the secrets of the universe, had made the point
that lying spreads confusion because it is nonsimple. "If *falsehood*
had, like *truth*, but one face only," he wrote in his essay "Of Liars," "we
should be on better terms; for we should then take for a certainty the
contrary of what the liar says. But the reverse of truth has a hundred
thousand forms, and a field indefinite, without bound or limit. The

Pythagoreans make *good* to be certain and finite, and *evil* infinite and uncertain." There are myriad ways to miss a bull's-eye, but only one way to hit it. For Descartes, the best examples of unique truths were the operations of arithmetic and geometry, which, being simple, could be applied extensively to other domains of knowledge. "My whole physics," he said, "is nothing but geometry."

Newton, an early admirer of Descartes, did not agree that geometry is all. There were states of motion, of speeding up and slowing down, which only his newly invented and rather complicated calculus could pin down satisfactorily. Yet Newton, too, trusted nature to be parsimonious. Rule One of the *Method of Natural Philosophy* was in the spirit of Ockham's razor: "Nature does nothing in vain, and more is in vain when less will serve; for Nature is pleased with simplicity, and affects not the pomp of superfluous causes." That is just fine as long as a scientist is studying the behavior of inanimate objects through the medium of an elegant instrument like mathematics. It was easy for Newton's contemporaries to admire the neat world revealed in the symmetry and coherence of his equations as it was difficult, two hundred years later, for the Victorians to respect the savage and blood-spattered saga of Darwinian evolution. All the ungainly and banal features had been removed. In Voltaire's words, nature "had been covered by an ugly veil and completely disfigured during countless centuries. At the end have come a Galileo, a Copernicus, and a Newton, who have shown her nearly naked and who have made men amorous of her."

In the explosion of scientific innovation that took place in the seventeenth century, the "century of genius," there was a discernible influence of Puritan ethics, especially the ethic of plainspeaking, simplicity, and disdain for the finespun cobwebs of speculation handed down by the medievals. Unvarnished truth was a capital virtue for Puritans. As the historian Perry Miller put it: "Puritanism allowed men no helps from tradition or legend; it took away the props of convention and the pillows of custom; it demanded that the individual confront existence directly on all sides at once, that he test all things by the touchstone of absolute truth, that no allowance be made for circumstances or for human frailty. It showed no mercy to the spiritually lame and the intellectually halt; everybody had to advance at the double-quick under full pack. It demanded unblinking perception of the facts, though they should slay us. It was without any feeling for the twilight zones of the mind, it could do nothing with nuances or with half-grasped, fragmentary insights and oracular intuitions." Puritan sermons had to be lucid and spare, a transparent medium to let in the light of revelation. William Ames, American author of a standard textbook of theology, taught that the efficacy of the Holy Spirit "doth more cleerely appeare in a naked simplicity of words, then in elegancy and neatness."

It was during the Puritan revolution, around 1645, that groups of scientists began to meet regularly in London. One of them was led by John Wallis, a mathematician who won the respect of Oliver Cromwell for his ingenuity in breaking coded messages sent to Charles I by his military commanders during the civil war. Wallis provided Newton with some of his most productive mathematical ideas. Another set called itself the "Invisible College," and revolved around Robert Boyle, a deeply religious person who discovered the law governing the elasticity of gas. Many of these men had advanced their fortunes under Cromwell. At the Restoration of Charles II, they coalesced to form the Royal Society, of whose original members a good two-thirds were clearly Puritan. By contrast, Puritans were a fairly small minority in the general population. "Science had a new charm, and scientists a new prestige," Jacob Bronowski wrote of this period. "And part of the prestige may already have come from their sense of mission and the aura which they were beginning to carry of being dedicated men. Most of them were Puritans by birth, and came from the families of merchants and smallholders who were thrusting their way into the world. But, intellectually, their Puritanism did give them a special devotion to the truth as they saw it for themselves, and a grave indifference to the authority of the past, both of which are still summarised in the word 'nonconformist.'"

The emphasis on speaking the *literal* truth at all times, which was part of the Puritan code, left its mark on the ethos of the Royal Society and its explicit commitment to plain language. Charles II, whose imprimatur lent considerable status to the Society, even if he proved less than unstinting in the matter of funds, conferred on it a coat of arms with the motto *Nullius in Verba*, reminding the members that science should deal in facts, not words, and if in words, nothing fancy or poetic.

The English masters of Renaissance prose, after an initial flirtation with simplicity, notably on the part of Erasmus, who insisted that scholarship return to the purity of original sources, had aimed at maximum variety, at copious adornment. Elegance, and then more elegance, was the goal. Cicero, not Aristotle, was the model. Since the fashionable path to truth lay in analogy, the more images the better. A reaction set in during Descartes's century, however. There was a turn to Aristotle, who did not commend lavish embroidery in language. There was even a suggestion that decoration is immoral, obscuring the core message, perhaps using beauties as contrivances to communicate untruth in the guise of truth. It was a modern version of the old Athenian animus against the sweet-tongued but duplicitous Sophists. Thomas Sprat, who wrote the history of the Royal Society, warned against the sort of excellence in speaking that the Greek Sophists cultivated, as being harmful to science. It floated too loftily above the world of hard fact and close observation, in which true scientists should have their noses firmly planted. Such eloquence was too facile. Of all the skills of men, Sprat said, "nothing may be sooner obtain'd, than this vicious abundance of *Phrase*, this trick of *Metaphors*, this volubility of *Tongue*, which makes so great a noise in the World." The policy of the Royal Society would be to "reject all amplifications, digressions, and swellings of style: to return back to the primitive purity, and shortness, when men deliver'd so many *things*, in almost an equal number of words."

Ultimately, the idea that simplicity is natural and nature truthful began to wobble in the face of evidence that the world, especially in its biological aspects, was not simple at all. Descartes had gaily assumed that nonhuman animals were mere robots, relatively simple clockwork machines—he modified this view later on—which obeyed the laws of physics. As for humans, they were machines with minds. The rise of experimental, as distinct from theoretical, science put a damper on that sort of thinking. In 1665, fifteen years after

Descartes died, Robert Hooke, curator of experiments and secretary to the Royal Society, peered into a primitive microscope at a sliver of cork, smooth and uniform to the naked eye, and saw it was actually full of tiny holes, which he named "cells," after the little bare rooms in a nunnery. It began to dawn on investigators that all living tissue was constructed in this way. Under stronger and stronger magnification, Hooke's simple cell, the most basic entity that can sustain life, turned out to be remarkably complex, replete with the most intricate structure. Most of its parts were so small it took the invention of the electron microscope, magnifying an image 500,000 times, to observe them. "It was now obvious," says the historian Norman Hampson, "that the functional organisation of the housefly was as complicated as human physiology had been assumed to be a century earlier. More generally, microscopes showed that the 'clear and distinct perceptions' received through the eye, which Descartes had taken as a criterion of truth, were sometimes a mere product of low magnification."

In time, the creative vitality of the Royal Society began to dry up and stagnate in an atmosphere somewhat indifferent to science. Leadership fell into the hands of aristocrats and dabblers rather than practical investigators. Traditionally, a gentleman had been regarded as especially immune to delusion or self-deception, and there was a custom that an aristocrat could testify in a court of law without supporting witnesses or payment of a bond, just by his word alone.

Richard Braithwaite, a Puritan author, spoke for his seventeenth-century brethren when he said that a gentleman should shun all "fabulous relations," all tales that might be factually correct but which gave the impression he had invented them in order to show off. A gentleman should take pains to speak in such a style as to leave no suspicion in the minds of his listeners that his account was anything but the literal truth. But if the "truth" of nature might now lie in optical enlargement, or some other device for heightening observation, the exceptionally reliable eyes and ears possessed by a person of aristocratic birth could be surpassed by any old bumpkin or peasant equipped with a microscope. One reason for the decline in the importance of the Royal Society may have been that too much faith was placed, not in hard-core experiment and observation, but in what was then regarded as a complete "Theory of Everything," namely, Newton's compact and neat laws of motion, which seemed to offer ultimate truth about the physical world. The Society tended to resist new ideas, such as the idea of energy, which came from outside investigators. Early on, there had been a certain shying away from symbolism. Robert Boyle, whose first contact with the work of Galileo instilled in him a deep hostility to Roman Catholicism, did not wholly trust logical methods and models written down on paper, and was apt to frown on "thought experiments," the mental manipulation of nature. His first priority was observation. Abstruse mathematics amounted to a form of pride or boasting, comprehensible only to a handful of the elect.

Until the big upheavals at the end of the eighteenth century, the single Truth ideology held people's minds in a powerful grip. It led to certain unrealistic hopes for a reduction of such complex entities as human beings to a simple, basic calculus. If Newton could explain celestial motions by writing marks on paper in his ivory tower at Cambridge, why could not a science—a "physics"—of society be developed along similar lines, deducing grand conclusions from a handful of spare, definitely true axioms about human nature? This "geometrical" approach was used to rationalize the English Whig revolution of 1689 and the French Revolution as well. There was actually an expectancy that experiment would become superfluous. Once you had the correct method—and Descartes had shown how to use it—the sky and everything beneath the sky was the limit. "All knowledge," Descartes wrote, "is of the same nature throughout, and consists solely in combining what is self-evident. This is a fact recognized by very few." Bernard Fontenelle, a French philosopher and man of letters who did much to popularize Descartes, said that "A work of morals, of politics, of criticism, perhaps even of eloquence, will be the finer, other things being equal, if it is written by the hand of a geometer."

The dream of a social physics, based on the notion that society is essentially simple, was promoted by John Locke, a dedicated Newtonian who had grown up in a liberal Puritan household which placed a high value on simplicity. John Herman Randall writes with-eringly of Locke as being a typical specimen of thinkers "always start-ing from a quite inadequate knowledge of the complexity of human society, always convinced that a few simple truths could be discov-ered and from them a complete science developed, always arriving at a social theory able to break down traditional beliefs but incapable of substituting a more comprehensive system." For that reason, the social sciences of the eighteenth century grew sterile, not up to the task of coping with the new and different predicament brought on by the industrial age.

As the heyday of the Enlightenment passed, other thinkers began to suggest that science, let alone society, was not as "natural" as opti-mists like the marquis de Condorcet had supposed, nor nearly as simple. It might even be forbiddingly abstruse, inhospitable to minds that lacked formal training. Newton had his popularizers, who avoided difficulties by leaving out the mathematics, concen-trating on the *Opticks*, which Newton wrote in graceful English, rather than on the *Principia*, composed in daunting Latin. After New-ton's death in 1727, a huge commercial enterprise sprang up devot-ed to his memory, including poems, statues, and a simplified version of his ideas for gentlewomen, entitled *Newtonianism for the Ladies*, which did not so much as mention the laws of dynamics. Voltaire also came out with *Elements of Newton's Philosophy Made Accessible to Everyone*, keeping the difficult stuff for the latter half of the book so as not to scare off his readers. In 1762, there appeared *The Newtonian System of Philosophy Adapted to the Capacities of Young Gentlemen and Ladies and Familiarised and Made Entertaining by Objects with which they are Intimately Acquainted*. Newton had deliberately made the *Principia* arduous to read so that his ideas would not be subjected to attack by half-baked amateurs of science. The simplicity of Newton's equa-tions of motion was in any case misleading, since it masked a formi-dable sophistication and the mind of a unique genius.

The Marquis de Condorcet, one of the intellectual parents of the Victorian belief in progress, had been confident that the easy assim-ilation of knowledge would ensure a democratic society, improving itself steadily from year to year, freeing mankind from nature, a development he regarded as entirely natural. John Locke, Jeremy Bentham, the French moralist Claude Helvitius, and others were not of one voice, however, as to the inevitable arrival of a democracy of wisdom. A certain liberal elitism hovered around the edges of the scientific enterprise, encouraging the snobbish restriction of "truth" to a select and special few, whose task was to filter and dilute it for consumption by the uninitiated populace, making easily digestible myths out of a reality too opaque for the common understanding.

In the twentieth century, there was a tendency to stress that science, like democratic government, is a profoundly *unnatural* activity. Physicists in general do not celebrate the fact that their theories are esoteric, but they acknowledge that those theories cannot be formulated, and certainly cannot be understood, except in the highly specialized language of mathematics. "With each freshman class, I again must face the fact that the human mind was not designed to study physics," is the bleak conclusion of Alan Cromer, a professor of physics at Northeastern University. There is a Principle of Simplicity that can be used as a rule of thumb by physicists: when faced with a number of possible laws which can all be induced from the same data, choose the least intricate one. But there may be a profusion of possible laws, all roughly as simple as the others. What scientists usually do is decide on the basis of a theory, and the theory may not select the simplest option at all. "There can be no doubt that the history of science shows the laws of nature are always more complex than we originally thought," is the conclusion of Rom Harré. "The Principle of Simplicity as a *blanket* principle can hardly be accepted. Of course at each stage of knowledge it would be mad to choose any more complex hypothesis than one has to, but that is hardly a methodological principle of the portentous epistemological status assigned to the Principle of Simplicity."

There is a suspicion today that behind the desire for unity, for the one Truth, lurks a yearning for metaphysical simplicity, the superstitious dream that if theories and laws are simple, they are more likely to be correct. Hovering over this tradition is the shade of Leibniz, whose God made a world that produced a cornucopia of variety but made sure it all had an explanation that was ultimately simple.

"I know of no other reason for thinking simplicity a guide to the truth," the historian of science Ian Hacking has said. "I suspect that many admirers of unity have, *au fond*, a thoroughly theological motivation, even though they dare not mention God. I wish they would! It would get things out in the open."

Einstein, believer in a Supreme Being whose taste was impeccable, defined that ruling intelligence as a God of Parsimony. The surface prodigality of the world is something a creative thinker aims to peel away so as to construct a more austere kind of symmetry, where deeper meanings are to be found. "Man tries to make for himself in the fashion that suits him best a simplified and intelligible world; he then tries to some extent to substitute this cosmos of his for the world of experience." On the face of it, the world does not possess these qualities. There is more than an echo in Einstein of the Cartesian proviso that God only illuminates our understanding when we have exerted the maximum effort to make our ideas simple and distinct. His deity is just as economical as Aristotle's and every bit as philosophical as that of Descartes.

Max Born, however, in his book *Natural Philosophy of Cause and Chance*, pointed out that whereas the logical underpinnings of Einstein's law of gravitation are simpler than those of Newton, the formalism itself is nightmarishly complicated. Einstein wrote in the margin of his copy of this book: "The only thing that matters is the *logical* simplicity of the *foundations*." The equations of Einstein's theory of general relativity are in most cases famously forbidding and his theory of gravitation requires fourteen equations whereas that of Newton needed only three. Yet of the two Einstein's is the more aesthetically pleasing, partly because of the simplicity of his key concept that gravitation and inertia are equivalent. Einstein's guiding principle has been called the "myth of simplicity," the attainment of simple results by means that are not simple at all.

"How unfashionable Einstein was," says Yehuda Elkana, "became somewhat hidden by the seeming similarity between Einstein's demand for his simplicity and the very fashionable demand for simplicity by the various idealistic schools, such as positivism, behaviorism and reductionism. But for these schools, simplicity consisted of reducing all metaphysics to sense experiences. For them, 'simple' is whatever is directly available to the senses; all so-called theoretical statements are reduced to so-called observational ones."

The sciences of the past half century have been called "a revolt against simplicity." One mark of this revolt is that scientists no longer take for granted that truth lies in the depths, or that the depths are simpler than the surfaces. There is an even stronger tendency to say that we make things more simple at the price of making them more strange. Theories of complexity and chaos have shown not only that hugely complex results can be produced by simple causes, but also, vice versa, that complex causes may lead to simple effects. It is no longer a straightforward matter to say whether something is *genuinely* simple or not.

Systems that are chaotic and wildly intricate may give rise to large-scale simplicities that are quite a surprise: they seem to take on a life of their own, independent of the circumstances from which they emerged. For example, the very economical lattice structure of salt crystals needs to be immune from the motion of particles that swarm about chaotically on the atomic scale, paying no heed to what is going on down there. Otherwise, salt could not crystallize in the regular way that it always does. This autonomy of structure from the fine details of its origin has been called a "complicated simplicity." In a sense, there is a serious rupture between cause and effect, making both more problematic than was ever dreamed of in David Hume's philosophy.

That hiatus dividing emergent features from the systems that give birth to them tends to subvert the once firmly held belief that the closer we approach the single, simple "secret of the universe," Einstein's Old One, the *arche*, the Logos, the unique principle that governs all the operations of the cosmos, the more we are converging on truth. What use is a Theory of Everything if there is a disconnect between its compact little recipe and the way things are at a higher level of less abstraction? Would a complete mathematical description of how the universe began lead to a new understanding of the mind of the Maker, as some of today's physicists suggest? The suspicion that it would not is at the root of some of the millennial dissatisfaction with the lofty claims of science. A rock-bottom unifying principle of great simplicity would be awfully interesting but of no practical use whatever. A question arises: Is meaning to be found in the middle range between the macrocosm and the microcosm, on our own familiar scale of things, where things matter because we make them matter?

In the new sciences of complexity, precipitated by the late twentieth century's fixation on computers, information, language, and things close to the middle scale—macroeconomics, weather, ecosystems, population control, politics, the brain—the term "transparent," which in the eighteenth-century Enlightenment meant plain, unencumbered, opening a clear window onto truth, acquires a different sense. A piece of computer software is called transparent if it can be put to work without the user having the foggiest notion of how it works. It could be monstrously complex in its inner details, thoroughly opaque to the untutored eye, but once installed is simple to operate, just as a novice motorist presses the pedals and turns the steering wheel in blissful ignorance of what is happening under the hood. That is a new version of the myth of simplicity.

Complexity confounds common sense. Chaos theory, which probes intricacy in the middle scale, shows that very simple equations can generate unpredictable behavior. In the case of certain computer programs, consisting of just a few lines of code, it is impossible to say ahead of time whether or not the computer will arrive at an answer. On the other hand, it is the violation of one of the classic "laws of simplicity," specifically, the law of symmetry—which says that the mathematical description of a system is the same whether it is going forward or backward in time—that enables large-scale, novel simplicities to appear out of chaos.

"The idea of simplicity is falling apart," says Ilya Prigogine, one of the authors of chaos theory. A new dualism, a surprising distinction between the simple and the complex, is introduced, such that the simple can give rise to complication so mind-boggling it seems incredible that one could have produced the other, and complexity that produces simplicities so emancipated and sui generis it is a wonder that such a parent could have birthed such an anomalous offspring. So simplicity is not just a matter of getting to the bottom of things, of stripping Nature to the buff, as Newton was thought to have done; rather, it is a way of looking at the world that assumes a vast amount of complexity, but treats it as transparent and beside the point for the task at hand. Whether something is simple or complex depends on the kinds of questions we ask, and it is never *simply* simple. Truth often lies at the intersection of the two.

CHAPTER NINE

The Inner Light

When people invited the Duchesse de Guermantes to dinner, hurrying so as to make sure that she was not already engaged, she declined for the one reason which nobody in society would ever have thought: she was just setting off on a cruise in the Norwegian fjords, which were so interesting. The fashionable world was stunned, and without any thought of following the Duchess's example, derived nevertheless from her action that sense of relief which one has in reading Kant, when, after the most rigorous demonstration of determinism, one finds that above the world of necessity there is the world of freedom. —Marcel Proust

What a strange contrast did this man's outward life present to his destructive, world-annihilating thoughts! —Heinrich Heine

S TRUTH DISCOVERED, SOMETHING THAT suddenly sheds radiance on us, like a light bulb going on in a comic strip? Or do we make it ourselves, as we make meanings in a life otherwise devoid of them? The theory of the Logos suggested it was possible just to sit back and tune in to the truth of the cosmos. In the eighteenth-century Enlightenment, it was thought that a reasonable world contained an order of everlasting truths that could be grasped directly by the rational mind. But a suspicion began to dawn that this was obtaining truth on the cheap, too easily and neatly, that the Age of Reason actually suffered from a smug and artificial sense of security. It tended to miniaturize truth in a world that was richer, larger, grander, and more mysterious than those thinkers gave it credit for being. An explosion was on the way.

In the inhospitable writings of a bachelor professor of regular habits living quietly in the East Prussian city of Königsberg in the confident noon of the eighteenth century, there can be detected what has been termed "the tremor of a coming earthquake." This shift of the tectonic plates of the Age of Reason, seemingly quake-proof due to the stabilizing power of orderly thought and the laws of a fully comprehensible universe, was the Romantic revolution. In the words of Isaiah Berlin, it brought about "the destruction of the notion of truth and validity in ethics and politics, not merely objective or absolute truth, but subjective and relative truth also—truth and validity as such—with vast and indeed incalculable results." The staid genius, whose life was as lawlike and predictable as the celestial bodies in Newton's theory of the heavens, was Immanuel Kant.

One and only one picture hung on the wall of Kant's sparsely furnished study: a portrait of Jean-Jacques Rousseau, another herald of the coming tumult. Rousseau, Kant was to say, "set me straight," showed him that the true moral worth of a person does not reside in the intellect, but rather in the deeply hidden center where desire for the good is to be found. Kant interpreted Rousseau as meaning that the autonomous moral law is as necessary, and just as objective, as the laws of Newtonian mechanics. That was to be the core of his philosophy, culminating in the unexpectedly anti-Enlightenment assertion that error is essential to a virtuous life, that true moral action can flourish only in a universe that is ultimately beyond our comprehension. "Newton first saw order and lawfulness going hand in hand with great simplicity," Kant wrote, "where prior to him disorder, and its troublesome partner, multiplicity, were encountered, and ever since then the comets run in geometrical paths; Rousseau first discovered amid the manifold human forms the deeply hidden nature of man, and the secret law by which Providence is justified through his observations."

There is an important difference between what the lay person means by "necessary" in this context and what philosophers, in particular Immanuel Kant, mean by it. Newton showed that the planets move as they do in obedience to inflexible laws of nature: there are no exceptions, ever. On the other hand, Plato had allowed that in his ideal Republic, rulers, the very topmost executives of the state, might find it "necessary" to lie for the good of the community, and Machiavelli most wholeheartedly agreed with him. For Kant, brought up in a Pietist household, telling the truth was more like a Newtonian law than something with a convenient loophole for hard-pressed heads of state. He did not, however, insist that we always tell the truth.

There are forms of expression that do not communicate a specific message to another party: keeping silent, not being pinned down, sidestepping, equivocating, exercising common courtesy. But if we do commit ourselves to saying something definite, we must never lie about it. Otherwise all contracts and covenants would be suspect, and so worthless; the whole basis of a just society would totter.

There was an occasion when Kant was thrust willy-nilly into the dilemma of deciding whether to tell a harmful truth or resort to something less than the whole truth to avoid injuring another human being. In a biographical sketch by Thomas de Quincey, we are told that Kant in old age began to be bothered by the disrespectful, and perhaps worse than disrespectful, behavior of his footman, Lampe. Like Lord Peter Wimsey's servant Mervyn Bunter in the detective novels of Dorothy L. Sayers, Lampe had entered Kant's household after serving in the army, in this case the Prussian army. But there the similarity ends. For many years, Lampe was as correct and scrupulously punctual in his habits as his master. Sharp at five minutes before five in the morning, he would march into Kant's bedroom and call out, in a parade-ground voice: "Mr. Professor, the time has come." Kant would obey the command as if taking orders from a drill sergeant, rising at once and seating himself at the breakfast table as the clock struck five. When Kant took his afternoon walk along the same linden avenue every day, up and down eight times in good weather and bad, Lampe trudged anxiously behind him with a big umbrella under his arm if rain was in the offing. It is said that Kant made room for the existence of a God in his second *Critique* just to keep old Lampe content.

As Kant's faculties began to decay, however, Lampe, "presuming upon his own indispensableness from his perfect knowledge of all the domestic arrangements and upon his master's weakness, had fallen into great irregularities and habitual neglects." Among other things, he was cheating the great philosopher of his money. Kant came to think he must dismiss the man who had performed his duties for some forty years. Once the decision was made, there was no going back, because "the word of Kant was as sacred as other men's oaths." Lampe had deterioriated into an old ruffian who was apt to keel over when in his cups. He warred continually with the cook. One January morning in 1802, Lampe did something so shocking, so "shameful," Kant could not bring himself to say what it was. Biographers can only speculate. But the die was cast: Lampe must go. A new servant, Kaufman, was engaged. Lampe was sent on his way with a handsome pension.

Now, however, came the moral quandary. Lampe had the nerve to call and ask for a reference of good character. "Kant's well-known reverence for truth, so stern and inexorable," was at loggerheads with his essential kindness and good manners. He sat frowning for a long time at his desk, staring at the paper, wrestling with his conscience. At last he took up his pen and—to put it bluntly—fudged the facts. Lampe, he wrote, "has served me long and faithfully, but did not display those particular qualifications which fitted him for waiting on an old and infirm man like myself."

Kant gets shot at from both sides for his emphasis on the moral core of human nature. He has been called an anti-intellectual for subordinating the thinking part of our makeup to the ethical, making morality central and basic. The epithet "prig" has been flung at him for his inelastic attitude toward duty and codes of behavior. He is accused of being a hidebound stickler for truth and, conversely, of opening the philosophical floodgates that undermined the whole concept of truth. When push came to shove, he gave a manservant who had acted unspeakably a euphemistic certificate of merit, because the man needed one.

Human needs play an important role as barriers to truth in Kant's philosophy. His idol Rousseau had taken up the question of needs and how they may distort or falsify the once axiomatic "true fit" between mind and world, as in Hume's work the need to make sense of the world of everyday, even if it means being deceived as to its true nature, is an overmastering priority. Lying, dissembling, and guile flourish, not just because they are easy and tempting, but for the added reason that they are necessary for survival. And we acquire needs that are superfluous to survival. Rousseau was a forerunner of Freud in that respect. He thought that if a person habitually wears a mask, that person might grow to become the false facade, while the real self dwindles, erodes, and finally disappears. Artificial wants edge out and replace the genuine, natural ones. Lacking a core of true desires, the individual becomes a flunkey to the whims and needs of others.

Hume had put a cloud over reason by saying it cannot provide us with true knowledge, since it operates only with information that has come to us via the senses. A belief is warranted as "true" by these impressions of sight, hearing, touch, but that is not a terrific guarantee, since they are impressions unique to myself. The belief only seems true to me. It is not universal; it cannot be an eternal verity. A specific cause "produces" a specific effect, not by virtue of some necessity in nature, but as a result of a connection between my ideas, the links of habit and custom. And we need habit, in order to make sense of the world.

Kant, who said Hume's dagger-strike at reason roused him from his "dogmatic slumber," set out to determine, in his *Critique of Pure Reason*, what reason can and cannot do to set us on the road to truth. Kant recognized three types of true assertion. The first is a statement such as "All triangles have three sides," which cannot be anything else but true, because it is completely independent of external facts, which may or may not be correct. It simply defines the meaning of the word "triangle" as a dictionary might. The sentence cannot possibly be false, but it tells us nothing we do not already know. It is true a priori, in its own little world. The second type of assertion is "synthetical." In the sentence "Gentlemen prefer blondes," we are told something that is not part of the definition of the word "gentlemen." We are stepping outside logic and language into the great world, observing certain particular facts and making general statements about them. This extra information, however, is not certain, but only probably true. It would be undone by the discovery of a single gentleman who is partial to redheads.

A third type of truth Kant called the synthetical a priori. Here the predicate does add new knowledge, but the knowledge does not come from outside, from the unreliable world of experience. It is contributed by the mind, and it is both universal and necessary, not local and accidental. "Matter is convertible into energy by the equation $E = mc^2$" is a sentence of this third kind. Such an assertion is objectively true, but not in the usual sense. We say things exist in space and occur in time, but in Kant's system, space and time are just mental categories. They are not "real." Yet they are categories possessed by every human mind, and therefore are universal, and the fact that we structure our experience in terms of space and time is an objective fact, not an empty tautology.

Unlike Hume, Kant was not doing psychology. The operations of the mind are not peculiar and different in each person, since they are not based on the senses. They are necessarily the same for everyone. So necessary, that instead of saying the mind conforms to the structure of things in the world in order to know them, we could put that statement into reverse and assert that things as we experience them conform to the universal structures of the mind. That is as quake-making and revolutionary as the Copernican discovery that, against all the evidence of common sense, the Sun does not revolve around the Earth; instead, the Earth orbits the Sun. It alters the job of philosophy from one of investigating the Being or essence of things, things as they are in themselves, to the very different project of considering the built-in rules of the mind. And these rules or principles are "transcendental," in the sense that they transcend or go beyond experience.

That has an upside and a downside. The upside is that we can have an objective, unexceptionable basis for a new kind of Logos, a relationship of intelligibility between the mind's innate rules of operation and the predictable, unified, and stable world they construct. This world must be intelligible, because the mind organizes it. Kant called these rules "categories," and they include substance, cause, unity, totality, reality, and limitation, among others. The downside of such an arrangement is that we are unable to have any kind of experience except for the ones the categories construct. We are totally unequipped to experience the "essence" or core reality of things, what Kant called the "noumenon," as opposed to the "phenomenon" of outward appearances, so that the Holy Grail of traditional philosophy, ultimate truth, which is veiled by mere surfaces and appearances, is forever closed to us. We may think we can know it, but that is an illusion, a mirage.

That banishing of philosophy from the paradise Garden of Ultimate Truth was regarded as a scandal by some. The poet Heinrich Heine portrayed Kant as a sort of intellectual bomb thrower, a terrorist of the order of Maximilian Robespierre. Heine saw in both men the same "talent of suspicion," the same absence of poetry in their makeup. "God, according to Kant, is a noumenon," he sniffed. "As a result of his argument, this ideal and transcendental being, hitherto called God, is a mere fiction. It has arisen from a natural illusion. Kant shows that we can know nothing regarding this noumen, regarding God, and that all reasonable proof of his existence is impossible. The words of Dante, 'Leave all hope behind!' may be inscribed over this portion of the *Critique of Pure Reason*." Heine blamed Kant's philosophy for casting the baleful influence of its arid "packing-paper" prose style over literature and the fine arts. Thank goodness, he added, it did not interfere in the art of cookery.

The categories impose limits on what we can know. Without the constraints of the universal rules of the mind, we could know nothing. The world would be nonsense, a meaningless chaos. Yet we are so constituted that we chafe at the very restrictions that make coherent experience possible. Human nature is such that it grows dissatisfied with meanings that make the world intelligible but do not disclose truth, that actually shut us out and bar the gates of truth. We are given phenomena, but we crave noumena. The categories cater to the sort of needs that Darwin investigated, of "adapting to the environment"—in this case, the environment of the categories—in order to live in the world. But Kant fully recognized that human beings have other needs, and one of the most potent of these is the desire, so deeply entrenched in consciousness, for metaphysical speculation. That is risky business, because pure reason, by which Kant meant intellect completely divorced from all other faculties, is a flighty vehicle that tends to run away with us, trespassing beyond the limits that keep us safely moored in experience, like a dove that finds it so effortless to fly in Earth's atmosphere it assumes it must be that much easier to soar in empty space. This Kant called "the scandal of reason."

Against all the odds, reason insists on making the futile attempt to pry into the "really real," a region outside our mental atmosphere, hoping to discover the way the world ultimately is, behind and beyond the categories, thus lurching into fallacies and fabrications. Reason uses its "ideas" to overstep the limits of what the mind is made to know. Infinity is one of these ideas, God another, and immortality a third. Kant constantly plays on the theme of illusion, of falsehood masquerading as truth, of the temptation to go blundering up the blind metaphysical alley that leads nowhere. Pure reason longs to escape the conditions that constrain what we are able to know, in spite of the wealth of knowledge those very conditions make possible. The categories become vehicles of deception. It is a disease of the understanding that pure reason should have such impossibly rarefied ambitions. Writing of the region of genuine knowledge, Kant said: "This domain is an island, enclosed by nature itself within unalterable limits. It is the land of truth—enchanting name!—surrounded by a wide and stormy ocean, the native home of illusion, where many a fog bank and many a swiftly melting iceberg give the deceptive appearance of farther shores, deluding the adventurous seafarer ever anew with empty hopes." Pure reason, in fact, is a sort of philosophical *Titanic*.

And yet, and yet. If an inclination is so firmly lodged in us, so ineradicable and vital, can it be dismissed as a mere nothing, an empty falsehood? Is it of no significance whatever? In a provocative passage of his *Logic*, Kant remarks that the primary question of philosophy is not so much "What can I know?" as "What is the human being?", a relocation of emphasis that bears the marks of Rousseau's influence. Seen from the human perspective, metaphysical conjecture cannot be pushed out of sight. It is both important and necessary. "That the human mind will ever give up metaphysical researches is as little to be expected as that we, to avoid inhaling impure air, should prefer to give up breathing altogether," Kant wrote in the *Prolegomena to Any Future Metaphysics*. "There will, therefore, always be metaphysics in the world; nay, everyone, especially every reflective man, will have it and, for want of a recognised standard, will shape it for himself after his own pattern. What has hitherto been called metaphysics cannot satisfy any critical mind, but to forego it entirely is impossible." The demon of deception is all the more potent because so deeply embedded in our nature. Even after the deception is unmasked, the illusion "will not cease to play tricks with reason and continually entrap it into momentary aberrations ever and again calling for correction." Susan Neiman uses the word "neurosis" in discussing the libidinous character of this sort of metaphysics.

It has been suggested that Kant himself never quite realized the extent to which he had taken reason off the leash. He recognized that, while metaphysics can be dangerously deceptive, it is a genuine need and cannot be eliminated without harm to psychic health and well-being. The questions it restlessly explores are of profound importance to the life of mankind. And its goals are quite unlike those of experimental science. The distinction made by Kant between *Vernunft*, "reason," and *Verstand*, "intellect," was to reverberate to the end of the millennium. The intellect wants to grasp experience only as it is provided by the senses of sight, hearing, taste, and touch. Reason, by contrast, strives to understand its meaning, and this is a craving as urgent and insatiable as sexual desire, almost Darwinian in its irresistible momentum and its priority as a universal characteristic of the human species.

"The need of reason is not inspired by the quest for truth, but by the quest for meaning," Hannah Arendt wrote in her comments on Kant. "And truth and meaning are not the same. The basic fallacy, taking precedence over all specific metaphysical fallacies, is to interpret meaning on the model of truth." It is the activity of thought on its own, regardless of the particular forms it takes, that is "probably the aboriginal source of our notion of spirituality." Useless to protest that down-to-earth reality must rein in such speculation, as, in Darwin's world, the constraints of the physical environment ensure that only certain types of biological organisms survive. That would be to suppose that all activity of the mind is based on common sense. But thoughts "transcend all biological data." It was thought that destroyed Descartes's trust in accepted wisdom and made him doubt the most obvious things. The function of common sense is to fit us to the world of appearances, of phenomena, so that we need not bother our pretty little heads about what it all may mean.

Vernunft is the faculty that makes us feel at home in the world as it seems to us, the humdrum, reliable world of everyday. It was one of the achievements of the eighteenth-century Enlightenment, and to a certain extent of the Romantic movement that followed, to take the strange, the uncanny, the exotic, and make it familiar, domesticated, and homey. The cosmic spaces that frightened the seventeenth-century mathematical prodigy Pascal with their vastness were brought down to the scale of the human mind, making them manageable. Newton reduced the majesty of the heavens to sets of equations that may have intimidated minds as capacious as those of John Locke and Richard Bentley, but carried the promise of becoming accessible to the lay understanding. Later, Darwin was to render almost banal the age-old mystery of the emergence of species.

Verstand, by contrast, tends to deprive us of the comforts of home and the easy tranquility of custom and habit. Our feeling of realness is a matter of biology, whereas thinking undermines that confidence; in our age it has produced a physics, an art and literature, which make us uncomfortable, cause us to doubt reality. It flies in the face of common sense and reverses the *geist* of the Enlightenment by taking the familiar and making it strange.

In the later Middle Ages, meaning had been given priority over literal truth. The world was not a big machine to be taken apart and explained, but an allegory, a parable. Its innermost secret was not describable as a chain of causes and effects. Rather, it held a sacred meaning, which could transform the life of a person able to grasp it. That might involve accepting some pretty wild stories, bizarre fables that were flatly at odds with nature as common sense construed it. The widespread medieval belief in miracles came out of this readiness to put meaning and purpose ahead of truth. Poking and prying into the material operations of the world was seen as antagonistic to this more elevated pursuit, implying a doubt, a suspicion, totally lacking in the sacramental view of nature. Since the whole point and aim of philosophy was to reveal the architecture of a world whose highest meaning and reason for existence was God, it was of minor concern whether nature was truly described or history accurately written. "To the mind of the scholar," says John Herman Randall, "it was meaningless to inquire whether the pelican really nourished her young with her own blood, or there really existed a phoenix who rose from the ashes, so long as these creatures, whether of God directly, or of God through the imagination, made manifest the Saviour who shed his blood on the cross and rose the third day. Indeed, a knowledge of natural history for its own sake would have been regarded as almost blasphemous, taking men's thoughts away from its essential meaning for man."

Kant uses the word "truth" quite sparingly in his writings, preferring to talk about "knowledge" or "reason," a new departure for philosophy. In a vastly different way and with all his critical faculties on the *qui vive*, he made a case for the importance of talk about transcendent matters in terms of a "meaning which could transform the life of an individual able to grasp it." Where previous thinkers aimed to demonstrate the noumena by metaphysical argument, Kant turned that topsy-turvy and said metaphysics itself must rest on a foundation of moral beliefs, and be essentially practical. There is not a glimmer of a chance that we can show, by logical reasoning, or by amassing "facts," that the universe was created by an all-powerful and utterly good Author, or that we are perfectly free and rational creatures. We cannot even claim to "know" the world as a whole, since we experience only a small segment of it. Neither is there the slightest hope of disproving any of these theses. We must, said Kant, seek in the practical use of reason sufficient grounds for the concepts of God, freedom, and immortality. These are not theoretical dogmas, but presuppositions. They are a product of *moral* intuitions. We entertain them as possibilities, and that is as objective as they are ever likely to get. Only by virtue of practical reason, Kant said, is our speculative thinking "justified in holding onto concepts even the possibility of which it could not otherwise presume to affirm."

We "need" the idea of a soul, as a guide in the workaday task of becoming a successful human being, even if it is just a bedtime story.

Pure reason is a snare and a delusion if it presumes to describe reality, but it can be useful in the form of what Kant called "regulative principles," not literal facts, but a kind of fiction; "as if" statements, which point us in the direction of genuine knowledge about how life should be lived, just supposing there is something to these high-flown notions. They should not be likened to the obsolete and defunct organs noted by Darwin as relics of an earlier stage of evolution and now useless. The regulative principles are a road map for living, now, today. They function as the basis of morality and religion. The way we act under the conjecture that we have free will is likely to be quite different from the sort of choices we would make if we believed everything we do is determined by an ironclad necessity. A life spent in the faith that there is a God and that the soul is immortal, even if such certitude has no basis in science and does not even entail genuine knowledge, would surely not be the same as a life dominated by the conviction that the world "just is," and has no author, no point, and no meaning.

The whole of Kant's philosophy revolves around the notion of the good will. He shared with Rousseau a belief that human beings are potentially freer than nature, unique in possessing a will that speaks through the voice of conscience, the inner light, and is able to resist the importunate, clamoring demands of the material world. In his hands, that became the theory of the absolutely free moral will. What is odd about this Kantian entity is that it acquires its metaphysical importance only in a world that is not fully understood. It is the source of action, but what would be the point of action if, like God, we knew all there is to know about everything? Paralysis would set in. As it is, through obeying the moral law, we transcend the limits of the phenomenal, lift ourselves clear of the laws of natural necessity, of space and time, cause and effect, that rule the world of ordinary experience, in a feat of levitation that pure reason could never accomplish. In the domain of the good will, we are absolutely free. We have conquered the Darwinian imperative of mere survival and by doing so have come closer to the ultimate meaning of the world than science or philosophy could ever take us.

You might think that, now we hold in our hand the key to the door which had shut reason out, we could ambush truth. Yet Kant still denies us entry. He does so because if all were understood, if we became as wise as God, there would be no more moral striving, and, as he makes clear, exercising the moral will is a higher and nobler thing than mere knowledge. Falsehood and error must remain so that we may go on struggling to be virtuous. There is always the possibility that if we were omniscient, if we relaxed and sat back in metaphysical ease, we would not be godlike, but diabolical.

The Kant scholar Richard Kroner calls this a case of anti-intellectualism carried to awesome extremes. We are left with this curious outcome of Kant's Copernican revolution in ethics: morality makes the world incomprehensible. The Kantian, as opposed to the Cartesian, dualism proposes that human beings are at one and the same time creatures of nature and also beings whose inner light enables them to take part in the nonnatural moral order. Meaning takes precedence over truth. The world has significance only if human actions are significant. The "meaning of the world" is not a matter of theory but of practice, of making decisions, having experiences, doing things. What Kant is saying is that only where nature and freedom are two separate things can the world be described as "philosophical." Absent that separation, "the world would be devoid of meaning. It could never satisfy the human longing for meaning. Such a world would not even give us a clue to the riddle of why we puzzle about ourselves or how beings like ourselves are possible at all. Such a world would never give rise to any philosophy whatsoever." In that case, the world is meaningful only if it is meaningful to us. It is the will, not the intellect, that reaches to the very limit of human experience.

Kant, who excluded nature from the world of the free, rational will, also put off limits aspects of nature that most moral philosophers since Aristotle held to be cardinal for any system of ethics: solicitude, warmth, sentiment. He placed all these qualities under the umbrella term "inclinations" and subordinated them to Duty, a word with wintry overtones that captured the allegiance of Victorians but chilled Romantics to the bone. His "categorical imperative" is a rule of moral action our reason requires us to follow absolutely, never mind our inclinations. That is something quite different from acting out of prudence, or self-preservation, worsting a business rival or beating another person to a taxi in the rain. In that case we are obeying our natural wants and needs, our biological and psychological urges.

The categorical imperative is a principle that commands us to put inclinations totally out of the picture. We act according to Duty and Duty alone, and that requires the use of the will. Kant insisted that there cannot be multiple versions of morality, contingent on culture and fashion, on history, on feelings. Telling the truth is incumbent on every person no matter where or when. He envisages a Utopian Kingdom of Ends, in which harmony reigns perpetually, since all its inhabitants act rationally all the time. Here a rule against lying is not a pragmatic convention, designed to avoid the disruption to society caused by falsehoods, but an a priori maxim derived logically, independent of experience. A philosopher of today, Robert Solomon, professes to be shocked—shocked!—at the fact that Kant thus made the consequences of our actions secondary to our intentions, subordinating the effect on others to our own purity of motive, losing the sense of belonging to a specific community. "Unfortunately," says Solomon, "this encourages moral self-righteousness and celebrates the moral prig who obeys all the rules and makes everyone miserable."

In a real-life situation, however, Kant did to a certain degree surrender to his inclinations, to the obligation, not of Duty alone, but to a fellow human being. He wrote a character reference for the old rascal Lampe that does not bear the mark of a prig, that did compromise a little with the categorical imperative and that embodied what Iris Murdoch, a Platonist, concluded on this subject: that compassion, "the great mystery of ethics," cannot always tell the truth.

CHAPTER TEN

Truth at Arm's Length

An ironic person does not commit suicide. —Jacob Golomb

Irony removes the security that words mean only what they say. So too does lying, of course. —Linda Hutcheon

HEN REASON LOST ITS SUPREME STATUS as the key to all mysteries, interest began to focus on other parts of the human psyche, less respectable, less trustworthy and rational. Whereas reason had been the vehicle of truth, these murkier faculties might deliver falsehoods, outright lies, in such a devious way the intellect would not even suspect it was being tricked. The biological aspects of our makeup may override the purely psychological, by brute force, reminding us that life can be more powerful than mind, and less fastidious about getting what it needs. It will opt for a lie if that is more beneficial than truth. One of its instruments for riding roughshod over intellect is the will, whose reputation as an upright character went into serious decline as the nineteenth century went forward.

Immanuel Kant gave us the good will, and on that score alone he can be commended for making a fresh start in moral philosophy. He made it clear that the standard virtues, many of them held in high esteem by thinkers of antiquity—bravery, stamina, continence, resolve—can all be put to the service of immoral causes, whereas the good will is good in itself. As Kant put it: "There is no possibility of thinking of anything at all in the world, or even out of it, which can be regarded as good without qualification, except a *good will*."

The seeds of revolution skulk in this otherwise un-Romantic, rational, quiet tongue of conscience, with its inexorable codes and its categorical imperatives. This sovereign voice of the inner light helped to set the torch of Romantic turbulence aflame. That was due in part to the very fact of its radical freedom, which Kant insisted was indispensable when it comes to making a moral choice. If I abstain from pushing old ladies off the sidewalk, not for reasons of ethics but because I know there is a police officer prowling nearby in a patrol car, or refrain from stealing money from a blind man out of a suspicion that he may not be sightless and could even possess a gun, neither action constitutes a moral choice. To be affected by extraneous circumstances in this way is being a "turnspit," in Kant's contemptuous term. The good will operates without taking notice of desires or inclinations, fear of punishment or reprisal, prudence, or consideration of one's own well-being. Duplicity is at the remotest opposite extreme from this principle of moral action, which is why Kant regarded lying as one of the worst offenses a person can commit.

A hallmark of the Kantian inner voice is that its commands are not statements of fact. Therefore, they cannot be true or false. Kant tucked the voice away in a place safe from the intrusions of external authority and from the prying eyes of scientists. It was a noumenon, not existing in space or time, immune from the laws of cause and effect. Moral action proceeds from this sheltered sanctuary, so that nothing in nature, not even the strongest blast of urgency wafting in from the senses, can alter its absolute priority.

This helped to weaken the idea, embedded in a robust philosophical tradition, that truth is correspondence with the facts. Kant had bypassed the skeptical heresies which doubted that we can have "truthful" knowledge of the world with his Copernican revolution, the theory that the mind does not correspond to the world, but just the reverse: the world as we experience it corresponds to the built-in structures of the mind. That was a drastic reinterpretation of the very concept of truth. It proposed that the really crucial facts are not outside the head but inside it, in the form of mental categories, which are given a priori, not learned. We actively organize the data of the world according to the rules that come already installed at birth, but it makes no sense to say the rules are true. They serve us well, but so might a completely different set of rules. It was the possibility that a child might invent its own idiosyncratic rules of grammar on the basis of the corrupt fragments of speech it hears from adults in its vicinity that led the twentieth-century linguist Noam Chomsky to his theory of a universal grammar, an organ of the mind as "natural" as the heart or lungs. The Chomskyan grammar is likewise neither true nor false. It is simply the only one we have.

In the case of the good will, too, facts are immaterial and truth is beside the point. If the will takes its canons from outside itself, it is no longer authentic, no longer autonomous. Kant described virtue as duties firmly settled in the character. "Autonomy is the ground of the dignity of human nature," he insisted. The good will must be an independent source of commands. "Perhaps Kant did not, like Hume, consciously intend to draw a sharp distinction between imperatives and statements of fact," noted Isaiah Berlin. "But in any case his formulation had revolutionary consequences. Commands or imperatives are not factual statements; they are not descriptions; they are not true or false. Commands may be right or wrong, they may be corrupt or disinterested; they may be intelligible or obscure; they may be trivial or unimportant, but they do not describe anything; they order, they direct, they terrify, they generate action. Similarly, a goal or value is something that a man sets himself to aim at, it is not an independent entity that is stumbled upon." Berlin believed that for all Kant's vision of a unified, harmonious Kingdom of Ends, his thesis of moral freedom shook, even sabotaged the classical idea of a single Truth, one that is immune from the caprices and whims of current fashion.

The doctrine of an inner voice so sovereign it owes no obligation to the truth is a potent one that could be highly destabilizing if it fell into other hands. Kant was a child of the Enlightenment and subscribed to its codes of reason, restraint, and universal truths, its belief that all questions have good answers if only we can discover them. But his successors were inhibited by no such qualms. Kant's theory of the inner voice was exaggerated, stretched, travestied. If values and goals are decreed by the individual conscience, they are not objects we discover, but artifacts we make, so the argument went. They are creations, like works of art, expressions of the self. They are not a copy of anything, not an imitation or even a representation. The inner voice makes every man and every woman an artist, an author, with that extra ration of license and liberty which is a core element of the artist's basic accoutrement.

One of Kant's acquaintances in Königsberg was a highly strung theologian and philosopher named Johann Hamann, a person given to emotional excesses and an exaggerated hatred of the sober canons of the Age of Reason. Sometimes known as "the Wizard of the North," Hamann was one of the leaders of the *Sturm und Drang* movement that emerged in Germany during the 1770s, which rebelled against the growing dominance of science and scientific thinking. The movement championed cultural diversity, the social context of anything that sets itself up as an eternal verity, non-highbrow art and the principle that thought cannot be separated from language, which itself was deemed a cultural product. For Hamann, there were only singular truths, not universal ones. As for reason, it can make models of reality, but a model is just a model: it does not coincide with the world as the world really is. We cannot hope to understand what the world is all about by using our intellect. Love alone provides the key to knowing its true character—love and the voice of God, who communicates through his works.

Like Descartes, Hamann experienced a mystical disclosure which some might call a breakdown, or at least a spiritual crisis. It helped to turn him from an adherent of the Enlightenment to one of its most savage opponents. In 1757 he was sent to London by the House of Berens, a merchant company in Riga, on a delicate mission, its exact nature unknown. Possibly it was to float an idea that the Baltic region should break away from the Russian Empire and set up as a separate state. In any case, the mission was a disaster. Hamann was treated with mockery by the Russian Embassy and lost all his confidence. He blew about £300 worth of Berens money on riotous living and took up an emotional relationship with a dubious character, supposedly a nobleman, only to fall into an orgy of jealousy when he discovered that his companion was being kept by a wealthy man. Financially spent, not in the best of health, he called a halt to all his indulgences, rented a simple room, subsisted on a Spartan menu, and read the Bible. He took Scripture very personally. He studied the distresses of the Jews, which seemed to mirror his own. In a "shattering mystical experience" while reading the Old Testament, the idea came to him that he was the murderer of Christ. His heart thumped, his hands shook. He felt the spirit of God stirring in him, revealing "the mystery of love." The inner voice became the voice of God himself, speaking to him alone. Hamann was bowled over by the thought that everything, the whole content of his waking experience, contained a secret message from God.

These spiritual crises. They tend to throw philosophy into channels that are more interesting than plausible. In the case of Hamann, divine communication, conferred when he hit rock bottom in London, helped to mobilize his opposition to the Enlightenment. Privileged to know the secrets of the Almighty, he was not disposed to endorse the Age of Reason's belief that man is the agent of his own salvation, that he is autonomous. We cannot think our way to the truth. We need the supernatural, the transcendent, the intervention of a higher power. "The breath of life in our nose," he said, "is also the exhalation of God." The *cogito* of Descartes, thanks to a very different kind of manifestation from the one Descartes experienced in a similar period of solitude, went glimmering.

One summer evening in 1759, Hamann had dinner with Kant at the Windmill, an inn on the outskirts of Königsberg. The idea was to bring Hamann back to the fold of the Enlightenment, to restore his respect for reason. The occasion was not a glorious success. The mood was stiff and awkward. Kant was less relaxed and genial than at his famous lunch parties at home. He persisted, however, proposing that Hamann translate some articles from Denis Diderot's *Encyclopédie*, the classic text of the Enlightenment, as an antidote to irrationalism. Another meeting was suggested, but Hamann wrote Kant a pungent letter tilting at the tyranny of reason and sending the insulting message that Kant had a crippling defect: he could not understand the "language of feeling." The very idea that a philosopher could turn him back to the Enlightenment was laughable. We do not need more reason, he went on, but more faith. Some thank-you note! But Hamann unwittingly did Kant a favor. He launched into a hymn of praise of David Hume, for showing that reason is impotent to prove anything worthwhile, cannot make us wise, cannot even give us the confidence to carry on our daily lives: "we need faith to eat an egg or drink a glass of water." That is the first recorded connection between Kant and Hume, whom Kant commended for rousing him from his dogmatic slumber.

Hamann set the stage for a thoroughgoing Romantic war against reason as an autonomous faculty, independent of all others, not excluding the way we speak, the culture which forms us, history, and even our desires and instincts. There is a hint of Darwin here. Where Kant had made the categories, the structures of the mind that make coherent meaning out of the chaotic signals coming from the outside world, universal, the same for everyone, the Romantics tended to reinterpret them as cultural artifacts, the products of history and of a specific society. They were no more "truths" than they were in Kant's scheme, but they were not a natural endowment either. They lost their radical autonomy. As for the hidden reality of the noumena, the things in themselves to which we are structurally unable to gain access, they were just a figment of Kant's imagination; he never was able to give a consistent account of them. The noumena do not exist, so let's not talk about them any more. That was one of the post-Kantian lines of argument.

As for reason, it turns out to have a past, perhaps a checkered one, which makes it suspect. If the thought processes of the mind are shaped by local and historical forces, can that sort of mind be trusted as wholeheartedly as the universal Kantian one, whose categories were as permanent and unaltering as God himself? That was a bothersome dilemma. One answer to it was the Romantic device of irony.

Irony in the Romantic era was used as a way of acknowledging the elusiveness of Truth with a capital T. We humans are in an ironical situation, because we are limited creatures in a universe that has no limits. Hamann used to carry on about how silly it was to suppose we can say anything true about the world, as if we were standing outside it, when any fool knows we are inside the world and will never be anything other than inside it. We are not God. If the mind is a cultural entity with a history, perhaps it suffers from the delusory need to convert the universe into a cultural entity. Like an old-fashioned historian, it cuts up the world into arbitrary pieces for its own convenience, trying to make it stand still when in reality it is mutable and fugitive. Nature herself is ironical, deceptively seeming to offer a sturdy sameness on which we can rely for definite knowledge, only to unravel and destabilize. That was the line spun by Friedrich Schlegel.

Romantic irony, says Anne Mellor, emerged from a post-Enlightenment distrust of consciousness, and a belief in the inevitable incompleteness, and therefore the falsity, of our ideas and myths. We can live with that distrust by acknowledging the fictional character of the theories and schemes by means of which we make sense of the world, yet enjoy the enterprise of inventing ever new ones, cheerfully doing what Kant said we should not do, namely, voyaging out beyond the limits set by the constitution of our minds. Still, philosophical irony is worldly enough to know that ultimate truth is out of reach. It is not deceived into confusing the inventions with eternal truths.

That involves an odd kind of doublethink. We treat the inventions "as if" they are truths (didn't Kant use this device for his regulative principles?). And yet we keep a mental distance from them, since of course we are grown-up enough, sophisticated enough, post-Kantian enough, to know they are not truths. We could say that irony is a sort of lie, albeit an out-in-the-open kind of falsehood, useful in a world where reality is very different from appearance and where truth may turn out to be not what it seems. In classical Greece, *eironia* meant a devious way of fooling someone by adopting a false front, or a tricky use of language.

Millennia before today's critics detected a flavor of irony in twenty-first-century science, a Greek writer noted that "it may perhaps be that nature has a liking for contraries." According to the Roman grammarian Donatus in the fourth century A.D., *Ironia est tropus per contrarium quod cognatur ostendens*—"Irony is a trope that shows the opposite of what one perceives." Its medium was incongruity and disparity, which distinguished it from metaphor, a dealer in samenesses. Socratic irony, in which the disingenuous Socrates pretends to need information and professes mock admiration for his intellectual inferiors, was related to the codes of Greek comedy, in which a character simulated humility in order to outwit a boastful but dimwitted confidence trickster. It is also a means of self-protection. In the *Symposium*, Alcibiades uses the word *eironia* to describe this distancing strategy, complaining that Socrates spends his whole life pretending and playing with people. "It is an outward casing he wears," says Alcibiades. "But if you opened his inside you cannot imagine how full he is, good cup-companions of sobriety."

In England, the use of irony was connected with the desire to be sophisticated. Chaucer's admired master, Geoffrey of Vinsauf, advised that when dealing with foolish people, one should "praise, but facetiously," calling a person who is stunted and malformed "Paris" and someone of rude speech "Cicero." Such a ruse suggests an urbane detachment; one is too civilized to engage in a direct insult, yet wishes at the same time to deflate by making a contrast between the "true" ideal and the inadequate reality. "An irony," according to a seventeenth-century grammarian, "hath the honey of pleasantness in its mouth, and a sting of rebuke in its tail." The term "irony" came into popular use in the eighteenth century and meant saying the opposite of what you mean, intending a strong opinion by voicing a weak one.

In all its various manifestations, irony implies that a speaker or writer wants to keep truth at arm's length, for one reason or another. It disrupts the correspondence between word and world. Perhaps irony is used because the truth is too obvious, too banal or simplistic to be spoken in a straightforward way. Hovering on the fringe of the "naked" truth may be cloaked truths just out of view, in the noumena where the ordinary rules do not apply; truths infinitely more important and transcendent than the literal facts language is equipped to capture. Henry James may have had something like that in mind when he said that irony "implies and projects other possible cases." In any case, irony is a saboteur of the correspondence theory of truth according to which words are a snug fit with facts. A word can mean more than it says, or less. In that respect, irony is first cousin to lying, even though the intention is often entirely different.

Thanks in part to Kant, the reliability of knowledge was subverted, making thinkers who came after him more open to the noncommittal features of irony. Language came to be seen as precarious, meaning unstable. Irony is "language drawing attention to its own limitations." It, too, joined the reaction against reason. In the Enlightenment period, irony tended to retain the idea that every question has a definite answer. It made room for the existence of truth and moral absolutes. When a traditional ironist says the reverse of what he means, he is confident that he knows what he means is the truth.

By contrast, Lilian Furst points out that post-Kantian irony "is not used to differentiate the true from the false because for the romantic ironist all options may be true, or false; nor can he manipulatively say the opposite to what he means because he cannot be sure of any meaning." Later, Friedrich Nietzsche was to say that irony is a mark of decadence, resorted to by a person who no longer curses and scolds, who dislikes having to say yes as much as he shrinks from saying no. "The habit of irony, like that of sarcasm, spoils the character," Nietzsche thought. "It gradually fosters the quality of a malicious superiority; one finally grows like a snappy dog, that has learned to laugh as well as to bite." Romantic irony is a recognition of the contrast between the confined scope of the mind and the immense complexities of experience. That may be one reason why poetry, a prime vehicle of Romantic irony, is said to observe, not the correspondence theory of truth, but the coherence theory, which requires only that the parts of a system fit together internally and need not match external reality. A poet "nothing affirmeth, and therefore never lieth," said Sir Philip Sidney.

Irony is a device that tends to confer autonomy. Sophistication, urbanity, which irony supports, is a form of self-sovereignty. That was a Romantic theme, a travesty of Kant's theory of noumenal freedom. It leaves all situations open. It helped prepare the way for the eventual conversion of the inner voice into pure, irrational will. Kant had turned inward, privileging the quest for righteousness over the search for truth. "After centuries of abuse by metaphysicians," says Robert Solomon, "the Truth acquired a foul taste." Will, like irony, became an alternative to truth. "In proportion as the Will has gone up the philosophical scale," wrote Bertrand Russell, "knowledge has gone down. This is, I think, the most notable change that has come over the temper of philosophy in our age."

The doctrine of the bad will, revived after Kant's death in 1804, had been publicized in the Renaissance by Machiavelli, a theorist of the will as an agency selfish, rapacious, and all-powerful, constantly wanting more, taking precedence over reason and intelligence, never altering in the strength of its appetites, agreeing to the restraints of authority only in order to enjoy in safety its possessions and pleasures. The Machiavellian will, epitome of the needy underside of human nature, is ever unsatisfied: sooner or later this leads a society down the slippery slope into decadence, making it too self-indulgent and hedonistic to resist reversals of fortune. Utopia is out of the question.

It may be no coincidence that the word "sincere" entered the English language only during the sixteenth century when Machiavelli, "Old Nick" to those who thought him diabolical, was in his prime. Lionel Trilling records that sincerity came into the lexicon at a time when society was "preoccupied to an extreme degree with dissimulation, feigning and pretence."

Machiavelli's refusal to endorse a simple set of moral principles has been attributed to the "ruthless and suspicious character of the diplomacy of his era, riddled with treason and betrayal, in which money and threats seemed the only effective instruments." In public life, insincerity is part of the equipment of a ruler, who may opt for the beneficial lie rather than the inconvenient truth. "Reasons of state" (not Machiavelli's phrase) often require craft and trickery. "A Prince must be a great feigner and fraud; people are so simple," he advised. In the notorious eighteenth chapter of *The Prince*, he notes that while "everyone" realizes how praiseworthy it is for a prince to honor his word, experience shows that princes who have achieved great things are those who give their word lightly, who know how to fool people with cunning.

Kant, hostile to unbuttoned self-intoxication of any kind, had kept the will in its place by linking it firmly to reason. It was free only to the extent that it obeyed the prescriptions of reason. The later German assertion of the will as untrammeled and on the loose was what *Sturm und Drang* was all about. Many of Kant's followers were young, radical, and Romantic. They took free will out into the murky badlands where the darker aspects of human nature lurked. The playwright Friedrich Schiller, who died in 1805, was an apostle and popularizer of the Königsberg maestro and soon cut freedom away from the moorings of reason, speaking of "the legislator himself, the God within us," and "the proud demon within man," a sort of imp or rascal rather than the high ethical entity of Kant's philosophy. The heroes of Schiller's early writings feel free to lie, cheat, and steal as acts of reprisal against a lying, duplicitous society. This was all of a piece with the Romantic notion of the "irony" of the cosmos. Where Kant had described the human mind as essentially uniform, each person experiencing the world in terms of the same mental categories, Schiller boldly declared that each poet interprets the world differently, according to temperament. Scientific judgments are as personal as moral ones, since they are inventions, stories we fabricate to make sense of what is ultimately unknowable, whose trustworthiness does not depend on whether they correspond to the "facts" of nature, but on their internal consistency and how they answer to human needs. Needs, whose power Kant acknowledged, became front and center in the drastically personalized worldview of these thinkers.

Johann Fichte, an ardent German nationalist and career academic, annoyed Kant considerably by extending his ideas in a Romantic, anti-Newtonian direction, brashly inflating the "Copernican revolution" as if it were the equivalent in philosophy of the French Revolution, which he admired excessively. Kant was bothered both by admirers who twisted his ideas with the best of intentions, and by opponents like Hamann who "misrepresented the *Critique of Pure*

Reason to a quite fantastic degree." In Fichte's philosophy, everything begins with the self, and truth plays little more than a cameo role. A person wills rather than knows, and will is first and foremost struggle. It is the need to act, rather than the operations of thought, that produces consciousness, and consciousness constructs the world. The French Revolution had impressed on Fichte that history does not just happen; it is made. The poet Heine, in one of his acidic deflations, commented: "Himself as everything! How does Mrs. Fichte put up with it?"

Among the audience for Fichte's lectures in the newly founded University of Berlin was a former medical student named Arthur Schopenhauer, who had arrived in the city in 1811 mainly to hear the famous man who claimed to understand Kant better than Kant understood himself. Schopenhauer was bitterly disappointed by the performances he witnessed, scribbling insults in his notes, calling Fichte pompous, obscure, a windbag, his writings humbug. A naturally distrustful person, he was intensely suspicious of consciousness, Fichte's almighty author of worlds. He decided that the will, which he regarded as the inner, true, and indestructible essence of the human person, is not conscious, and there are times when consciousness does not trust the will. What makes consciousness suspect, in Schopenhauer's view, is that it is conditioned by the intellect, and the intellect is nothing but an accidental outgrowth of the body, a parasite, which is not involved directly in the inner workings of the organism. The will is primary, older and far more robust than consciousness, revealing itself in the shape of "a great attachment to life, care for the individual and the species, egoism and lack of consideration for others." Even in the smallest insect, bereft of intelligence, the will in its simplicity is present, complete and entire. It is a brute force, uncivilized, amoral, an oblivous contending force, and unlike God, has no plan for the salvation of the world.

The will is the core and essence of a person, Schopenhauer repeated over and over again. The intellect is secondary, a mere tool and instrument of the will. It appears in every blindly acting force of nature, as well as in the deliberate conduct of human beings. The difference between the two is just the extent of the end result, not the inner character of the driving energy.

And the will is a source of falsehood, because its "secret decisions," its desires, plans, and demeanor, are tucked away from awareness, even though they control behavior. The intellect is essentially a stranger to the decisions of the will. It provides the will with motives; but only after the fact does it learn how these have turned out. Suppose I have devised a plan, but have reservations about its feasibility. I let the matter rest for the moment. Often, I do not know how firmly I am already attached in secret to this plan, how much I desire to carry it out, in spite of my scruple. But once a piece of information reaches me, conducive to putting the plan into action, "at once there arises within me a jubilant, irresistible gladness, diffused over my whole being and taking permanent possession of it, to my own astonishment. For only now does my intellect learn how firmly my will had already laid hold of the plan and how entirely it was in agreement therewith, whereas the intellect had still regarded it as entirely problematical and hardly a match for that scruple."

The covert operations of the Schopenhauerian will, furtive, restless, and unmanageable, lead to deeply rooted deceptions and illusions in the life of the individual. Consciousness often cannot even guess at the real motives for an action. The intellect "does not penetrate into the secret workshop of the will's decisions," but tends to interpret motive in the most flattering light to bolster our good opinion of ourselves. As La Rochefoucauld said: "Self-esteem is cleverer than the cleverest man in the world."

For Schopenhauer, self-deception is not an unusual or accidental state of mind, but part of its normal functioning. In that respect, he has much in common with today's evolutionary psychologists, Darwinians who "come close to calling into question the very meaning of the word truth." Schopenhauer's main work was published some forty years before the *Origin of Species*, which he read only at the end of his life, deciding it was a lightweight "soapsud or barber" book. He did, however, share with Darwin the notion that there are invisible constraints on how we act and think, how we view the world, and that these curbs are connected with the most basic forces of brute survival and the perpetuation of the species. A certain amount of trickery, deception, and illusion will be used in the service of the greater goal. Many of the "things more important than the truth" are buried deep in the underground of the psyche. And because the constraints are below the level of awareness, we suppose we are freer than we actually are.

The view that the mind is a biological organ waiting hand and foot on the will, helping it to survive, its aim not knowledge but action, content to cope with reality rather than discover ultimate truths about it, was taken up by Hans Vahinger, a German philosopher who was seven when the *Origin* burst upon the scene and eight when Schopenhauer died. Vahinger was renowned as a Kant scholar, a student of evolution who believed, as many others were to do in the later nineteenth century, in the biological character of the mind. He was greatly impressed as a young student by Kant's discovery of the contradictions thought encounters when it roams in the Oz land of metaphysics, and by his doctrine that action, the practical, must take precedence over mere reason. Vahinger was also drawn to Schopenhauer, then out of fashion and actually despised at the University of Tübingen. He was vastly impressed by that philosopher's pessimism, irrationalism, and voluntarism. Vahinger foresaw and prophesied World War I, mainly because he believed that Germany's unrealistic idealism and optimism, both diametrically opposed to Schopenhauer's thinking, would lead to disaster.

Linking Schopenhauer's conception of the will to the theory of evolution, Vahinger set out as a basic principle that a means, originally working toward a definite end, tends to cut up, become independent, and emerge as an end in itself. At first, thought is only used by the will as a means to survive and dominate. But in the course of time, it evolves to an extent that is in excess of what is necessary for its function. It breaks loose and goes its own way. A device initially equipped for the practical task of survival, it outstrips that basic role and indulges in theoretical speculation for the sake of speculation, puzzling over such pointless questions as the origin and meaning of the universe. Other animals have quite small brains which are sufficient for their function as a vehicle of the will and its interests. In the human species, however, hypertrophy sets in, enlarging the brain out of all proportion to the rest of the body. Kant's theory, that human thought hankers after metaphysical truths it is entirely unsuited to understand, now seems to be a natural and necessary result of the fact that thought outran its original function, which was to serve the basic purposes of life. Emancipated from spending all its brain power on staying alive, it uses the surplus to conjure with questions that are unanswerable, not just by human thought but by any form of thought whatever.

Given these impossible aspirations of the intellect, Vahinger suggested it would be better not to chase after absolute truth, but rather to acquire knowledge by means of ideas that we know to be false, but nevertheless are of great practical usefulness in accessing reality. These ideas he called "fictions." They are needed because many thoughts and ideas are not the product of reason but have biological origins. They are consciously false assumptions, even self-contradictory ones, formed in order to overcome difficulties of thought by an artifical digression, reaching the goal of thought by "roundabout ways and bypaths." Vahinger saw an intimate connection between these serviceable untruths and "what Darwinism calls useful illusions formed by natural selection." He called his theory of conscious fictions "the philosophy of As-if." The world of such figments is just as important as the world of the so-called real or actual, he stressed, and far more consequential when it comes to ethics and aesthetics.

One of the most important ethical fictions is the notion of freedom, of human actions which are regarded as free, and therefore as "responsible," in contrast to the "necessary" course of physical nature. That whole notion, Vahinger said, is contradictory, since an absolutely free act, caused by nothing, is just as worthless ethically as a completely necessary one. Nonetheless, we still make use of the concept of free will in ordinary life when we judge a moral action, and it is the basis of criminal law. Without that assumption, it would make no sense to punish any wrongdoer. At the same time, it is a logical monstrosity, a kind of controlled lie, not even a hypothesis. There is nothing in the "real" world corresponding to liberty. It is like an imaginary number in mathematics. The square root of minus one is a mathematical fiction, an unjustified extension of a logical operation having no existence in reality, and so meaningless from that point of view. But mathematics needs the idea and proceeds *as if* it did mean something.

An example of a modern As-if is the concept of "rational man" in economics, an imaginary character who always chooses in such a way that the expected benefits of his choice will exceed the expected costs. Rational Man is a cornerstone of economic theorizing. He is a sort of robot, acting in a perfectly consistent fashion, knowing the things he prefers, aware of all the alternatives open to him, selecting the ones that give him most satisfaction, unlike any creature that ever drew breath in the real world. He represents a highly restricted and even warped conception of human life. Yet economists find the idea useful for the very reason that it rules out other, less rational kinds of behavior, and thus simplifies and directs their thinking.

Thomas Mann at once deplored and commended the anti-intellectualism of his day, the glorification of instinct, even the bad instincts, because, though false and one-sided, it was a means of looking from a new angle at perennial questions of human nature. "We have seen instead of pessimistic conviction deliberate malice," Mann wrote. "Intellectual recognition of bitter truth turns into hatred and contempt for mind itself. Man has greedily flung himself on the side of 'life,' that is, on the side of the stronger, for there is no disputing the fact that life has nothing to fear from mind, that not life but knowledge, or rather, mind, is the weaker part and one more needing protection on this earth. Yet the anti-humanity of our day is a humane experiment too in its way. It is a one-sided answer to the eternal question as to the nature and destiny of man."

CHAPTER ELEVEN

The Pleasures of Falsehood

Truth is contrary to our nature, not so error, and this for a very simple reason: truth demands that we should recognize ourselves as limited, error flatters us that, in one way or another, we are unlimited. —Goethe

Anything that raises the human spirit is basically good, even if it's false.
—Joe Queenan, critiquing *The Oprah Winfrey Show*

 S TRUTH BAD FOR ONE'S HEALTH? SHOULD it carry a warning from the U.S. Surgeon-General, and might it be less harmful if we did not inhale? The notion that the will is stronger than the intellect, especially after Darwin's writings captivated the Victorian imagination, merged, in the hands of an iconoclastic invalid named Friedrich Nietzsche, into the theory that lying is more natural than truth. The will is more deepseated and sturdy, because based on the instincts, those ancient forces of survival, whereas consciousness is a recent arrival, a newcomer weak as a kitten, and therefore delicate and easily indisposed. Nietzsche held up to ridicule the idea of a moral realm out of reach of the inclinations that are a core element of our biological heritage:

A new take on morality and its vicissitudes was Nietzsche's patented philosophical product. Politeness is not equal to goodness in his ethical universe, for sure. One may get the impression that Nietzsche is a bit of a bully, especially with women, hurtful and rude, an enemy of all the amiable virtues. His defenders say, however, that this is a misreading of the man. In spite of passages in which "ruthlessness, cruelty, and suffering are commended and kindness and charity are

157

condemned," writes Arthur Danto, "there is overwhelming evidence that he was a gentle person, of sweet disposition and capable of great considerateness and courtesy—a softspoken man with a disarming sense of humor." He was cranky, we are told, only in matters of diet. But if Nietzsche spoke softly, he carried a hefty philosophical stick, or as he preferred to call it, a hammer. In one of his most hard-edged, blitzkrieg attacks on conventional morals, Nietzsche writes with scorn of the process by which meekness, modesty, humility, self-sacrifice, diffidence, have become virtues, highly prized values. However did such an unnatural state of affairs come about? Surely it is natural for people to cultivate "masterly" traits, like health, good looks, strength, wit, enthusiasm, stamina, and so forth. Nietzsche constructed a parable to explain what happened: During the history of mankind, the physically weak, the frail and underdeveloped, the talentless and ungifted, individuals of low spirits and poor health, retaliated against the strong by elevating these very deficits into virtues. Pride, once regarded as "good," became "bad." A weak sexual drive was sublimated into saintly asceticism.

Compassion, that "great mystery of ethics," which must at times speak falsehoods in order to do its work, is one of the inferior traits transformed by sophistry and hatred of the strong into a virtue. By contrast, cunning is a mark of the robust and healthy person; it was dragged down and branded a defect by the weak and disadvantaged, those who lacked the wit to be crafty and underhand but turned the tables on those who were. These are two kinds of lies which reversed their status in Nietzsche's allegorical history of morals.

It is hard to imagine a personality more unlike Kant, the sociable but rather prissy Königsberg professor, than Nietzsche, an intemperate smasher of idols, God's funeral director, itinerant invalid and one of the loneliest men on the planet, but he did inherit one of Kant's dilemmas: how to reconcile the "truth" (Nietzsche often put the word in scare quotes) of science with those beliefs that cannot be proved by mathematics or logic, yet support our deepest values and keep at bay a suspicion that the world is meaningless. Kant's answer had been to revive Aristotle's theory of the practical reason as distinct from the theoretical kind. Aristotle had placed the practical mind in that part of the soul that initiates movement. "Thought by itself moves nothing," he said in the sixth book of the *Nicomachean Ethics*, "but only thought directed to an end and concerned with action."

In Kant, theoretical reason may aim at truth, may tell truth apart from falsehood. Practical reason, on the other hand, is concerned with propriety, with duty and right conduct. These are two different kinds of reality, two separate worlds. The mistake thinkers of the Middle Ages made was to muddle the two together, trying to appraise facts through the lens of value, which meant they could never create the sort of science that emerged belatedly in the seventeenth century. Kant warned that the reverse procedure is just as wrongheaded, to assess values as if they were facts which are either true or false.

Kant had put a tremendous strain on the concept of truth by splitting the world of experience in two. But he did not question the *value* of truth. Nietzsche broke new ground by doing exactly that, and we are feeling the aftershocks of his particular Copernican revolution to this day. He asks point-blank: Is truth really worth more than falsehood? And if so, why? "That celebrated veracity of which all philosophers have hitherto spoken with reverence; what questions this will to truth has already set before us, what strange, wicked, questionable questions!" he exclaims at the outset of *Beyond Good and Evil*. "What really is it in us that wants 'the truth'? We did indeed pause for a long time before the question of the origin of this will, until we finally came to a complete halt before an even more fundamental question. We asked after the *value* of this will. Granted we want truth: *why not rather* untruth? And uncertainty? Even ignorance?"

The value of truth, Nietzsche decided, must be measured by the extent to which it promotes the flourishing of life, which is a "masterly" role for it to play. His thesis was a variant of the teaching of the Greek Sophist Protagoras, but in this case it is life, rather than man, that is the measure of all things. Health, mental and physical, is always Nietzsche's criterion, perhaps in part because his own health was so persistently rotten. During the Franco-Prussian War, as a medical orderly, he had contracted dysentery and malaria from contact with six wounded men he tended, unrelieved, for three days and nights in a railroad boxcar. The legacy of that experience was ten years of wracking migraine headaches, sleepless nights, and painful vomiting.

As a source of well-being, truth may be less effective than certain types of falsehoods, including the falsehoods of art. Truth does not come *naturally* to human beings, because nature operates in terms of survival and strength, not authenticity and openness. That is an important part of Nietzsche's message. We lack an "organ" for truth, but perhaps we inherit one for falsehood. Our frailty as a species, quite apart from the large number of inferior individuals comprising it, often makes the counterfeit more serviceable than the genuine. The bulk of people are constitutionally unfit to live with truth. They can take it only in small doses, sweetened with plenty of illusion. They are not rugged enough, mentally or morally, to imbibe it straight. "Those who can breathe the air of my writings know that it is an air of the heights, a *strong* air," Nietzsche wrote in *Ecce Homo*, the year 1888, his last productive year before madness closed in. "One must be made for it." Going all-out after truth involves the sort of discomfort endured by heretics and martyrs. "Only great pain, the long, slow pain that takes its time—on which we are burned, as it were, with green wood—compels us philosophers to descend into our ultimate depths and to put aside all trust, everything good-natured, everything that would impose a veil, that is mild, that is medium—things in which formerly we have found our humanity. I doubt that such pain makes us 'better' but I know it makes us more profound."

To "put aside all trust." That was Nietzsche's watchword. "The philosopher," he wrote in *Beyond Good and Evil*, "as the creature which has hitherto always been the most fooled on earth, has by now a *right* to 'bad character'—he has today the *duty* to be distrustful, to squint wickedly up out of every abyss of suspicion."

A cultural vogue for such mistrust was in full swing in Europe at about the time when Nietzsche was writing his mature works, his brain still seemingly unclouded by the approaching breakdown. There was a movement in opposition to naturalism, surfacing in the literature, painting, and music of the period, including the work of the English Pre-Raphaelites and the French Symbolists, reflecting the fact that the Industrial Revolution, with its smoke and clutter, had drastically altered our once close rapport with nature, that rapport which had been a dominant inspiration of Romantic poetry. Life was much more artificial than it had been earlier in the century. The natural world was seen through the filter of aestheticism, and as being in decline rather than evolving toward new and interesting forms of life, as certain adherents of Darwin believed was the inevitable course of things. There was a widespread interest in the irrational and in the exploration of the mysterious subterranean depths of the mind. Modern psychoanalysis developed alongside this "unmasking" trend, the suspicion that what a person says he (or she) thinks may be vastly different from what he "really" thinks in the hidden recesses of his psyche. Dostoevsky and Ibsen pursued this unmasking theme in fiction and the theater.

Suspicion was a woven strand of Nietzsche's personality, a trait he shared with Schopenhauer. The cult of artificiality meant that everything could be a lie, including God and what passed for nature in a decadent age. Nothing should be taken at face value. That was part of Nietzsche's early training. The son of a Lutheran pastor, he showed brilliant promise as a student of classical philology and was named to a chair at the University of Basle at the age of only twenty-five. Years of close scrutiny of ancient manuscripts, whose authenticity was open to question, reinforced a habitual tendency to look askance at anything that was put in front of him. "All our so-called consciousness is a more or less phantastic commentary on a text which is unknown, perhaps unknowable," he once wrote. Among the early influences on the young Nietzsche were the French moralists, with their acutely sensitized antennae for picking up tokens of self-deception. "My writings have been called a school of suspicion," Nietzsche wrote in the Preface to *Human, All Too Human*. "Indeed, I myself do not think that any one has ever looked at the world with such a profound suspicion; and not only as occasional Devil's Advocate, but equally also, so to speak theologically, as enemy and

impeacher of God." Such a temperament made him liable to "chills
and anxieties of loneliness," brought on simply by being a person
with an uncompromising difference of outlook.

Nietzsche was suspicious even of nature. He made fun of the eighteenth-century and Stoic doctrine of "Follow nature" as laughably
counterfeit. Nature is a deceiver. She needs to be, in a world where
total truth would be as dangerous to a fragile species like *Homo sapi-
ens* as trying to stare down a tiger. Even plants are "masters of cunning," a remark that makes us wish Nietzsche could have had access
to the wealth of research by natural scientists into the widespread
deviousness of living things. In an essay *On the Pathos of Truth*, presented to Cosima Wagner as a Christmas gift in 1872, thirteen years
after the publication of the *Origin of Species*, Nietzsche pointed out
that nature conceals most things from us, even something as close
and intimate as our own bodies, of which we have only an illusory
awareness. We are locked inside this consciousness, and nature
threw away the key. "Oh, the fatal curiosity of the philosopher, who
longs, just once, to peer out and down through a crack in the chamber of consciousness." And people talk about nature as if she were a
source of wisdom, a muse, a guide to truth. What a joke! Nature is
sublimely indifferent to us. She doesn't care whether we live or die.
How could a person act or think in accordance with such a vast
unconcern! If we were honest with ourselves, we would admit that
we want to be different from nature. Geniuses of self-deception, we
read into nature our own human values and ideals. In notebook
entries to *The Philosopher*, written in 1872, Nietzsche wrote: "The man
who does not believe in the truthfulness of nature, but instead sees
metamorphoses, disguises and masquerades everywhere—the man
who catches a glimpse of gods in stones and nymphs in trees: now
when such a man sets up truthfulness as a law for himself, he also
believes in the truthfulness of nature toward him."

Nietzsche had a prickly attitude toward Darwin. He did not agree
with the *Origin*'s emphasis on self-preservation, which he thought
misread the character of nature. Self-preservation is a symptom of
distress, a curb on the core principle of life, which is just the opposite: expansion, enlargement, mental hardihood, creative verve. Liv-

ing things hazard their own survival to make the most of their potential. The doctrine of the "struggle for existence," a hallmark of Darwinism, he ascribed to a quirk of the English class system: most natural scientists in that damp little island came from blue-collar backgrounds, descendants of poor, obscure folk living in cramped conditions, scraping by, learning the art of survival perforce at first hand. "The whole of English Darwinism breathes something like the musty air of English overpopulation, like the smell of the distress and overcrowding of small people," was Nietzsche's scathingly aristocratic assessment. The mistake these timid, hard-pressed people made was to accept the outmoded fallacy that nature "does nothing in vain," whereas in fact what we see in nature is not niggardliness, but superfluity, overproduction, and squandering, even to an absurd degree. The struggle for existence is only a temporary aberration.

All the same, Nietzsche took seriously Darwin's argument that the human species emerged from humble origins. He recognized that falsehood may have been the primary mode of life, not just for brute subsistence but for exactly that flourishing and augmentation which was at the kernel of existence; the "will to power," as he called it. Truth could have been a later evolutionary development, parasitical on falsehood, a synthetic overlay or by-product. The laws of "truth" would have been invented as a social convenience, and then only in the form of an agreement to abide by certain beliefs, a sort of conventional Krazy Glue whose function is to keep the community together. They could be just a useful illusion.

Nietzsche also shared Darwin's doubt that human consciousness, given its emergence by random accidents from primitive life forms, is equipped to deal with deep metaphysical questions, among them the eternal one: "What is truth?" Descartes had rested his case for the reliability of human knowledge on the guarantee that God would not deceive him. Falsehood was a Satanic ruse, and Satan was a loser. Nietzsche had no such fallback position. The "simple" truth, in his book, is somehow diabolic. The argument that truth has a divine warranty reveals an attitude that is actually hostile to life, since all of life is based on semblance, art, deception, points of view. Take away perspectives, take away error, and you are left with nothing. If "one wanted to abolish the 'apparent world' altogether, well, assuming you could do that at any rate nothing would remain of your 'truth' either." In the *Genealogy of Morals*, Nietzsche puts a question mark over the whole tradition that God is truth: "what if this belief is becoming more and more unbelievable, what if nothing turns out to be divine any longer unless it be error, blindness, lies—if God himself turns out to be our *longest lie*?" We are on the brink of the arrival of a new doctrine, the gospel of the holiness of falsehood.

Nietzsche himself was apt to assume disguises and false fronts. It was one of his ways of coping with a recalcitrant world. He may or may not have contracted syphilis in his student days, which may or may not have been responsible for his abrupt decline into insanity. Even unhinged, Nietzsche left some in doubt as to whether the breakdown was entirely genuine, or merely a protective camouflage. One morning in early 1889, he walked out of his lodgings in Turin and saw a cabbie thrashing his horse in the Piazza Carlo Alberto. Weeping, he threw his arms around the horse's neck, then fell unconscious to the ground. Coming to, he began to clown, singing and shouting, banging away at the piano. He wrote letters to the king of Italy, to the Vatican. Other letters he signed "The Crucified" and "Dionysus." He called himself the successor to the God that was dead. His antics grew steadily more bizarre, but at the beginning of 1890, Peter Gast, a musician friend of long standing, on the basis of extended walks with Nietzsche every day, had the impression that his friend was merely feigning madness, as if that were the preferred last act of an extraordinary life. Another friend, Franz Overbeck, a professor of theology, came to see the self-proclaimed new God and did not take the deranged vaudeville act at face value. He knew the man too well. "I cannot escape the ghastly suspicion," said Overbeck, "that his madness is simulated. This impression can be explained only by the experiences I have had of Nietzsche's self-concealments, of his spiritual masks."

Nietzsche in his prime regarded consciousness, which early modern philosophy banked on as bedrock, as just another product of evolution, with its roots in the subhuman. It proceeded under the mistaken idea that it could forge the key to unlock the secrets of the universe. Consciousness, too, suffered from delusions of grandeur. Probably, it had emerged out of the need to communicate, which meant it was merely utilitarian, inviting his contempt. As an instrument of social cohesion it catered to the mentality of the crowd, "the herd," in his disdainful term. As a recent innovation, consciousness was also the most fragile and incomplete of faculties. It gave rise to innumerable errors, some of them life-threatening. It is only thanks to the superior force of the instincts, far more ancient than the *arriviste* consciousness, that humanity is still around today. We exaggerate wildly its capacity for truthful knowledge, and this "ridiculous overestimation and misunderstanding" prevents consciousness from developing at a rapid rate: assuming that we already possess consciousness, we do not exert ourselves greatly in order to cultivate it. What little we do have has made us frail by comparison with other species; delicate, irritable, suffering, and in need of the consolation of chimeras and fantasies.

This downgrading of truth, and the boosting of life-enhancing illusions, was contemporary with a similar upending of traditional priorities; the neo-Romantic, end-of-the-century notion that the artificial is more replete with meaning, more "real," than the natural. In 1878, Henry James explored this idea in his novel *The Europeans*, which deals with a New England family, the Wentworths, who live a life of "unpretentious" simplicity in a Puritanical milieu, where nature has not been excessively improved upon by art. The Wentworths are deeply suspicious of a visiting European couple, Felix Young and his sister Eugenia, seeing them as poseurs and role players, too witty by half and strangers to sincerity. It turns out, however, that it is the Wentworths who are pretentious, and the European Youngs, with their cultivated gaiety and fashionable clothes, are the ones who accomplish the difficult feat of being themselves. Gertrude Wentworth blurts out that she seeks the company of Felix because she is "trying for once to be natural." She has only been pretending to be natural all these years. Tony Tanner, in a critique of the novel, comments: "The Puritans' self-conceit was that their way of life represented something nakedly simple and natural, whereas the amoral Europeans were given over to concealment and pretence. But here is a spirited child revealing that it is those honest, simple Puritans who have imposed a life of concealment and pretence on her, while it is with the adorned and eloquent Europeans that she feels most 'natural.' The paradox is a deep one. Perhaps it is precisely with the aid of art that we may most readily discover, and be, our natural selves."

Oscar Wilde, with whom Nietzsche has often been compared, promoted a drawing-room-comedy version of this thesis, throwing violently into reverse the cliché that art should mirror nature. The "truth" of nature unadorned, stripped naked, is not sufficiently interesting to make us care about it. In Wilde's dialogue "The Decay of Lying," a character named Vivian talks about nature's "extraordinary monotony." Vivian, who hates to be interrupted when he holds the conversational stage, enlarges on the theme that nature imitates art. Sunsets, he asserts, "are quite old-fashioned." They belong to the time when Turner was the last note in painting. To admire sunsets is a distinct sign of provincialism of temperament. "Yesterday evening Mrs Arundel insisted on my going to the window and looking at the glorious sky, as she called it. Of course, I had to look at it. She is one of those absurdly pretty Philistines, to whom one can deny nothing. And what was it? It was simply a very second-rate Turner, a Turner of a bad period, with all the painter's worst faults, exaggerated and overemphasized." Later, he complains: "I wish the English Channel, especially at Hastings, did not look quite so often like a Henry Moore."

Another heretical reversal, an overturning of what seemed most settled and impregnable in Western philosophy, was the assertion that surface may have priority over depth. Art periodically rebels against such distinctions. Frederic Jameson has noted trends in *fin-de-siècle* twentieth-century architecture which emphasize the "epidermis," or outer membrane of structures, shunning dimensions of depth. He speaks of "a new kind of flatness or depthlessness, a new kind of superficiality in the most literal sense—perhaps the supreme feature of all postmodernisms." Alan Wilde (no relation to Oscar) finds in the late work of E. M. Forster a celebration of a world without "causality, sequence or depth," and the feverish acceptance of surface. Late modernism did not know quite which to value more, depth or surface, and postmodernism discovered "horizontal depth," a surface without superficiality. Early in the twentieth century there was in the novel an almost obsessive concern with profundity, which gave way in the 1930s to a "noticeable, if somewhat ambiguous shift to surface that amounted to something like a new sensibility." It was a major reversal.

Ezra Pound, the Imagists, Wyndham Lewis, George Orwell, Evelyn Waugh, were all exponents of surface. This was a reaction against modernism. "The early modernist tendency to connect truth with depth, and at times to sacrifice the phenomenal for the reality that is presumed to underlie it, gives way to a counterassertion that truth inheres in the visible," in the view of Alan Wilde. "Thus the repeated announcements that things *are* what they seem—provided, of course, that the seeing eye is clear, unclouded by the mists of convention and tradition, free from the deliberate evasions and sentimentalities of the past and from the still more insidious deceptions of the self. The trick, then, is to see not more deeply, but differently." It is as if the *cogito* of Descartes is now optical rather than intellectual, but still the sworn enemy of custom and tradition.

For much of his career Nietzsche did not deny the possibility of a hidden truth beneath the epidermis, but he regarded such a truth as possibly dangerous, unnatural, unhealthy (health obsessed him), and antithetical to our deeply implanted needs and desires. At this late stage of civilization, when we are sophisticated enough to question how much truth is really worth, might it not be better to keep some things decently concealed? Could it be a sign of immaturity, of being behind the times, to hanker after ultimate reality? In his 1886 Preface to *The Gay Science*, Nietzsche wrote: "This bad taste, this will to truth, to 'truth at any price,' this youthful madness in the love of truth, have lost their charm for us: for that we are too experienced, too serious, too merry, too burned, too *profound*. We no longer believe that truth remains truth when the veils are withdrawn. We have lived too much to believe this. Today we consider it a matter of decency not to wish to see everything naked, or to be present at everything, or to understand and 'know' everything." A little girl, told that God the all-knowing is present everywhere at all times, gave the answer of a perfect aesthete, so old-fashioned now to us with our hidden cameras, our reality television shows, our paparazzi: "I think that is indecent."

Nietzsche would surely have agreed with Oscar Wilde that "Lying, the telling of beautiful untrue things, is the proper aim of art," though his attitude to art was much more complex, more contradictory and wayward, than Wilde's. The morning-after hangover from his infatuation with Richard Wagner had left a toxic residue. He did say that art is only possible as a lie. But these lies are of a special kind: they are not really intended to deceive us. Art treats illusion as illusion, so that in a sense it is sincere. Yet its truth is a surface truth. "Oh those Greeks! They knew how to live. What is required for that is to stop courageously at the surface, the fold, the skin, to adore appearance, to believe in forms, tones, words, in the whole Olympus of appearance. Those Greeks were superficial—*out of profundity*."

The "great sweep of life," Nietzsche insists, has always been on the side of the most unscrupulous, wily, and resourceful deceivers. He uses the word *polytropoi*, applied to Odysseus in the first line of the *Odyssey*. Life itself, in Nietzsche's view, seems to aim at semblance, mirage, simulation, self-delusion. Odysseus is the prototype of Darwinian man. His strength comes, not from truth, but from the skillful deployment of error.

Nietzsche, it has been said, perhaps unfairly, was a moralist whose criteria of better and worse were inseparable from feeling better or worse. They fluctuated with the condition of his body. Truth may have seemed too harsh for his precarious state of health, like a purgative medicine or a bloodletting. Prozac might have been more beneficial. He thought it aristocratic to be solitary, to "live almost always in disguise, to travel *incognito*," but might it be that solitude, like the masks he wore, protected him from the exertion of social intercourse? He liked the anonymity possible in a crowded resort like Nice, where he told his friend Peter Gast they should both settle: "As hardworking and solitary animals, we will keep tactfully out of each other's way, except for an occasional celebration of togetherness." Holed up in a pleasant room with a view of eucalyptus trees and the Mediterranean at the Pension de Genève in the year 1885, he worked on his pivotal book, *Beyond Good and Evil,* where he definitely rejects the idea that truth is of the highest worth. Being a religious tenet, it is anti-life. Q.E.D. Self-preservation dictates that we be superficial, that we accept falsehood, and this, as a biographer has pointed out, comes from a man in whom the instinct of self-preservation had become remarkably feeble.

In 1888, Nietzsche wrote the last book he saw printed, *Twilight of the Idols.* He was at the end of his tether. He wrote to Overbeck of "grim hours, entire days and nights when I no longer knew how to go on living, and when a black despair, unlike any I have known, took hold of me." He complained of a draining away of his stamina, keeping himself on his feet only by means of great art and caution. There were symptoms of a profound nervous exhaustion "in which the whole machine is worth nothing." His breakdown was only months away. *Twilight* demolished completely the notion of a "true" world behind appearances. It aimed to smash "with a hammer" the notion that one can dehistoricize, "make a mummy" of anything, remove the world of Being from the world of becoming. Being is an empty fiction. The "apparent" world is the only one. The "real" world of hidden truth "has only been lyingly added." All talk about an alternative, truer world, Nietzsche decides, is a waste of time. It slanders and disparages our actual existence. It is a form of revenge against a life which does not meet our needs, a mark of decadence, a symptom of decline. Abolish that alternative universe, and the world of everyday, of common sense, can be redeemed. It can be taken seriously. But it still does not cater to us, which is why we tell so many lies about it.

"We have become cold, hard and tough in the realization that the way of this world is anything but divine," he had written in *The Gay Science,* finished two years earlier. "Even by human standards it is not rational, merciful or just. We know it well, the world in which we live is ungodly, immoral, 'inhuman'; we have interpreted it far too long in a false and mendacious way, in accordance with the wishes of our reverence, which is to say according to our *needs.*"

Nietzsche knew that we hanker after truth and yet long to satisfy the whole of our being, and we cannot have both. That is part of his gripe with the majority of philosophers. What they present as the answers to the great metaphysical questions are actually disguised versions of their deep inclinations, perhaps even of something as crassly Darwinian as the need to protect a certain kind of life. The artist in Nietzsche recommended keeping a safe distance from things because "in themselves" they are seldom or never beautiful, attractive, or desirable. We should be "poets of life" first of all in the smallest, most everyday matters. He called art "the goodwill to appearance," the cult of the untrue, softening the bad news that delusion and error are the conditions of human knowledge.

In fact, Nietzsche's strongest legacy to the twenty-first century is his decision, sometimes tacit, to treat the world, not as an object of the kind that science investigates, but more like a work of art or literature, where there are no "facts," only interpretations, the more the merrier. It was an elaboration of his 1873 thesis that "Truth cannot be recognized." As in philology, commentary can obliterate the text altogether. Just as there is no single Truth, there is no pure self, no observer who is wholly neutral, who comes with no cultural baggage, unaffected by circumstances of place and time and upbringing, innocent of all proclivities, leanings, desires, memories. God might be so unencumbered, but we are not.

The problem of placing confidence in life is a tremendous one. To solve it, Nietzsche said, man must be a liar by nature. He must be above all an artist. "The pleasure of lying is an artistic pleasure; otherwise, only truth would possess any pleasure in itself. Artistic pleasure is the greatest kind of pleasure, because it speaks the truth quite generally in the form of lies." Existence with all its horrors is endurable only as an aesthetic fact. Art is a counterpoise to honesty, whereas honesty by itself would lead to disgust and suicide. It is the goodwill to illusion, the only sure antidote to that itch to chase after absolute truth, with all the "metaphysical nausea" that goes with it. In *The Birth of Tragedy*, written some sixteen years earlier, while he was still infatuated with Wagner, Nietzsche had theorized that the Greeks of antiquity invented the gods of Olympus in order to make life bearable. "The Greek knew and felt the terror and horror of existence," he wrote. "That he might endure this terror at all, he had to interpose between himself and life the radiant dream-birth of the

Olympians." The gods formed a "middle world" of artifice, of fiction, which acted as a sort of theatrical and poetic demilitarized zone, mitigating the terror. It was in order to be able to live that the Greeks had to create these gods from a most profound need. The gods justify the life of mankind simply by living it themselves: "Existence under the bright sunshine of such gods is regarded as desirable in itself."

Montaigne—a favorite author Nietzsche read to cheer himself up when the discomforts of rented rooms pressed hard upon his spirits—had hated falsehood because of the sheer quantity of untruths that are available on any given matter. By contrast, Nietzsche saw this very kind of anarchy and confusion, the Dionysian element of life, as the raw material of new creations. "One must have chaos in one," says Nietzsche's hero Zarathustra, "to give birth to a dancing star." Safety might suit a logician, but it starves an artist, who must venture out onto the open seas of dangerous but fertile new possibilities. Nietzsche himself was extraordinarily restless in his anchorless wanderings, always seeking new surroundings. Here is his itinerary for a single year, 1887. He changed his lodgings in Nice from the Pension de Genève to a room in the rue des Ponchettes, the twenty-first room he had occupied during seven winters in Genoa and Nice. In April of that year he left Nice for Cannobio, on Lake Maggiore, staying only three weeks. The bright sun bothered his eyes and he lacked a stimulus. Should he take a cold-water cure in Switzerland, or return to Venice? He finally chose Zurich. After ten days he was off to Chur and walked in the woods to soothe his eyes, but soon tired of that. He quit Chur early in June, spent four days in Lenzerheide, intending to stay there for the summer. But another four days later he was in Sils-Maria, headachey and throwing up. In September he moved to Venice, intending to stay for two months, but four weeks later he shuttled back to Nice, pleased to note that the food in hotels had improved, settling in there until the following April.

The theme of not playing it safe, of not staying put, caught on at the turn of the century. The word "adventure," with its connotation of risk and the unknown, became one of the key terms of the post-

Victorian age. Suspicion, distrust, and falsehood all had the virtue that they open up possibilities, whereas truth closes in, seals in, slams doors shut. Nietzsche, having proclaimed that truth is a late and rather fragile invention growing out of a more basic and robust accumulation of beneficent falsehoods, comes close to saying that the world, or at least all of it that could possibly be of interest to us, is a human creation that supersedes nature. That is a variation of the Romantic doctrine that art and literature do not represent reality, as common sense would suggest, but instead make it a more important kind of reality.

The concept of adaptation, of simply adjusting to one's niche, is anathema to this way of thinking. It was one of Nietzsche's chief grumbles about Darwin's theory of evolution. An artist, a poet, does not adapt, but invents his or her own world and justifies it through the work itself. "Nietzsche stands as the founder of what became the aesthetic metacritique of 'truth,' wherein 'the work of art,' or 'the text,' or 'language,' is seen as establishing the grounds for truth's possibility," says the Nietzsche scholar Alan Megill. It is not a question of whether what is written or painted "corresponds" to actuality, since the connection is an aesthetic, not a logical one. "The truth, such as it is, refers only to how we comprehend the world as a work of art."

CHAPTER TWELVE

A Cloak for Quite Different Impulses

You must not be frightened by words, Ernest. What people call insincerity is simply a method by which we can multiply our personalities. —Oscar Wilde

It was so sincere, that nineteenth century, it pronounced the lie, the lies of life, to be indispensable. —Thomas Mann

O THOSE WHO DREAM OF DRASTIC ALTER-
ations in the fabric of society, truth may not be grand or
inspiring enough to mobilize the necessary energy and
enthusiasm to overthrow an entrenched regime. Something fabulous may be called for, narratives in the heroic vein that
tell of deeds impossible but glorious, drawing minds away from a fixation on the merely possible. A myth of this kind makes contact with
those parts of the psyche that are apt to ignore the difficulties that
loom if seen with a strictly rational eye. The "lies" of myth acquire a
political power through their contact with the will rather than with
the intellect, rich in meaning if poor in the literal truth.

That theory of the galvanizing untruth was espoused by one of
Nietzsche's devoted admirers, Georges Sorel. Sorel was a man struck,
like his hero, by the spiritual sickness of society and in particular the
moral decadence of France. Georges Sorel led as quiet and
respectable a life as Nietzsche's was turbulent and untidy. He has
been called variously a prophet, a modern-day Machiavelli, a "mere"
romantic journalist, an amateur, a genius, and, with Marx, the only
original thinker of which socialism can boast. Lenin referred to him

cuttingly as a notorious muddlehead. Isaiah Berlin said Sorel is one of the fathers of the culture of protest in America in the 1960s, with his belief in absolute moral ends and the power of the collective will.

Born in Cherbourg in 1847, three years after the birth of Nietzsche, to middle-class Catholic parents, Sorel, like the twentieth-century philosopher Ludwig Wittgenstein, was trained as an engineer. He spent much of his life as a government official in the department of bridges and roads. A narrative of these years provides not much in the way of enthralling reading. Sorel was posted to Corsica. He fell ill at a hotel in Lyon in 1875, where he met a chambermaid, Marie-Euphrasie David, nearly illiterate, who nursed him back to health and became his lifetime partner, though they did not marry and it is said that even close friends could only guess at their relationship. It provided a measure of social isolation which enabled him, like Nietzsche, to concentrate on his work. When Marie-Euphrasie died, Sorel wrote all his letters on black-bordered stationery for the rest of his life and shared his house with the family of her nephew, a masseur and bicycle racer. Once he resigned from the civil service, he was as stay-put as Nietzsche was restless. Ensconced in a modest house in a suburb of Paris, his outward behavior was curiously akin to that of the respectable middle class he despised. He cultivated his garden (wearing a disgraceful old straw hat and carpet slippers) and asserted that every person ought to have only one house as they have only one mother. Yet it was here, in retirement, that he discovered the work of Karl Marx.

Sorel shared with Nietzsche a distrust of the "vices" of rationalism. He, too, was a Master of Suspicion. Woe betide a civilization if the intellect comes to be prized above the manly virtues of valor, the doing of great deeds, virility, glory in battle. The Greeks went down the slippery slope of decline once philosophers in armchairs came into their own. Sorel, in an early work, portrays Socrates as the enemy of the heroic ideal exemplified in the *Iliad*, of bravery and discipline, and disputes the view that the death sentence, the hemlock verdict on him, was a crime. Socrates represented decadence, undermining the moral order of the Homeric world, preaching a sophisticated indifference, epitomizing the "little and illusory divinity of

Reason." And, like the author of *Beyond Good and Evil*, Sorel insists that human beings are not Darwinian organisms merely adapting to circumstances, just surviving, no matter with what devious cunning and guile, with what Machiavellian ingenuity. They make their own circumstances.

Sorel was obsessed with the future of European society and the unrest he saw brewing and building. The twentieth century was not six years old when he predicted that a foreign war could put new energy into a lethargic bourgeoisie, and six years after that he predicted a bright future for the young Mussolini. He was that dangerous character when let loose in the world of politics, an immoderate moralist with a vituperative pen, a gift for invective, and a tendency to ignore social realities. Such a person tends to decide that democracy is stupid and mediocre, that it lacks grandeur. "One cannot understand Sorel," wrote Isaiah Berlin, "unless one realizes that what caused the ferment in his mind was a passionate conviction which he shares with some of the early romantic writers, that the pursuit of peace or happiness or profit, and concern with power or possessions or social status or a quiet life, is a contemptible betrayal of what any man, if he takes thought, knows to be the true end of human life: the attempt to make something worthy of the maker." It was a different take on the Nietzschean theory of the world as a work of art.

The "something more important than truth" for Sorel was the discovery of a new moral principle to revive a tired, corrupt, fraudulent, and decadent civilization. He wanted a "true" society; but the means to bring about such a thing need not be true in the ordinary sense of the word, any more than the legends that inspired the Greeks in their political achievements had to be actual, literal fact. Times were so rotten, Sorel considered, that nothing less grand than a legend would suffice.

What makes him interesting for us is his explicit approval of fictions, or "social myths," artifices entirely independent of truth or falsehood, to operate as engines of history, inspiring individuals to create a more moral society. A myth, Sorel stressed, is quite different from a lie. Totalitarian regimes may hoodwink a naive populace into swallowing rank falsehoods, invented by the ruling powers for their own benefit. Myths, on the other hand, are untrue by normal standards, but are not simply concocted out of thin air. They exist in embryo in the unconscious minds of the people. Sorel believed strongly that the results of any social action must first be imagined as a fully accomplished fact before the action is undertaken. "When we act," he said, "it is because we have created an entirely artificial world, placed in advance of the present, formed of movements that depend on ourselves."

Myths, by this definition, are synthetic realms created by the will as an explanation of its own action. And the artifice not only expands one's horizons; it also acts as a constraint, forming a defined, mythical world of order and parsimony amid the chaos and profusion of nature. As an engineer, Sorel knew all about the Second Law of Thermodynamics and its principle of entropy, the tendency of all things to decay into disorder, randomness, and nonsense. The constraints of myth provide a little clearing in the forest, some orderliness, where human beings can hope to be masters. The world created by modern scientists, as artificial as any, is an example of such a useful fiction.

Sorel was strongly opposed to certain key values of the Enlightenment, especially its belief in the inevitability of progress, its faith in the ameliorating effect of laws and education, and its celebration of liberty, equality, and individualism. He hated utopian blueprints based on the principle of the rightness of reason. He regarded middle-class democracy as a kind of cloak that hid the arrogance of ruling-class coercion and celebrated the class struggle as "the alpha and omega of socialism." The middle class acts to defuse and emasculate class warfare in the name of liberalism and democracy. It blunts the sharp blade of violence with bromides and clichés. Democracy is "an economic tactic of the weak." It perpetuates the status quo. "In all countries where democracy can develop its nature freely, the most scandalous corruption is displayed without anyone thinking it even necessary to conceal his rascality." Mass action, impromptu and unpremeditated, is the best instrument against the domination of the state, and violence becomes an end in itself.

Civilization, Sorel thought, was not on autopilot toward better times, as the Enlightenment optimists had supposed. It was a task of socialism to demolish "the entire structure of conventional false-hoods and to ruin the esteem which those who popularize the pop-ularizations of the eighteenth century are still held." He read voraciously in studies of *fin-de-siècle* periods of the past: the glory and the fading of the glory of Greece, the vicissitudes of the Roman Empire, the story of Christianity in Europe. Civilizations emerge, rise, thrive, then sink, rot, decompose. There is no predetermined future where all will be well. Sorel had a contempt for Utopian thought, a typically wrongheaded hobbyhorse of the Enlightenment which had an insatiable desire "to fix dates for the arrival of the mil-lennium." He abhored the utilitarian ethic. He vehemently denied the Enlightenment say-so that reason is a more effective tool of social betterment than violence and revolution, which the rational thinkers of the eighteenth century considered to be mere reflex actions of the lazy-minded masses. For Sorel, violence was a test of manliness and tenacity in the pursuit of class interests. It was a cleansing agent. It was heroic. Pacifism was a symbol of decadence, violence of virility. "It is to violence that socialism owes those high ethical values by means of which it brings salvation to the world." He saw the future of socialism in the organization of workers into mili-tant trade associations, or *syndicats*.

History, Sorel decided, is driven primarily by psychology, not by politics, or economic and social forces. "Subjective distortions rather than objective laws" govern its workings. And the distortions need not be conscious. He read widely in the literature of individual and group psychology, trying to understand what makes a person or a collective act as they do. In particular, he was drawn to the work of Gustave Le Bon, who theorized about "collective hallucinations," which motivate people to do risky things, "fictions" that provide the impetus for altruistic and unselfish behavior. The trouble with Marxism as it existed then was that it lacked such a psychological theory of history, or at least one that could be called scientific. Marx-ism was too exclusively economic and social. Sorel did not think that revolutions could be accounted for without reference to the ideals, or "myths," that egg them on. Which was more likely: that a person sacrifices his life, dies on the barricades, for an economic principle, or that he dares death in the pursuit of a dream, an ideal, an imagined future that is not literal fact but an inspiring fiction? "Social poetry" rather than dry logical arguments was the spur to such otherwise inexplicable heroism. "It is often the case," says James Gregor, "that such myths are in fact unintelligible, having of themselves no cognitive yield whatsoever. They may be little more than bits of transparent foolishness and sometimes literal contradictions. None of this impairs their effectiveness, under appropriate conditions, as a means of mobilizing the sentiment that informs the will."

This way of thinking had a considerable appeal to Italian intellectuals, who tended to emphasize psychological factors in the exercise and maintenance of power. There were radicals in Italy opposed, like Sorel, to Socialist orthodoxy, who read him with enthusiasm. His ideas were to influence their agenda, and they expounded them in the pages of the *Avanguardia socialista*, published in Milan, which also gave space to the writings of a young revolutionary and anti-parliamentarian whose name was Benito Mussolini. Like Sorel, Mussolini believed people undertook radical political action at the behest of an ideal—patriotic sentiment. And, again like Sorel, he was interested in moral revival as much as in economic forces. In 1909, he reviewed Sorel's *Reflections on Violence*—he was to call it "my bedside book"—and made the point that only in heroism, in strife, do people show those heroic virtues, the readiness to give up their life, that the warriors of pre-Socratic Greece had in abundance. To implant such a spirit in the masses, he wrote, is a task "grave, terrible, sublime." Since his youth, Mussolini had shown an interest in the psychology of crowds, the force of sentiments that activate the will. He, too, had read Le Bon on collective fictions. And he subscribed to the view that violence is a necessary part of real social change. Of Mussolini, Sorel said in 1912: "He is an Italian of the fifteenth century, a condottiere! The world does not know him yet, but he is the only energetic man capable of redressing the feebleness of the government."

Reason, in Sorel's view, is an impediment to the creation of a better society. It insists on truth, and truth is a chimera; the search for it, the notion that one must first have truth before one can have action, tends to reinforce conservatism. Cartesian doubt leads to paralysis. Imaginary futures, on the other hand, are dynamic and productive. Sorel was attracted to the radical wing of French labor, the *syndicats*, because they did not treat Marxism as an empirical science, but applied it as a myth. Truth is simply not brawny or potent enough to accomplish the tremendous task of transforming society. The Greeks had the myth of "glory," the ancient Romans the myths of "frightful inequality and suffering," and the early Christians that of the Second Coming of Christ and his kingdom. The Gospel of St. John was on his recommended reading list for good revolutionaries. The myth of Napoleon buoyed up the courage of French soldiers; the dreams of Mazzini helped to make possible the unity of Italy.

The *syndicats*, Sorel thought, had the wind of myth at their backs. They had dreams as to what lay ahead. Those dreams might be entirely false, quite unscientific, yet still have a unique type of focus and incentive to action. Such images are "a present morality stated in the future tense." Unlike utopian theories, they are immune from refutation, from logical challenge or caviling as to whether they are literally true. They are not at all discredited if the believers in a social myth do not attain their objectives. Man, Sorel said, "would probably never abandon his inertia if he had a perfectly clear view of the future, and if he could calculate exactly the difficulties in the midst of which he ventures."

The central Sorelian myth is the general strike. It promotes a sense of unity and harmony of purpose, inspires a vision of total catastrophe and breakdown, intensifies the sense of class struggle. Critics might talk about "general rubbish" in connection with this theory, but workers under the spell of the myth regard themselves as "an army of truth fighting an army of evil." Start a general strike, so went the dream, and the capitalist state would collapse. It might be objected that if every worker is ready to come out on strike, the war is already won, so why bother to have a strike in the first place? Sorel's answer is that it is not the function of a myth to speak truths about the future, but to embody the aspirations of the masses. "Social poetry" should not be read as textbook prose.

The promotion of sublime falsehoods, of energizing fictions, was a reaction to the prevailing late nineteenth-century mood of disillusion, of disgust with the moral temper of society. Life in Paris in the Third Republic, in Isaiah Berlin's words, was "commercialized, jaunty, insolent, dishonorable, easy-going, cowardly, mindless, bourgeois." A spiritual crisis had dawned. And education, reason, knowledge, the advance of science, all those Enlightenment virtues, did not seem to improve the situation. Might it be better to turn a blind eye to the unpleasant truths such instruments of progress revealed by sticking to the fictions that are so much more palatable? "Ignorance," wrote Anatole France in *Le Jardin d'Epicure* in 1895, "is the condition necessary, I do not say for happiness, but for existence itself. If we knew all, we could not endure life for an hour. The feelings which make it either sweet, or at least tolerable, are born of a lie and are nourished on illusions."

Several strands of thought were coming together at this time to suggest that the amenities of civilization were a facade, highly artificial, precarious, out of kilter with the more basic and firmly established aspects of the psyche. The European intelligensia was making its first head-on assault on the hypocritical morality of the middle class and Oscar Wilde was shocking it with his Nietzschean epigrams about the superiority of illusion to truth.

In England, the liberal journalist and member of Parliament John Morley famously castigated Victorian society as a big lie, "a community where political forms, from the monarchy down to the popular chamber, are mainly hollow shams disguising the coarse supremacy of wealth, where religion is mainly official and political, and is ever ready to dissever itself alike from the spirit of justice, the spirit of charity, and the spirit of truth." It was an age of fragile beliefs, weak creeds, masked by robustly proclaimed moral attitudes, all the more stridently asserted in public because of the effete state of private convictions. There were, of course, many notable exceptions, occasions when uncertainty came charging out into the open. T. S. Eliot said of Tennyson's *In Memoriam* that it was religious "not because of the quality of its faith, but because of the quality of its doubt. Its faith is a poor thing, but its doubt is a very intense experience."

Leslie Stephen, father of Virginia Woolf, was a cleric who resigned his tutorship at Cambridge after he lost his faith, a Bloomsbury Group precursor, prophet of the modern secular society whose members, "bereft of Christianity's consolations, but determined nonetheless to live and die like gentlemen, admired men who would go to the stake for their beliefs, with the hoots of society ringing in their ears." In America, Stephen once met the abolitionist W. L. Garrison, who had been hauled through the streets of Boston for preaching abolition and was only rescued by the daring intervention of the police. Stephen thought Garrison a muddle-headed pacifist, but pointed out that "it is impossible not to feel some respect for a man who has been dragged through the streets by a rope."

There was a tendency to subscribe to the Sorelian idea that belief by itself is a virtue, even if it is mythical, even if it is unsound and its foundations flimsy. Better that than be bereft of all convictions. A belief could be a species of falsehood, and still be useful, still have a bracing effect on character. It tended to produce model citizens and to have beneficial effects on society, steadying and taming inclinations to anarchy, the reverse of Sorelian myths, which were intended to shake up and disconcert the establishment. Stability was highly valued in a country like England where there had never been a proper blowoff along the lines of its Continental neighbors. The fear of social explosion was rampant in nineteenth-century Britain. Bertrand Russell's grandfather, lying on his deathbed in 1869, heard a noise in the street and immediately deduced that the expected revolution had begun. "Victorian society," said Walter Houghton, "particularly in the period before 1850, was shot through, from top to bottom, with the dread of some wild outbreak of the masses that would overthrow the established order and confiscate private property."

One review of Darwin's *Descent of Man* chastised the author for "revealing his zoological conclusions to the general public at a moment when the sky of Paris was red with the incendiary flames of the Commune." A collapse of trust in the official doctrines of religion was something better hushed up, kept hidden, like a mad wife in the attic. "I pray that Mr. Darwin's theory is not true," a Victorian woman said. "But if it is true, I pray it may not become widely known." That sort of thing fed, of course, the hallmark Victorian vice of hypocrisy, and its first cousin, dogmatism.

An age "destitute of faith but terrified of skepticism" is how Thomas Carlyle summed up the atmosphere of the time. It has been noted that whereas Carlyle's published works exude confidence in the eternal verities, his letters disclose unsettling visitations of doubt. Bravado papered over inner waverings. It was an unspoken premise that to express pessimistic reservations as to the truth or otherwise of traditional doctrines was somehow effete. The muscular Christian Charles Kingsley was known for his hectoring style of conversation, which brooked no unmanly questionings of what strong, upright men ought to believe. He had a way of talking "with the air and spirit of a man bouncing up from the table with his mouth full of bread and cheese saying he meant to stand no blasted nonsense." Putting on a bold or even brash face was sometimes the safest option if one were to avoid the traps and snares lying in store for anyone who ventured to give a closely argued defense of Christian teachings. There was a constant tug-of-war between the pragmatists and the purists. John Stuart Mill held that a religious belief may be morally useful without being intellectually sustainable, but that was a position John Morley scorned as lazy and cowardly.

The importance of artifice as a refuge from simply doing what comes naturally—and that includes telling the truth when truth is just a reflex action akin to a facial twitch—is a theme that surfaces repeatedly in the literature of the latter part of the Victorian era. In the early 1880s, when Nietzsche was still in command of his faculties and had yet to publish *Beyond Good and Evil* and *The Gay Science*, Henrik Ibsen was writing about the antagonism between impersonal truth which, like nature, can be violently destructive, and the falsehoods that are indispensable to the human attempt to prevent such desolation. Gregers Werle, a character in Ibsen's play *The Wild Duck*, is imbued with the compulsion to tell other people the unvarnished truth about themselves, in order, as he fondly supposes, to free them from illusion and enable them to live more authentic lives. He is taken to task by the cynical Dr. Relling, who stands up for the right of the average person to retain the "life lies" that make possible the limited amount of happiness and confidence without which existence would be unbearable.

Gregers, apt to talk portentously about the "claims of the ideal," takes it upon himself to inform his boyhood friend Hjalmar Ekdal that his wife, Gina, was the mistress of Gregers' father. That man had helped to ruin Ekdal's father, who was his former business partner. The disclosure leads Ekdal to doubt whether Hedwig, his fifteen-year-old daughter, whom he worships, is really his own child. The results of such truth-telling are catastrophic. Hedwig commits suicide. Gregers is shown as harboring, behind an ostensible desire to emancipate others from self-deception, the ulterior motive of avenging himself on his father. Relling, who has tried to bolster Ekdal's confidence with false notions that he would some day restore the family fortunes, taunts Gregers for having "an acute case of inflamed scruples." At the very end of the play he blurts out: "Oh, life would be all right if we could only be rid of these infernal fools who come to poor people's doors presenting their demands of the ideal."

Here, in dramatic form, is a working out of Nietzsche's terse epigram, in a work he kept secret, *On Truth and Lies in a Moral Sense*: "Truth as a cloak for quite different impulses and drives." Truth can be sinister, selfish, ulterior, a smoke screen for submerged intentions, untrustworthy and dangerous in the highest degree. Earlier in his career, Ibsen had embraced the obtrusive Victorian aspiration to base life on a foundation of truth and sincerity. It is even suggested, in *An Enemy of the People*, that liars should be excluded from decent society. But in *The Wild Duck*, Ibsen, in Herman Wiegand's words, "examines the status of the average run of men with regard to their capacity for truth and records as its finding that, far from truth affording the foundation on which the life of the average man can thrive, life is so steeped in make-believe that the habit of fostering illusions can better afford cultivating than destroying." Henry James thought the whole truth, told regardless of the consequences, could "destroy civilization."

Thus, Sorel's theory of the potency of fictions to renew and cleanse civilization had a certain allure. In America, the theologian Reinhold

Niebuhr also turned a hostile face to liberalism in religion and politics, also rejected the notion that human beings, left to themselves,
are rational and well intentioned, and that science, law, ethical teachings, will lead to the good society. Niebuhr decided that the use of
force is sometimes necessary in the struggle for a just community,
and violent revolution is acceptable if all other measures fail. He
argued that the workers will engage in militant action only if they are
given nonrational psychological inducements, such as symbols and
"emotionally potent oversimplifications." Without the exercise of
religious imagination, no society would have the boldness and daring to overcome despair and attempt the impossible. The vision of a
just society is an impossible one, and it can be put into practice only
by those who do not think it is impossible. "The truest visions of religion are illusions," Niebuhr said, "which may be partially realised by
being resolutely believed. For what religion believes to be true is not
wholly true but ought to be true; and may become true if its truth is
not doubted."

Here truth is actually equated with illusion. In Sorel's scheme, a
myth is not true in the literal sense, but it is armor-plated against all
attempts to prove it false, since it must be seen as an organic whole
that cannot be taken apart and broken down into logical elements.
"People who are living in this world of myths are secure from all refutation," Sorel wrote in *Reflections on Violence*. Myths trigger unconscious sentiments that are large enough, grand enough, to do justice
to the enormity of the task of regeneration. The myth of the general
strike, for example, produces an "epic" state of mind.

Behind the paradoxes of Sorel's ideas stands a pregnant fact: he
had a "contempt" for the correspondence theory of truth. He actually despised it, as he despised intellectuals, fashionable talkers,
moderate politicians, all the star turns of Enlightenment thought.
For him, "truth" was merely the relation of one statement to another. It was an artifact of language. He was that most incongruous of
characters, an anti-intellectual who was also a man of ideas; an
enthusiast of action who spent his time in sedentary pursuits. Truth,
such as it is, would emerge as a result of action.

Myths, the irrational, the life force, the products of the unconscious mind, are adjuncts of the will rather than of reason. And the will gives birth to monsters as well as to comely offspring. Fascism, with its overt irrationalism, was a child of the philosophy of the will. Mussolini defined the state as "the universal ethical will," a phrase that is Sorelian to the core. Sorel himself underwent repeated disenchantment at the outcome of his hopes for a transformation of society. Early on, he shifted from orthodox socialism to revolutionary labor agitation. Just before World War I, he soured on that and flirted with the far right, with monarchists in the royalist *Action Française* and with ultranationalists. "Socialism is becoming a demagogy," he wrote; "consequently it no longer offers anything of interest to philosophers." After the war, he became interested in Italian fascism and waxed enthusiastic about Bolshevism. He was still searching for a myth that would restore the virtues and the morals of a vanished era. Lenin he saluted as if he were the Second Coming itself: the myth of Lenin acted like the myth of Napoleon to invigorate the heroism of the Red Guard in its struggle against the intervention of the Western powers. But the Lenin myth turned into the Soviet reality. And the irony of that mutation is that Soviet ideology, as has been noted, did not deal in the irrational, with myths lurking deep in the unconscious setting off great spontaneous bursts of moral grandeur. It advanced by deliberate planning, by an eyes-wide-open awareness of the class struggle. Consciousness was a key element in the survival of the system; it promoted responsibility, structure, and method.

Sorel died in 1922, when the full horrors of the Soviet regime were in the future and the world-wrecking consequences of the Fascist myth had not yet matured. Looking back from the vantage point of the post–World War II period, Thomas Mann, with Nietzsche in mind, but passing a judgment that would apply equally well to Sorel, asked "whether it would not be better to maintain in the masses respect for reason and truth, and in so doing honor their longing for justice—far better than to implant mass myths and turn loose upon mankind hordes dominated by 'powerful illusions.' "

CHAPTER THIRTEEN

Curing by Fiction

We possess the truth. I am as sure of it as fifteen years ago.
> —Freud in a letter to Sandor Ferenczi, May 1913

Truth is unobtainable; humanity does not deserve it.
> —Freud in a letter to Arnold Zweig, May 31, 1936

F GRAND MYTHS DRIVE ORDINARY PEOPLE on to perform "impossible" deeds, fill them with a sense of power that truth could never match, the petty false-hoods people tell themselves and others every day ful-fill a more mundane purpose: to provide a buffer against the cruelties of existence which arise in even the most democratic and enlightened societies. Again, untruth is a means of power, but of a very different kind. Lying may not be as antisocial as we might sup-pose, but rather the price to pay for the fact that the individual is not at liberty to do anything he or she likes. "Lies are an index of powerful propensities and passions. And, equally important, lies are an index of the conflict between civilization's morality, saturat-ed with hypocrisies and protected by sanctions and sanctimony, and the powerful longings, both affectionate and domineering, of individuals."

Sigmund Freud was a child of the Victorian Age, and as such he could not be a lifelong disbeliever in the possibility of truth. And yet this archeologist of the human mind, this bathyscope of the psychic depths, came to discover that lies and self-deception are a key to understanding human character.

People need illusions. That principle is an *arche* of Freud's world-view, a starting point for any investigation of what makes human beings tick. A person, Freud said, is in important respects an enemy of civilization, chafing at its tyranny, resenting the way it curbs and thwarts his selfish impulses, expecting him to sacrifice his own interests for the benefit of the community. Every civilization is built on coercion and the bridling of instinct in individuals who harbor anti-social and anti-cultural bents, some more than others.

Freud had contempt for the ordinary run of the human species. The masses "are lazy and unintelligent; they have no love for instinctual renunication, and they are not to be convinced by argument of its inevitability." They must be made to rein in their desire for endless gratification by the intervention of an elite which stands guard over the welfare of civilization. This elite needs to have its hands firmly on the reins of power, since it is continually tempted to surrender to the craving of the masses for more pleasure and less work in order to hold onto its leadership status. An immense amount of coercion would be needed to transform the anti-cultural majority into a minority, and that in itself would be about all a society could ever hope to achieve.

During the history of mankind, Freud said, external coercion to domesticate the unruly instincts became internalized in the psyche, in the form of the Superego. Thanks to it, the vast majority of people are able to say no to such basic social transgressions as murder and incest. They are less apt to abstain from indulgences that stand a chance of going unpunished, including greed, lust, fraud—and lies. But the effect of such oppression of the "natural" instincts by the instruments of culture is finally to make reality unsatisfying. It kindles a desire for fantasy, for illusions and myths that might be able to make civilized life bearable.

As a Master of Suspicion, Freud, like many philosophers, had a strong distrust of what people think they know. He harbored a certain disdain for philosophy, however, in particular for its tolerance of what Kant called regulative principles which we cannot show to be either true or false, but which guide human thought and conduct. The argument that we agree to fictions, knowing them to be mere artifacts but acting as if they were true, Freud said, "is one that only a philosopher could put forward. A man whose thinking is not influenced by the artifices of philosophy will never be able to accept it." Illusions are illusions. That was the Freudian decree. The secret of their strength is to be found in the strength of the wishes that give rise to them. An illusion is not the same as an error and it need not be an error. Christopher Columbus' belief that he had discovered a new sea route to the Indies, on the other hand, was an illusion, one in which his wishes played a very important part. "We call a belief an illusion when a wish-fulfilment is a prominent factor in its motivation," Freud said, "and in doing so we disregard its relations to reality, just as the illusion itself sets no store by verification."

Freud classified religion as an illusion, and then castigated it for not doing more to make people happy, give them comfort, reconcile them to the austere burden of denying the instincts, reconstitute them as vehicles of civilization. What do we see instead? "We see that an appallingly large number of people are dissatisfied with civilization and unhappy in it, and feel it as a yoke which must be shaken off." Each person is "obliged to live psychologically beyond his income," knowing that the rewards provided by society do not fully compensate for the loss of instinctual satisfaction.

Late in life, Freud declared that throughout his career, his single motive had been the love of truth and the pursuit of truth. Yet it has been well noted that in his writings the concept of truth is not explored in any depth and does not even appear as a main element in his theory of the mind. Equally striking is Freud's discovery that the mind is a more habitual liar than mere nature could ever be. For that reason, it should be approached with unceasing suspicion and mistrust. As a guide to knowing what the mind is all about, moreover, the sort of lies it tells are often more instructive than its unblemished truths. "Primitive and infantile man (and every man is in some way primitive and infantile) cannot stand much truth, and yet he has to believe that his very self-deception is truth. This he accomplishes by rationalization, giving himself good reasons instead of true ones—a deceptively successful accomplishment, which, just because it works for the moment, will destroy him in the long run."

Freud treated a patient's narrative account of his or her life history somewhat as Nietzsche the philologist had scrutinized ancient manuscripts, taking nothing for granted, nothing on trust. Each reading was an interpretation, one of many possible interpretations, never final. Likewise, Freud believed that a dream is always open to a more complete interpretation, as are works of literature. The trade of Lit. Crit. will never come to an end. No biography can capture a life in its entirety, an assertion Freud made with force to an author aspiring to write his own: "Anyone turning biographer commits himself to lies, to concealment, to hypocrisy, to flattery, and even to hiding his own lack of understanding, for biographical truth is not to be had, and even if it were, it couldn't be used."

Freud was shaken to discover that a number of the "texts" of his patients' unburdenings were counterfeit, deceitful, without intending to be. He saw human beings as torn between the frankness and simplicity of their instincts and the hypocrisy of their culturally conditioned intellects. To heal this fissure, a person must be educated to be profoundly suspicious of the falsehoods that such a conflict entails. This process of stripping away the masks that civilization imposes on the barbaric impulses seething within the psyche has been linked to another trend in twentieth-century literature, a "drive toward disenchantment."

People protect their well-being by keeping unwelcome facts a secret from themselves. Psychoanalysis is in large part a theory of self-deception and systematic misreadings of what is "really" going on in the mind. In the last article he wrote, Freud was still wrestling with the anomaly of a mind that is able to lie to itself, suggesting a deep rift within the psyche. Like Nietzsche, he regarded most individuals as insufficiently robust for the task of coping with the strain of sorting out the genuine from the fake in their makeup. In the consulting room, he turned upside down the moral code of civil converse that assigns a useful role to hypocrisy, considering it immoral to hold back ugly impulses or hurtful truths, and ethical to blurt them out unvarnished, with the skin off. Secrecy "is the category of moral illness, for it provides a hiding place for false motives." On one occasion, a complete breakdown in treatment occurred when a high government official, undergoing analysis, refused to divulge certain state secrets he had sworn never to communicate. An element of malice has been detected in this ruthless unmasking of considerate lies that normally would be commended as good manners.

On the other hand, it is only too apparent that a patient's fantasies and illusions are as much fodder for the analyst as the naked truth. They are "mental facts" on which he or she can work. "Psychoanalysis sets up the conditions for a scientific study of lies," in the view of the historian of science John Forrester. "In order to defuse the question of deception, which is so pressing for other human sciences, the psychoanalyst first of all places the patient in a situation where she has minimal incentives *either* for telling the truth *or* for telling lies. Which way she goes is entirely up to her. The analyst is professionally disinterested in the difference between truth and lies. This attitude goes hand in hand with the highly idiosyncratic place of reality in psychoanalysis. The extent to which psychoanalysis takes no account of reality has perennially been seen as something of a scandal, but acutely so in the 1980's."

Just as Darwin saw no preestablished harmony between the mind and the world, and certainly no natural intuition into profound metaphysical questions, Freud regarded reality as somehow not helpful to the psyche, at odds with and even antagonistic to its deep needs and wishes. The psyche has to resort to ruse and artifice in order to shield its interests and appetites from domination by the uncooperative environment. As a result, for all the emphasis on truth-telling, straightforwardness, and keeping no secrets back, the fictions invented by the psyche are so sturdy and vigorous, so needed by the patient, that they are extremely difficult to break down. That is no less the case in the post-Freudian world. At a conference of three dozen psychoanalysts at Mount Sinai Hospital in New York in 1998, a consensus was reached that the hope of eliciting a reliable, nonfiction account of a patient's life and traumas is more distant today than it was a century ago, when Freud was in his prime. The analysts described themselves as experts, not in helping patients to learn facts, but rather in assisting them to construct useful myths.

"We are fantasy doctors, not reality doctors," said Robert

Michaels, one of the participants. "We don't help patients decide what is true. It is important to show them that they can organize their experience in many ways, that they can become more comfortable, not about what happened in the past, but about living with uncertainty and ambiguity." Many patients do in fact want to know what "really" happened to them, but there is general agreement that this is precisely what they must be taught not to expect. "Everybody wants certainty about history," another analyst was quoted as saying. "And that may be the first thing to get rid of in therapy." Instead, they should be given a "reasonable narrative."

The issue of historical truth emerged as a central controversy early in the career of psychoanalysis. In the autumn of 1900, an eighteen-year-old girl, identified only as "Dora," was brought to Freud by her father, a wealthy manufacturer. Dora, whose real name was Ida Bauer, was suffering from migraine headaches, shortness of breath, periodic spasms of nervous coughing, fainting, and thoughts of suicide. Her symptoms also included a feverish spell that mimicked appendicitis, and an occasional limp. Dora told Freud her father was involved in an adulterous relationship with a family friend, whose husband, Herr K., had taken a sexual interest in her since she was fourteen years old. While she and Mr. K. were taking a walk by a lake in the Alps, Dora said he "had the audacity to make a proposal." She slapped him in the face and hurried away. Mr. K. vehemently denied doing anything of the sort, suggesting that Dora, who had been reading Mantegazza's *Physiology of Love* in the family's house by the lake, invented the entire scene. Dora's father, to her disgust, agreed. He handed her over to Freud with the instruction: "Please try to bring her to reason."

Freud attempted to persuade Dora that it was hysterical on her part to rebuff the man who kissed and pressed his affections on her, that she had been in love with him all the time, and that by repressing her sexual fantasies she was in large part to blame for her present unhappy situation. He wrote it up as a "Fragment of an Analysis of a Case of Hysteria." But was it? Frederick Crews thinks Dora may have been suffering from an organic disease: asthma, tuberculosis, and syphilis were present in her immediate family to an extent that "would have set off alarms in the mind of a responsible physician." As a Master of Suspicion, however, Freud assumed that Dora's consciousness was false. He made no attempt to find out if Dora was in fact a hysteric, but instead, as Crews puts it, "leaped to a conclusion that would permit him to put his trademark suppositions into play and then hold to them like a pit bull—later, however, portraying himself as having gradually solved the case with all the prudent objectivity and uncanny astuteness of his favorite literary character, Sherlock Holmes."

In a notorious passage which has given critics of Freudian analysis plenty of ammunition, Freud insisted that the more strenuously Dora rejected her interpretation of her "real" emotions and desires, the greater the likelihood that his version was the correct one. A "no" signified an emphatic "yes." Freud was collaborating with the drift that since Kant had tended to give meaning priority over truth, because life is too complicated, too ambiguous and conditioned by all sorts of hidden or ignored factors to be dealt with by a single explanation. Freud talked about "overdetermination," by which he meant we had better be ready to accept that there are multiple causes for the things we do and say. We live in a world "in which everything has a meaning, which means that everything has more than one meaning."

The calamitous and abrupt collapse of Freud's seduction theory was a turning point in his attitude toward the truthfulness of a patient's testimony. As late as 1896, Freud said he had found the key to hysteria: all hysterics were seduced as children. No shrinking violet when it came to his own reputation, he announced that he had solved a thousand-year-old problem, had in fact found the "source of the Nile," in deciding that early experiences of that kind were specific causes of later adult illness, and that the sort of childhood occurrence determined the type of adult disorder. He thought his discovery would make him rich and famous. The very next year, however, he reversed himself, asserting that fantasies of seduction, not actual seductions, were the cause of hysteria, though he did not publicly abandon the seduction theory until 1905. For the purposes of diagnosis, reality was now divided into two kinds: physical and psychical. Freud reinterpreted the clinical data to theorize that patients in childhood conceived incestuous desires and then suffocated them. He decided he had been told a collection of tall tales instead of genuine life histories. He acknowledged that he probably suggested such fictions to his patients himself.

From this fiasco, however, he made an adroit recovery. Taking a hard look at himself while on a walking tour of the mountains of northern Italy, Freud realized that his suspicions about his father, Jacob, whom he had conjectured to be a prey to warped impulses, were entirely without foundation. He had imagined the whole thing. What now came under suspicion in his mind was the unconscious itself, where fact could not be distinguished from emotionally charged fiction. What if the stories of seduction were untrue? Was it not the case that they were real in the consciousness of his patients, genuinely felt, and were invented for some specific, deep reason, which when elucidated might lay bare the actual cause of hysteria or neurosis? Tales of seduction could be elaborate cover stories masking the fact, that, as a child, a patient had sexual yearnings for a parent. The tables were turned. The suspicion now was that instead of adults being sexually attracted to children, the children were in love with father or mother, and, hey presto, the Oedipus Complex was born. Freud's biographer Ronald Clark thinks his failure to admit publicly his "first great error" over the seduction theory was due in part to his invention of the Oedipus Complex so soon afterward. "He was impatient of society's unwillingness to face unpleasant truths and contemptuous of its hypocrisy, which cloaked the subject in Vienna as in Victorian Britain, Calvinist Switzerland or the Godfearing homes of New England."

Freud railed against the illusions that make life more congenial, that see society as basically good and reasonable, the world full of purpose and meaning. What bothered him was the endless capacity of the mind to dupe itself. The key to a healthy society was clear-eyed rational honesty. Oddly, Freud did not attach excessive importance to the premeditated lie, the intentional untruth calculated to mislead another person; he saved his censure for the habitual devices of self-deception that the mind uses against its own integrity, a theme that had been developed with a considerable amount of biting wit by the seventeenth-century French *moralistes*. Freud was an enemy of the kind of sanitized discourse one trades over teacups when on one's best behavior. On the analyst's couch, a patient must dispense with the polite rituals and mealy-mouthed clichés that are *de rigueur* in ordinary converse. He or she must be thoroughly unicivilized and boorish, if need be. Nietzsche had inveighed against the "shamefully *moralized* way of speaking which has gradually made all modern judgments of men and things slimy." The most distinctive feature of modern life, he said, is not lying, but a kind of deepseated innocence which makes do with fake moral attitudes, a mendaciousness that is abysmal, but sincere, blue-eyed, and maidenly. "Our educated people of today, our 'good people,' do not tell lies—that is true; but that is *not* to their credit! A real lie, a genuine, 'honest' lie (on whose value one should consult Plato) would be something far too severe and potent for them: it would demand of them what one *may* not demand of them, that they should open their eyes to themselves. All they are capable of is a *dishonest* lie."

Freud has been seen in this respect as very much the heir of Nietzsche, doing more than anyone else to alter the style of the twentieth century. Freud insisted on using the explicit term "sexual" rather than the more polite "erotic" and fought against the "slimy" euphemisms of the age. "Civilization being necessarily hypocritical," Philip Rieff noted, "a certain terminological vulgarity, Freud calculated, was a moral imperative and a positive value." This did not not go down well with the public. A man once accosted Freud on the street and shouted in his face: "Let me tell you what a dirty-minded, filthy old man you are."

Freud has been described as "a tough old humanist with a profoundly skeptical mind." There was a residue in him of the Enlightenment, with its high respect for reason and the redeeming force of science. He shared with certain eighteenth-century thinkers the idea that if we are in possession of the truth, goodness will follow as the night the day. Truth is therapeutic and leads to virtue, though perhaps not the kind of virtue Victorian England prized. The relationship between analyst and patient Freud described as "based on a love of truth—that is, a recognition of reality." It precludes any kind of sham or deceit. A person who has succeeded in educating himself to the truth about himself is "permanently defended against the danger of immorality." In that case, why not let up a bit on curbing the instincts and go all out for truthfulness as to what our real desires and cravings are all about? Nietzsche had put a question mark over this theory of the power of truth to liberate and make us happy, and even Freud in the early *Studies in Hysteria* stated as an ideal goal of treatment the replacement of acute neurotic misery with the plain, ordinary blues. "If truthfulness about sexuality is supposed to make us less nervous, less needful of psychological medicine," says the philosopher Barry Allen, "the result of the experiment is negative."

Talking dirty did not necessarily mean talking truth. The unconscious is so devious and ulterior it does not even respect the basic, logical rule of the truth or falsity of propositions. Logic dictates that a statement is either true or false; there is no third alternative. In dreams, the land of the unconscious, the true and the false can exist side by side and be equally meaningful. Asked who a particular person is in a dream, a patient might reply: "It's not my mother." Whereupon the analyst immediately thinks: "So it is his mother." Freud wrote that there is no evidence of reality in the unconscious, which makes it impossible to tell the difference between a truth and a fiction coated with emotion. There is no way to decide which is which just by listening to a person talk on a couch. The analyst cannot be a lie detector, but he can detect important clues to the hidden truth about a patient in what she says, regardless of whether or not it is factually correct.

False memories, invented connections between unconnected things, might be more useful than the literal truth in guiding the analyst to the discovery of psychic reality. To repeat a theme that is becoming ever more obtrusive as our narrative moves forward, the emphasis shifts toward meaning and away from truth. Everything that the cunning psyche throws up to consciousness has meaning, even though it may be an outright lie. The unconscious is a law unto itself and a moral world to itself. Freud allowed himself tremendous latitude in his interpretations of a patient's narratives, in part because of this belief in the disclosing power of fictions. Some "over-interpretation" is always called for. Philip Rieff contends that the flowering of modern literary criticism, which certainly has been influenced by the Freudian method of deciphering, "follows closely this model relation of neurotic symptom and medicinal interpretation. Works of art are esteemed for the ambiguity, or richness of texture; and some of the great modern pieces of fiction seem deliberately unfinished (*vide* the novels of Kafka), as if inviting the completion of an interpretation, or are themselves constructed as many-layered conundrums, inviting (as James Joyce said of his own works) a lifetime of interpretative meditation to decipher them."

The analyst is in a position of asserting authority, since his interpretation of what the patient says about dreams, memories, childhood, is closer to psychic reality than what the patient thinks is actually the case. According to Freud, the dreamer never knows the meaning of a dream. He or she is hung up on the literal content, which is just a cloak concealing more important information. In one of Freud's own dreams, he felt affection for "my friend R" but interpreted it as envy and rivalry. Memories as well as dreams were open to decipherment, tempting the analyst always to go overboard with his interpretations, making him at all times "suspicious of the obvious."

Lately, there has been harsh censure of Freud for separating meaning so drastically from truth, for elevating interesting falsehoods constructed by the patient above historical fact. Mistaken memories were regarded as more potent for the psyche than events that actually happened. Jeffrey Masson, who was projects director of the Sigmund Freud Archives, is particularly hard on Freud for dismissing out of hand the significance of hard reality versus psychic reality, the imaginative creation of his patients. It is a professional hazard for psychoanalysts to take more interest in fantasy than in fact. If paranoiacs can have real enemies, neurotics can have real memories of really awful things that actually happened to them. Masson views it as ironic that the ideal patient today is someone whose childhood is absolutely lacking in terrible experiences and severe traumas, since psychoanalysis after Freud is intent on the interpretation of fantasy.

No one calls it "lying" any more. Analysis is unsuited to the task of treating people with a history of genuine and serious emotional injury. By shifting the emphasis, Masson argues, from "an actual world of sadness, misery and cruelty to an internal stage on which actors perform invented dramas for an invisible audience of their own creation, Freud began a trend away from the real world that, it seems to me, is at the root of the present-day sterility of psycho-analysis and psychiatry throughout the world."

It is curious that Freud, who sang the praises of Truth the Redeemer, should now stand accused of repeated acts of dishonesty. "Though Freud loved to sermonize about courageously opposing the human penchant for self-deception," says another ex-Freudian, Frederick Crews, "it is no exaggeration to say that his psychoanalyt-ic career was both launched and maintained by systematic mendac-ity." There were lies told about the case of Anna O., a young woman suffering from various hysterical symptoms, including partial paral-ysis and the loss of the ability to speak German, her native language. She was treated by Joseph Breuer, a noted surgeon and friend of Freud's. Breuer put his patient into deep hypnosis, during which the "missing connections" between her symptoms and their causes were supposedly revealed. In one astonishing episode, Anna, whose real name was Bertha Pappenheim, talked about a hallucination she experienced while nursing her sick father—a large black snake which she tried to strike with her right arm. The arm was paralyzed, where-upon, terrified, she recited a prayer in English, the only one that came to mind. After Anna disclosed this incident under hypnosis, her arm regained its normal function and she was again able to speak German. According to Freud's admirer Ernest Jones, however, Breuer's description of this as a "cure" was exaggerated. Anna regressed several times into her previous state and spent some time in an institution. She continued to suffer from hallucinations.

Breuer had abruptly terminated his treatment after his patient showed signs of attachment to him and went into the throes of an illusory, hysterical childbirth. Breuer put Anna into hypnosis, ran out of the house "in a cold sweat," and next day took off for Venice on a second honeymoon with his wife. We are advised to treat both versions of the story with caution, however. Breuer wrote from memory some thirteen years after the event and altered certain facts in order to protect the anonymity of the patient, while Jones drew largely on hearsay and his account put Anna in a sanitarium that did not exist. In the end, Anna returned to health and became active in the women's movement, later doing highly distinguished work for orphans and unwed mothers. But she did not champion the cause of psychoanalysis. She would not permit the girls she looked after to receive the sort of treatment which allegedly had worked such miracles of healing. She described psychoanalysis as "a double-edged sword," like the priest's confessional, a healing instrument in the right hands and under the right circumstances, but harmful in others.

Two researchers friendly to Freud have judged nearly all Freud's fully described cases as manifest failures, yet Freud himself reported eighteen cases in *The Etiology of Hysteria* to be successful. He even acknowledged to friends that duplicity of this kind was essential if his enemies and hostile critics were to be kept at bay, an example of the "constructive" lie if ever there was one. Duplicity, in fact, is an essential component of hypnotism itself; the doctor himself makes suggestions that he knows are deceptive; he is like an actor playing a role in a drama. Within the very practice of hypnotism, says John Forrester, "lay the recognition that fiction can cure as well as truth." Hysteria was a disorder in which the body seemed to bamboozle the physician who was trying to relieve its distressing symptoms. Tit for tat, the physician responded by doing some deceiving himself. "The doctor began to play the same game as his patient: began to deceive his patient through the art of hypnosis," Forrester writes. "Hypnosis has this double edge: it was intended as a sure physiological means of duplicating and reproducing hysterical symptoms, thus bringing them under the sway of a physiological model in which nature cannot lie. On the other hand, it was intended as a means for securing total dominion over the patient's mind, through control of the body, and the suggesting away of pains and symptoms. Now, instead of the patient deceiving the doctor, it was the doctor who assessed his privileged relation to the truth by deceiving the patient."

Heinz Hartman, one of the most influential of the post-Freudians, altered the picture of the psyche with his theory of the Ego as being to a certain extent autonomous, not so dependent on the needy, obstreporous, uncivilized Id for its very origin and existence. The main role of the Ego in this version is to adapt to reality, and thereby survive—an evolutionary imperative—unlike that of the Id, which is a reckless pursuer of pleasure and a stranger to reality. The Ego is master in its own house within limits, especially in the realms of memory and language. As a result of this Ego sovereignty, a person is able to cultivate virtuous reflexes, overcoming base inclinations to lying, selfishness, and greed. It can develop a kind of "second nature." But it is still the case that truth is not an indispensable factor in constructing this second nature. In fact, it may be a liability. Someone who thinks she is a little stronger, smarter, more upright than is actually the case may in the end make a more successful life for herself than a person who habitually underestimates his own assets. The harmful effects of "the truth" have been called the skeletons in the closets of older psychoanalysts.

Another theorist of the dubious value of truth in the treatment of disordered psyches was Jacques Lacan, a "postmodern" Freudian who was active in the Surrealist movement in Paris in the 1930s. He was a friend of André Breton and Salvador Dali, and acted as Picasso's personal physician. Lacan, born in 1901, studied medicine, but kept up a keen interest in literature, art, and philosophy. His doctoral thesis was a study of paranoia, in the person of a woman named Aimée, who had tried to stab a famous Parisian actress, Huguette Duflos. Lacan argued that the woman, by attacking the actress, was punishing herself for not being a person as free, as admired by society, as Duflos. A person's identity, he suggested, does not end at the boundaries of the body or the mind, but incorporates elements of the social world surrounding her.

Freud's work, said Lacan, put truth into question. He apologizes for even using the term, "flinging this word in your faces, a word almost of ill repute, a word banished from polite society." Yet psychoanalysis is constantly remaking the discovery of the power of truth in our selves, "in our very flesh." That truth may be buried sixty

fathoms under the conscious part of the mind, it may be profoundly quelled and subdued, but it is the truth of our deep desires, the
"truth of the subject." And that truth may be revealed in speech which
contains an abundance of falsehoods. It is not only quite different
from reality, it may even be opposed to reality. Lacan protests that he
is "not reviving here the shoddy Nietzschean notion of the lie of life,"
the untruth that makes life more bearable. But he insists that truth
discloses itself, not in plain propositions, but in lies, mistakes, trickery, and tall stories. Lacan's truth has the structure of fiction. Truth
is that much truer for being mendacious. "There is in Lacan," says
the French theorist Mikkel Borch-Jacobsen, "a sort of privileging of
the lie, and this is because the lie, being inadequate to the thing it
speaks about, is better able to reveal the truth of the subject."

Lacan considered the Ego to be inherently falsifying, papering
over the gaps and holes in what masquerades as a unified and coherent self, which in fact is nothing of the kind. It puts up a facade of
completeness that cannot be trusted. An analyst who treats it as honest is engaging in mutual deception. Lacan broke free entirely with
Freud's "biological" approach to the mind, especially the unconscious mind, which Freud linked to mankind's evolutionary past. In
Lacan's system, the unconscious mirrors the shift in intellectual
fashion which caught hold as the twentieth century advanced,
whereby language, rather than ideas, occupied the center of the
stage. The Lacanian unconscious is structured like a language, but
with a twist: it tends toward the surrealism that flourished when
Lacan was swept up in the literary life of Paris between the two world
wars. It is a Parisian unconscious, surrealist in its predilection for
incongruities, jokes, puns, and words that do not mean what they literally say. Hamlet in his quirky, ellipitic, paradoxical moods, teasing
Ophelia with clever word games, exemplifies the surrealist style that
is the hallmark of this theory of the unconscious, its unspoken
premise that the way to "truth" is by paradox and contraries. A joke
is often the key that opens this region of the psyche to inspection. It
embodies the surrealist bent for negation, for being restlessly anti-
this or anti-that, rebelling against reality while professing a desire to
be absolutely sincere. Lacan refers to the venerable joke about two

men who meet in a railway car at a station in Galicia. Says the first: "Where are you going?" Replies the second: "To Cracow." The first man explodes with irritation: "What a liar you are! If you say you are going to Cracow, you want me to believe you are going to Lemberg. But I know perfectly well you are going to Cracow. So why are you lying to me?"

Whereas Freud was uneasy about the "recollections" by hysteric patients of dreadful experiences in their past under hypnosis, accounts which as often as not were figments, the "cure by fiction," Lacan rested easy in the confidence that language, speech, is itself prior to reality. The important thing is for patients to "verbalize" their myths.

Jane Gallop notes that in America, Lacan was taken up by literary critics before psychologists clambered onto the bandwagon. The "Freudian slip" was a new way of probing the nether realms of the mind on the theory that an error, a mistake, which disrupts what a person intended to say, contains more profound, more startling truth effects than could have been produced by the intention itself. This is the stuff of literary criticism, because according to Lacan, the truth reveals itself "in the letter rather than the spirit." It emerges out of the manner in which something is said, not from the intended meaning. Literary critics "learn how to read the letter of the text, how to interpret the style, the form, rather than just reading for content or ideas." Similarly, says Gallop, "the psychoanalyst learns to listen not so much to her patient's main point as to odd marginal moments, slips of the tongue, unintended disclosures."

Lacan was a forerunner of late twentieth-century deconstruction, the theory that there is an unstable relation between a concept and words that signify that concept. The traditional view, that a concept comes first and a word gives access to it, is reversed. The signifier has priority. It is sovereign over the signified. Lacan believed there is a barrier that obstructs the simple link between word and meaning. A word, a signifier, never holds still to ensure a fixed and stable meaning, but is always making connections with other signifiers in an endless chain. It is restless, like the surrealist artist. This makes language and thought highly artificial, in exactly the place, the unconscious, where we might expect to find the basic, biological, *natural* components of the psyche. Instead of the concrete and the literal, the Lacanian unconscious is the home of rhetorical devices: metaphor, metonymy (the part signifies the whole), and other dodges of the linguistic game. Also, in this basement realm, there lurks the Other, the alternative or extraneous self that is always present, which is why everything the unconscious says has an alternative, an Other meaning, that contradicts the apparent truth on the surface.

By this stratagem Lacan, the surrealist Freud, can get away with his seemingly whimsical pronouncements about truth and falsehood. A contradictory unconscious may open itself to a complete misconstrual, and real cures are effected by absolutely fabricated "memories." Freud's treatments seemed to "flirt dangerously with magic," but to accuse him of shamanism, Lacan asserted, is to mistake the potency of speech and its entirely symbolic character. "The ambiguity of the hysterical *revelation* of the past is due not so much to the vacillation of its content between the imaginary and the real, for it is situated in both. Nor is it because it is made up of lies. The reason is that it presents us with the birth of truth in speech and thereby brings us up against the reality of what is neither true nor false."

Freud's treatments, Lacan said, were actually more effective when his interpretations were awry, because it was then possible to indoctrinate a patient starting from scratch. He recommended a pragmatic "fictionalizing" of the truth, since the patient is nothing but what is said about him. "In this strange analytic universe, where there is no real reality and everything is reduced to a contractual interaction, *all* speech by definition will be active and effective—all speech and therefore *any* speech," says Mikkel Borch-Jacobsen. "Freud might just as well have said 'Abracadabra;' the beneficial effects of his speech would have been none the less evident."

CHAPTER FOURTEEN

𝕻𝖗𝖊𝖙𝖙𝖞, 𝕾𝖍𝖎𝖓𝖎𝖓𝖌 𝕷𝖎𝖊𝖘

From the point of view of art there are no concrete or abstract forms, but only forms which are more or less convincing lies. That those lies are necessary to our mental selves is beyond any doubt, as it is through them that we form our aesthetic view of life. —Pablo Picasso

To try and approach truth on one side after another, not to strive or cry, nor to persist in pressing forward, on any one side, with violence and self-will—it is only thus, it seems to me, that mortals may hope to gain any vision of the mysterious Goddess, whom we shall never see except in outline, but only thus even in outline. —Matthew Arnold

 WORLD FILLING UP WITH ARTIFACTS, WITH machines and houses, clothes and furniture, paintings, vehicles, ingenious cuisines and creature comforts, codes of polite behavior, is very different from the pristine wildlife park inhabited by Adam and Eve. "If nature had been comfortable," said Oscar Wilde, in a fairly typical dismissal of the idea that Eden could possibly have satisfied Victorian tastes for the unnatural, "mankind would never have invented architecture, and I prefer houses to the open air." Doing what comes naturally, saying what comes naturally, may no longer be adequate or fitting to what is increasingly a non-natural environment. The simple truth, which might (or might not) be sufficient to describe the world of physical nature but in any case cannot harm it, may be a source of disruption in the world of the artificial and tends to be regarded by that world with hostility and even fear.

The cultural revolution known as modernism, in which Freud was a major voice, reflected this triumph of the artificial and shifted the balance between truth and falsehood. That is understandable, since, as in the days of other major upheavals of thought, from the Reformation to the Romantic movement, it can be said, as Virginia Woolf famously remarked of the new climate of the arts in 1910, "human character changed."

Modernism lasted roughly from the final third of the nineteenth century to the middle of the twentieth. Scholars have lately tended to upgrade its importance, and that is a victory of sorts for the arts, since modernism was first and foremost a movement of artistic innovation. It suggests that literature, music, and painting may be as potent an influence in the shaping of history as economics and politics. Modernism showed that art on its own can be a world-changing, mind-altering force. The historian Norman Cantor thinks modernism must now be seen as at the core rather than out on the margins of the structural changes that took place in the twentieth century. Its impact has often been underestimated, in part because it never acquired a political ideology of its own, though attempts were made in the thirties to link it to Marxism. Instead, it "produced a host of ambiguities and ambivalences." Nevertheless, Cantor thinks, modernism represents a transformation as profound as the Reformation, the Enlightenment, or Romanticism.

After the French Revolution, the term "avant-garde," originally a term of military strategy, came into general use, designating a new kind of radical politics, one which looked to the future for the coming of a better society and had utopian overtones. Later, in the nineteenth century, the Romantics picked up the phrase and applied it to the arts. The inference was that in the new society, artists would be the leaders, in fact, well ahead of the commercial class and even of the scientists. Gifted with imagination, the writer or painter could envision a grander tomorrow, and thus help to bring it into being. Artists were the front-line troops, the vanguard, marching toward a more just and seemly, a more "poetic" civilization. A privileged élite would create a society without privilege, a paradox which can be detected in the ideology of Marx and Lenin. Buried in the notion of the avant-garde was the Romantic dream of the poet as prophet, as legislator, taken up in earnest around the middle of the Victorian period by a handful of cultural iconoclasts who made it their mission to wreak havoc on the formal traditions of art.

Two kinds of avant-garde confronted each other with a hostile glare. On one side was science and industry, hardheaded social reform, apostles of the useful and of the gospel of material progress. The other side was entirely different in character. It was aesthetic to the core, anti-middle class, antagonistic to modernity in the sense of mercantilism and technology. The antipathy between the artists and the utilitarians is beautifully summed up in a famous Max Beerbohm cartoon in which Rossetti is at work on a mural for the interior of the Oxford Union, depicting a congregation of Arthurian knights and immaculate ladies. Standing watching, his feet firmly on the floor, is Benjamin Jowett, the worldly and well-connected Master of Balliol College. "And what were they going to *do* with the Grail when they found it, Mr. Rossetti?" is Jowett's deflationary question.

The aesthetic mentality took a view of truth and falsehood which was very different from that of the Philistines the aesthetes despised. One of its leading figures was Walter Horatio Pater, whose Conclusion to his *Studies in the History of the Renaissance* included the notorious phrase "the love of art for art's sake," and was hailed by Oscar Wilde as "the holy writ of beauty." Jowett viewed such a worldview with intense suspicion, and at first regarded Pater as a pernicious influence at Oxford. The Conclusion was suppressed in the second edition of the book for fear "it might possibly mislead some of those young men into whose hands it might fall." In this short essay, Pater declared that the value of philosophy is not to bring closure to the eternal quest for the answer to it all, but "to rouse, to startle" the human spirit to a life of constant and eager observation. Exactly how it accomplishes this task Pater does not inform us, but he is anxious to divert us from the futile chase after Being, the One, which "to the majority of acute people is after all but a zero, a mere algebraic symbol for nothingness."

Each insight or intellectual excitement is real *for the moment only*. "Not the fruit of experience, but experience itself'" is the point and purpose of it all. It is a waste of time trying to capture Truth as a thing, out there, to be trapped like a butterfly in a net. Experience, Pater said, is ringed round for each one of us by "that thick wall of personality" that is impervious to the real, so that we can only conjecture as to what is actually in the external world. "Every one of those impressions is the impression of the individual in his isolation, each mind keep as a solitary prisoner in its own dream of a world." So truth is relative to the particular prison cell we happen to occupy. Objects are no more substantial than impressions, flickering and inconsistent. What is real for us are simply images and sensations that coalesce and dissolve unceasingly, and even the self, that seemingly coherent and enduring whole, is a "continual vanishing away." In *Marius the Epicurean*, Pater talked about the "flaw at the foundation" of every philosophy of the universe, namely, the "weakness on the threshold of human knowledge," which enforces the subjective approach. Forget about absolute truth, concentrate on immediate experience: "burn always with this hard gemlike flame."

Pater himself presented a striking contrast between the bold assertion of the cult of beauty in his writings and the "abnormal caution, hesitancy, reticence" of his social demeanor. "Life is infinitely seductive," he once said, in the bachelor kingdom of his rooms at Brasenose College, "but books are safer, much safer." Pater lived at one remove from the ordinary and was famously unpractical. "He liked the human race, one is inclined to say," recalled Edmund Gosse in an obituary notice, "liked its noise and neighbourhood, if it were neither too loud nor too near, but his faith in it was never positive, nor would he trust it to read his secret thoughts." In his way, Pater was another Master of Suspicion. He conversed from behind a mask that hid all that was most precious to him. Oscar Wilde warned a young poet on his way to visit the great aesthete: "He never talks about anything that interests him. He will not breathe one golden word about the Renaissance. No! He will probably say something like this: 'So you wear cork soles in your shoes? Is that really true? And do you find them comfortable? How extremely interesting!' "

Pater taught that a new "faculty for truth" must be acquired if the mind is to operate in a modern world of huge complexity. This faculty is decidedly an *aesthetic* one. Ancient thinkers, he said, tried to arrest objects, to fix thought and classify things by kinds or species. That is all well and good as long as we are dealing with the given, with nature, the worlds of physics and biology. It is a different matter, however, when it comes to a universe crowded with the products of humankind's brains and imagination and genius. Such intricacy presents everyone, including artists, with a new kind of difficulty. Oscar Wilde in 1889, sixteen years after the publication of *The Renaissance,* wrote that "There is something interesting in the marked tendency of modern poetry to become obscure. Many critics, writing with their eyes fixed on the masterpieces of past literature, have ascribed this tendency to wilfulness and affectation. Its origin is rather to be found in the complexity of the new problems, and in the fact that self-consciousness is not yet adequate to explain the contents of the Ego."

The realm of the man-made was expanding on a terrific scale at this time. England had been the leader and innovator in the Industrial Revolution, and such a headstart was the key to its prosperity and imperial power. Vicitorian cities were smoky and grimy, dusky gulags of brick and noise and sulphurous emissions that excluded nature altogether; the works of man shut out the works of God. Charles Kingsley, for example, could speak of London's picture galleries, artificial substitutes for the givenness of nature, as the townsman's paradise of refreshment, where "his hard-won heart wanders out free, beyond the bleak world of stone and iron, smokey chimneys and roaring wheels into the world of beautiful things." Of the Victorian city, J. Hillis Miller said: "Everything is changed from its natural state into something useful or meaningful to man. Everywhere the world mirrors back to man his own image, and nowhere can he make vivifying contact with what is not human. Even the fog is not a natural fog, rolling in from the sea, but is half soot and smoke." It was impossible to tell whether man had banished God by the creation of these urban monsters, or whether God had vanished, after which the cities were built to fill the vacancy left by his absence.

The new sort of truth that Pater espoused, a citified variety, was not the truth of the given, the God-made or the natural, in the sense of Plato's Ideas, which were simply there, prior to human history and every other kind of history, eternal, unalterable, absolute. The modernist aesthetic theory said that nothing can be rightly known except in relation to other, "ungiven" things. A truth of this sort is always conditional, a truth of relations that the mind constructs—not easily and naturally, but with intelligence and a certain amount of exertion. It is unashamedly subjective, multiple, local, and relative. Pater had no nostalgia for a vanishing Age of Faith. "Modern thought," he said, "is distinguished from ancient by its cultivation of the 'relative' spirit in place of the absolute." Relativism became a respectable aesthetic doctrine and set the scene for later modernist themes, including truth as a point of view, the narrator whose word the reader cannot fully trust, and obscurity as a literary device, among others.

One feature of Pater's thought, growing out of his relativism, was the notion that if one must pursue truth, the quest itself may be preferable to actual possession. It is better to travel open-mindedly on that sort of journey than to arrive at a destination encumbered with hopelessly limited horizons. There is an echo here of Lessing's famous affirmation that if God held all the truth in his closed right hand, and in his left hand the living aspiration and impetus toward finding the truth, with the proviso that this lifelong chase will always become bogged down in error, and asked him to choose, Lessing would kneel respectfully in front of God's left hand and say: "Father, give me this. Pure truth is for Thee alone!" Max Beerbohm's Jowett had a point. What, after all, *would* one do with the Grail, supposing one were to find it?

In *Plato and Platonism*, Pater recommended the literary form of the essay rather than the philosophical treatise as the best vehicle for "a mind for which truth itself is but a possibility, realizable not as a general conclusion, but rather as the elusive effect of a particular personal experience." The non-terminating quality of the Platonic Dialogue, a foretaste of the "interminable" Freudian analysis, lent itself to this inconclusive exercise, resulting in at best "a many-sided but hesitant consciousness of truth." The paradox of Plato was that he aspired to absolute and eternal forms of knowledge, but made it clear throughout the give-and-take of his "theater of ideas" that truth depends in large part on the person who opens his mind to it. "The philosopher of Being," Pater wrote, referring to Plato, "or of the verb 'To be,' is after all afraid of saying 'It is.' "

At times Pater gives the impression that he is bored with the whole question of truth as defined in traditional philosophy. That was a trademark attitude of many modernists toward the culture they had inherited. Boredom was the secret vice of Victorian England, the contagious disease, according to Matthew Arnold, of modern societies in general. Ruskin attributed the breakdown of faith to a condition of "jaded intellect." Pater himself spoke of "that inexhaustible discontent, languor and homesickness, that endless regret, the chords of which ring all through our modern literature."

Ennui, which Baudelaire identified as the "great modern monster," fed the creative engines of modernism. Oscar Wilde taunted Victorian society for its growing boredom, exacerbated by the "tedious and improving conversations of those who have neither the wit to exaggerate nor the genius to romance." In an essay of 1860, "The Painter of Modern Life," Baudelaire celebrated the new in art for the sake of its newness, as opposed to the "boring" realism of the academy. Life by itself, the "given," unmodified by the mind of the artist, was stultifying and uninteresting.

The classic statement of that creed was an observation by Henry James, who spoke of "clumsy Life again at her stupid work." He might just as well have spoken of "boring Truth again at its lifeless work." The occasion was as follows. James was seated next to a woman at a Christmas Eve dinner party. The woman made a chance remark, "a mere floating particle in the stream of talk," which set his novelist's imagination off on a flight that eventually resulted in a fiction, *The Spoils of Poynton*. The woman "spoke of such an odd matter as that a good lady in the north, always well looked on, was at daggers drawn with her only son, ever hitherto exemplary, over the ownership of a fine old house accruing to the young man by his father's death." Her entire communication was no more than ten words in all. But in this little "speck of truth," James recognized the germ of his story. At that juncture, the last thing he wished to hear was the lady proceed to narrate the rest of the actual chain of events. That would severely offend his novelist's sensibility. When she started up again, James recognized the inarticulate meandering of actuality, of tiresome life. He was concerned with art, not with life, and these were very different commodities. What is more, their "truths" were incompatible. At the first step beyond the little particle that art could use, "life persistently blunders and deviates, loses herself in the sand. The reason is of course that life has no direct sense whatever for the subject and is capable, luckily for us, of nothing but splendid waste."

Fighting off the listlessness induced by clumsy Life could mean making a work of art as *different* as possible from it. In literature, words need not be a passage to actuality. It was a core belief of modernism that the attunement between the order of the mind and the order inherent in social structures, traditions, and conventions, which are to the individual what the "environment" is to a species in Darwin's theory, had been ruptured, possibly beyond repair. Adjusting to this new, discordant state of affairs calls for strategies far removed from the old, straightforward codes of transparency and directness. Thomas Mann, for part of his career a modernist experimenter, depicts this dislocation in his novel *Doctor Faustus*, a reminiscence of one Adrian Leverkuhn, written by Serenus Zeitblom, a scholar and humanist. Adrian, a theologian turned composer, who bears some resemblance to Nietzsche, is haunted by the realization that the musical tradition which sustained so many great artists of the past has been worked to death. The artist must break free of that tradition, but to do so requires "ingenuities not thought of in heaven."

Adrian symbolically enters into a pact with the devil, who arrives in the form of a mentally heightening but physically wasting disease. He sells his soul for two dozen years of musical genius. He writes masterpieces "instilled with the poison of the angel from the deep." In a dreamlike scene, a bow-tied, nasal-voiced Lucifer, suave but "not a gentleman," tells Adrian that composing has become too difficult, in fact, "devilishly" difficult. It does not go along with *sincerity* any more. Adrian proposes that there might be a "spontaneous harmony between a man's own needs and the moment, the possibility of 'rightness,' of a natural harmony, out of which one might create without a thought or any compulsion." Lucifer, perched on a horsehair sofa, a pair of horn-rimmed spectacles on his hooked nose, goes off into a spasm of cynical laughter. Music, by conforming her specific concerns to the ruling conventions, is part of a "highbrow swindle." It is all up with the "once bindingly valid conventions." For four hundred years the high works of musical genius were based on the idea that there is a natural congruity of the rules of tonality with the psychological makeup of the listener, that a unity exists between the formal elements of musical composition, the "conventional universal law," and the necessary logic of the mind. The "law" no longer recognizes itself in the mirror of human inwardness, and the human heart no longer feels that any general order of things can be valid.

A theme of Mann's very rich, very disturbing *Doctor Faustus* is that in the Age of Modernism, the Age of Suspicion, art has become too difficult, and that is something to worry about, because we cannot separate matters of art from matters of truth, and of the value of truth in a culture whose art puts truth in question. The critic Erich Heller thinks the chief difference between Mann's treatment of the Faust legend and that of Goethe is its concern with the breakdown of attunement between mind and world. Goethe's Faust is protected from the schemes of Mephistopheles to lure him into Hell as long as he persists in striving for knowledge, for the truth. He "needs no savior, because he is safe in the preestablished harmony between the intellectual, moral and aesthetic aspirations of man and the real nature of things." In the case of Adrian Leverkuhn, however, there is no such safety net. The relation between the soul and the world it inhabits is not a harmony, not a guide to truth, but inane, meaningless. Dissonance is sublime, tonality belongs to the domain of Hell. Lucifer is a modernist figure who holds truth, truth for its own sake, in low esteem and champions the life-enhancing power of the strategically chosen falsehood. "What uplifts you, what increases your feeling of power and might and domination, damn it," he tells his purchased victim, "that is the truth—and whether ten times a lie when looked at from the moral angle. This is what I think: that an untruth of a kind that enhances power holds its own against an ineffectively virtuous truth."

Modernism came at the question of truth and falsehood from a peculiar angle, owing to certain of its basic tenets, which were in sharp antagonism to those of its early and mid-Victorian predecessors. The Victorians in general believed that truth had a history. They were powerfully influenced by the triumphs of evolutionary theory and the historical method. The key to understanding anything, natural or artificial, was to investigate its past, its origins. Nineteenth-century philosophy was dominated by Hegel, who took history with exceptional seriousness and regarded human nature as something that altered from one age to the next. Hegelian history is the evolution of the consciousness of freedom, and therefore of huge importance. "Truth" is a quarry we hunt over time, a continual testing of a timeless universal idea against a particular instance that occurs at a specific moment in time, setting up a certain rivalry between the two, then reconciling them to produce a new concept which is truer than the original one.

All that was anathema to modernism. Truth-finding became analytical, not historical. A modernist would not try to fit anything into a sequence stretching from the past into the future; instead, he would examine the thing itself, what it is here and now, never mind where it came from or where it may be going. Self-sufficiency enters as a theme and a guide to meaning that would have large repercussions in twentieth-century thought.

Analytic philosophy is quintessentially modernist, enjoying a revival at the turn of the century. It resisted all "top-down" ideologies such as idealism. In the early stages of the anti-idealist reaction led at Cambridge by G. E. Moore and Bertrand Russell, the world was thought of as consisting of simple propositions related in simple ways, each one independent of and isolated from all the others. Being simple, each bit of reality was knowable and each proposition must be either true or false. The notion of absolute truth, a bedrock axiom of analytical philosophy, was taken over from the old-hat idealists, but in an entirely different form. The rules of logic made truth an absolute concept. We cannot say of something that it is a little bit true or partly false, or truer than something else. It cannot be more or less true. Russell was especially adamant on this point: a single proposition had the status of the absolute that Hegel said could only be the pinnacle of a process of reconciling opposites.

Part and parcel of Russell's system of "logical atomism," inspired by the philosophy of Leibniz, was the correspondence theory of truth. The simple elements out of which knowledge of the world is made up are based on encounters with the actual world we inhabit. They are validated by matching them up with observation. There is a one-to-one correspondence of sentences with reality, and it is this conformity that shows the sentences to be true. There is no wobble or looseness in the fit, and that is thanks to the fact that a sentence is an autonomous, self-sufficient entity with a clear boundary, not open to question, as it might be if it were entangled with other sentences. By virtue of that stable agreement, logic becomes a key to the structure of the "real" world. Analyze logical form correctly and you accomplish what metaphysicians had groped their way toward for thousands of years: an insight into the true nature of the universe. For this task, clarity, precision, simplicity are essential.

Predictably, the modernist tendency to isolate truth from history, and to deal with knowledge in simple, separate units, helped to elevate the intellectual or aesthetic element over mere physical reality, and to sever connections between the two. Art became intensely artificial, and artists strove to make their work as different as possible from anything to which its content might allude. Truth was internal to the work, not a correspondence with anything external to it. In a poem, words were not a passage to actuality. Paintings did not portray nature. Some modernists wrote of nature as if it were an inert material of the sort one might purchase at a butcher's shop to be taken home and sliced up for conversion into an aesthetically pleasing form. "A Picasso studies an object the way a surgeon dissects a corpse," said the poet Guillaume Apollinaire. Cubist art drew its inspiration from a dead nature: the man-made became more animate than the God-given. Critics talk about modernist "cruelty" and "barbarism," a sort of reckless exuberance in the discovery of forms that disrupt normal expectations. There is a sense of overmastering the natural, an operating-theater vandalism "which mocks the humanist fetish of the unified body. The avant garde rejection of mimesis is now clearly linked with a dismemberment of the body and its translation into inorganic form as a prerequisite of 'original' aesthetic perception." This was the aesthetic counterpart of the denaturing inclinations of the modernist logicians.

As a result, such creations ceased to harmonize with anything outside themselves that might guarantee their truth. They must be understood exclusively on their own terms. W. H. Auden, for example, was adamant that a poem is not primarily "about" anything but the words that compose it. Painting was also about itself. It was radically autonomous. "Yours is a hellish craft," the painter Degas, who also wrote verse, once remarked to the poet Mallarmé. "I can't manage to say what I want, yet I'm full of ideas." To which Mallarmé replied: "My dear Degas, one does not make poetry with ideas, but with *words.*" In the same vein, Auden defined a promising poet, not as someone who has important things to say, but as a person who likes "hanging around words listening to what they say."

Cubism was celebrated as a new form of art which no longer imitated nature and which, "like a flame, has the sublime and incontestable truth of its own light." Just as each god creates in his own image, so does each painter. In 1913 Apollinaire, one of the firebrands of the modernist revolution in the arts and a close friend of Picasso's, laid it down as law that art spurns resemblance and sacrifices everything to a new sort of truth. Henceforth, painting is to be like music, which does not refer to anything outside itself, but is complete, sheer, needing no external world to describe or mirror. It would concentrate exclusively on creating "harmony with unequal lights."

Writing ten years later, Picasso, displaying the anti-historical bent of modernism, ridiculed the idea that art evolves, as if it were a species in a Darwinian universe. In art there is no past or future, no advance toward an unknown "truth" or ideal of painting. Somewhat in the manner of T. H. Huxley declaring an antagonism between ethics and nature, Picasso stressed the profoundly *anti-natural* character of painting. Nature and art are two quite different things; through art, an artist expresses his idea of what nature is not. And if nature is truth, art is something else entirely. Picasso stated this as an article of belief: "We all know that art is not truth. Art is a lie that makes us realize the truth, at least the truth that is given us to understand. The artist must know the manner whereby to convince others of the truthfulness of his lies." Both Picasso and Apollinaire subscribed to the Nietzschean dogma that God is dead, which meant the artist had a duty to affirm his role as a "microcosm of the universe," and rescue the known world for art. It was said that Apollinaire was dedicated to the task of becoming "a sort of illegitimate Christ saving the world through the Verb."

It is through the lies of art that we form an aesthetic view of life. That was the faith of Picasso and of many like him. And it is the aesthetic that becomes an absolute in the modernist universe. Art edges out metaphysics, religion, history. André Malraux talked about art museums as sacred shrines, holy temples, the only ones left in the modern age. "Though this art is not a god, but an absolute," he said, "it has, like a god, its fanatics and martyrs and is far from being an abstraction." Artists have this supreme status because they do not represent the visible world, but try to create a totally different world for their personal use.

Modernist literature's famous preoccupation with lies and liars was a side effect of its refusal to make its own truths easily accessible to a public whose taste and intelligence it did not respect. Like Pater discoursing on the virtues of cork soles to avoid talking about things close to his soul, writers in the Age of Suspicion did not trust their readers, who in turn were not inclined to take what an author wrote at face value, but were always sniffing about for concealed meanings and ulterior motives. The Victorians were apt to think that the realistic depiction of nature and life brought art close to "the truth," whereas the modernists agreed with Arthur Symons, who said: "I affirm that it is not natural to be what is called 'natural' any longer." By that he meant an artist should not succumb artlessly to the impulse to blurt everything out, sharing his secrets with the common herd.

There is detectable in certain modernist authors a suspicion of all earnest chasers after truth, and of truth itself as some kind of blundering, heavy-footed enemy of art and privacy. Joseph Conrad noted how "bizarre" it is that secrecy should play such a large part in the comfort and safety of people's lives. For that sort of reason, the critic Allon White argues, modernist authors such as Conrad, George Meredith, Henry James, were "fascinated by liars. They persistently return to explore situations in which people are forced to lie to defend themselves or to defend others. Their lies are rarely malicious or calumniating; they are defensive, often so vague or subtle that their relation to the truth is hopelessly perplexed. Lies are as old as the fictions to which they have been assimilated, but in late nineteenth century fiction lies and liars focus some complex issues of literary obscurity. Lies took on a special significance in a period when it was often felt that neither culture nor individual expression could be entirely sincere."

There was a sense that if society is held together and kept up as a going concern by artificially created deceptions, truth-telling may be terribly disruptive, irresponsible in the extreme. In Conrad's novel *The Nigger of the Narcissus*, able seaman Jimmy Wait, aboard a vessel sailing from Bombay to London, falls sick. He is dying, and his death would lead to chaos on the ship. So he pretends to be malingering, acting out a lie and hiding a secret that might have enabled the troublemaker Donkin to incite a mutiny among the crew. Wait stands by his falsehood even when it is public knowledge that he is lying, and by his steadfast loyalty to it emerges as a sort of hero who saves his ship from anarchy by refusing to take the ruinous path into truthfulness. Lying, secrecy, equivocation are prominent in Conrad's stories, due in part to the fact that culture and civilization are insecure, yet their very artificiality is necessary to preserve the decencies of everyday life.

Freud, Conrad's contemporary, sounded the same theme in *Civilization and Its Discontents*. It was not only religion that was losing its authority. The whole tradition of philosophy as an exploration of truth was fraying and growing irrelevant for ordinary human purposes. Ian Watt theorizes that Conrad's *Heart of Darkness*, published in 1902, is in part an expansion of this idea. Marlow, the narrator of the story, traveling in Africa for a trading company, hears of a Mr. Kurtz, a successful agent of the firm, dealing in ivory. He undertakes a two-month journey on a rickety steamboat to find this man celebrated for his exceptional abilities and mysterious power over the natives. Arriving, Marlow is horrified to discover that Kurtz has descended to a subhuman level of degradation, indulging in barbaric cruelty and ritual sacrifice to enforce his hold over the local people. His hut is surrounded with the evidence of his crimes: a row of severed heads on stakes.

Marlow tries to rescue Kurtz from his blood-spattered kingdom, but Kurtz, who has up to that moment spoken chiefly in platitudes about his life, dies with these words of truth on his lips: "The horror! The horror!"

At one stage in the novel, Marlow states that "I hate, detest and cannot tell a lie, not because I am straighter than the rest of us, but simply because it appals me. There is a taint of death, a flavor of mortality in lies—which is exactly what I hate and detest in the world." Yet he tells a number of lies in the course of his adventures. He exaggerates his influence in order to obtain needed rivets to repair the cranky steamboat that was to rescue Kurtz. He deceives by withholding the truth about Kurtz, and flatters him insincerely as a ruse to lure him to return to the company station. Arriving in Europe, Marlow destroys the single honest opinion scrawled by Kurtz on a report he drafted about the proper treatment of natives: "Exterminate all the brutes!" And he dissembles while visiting Kurtz's fiancée, making no response when the girl utters glowing commendations of her deceased intended. Asked what were Kurtz's last words, Marlow lies that he expired speaking her name.

These fabrications, contrary to centuries of philosophical cogitation about the value of truth-telling, are actually presented as forms of self-restraint, and self-restraint is a trait which separates humans from the rest of nature. T. H. Huxley, Darwin-intoxicated as he was, regarded it as an important, deep mystery. "In the perspective of intellectual history," writes Conrad's biographer, Ian Watt, Marlow's "whole series of deceptions, equivocations and silences can be regarded as part of a general trend towards the abandonment of the idea that the truths of philosophy could be applied to any of the practical problems of life." It is not the seemingly sturdy ideals of truth and goodness that maintain society, but the much flimsier facade of civilization and the deceitful character of our day-to-day attitudes and disposition. Raw nature, the wild ocean and the untamed jungle, are for Conrad more likely to outlast these makeshift illusions, "including, perhaps, the illusion of humanity's necessary survival."

It is because people in the normal course of affairs habitually lie to themselves that the rare individual who sees the world clearly, but also understands the insecurities of those who do not, is unable to bring himself to demolish their fantasies. In the case of women, creatures Marlow believes are out of touch with the truth and live in a make-believe world of their own, must—simply must—be allowed to continue in it. If their dream bubble bursts, the grittier and uglier world of the male might also be impaired. That, Conrad makes Marlow say in the original manuscript of the novel, "is a monster-truth with many maws to whom we've got to throw every year—or every day—no matter—no sacrifice is too great—a ransom of pretty, shining lies."

Just as the characters in the early modernist novel face the discomforting realization that being "sincere" leaves them open to the destructive intrusions and betrayals of other people, so the authors use various literary devices to avoid making themselves transparent to the reading public. Obscurity was one such device, creating a wall of difficulty and hindrance for the common reader to overcome, denying access to the multitude. And obscurity has a family resemblance to secrecy, which in turn is a blood relative of untruth. T. S. Eliot, speaking for the modernist sensibility, observed that "it appears likely that poets in our civilization, as it exists at present, must be *difficult*." The poet must be more allusive, more indirect than his nineteenth-century predecessors, "in order to force, to dislocate if necessary, language into his meaning." In language not at all indirect, Henry James confessed that difficulty was the only thing, at bottom, that interested him. "I hate American simplicity," he wrote. "I glory in the piling up of complications of every sort. If I could pronounce the name of James in any different or more elaborate way I should be in favor of doing so."

Modernism refused to accept the realities that history provides or nature offers. It insisted on a new Genesis and a new knowledge of good and evil. Transparency would have meant acknowledging that truth is simple, public, natural, and it is none of those things. "Man," said Jean-Paul Sartre, the modernist philosopher of the ubiquity of self-deception, "is the being whose plan it is to become God." Godlike, he creates from nothing. What is more, it is not possible to know him entirely from his works. His works resist full disclosure. This is a reversal of the famous doctrine of Vico in the eighteenth century, who said we can understand completely only what is made by human minds and hands, not what is given by the extrahuman. We know art, said Vico. As for nature, it must remain in part a mystery.

The obscurity of modernist literature is *different*, a new kind of non-illumination that cannot be illumined by close analysis of sentence structure, by looking up unfamiliar words in a dictionary or reading up on the cultural context of an author's life. "The obscurity of modernism," says Allon White, "is not susceptible to simple decoding. It is usually not a matter of information suppressed or omitted which the critic can patiently recover. It is rather that, despite a remarkable diversity of intent and effect, modernist difficulty signifies in and by the very fact of offering resistance." In other words, inaccessibility in itself acquires a meaning. It does not hide a clear, distinct message which in principle could be retrieved. Obscurity *is* the message. Things that cannot be said are of higher significance than the things that are spoken. One example is the letter that is burned unread and the letter that is never opened—both of which contain information crucial to the ending of the story—in Henry James's novel *The Wings of the Dove*. James refuses to communicate what the ordinary reader most desperately wants to know, for the very modernist reason that goodness is no longer linked to openness, plainspeaking, full disclosure, all the Cartesian virtues of a clear consciousness and a limpid mind, but to secrecy, the fog banks of opacity, the closed door, the sealed envelope. "Innocence in the late James is not granted by simplicity of utterance, but by an almost impenetrable reticulation of surface which envelops that which is desired and feared." Obscurity of information betokens purity; the overt delivery of it, the unbridled transmission of truth, heralds vulgarity, perhaps some kind of moral peril.

𝔄 𝔏𝔦𝔣𝔢 𝔬𝔣 𝔍𝔱𝔰 𝔒𝔴𝔫

Language is the main instrument of man's refusal to accept the world as it is.
—George Steiner

ODERNISTS ENCOURAGED THE PROVO-cative idea that the artificial is a source of truths that are more nourishing, more sustaining and interesting than the truths of the natural, and that the two are incommensurable. And after modernism was over, there arose a tendency of intellectual fashion, leaning to a certain Wildean taste for the paradoxical and perverse, to take this to extremes and turn upside down orders of precedence long accepted as obvious. It would hardly occur to the ordinary person to doubt that the natural, the simple, and the primitive are basic, while the artificial, the mature, and the complex are late arrivals superimposed on them. To a significant number of thinkers, however, these priorities are back to front. The latter so predominate over the former as to claim a sort of aboriginal status. Briefly expressed, these reversals of the normal order of things include the following:

- Culture is prior to nature, since nature is an invention of culture, and a relatively recent one at that.
- Society precedes the individual, and by a long chalk. The concept of the unique self materialized only in the seventeenth century,

when the bourgeois belief in individualism was in the ascendant.

· Meaning edges out truth, which is a metaphysical notion. Truth dissolves in the acids of a philosophy that puts culture and language first. Truth can no longer be defined as a correspondence between the world of signs and the world of things.

· We do not have a thought first, and then express it in the form of connected speech or text. Instead, thoughts do not and cannot exist without language, which brings them into being.

· The whole of language takes precedence over a single actual sentence, spoken or on the printed page. Writing is more faithful to the true nature of language than speaking.

· Man-made constraints and taboos inherent in the structure of society are more basic than "natural" liberties we assume existed prior to civilization, but which in fact are an illusion produced by the constraints themselves.

· It would be more accurate to say that language and social meanings make us, rather than that we make them. They are ultimate realities, necessary and unavoidable, a present-day version of the remorseless Fates of the Greek tragedies.

Oscar Wilde had announced some of these heresies in the early days of modernism, only more elegantly and with his tongue at least partly in his cheek: "The whole of Japan is a pure invention. There is no such country." They flourished in an atmosphere where language not only became the focus, even the obsession, of philosophers, but was granted almost total independence, a priestly autonomy from everything that lay outside its domain. This privileging and isolating of the word, the word closing in on itself, was carried to such extremes that the scholar Richard Harland could say: "Language, I suggest, is important not because it ties onto objects and states of affairs, but because it disengages from them. We don't need language in order to know actuality but in order to conceive of possibility." More or less the same could be said of falsehood, as we have seen time and time again in our overview of thought from Kant onward. It is a theme that will not go away.

The theorist who set the scene for this sort of contrariness was the

Swiss Ferdinand de Saussure, whose *Course in General Linguistics*, published in 1916, showed that no matter what common sense or scholarship might say, there is no direct correspondence of language to
the world. Instead, language is a network of signs, in which a particular sign has meaning only by virtue of its difference from other signs.
Outside this network, the "real" world acquires meaning insofar as
language as a whole throws significance onto it. There is a certain
haughty aloofness, a standoffishness and cultish condescension, on
the part of the linguistic system. Words do not refer to anything in
the realm beyond their territory. According to this view, truth is not
discovered; it is produced by differences between signs. It is a property of language, not of the world. A statement "is true when it conforms to certain norms that govern what a particular way of writing
takes to be true."

Saussure's provocative snipping of the umbilical cord between
words and the world undercut the traditional view that literature is
unique because it does not deal in facts, and therefore cannot be
accused of lying. Nonfiction, on the other hand, is supposed to
describe what "really" happened and is held accountable for its accuracy. But how can this commonsense definition of factual writing be
accepted if language does not correspond to the real? "Suddenly, all
forms of writing were revealed as being distant from the real world,
and as linguistically embedded, as literature had been thought to
be."

The Saussurian revolution shared with modernism an anti-
historical bent. It did not bother itself with the evolution and development of language, but only with its structural properties here and
now, just as they are. All that comes within its purview is a finite
number of constituents, which are manipulated according to a finite
list of rules. As in a game of chess, it matters not in the least who
invented the game, how it has altered during the course of its history, what material the pieces are made of, or what they symbolize. You
just play chess by moving the pieces about according to the existing
rules. No object that sits on the board, nothing that happens on the
board, has any "correspondence" to anything in the world outside it.
What matters is just that a particular chess piece is *different* from

other pieces, either in shape or position. And these differences are purely conventional. Difference, not identity, is the producer of meaning.

Later, there was to be a tortuous political interpretation put on Saussure's theory. Marxists in the overheated political atmosphere of France in the 1960s decided that Saussure's description of the linguistic sign as made up of two parts—the "signified," a mental concept, and the "signifier," the material mark or spoken sound—could be used to reinstate the importance of the material conditions and actual economic constraints that ruled the lives of ordinary people, as opposed to the dreamy idealism of the bourgeois, which relegated such gritty actualities to secondary status. The "liberation of the signifier" became a summons to the ideological barricades. Jacques Lacan saw the unconscious as a place where signifiers slide about, making meaning not by reference to anything in a person's conscious life, but by the position of a sign in the signifying chain.

The campaign to free the signifier had ominous implications for traditional ideas of truth and falsehood. According to George Steiner, the problem of the nature of truth entered a new phase in the modernist period, thanks in large part to the virtually uprecedented emphasis on language. There was a shift from an outward-looking concept of truth as something independent of personal intuition, but immediately accessible to the mind and to the will, to an inward-looking sort of truth as no more than a feature of logical form and of language.

There are three standard theories of truth: truth as pragmatic, as coherence, and as correspondence. The pragmatic theory, an invention of nineteenth-century American philosophy, to which a major contribution was made by Henry James's brother William, defines truth in terms of what it is useful for a person to believe, and being useful, an instrument of action. John Dewey, partly under the influence of William James, jettisoned his earlier belief that we actualize ourselves by tracing the outlines of an ideal, universal self, and went Darwinian, went biological, arguing that the mind is a product of a struggle by the human species to make a proper adjustment to the environment, so that its chief function is practical; it is meant to solve problems and act, not merely contemplate or indulge in dreams. James and Dewey both believed that the truth of an idea can only be shown by putting that idea to work in practice, and noticing what sort of results it obtains. It is results, not prior criteria, that determine truth. "If they succeed in their office they are reliable, sound, valid, good, true," Dewey wrote. "By their fruits shall ye know them. That which guides us truly is true—demonstrated capacity for such guidance is precisely what is meant by truth."

In the pragmatic theory there is a distinct inward bias, an emphasis on the utility of truth to us as believers. This smacks of relativism, since what is useful for me may be useless to you, and vice versa. Here the individual mind does not exactly "make" truth, but it certainly is not a detached observer. Pragmatism implies that truth, so defined, *matters*. It has value in a person's life. We note that Dewey equates truth with goodness, a throwback to the Greeks.

The coherence theory of truth, by contrast, defines a true statement as one that harmonizes with a consistent set of already existing beliefs. Whereas the correspondence theory, which bears the stigma of being compatible with ordinary common sense, says a proposition is true when it corresponds to facts or to the world, the coherence theory, held by such thinkers as Fichte and Hegel but jilted by Dewey in his Darwinian swerve in the 1890s, suggests that truth is strongly dependent on the mind, on a crucial relation between established beliefs and new knowledge. In the view of many, this falls afoul of the famous theorem of Kurt Gödel, published in 1931, which says that no system above a certain minimal level of complication can prove its own consistency without recourse to rules that lie outside its borders.

It was in the spirit of analytic philosophy that truth came to be seen, not as a connection between words and things, but between words and words. It was a rock-bottom axiom of the analytics that truth and falsity play an essential role in the meaning of any statement. But, in George Steiner's view, this tilted the balance too far in one direction. A theory of truth must also be able to deal just as effectively with falsehood. "None of the accounts of truth given by modern linguistic philosophy seems to me to fulfil this requirement,"

Steiner said. "Yet I believe that the question of the nature and history of falsity is of crucial importance to an understanding of language and of culture. Falsity is not, except in the most formal or internally systematic sense, a mere miscorrespondence with a fact. It is itself an active, creative agency. The human capacity to lie, to negate what is the case, stands at the heart of speech and of the reciprocities between words and the world."

This very modernist sentiment is diametrically opposed to that of the nineteenth-century colossus, Hegel, who was adamant that truth is primary, sovereign, and independent. Truth is the measure of things, including those things that are false. Untruth, lies, and error are not competitors or rivals for the crown, posing a danger to truth; they have no legitimate status with which to claim such a prize.

The new discoveries made in the past half century about the roots of syntax, how it works in the mind and on the page, have helped to disconnect language from its various anchors outside syntax, including the anchor of truthful intention. Language has lost any close coexistence with logic, where propositions are either true or false and it matters extremely which is which. The logical positivists, who aimed to detoxify philosophy by ridding it of metaphysics and anything that smacked of metaphysics, and decided that the meaning of a sentence was the procedure for showing it to be true, naturally took more interest in truth than in meaning. They wanted to be scientific, and meaning belongs more to psychology and literature than to science. Ordinary language was the wrong instrument for their purposes; it functions more as a vehicle of meaning than as a guarantor of truth. There is too large an element of the private and the personal, of the idiosyncratic, about it, whereas the criterion of science since the seventeenth century has been that it be public, impersonal, shared.

The philosopher Karl Popper, from his youth intent on marking a clear difference between science and nonscience, went to some pains to make a new kind of distinction between meaning and truth. As a very young man living in Vienna in the 1920s, Popper became a Marxist, only to suffer a bitter disillusionment at the age of seventeen, when he watched unarmed young Socialist demonstrators

being shot to death by police. The demonstration had been instigated by the Communists. The experience jolted him into realizing he
had accepted a complex doctrine like Marxism uncritically, as a "science," whereas it was more like Freudian psychoanalysis. It claimed
a privileged access to truth, but in fact was nonrational in the sense
that any new fact could always be made to confirm the theory but no
fact could ever disprove it. It was immunized against criticism. Popper decided that science is different from nonscience chiefly in its
openness to refutation, to falsification, to devastating criticism. Science has a defective immune system. And part of the strength of a
scientific theory is to rule out, to exclude, rather than to incorporate.
The more a theory prohibits, the more it tells us.

Popper went a long step beyond Cartesian dualism by introducing
not two, but three distinct "worlds" of knowledge, each with its own
special attributes.

World One is the universe of physical objects and states, of nature
in the traditional sense of the word.

World Two is reserved for mental states and dispositions to act. It
includes everything that goes on inside the human head.

World Three consists of those products of thought that are public, out in the open for all to discuss, to argue about, ridicule, or crit-
icize: theories, conjectures, texts, poems, scriptures. World Three has
much in common with Plato's supernatural realm of Ideas and with
Hegel's Objective Spirit, but also is unlike them in important ways.
It has a large degree of autonomy. If a global cataclysm wiped out all
machines and tools, together with our memory of how to make and
use them, yet spared all the books in all libraries, we would eventually be able to get civilization back on track. If libraries were demolished, however, it might take thousands of years to recover.

Knowledge in World Three is knowledge without a knower. Popper presents us with an anti-psychological thesis: we can learn more
about how the contents of World Three are produced by studying
the products themselves than by examining the mind of the person
who made them. That is a novel approach. It starts back to front,
with effects rather than causes. Products are prior to the producer.

World Two is the home of common sense, and for that reason is not free of bias and slanted perspectives. Its contents are personal and subjective: ideas, expectations, stereotypes, presuppositions which can and do distort and prejudice the mind. Common sense may put blinkers on our judgments. World Three's role is to tear off the blinkers and subject skewed opinions to merciless scrutiny. That explains why scientists are sometimes so cauterizingly rude to each other when a new theory is under discussion.

The contents of World Three are human inventions, the "made" rather than the given, which modernists sometimes treated as extrahuman, as if they were given. It is as if explorers were groping their way around a new continent without the help of maps, not knowing what to expect until they arrive at their destination. The number system, for instance, may be a mathematical artifact, but that does not mean we know all there is to know about it. Seemingly simple questions about the nature of numbers may present nightmarish difficulties. The innocent-looking conjecture that every even number is the sum of two prime numbers is in fact so disingenuous as to stump the best efforts of mathematicians for centuries. Logic also, once regarded as a tamed and settled province, turned out to harbor monsters, in the form of strange and deadly paradoxes. The difference between World Two and World Three in this respect is that World Three thrives and prospers on such exigencies, whereas in World Two the mind tends to look for evidence that will confirm its partialities rather than for unsettling new facts that are likely to disconcert them.

A core property of World Two—and here our central theme enters again like a leitmotif—is that it prefers meanings to truths. It is at home with interpretation, conjecture, opinion, belief. All these, in Popper's words, are "nets in which we try to catch the real world." What the mind catches in its nets is a seriously slanted version of reality; but the alternative, the fully open mind of World Three, would not be able to catch reality at all. Without the meanings, without conjectures and interpretations, it would not even know where to begin.

Language, as it emerges from the penetrating and subtle probings of twentieth-century thinkers, is likewise multidimensional. And it, too, has its private and public mien. In the theory of Saussure, a word has no definite import on its own, but only in relation to other words which might have been chosen instead, but were not. A word may be surrounded by a ghostly cloud of related words in a sort of vertical formation:

MUSCLE
RUSTLE
TASSLE
HASSLE
WRESTLE
SETTLE
METAL
MENTAL
SENTINEL

This may look like a simple game of word association, one word triggering others in the subterranean world of the Freudian unconscious. But the connections are not primarily mental. The situation is more like a game of chess, where a single, specific move logically implies all the other legitimate moves that could have been played, but were ruled out by the choice of a unique strategy. The entire system of chess lurks behind a decision, say, to move a pawn one square forward. And the system itself exists independently of the thoughts and desires of the player.

Yet, there is a certain private, individualistic quality to these vertical linkages that never allow one word to stand on its own. No two human beings share exactly the same context in which a word is embedded. "There are no facsimiles, no twin psyches," as George Steiner put it. In French, for example, there exists a vertical chord of associations which no one acquiring the language from outside, in a classroom, will ever fully master.

Another kind of linkage is horizontal. A word is followed by another word, and that word by another in a sequence that is organized in terms of syntax, not association. And syntax is preeminently a public, shared system of connections, the established rules of the game of language. In this case there *are* facsimiles: everyone in a linguistic community plays by the same rules. The theory of universal grammar is one of the twentieth century's Copernican revolutions, the conjecture that every human being is born with a "language acquisition device" in the head, a mental organ enabling a child to acquire just the one unique theory of syntax that everyone else is using, instead of concocting an idiosyncratic, private theory of his or her own. If there were no such inborn device, any number of different theories would be compatible with the fragmentary and incomplete evidence available to the child in the form of adult speech.

Grammar, the horizontal dimension of language, tends to reduce the copiousness of meaning to a manageable number of alternatives. Richard Harland points out that the greater the number of words in a horizontal sequence, the fewer there are in a vertical array. The public properties vanquish the private ones. The phrase "bulls in street" suggests innumerable possible meanings. Pamplona? Hemingway? Vertical connections run riot. "Bulls in street take heart" reduces that number radically, yet leaves open certain eventualities. All those options are drastically abridged with the grammatical sentence: "Bulls in street take heart as stock market rises 150 points in relief rally at no change in interest rates." We are in the domain of World Three. In a specific place, Wall Street, on a unique day, stocks turned in a once only performance that would likely never be repeated exactly. The complete sentence stabilizes a highly unstable linguistic situation. Yet it also conveys novel, perhaps surprising information.

Such information need not describe an actual state of affairs, however. The linear structure of syntax does not tie us down to the literal truth about things. In fact, language in the horizontal mode gains a large measure of independence from the actual world, projecting meaning as possibility as well as fact, constructing worlds that are not given in reality, nor custom-made by social convention. The constraints of syntax turn out to confer an exhilarating sense of freedom and detachment. And syntax is exactly the apparatus of rules and principles that sets human language apart from every other kind of message system.

Not only is language multidimensional. It is so constituted that a given dimension tends to take on a life of its own. That complicates immensely its role in dealing with truth and falsehood. It may be that primitive forms of language had fewer dimensions than ours today, which left it unable to transcend the literal, the factual, the here and now. Perhaps, as Peter Munz speculates, false beliefs, based on World Two suppositions, once had a social usefulness, binding tightly together members of a community who clung to esoteric doctrines and creeds that had no basis in truth. Because such beliefs were not shared by the rest of humanity, because they were private and unique to a specific community, they could serve to shut out unwelcome strangers, who would regard such eccentric ideas as alien and unacceptable. The weirder the belief, the greater the power of exclusion and the stronger the cohesion of the society that subscribed to it. Truth, being single and universal, would tend to break down the barriers that divide one culture from another, but falsehood is hydra-headed. Its very copiousness might have enabled little isolated societies to hold onto their autonomy.

The complexity of language had been underestimated. The mistake was to suppose it existed on just one level, where its "natural" and proper function was to convey information that is positively true or definitely false. That attributes to language a thinness, a parsimony, that is foreign to its nature. Language is in fact a dense, layered medium empowered not just to reflect reality but to transform it radically. In part, it is a message system, but only in part. Language communicates, but on the other hand it creates what it communicates. Its properties are not necessarily the same as those of the external world it purports to describe.

At a primary, prelinguistic level of the animal brain, the linguist Derek Bickerton argues, the brain makes a model of the world based on information from eyes, ears, taste, and touch, supplemented by memory. At the next level, with the use of symbols, the nervous system constructs a model of that model. Then, perhaps, syntax arose, and syntax is a device for giving symbols a definite structure, for making a model of a model of a model. Ascending these levels of evolved complexity, we notice an increasing distance between language and the world.

As Bickerton tells it, primitive language, emerging after the separation of the hominid line from other primates, had virtually none of the structural properties of language as we know it today. Maybe it survives in the grammarless speech of very young children and the behavior of specially trained primates. The cry of a vervet monkey, conveying the message: "A lion is coming," is tightly linked to present reality. But it is less powerful than true grammatical language, which is able to represent: "A lion was taken away in a net by three men with a van." The opportunity for lying is severely restricted in the first case, but offers prolific openings for mendacity in the second.

Language at a remove from reality is exemplified by the famous Liar Paradox. Epimenides the Cretan asserts that all Cretans are liars. It follows that if Epimenides is telling the truth, he is a liar. If he is lying, what he says is consistent with the truth. Paradoxes of this kind gave ancient philosophers many headaches, and are said to have caused the actual death of one of them, Philetas of Cos. Attempts have been made to dismiss the Liar Paradox as a freak of grammar: it is illegitimate to say, in one half of a sentence, that the other half is true or false. As Bickerton notes, however, that objection can be sidestepped by recasting it in the form of two sentences:

1. The sentence printed below is false.
2. The sentence written above is true.

If the second sentence is true, then the first is true; but if the first is true, the second is false. The upshot is that if the second sentence is true, it is also false. This shows that such paradoxes of meaning cannot be corrected using the purgative medicine of syntax. There is no way of disqualifying the sentences by saying that their grammar is wrong.

One way of dealing with the dilemma was suggested by the Polish logician Alfred Tarski. A theory of truth, Tarksi said, cannot be stated in the same language as the language we are talking about. It must be couched in a different, metalanguage, on a higher level. Consider the sentence: *"Snow is white" is true if and only if snow is white.* The phrase in quotation marks is on a higher semantic plane than the unquoted remnant. Tarski's solution was to propose a hierarchy of languages. Truth can be defined for one language, but it must be done in terms of another, which means that no sentence can state that another sentence on its own level is true. Epimenides the Cretan made the mistake of stating truth values and talking about them all on the same level. Tarksi's ascending ladder of languages is open-ended, potentially infinite, each level able to assert the truth of the level beneath it, but not of its own.

Tarski stressed that we must always connect the notion of truth to a specific language. The same expression that is a true sentence in one language could be false or meaningless in another. In spite of the fact that he called his famous paper "A Semantic Theory of Truth," a theory of truth is what he conspicuously failed to deliver. Instead, he gave a definition of the meaning of the word "true." In fact, Tarski changed the word "theory" to "conception" in the body of his paper. As for "true," it does not refer to things as other logical entities do, but describes a property of *sentences*. The focus is on language, not on facts. Ideally, we would identify, for each and every sentence in the language, a definite state of affairs which would "satisfy" that sentence, a formidable, perhaps a hopeless task. We set up the world to correspond to our language, a dangerously Platonic sort of enterprise and one that might make translation impossible.

Karl Popper praised Tarski, but not for giving us what many people suppose he gave: a criterion of truth, a method of deciding whether or not a given statement is true. Tarski's main achievement, in Popper's view, was to rehabilitate *talk* about correspondence and truth. Here "truth" plays a role similar to that of Kant's regulative ideas, reminding us that there is "something like" truth or correspondence, keeping us pointed in the right direction, even if it provides no means of finding truth "or of being sure that we have found it, even if we have found it." So there.

The Liar Paradox is an artificial creation made possible by the peculiar features of ordinary language. It is perfectly at home within the confines of that very rich, very elastic and malleable medium. Trouble looms when we insist on tying linguistic objects, entirely acceptable as such, to the extralinguistic world. We feel the urge to look for witches and flying saucers under the same linguistic compulsion that impels us to search for Truth, not realizing that language is multidimensional, that it possesses special properties peculiar to itself, properties that may not belong to the things language talks about.

Flush with intellectual gratification that there is so much more to language than we might suppose, some thinkers have fallen into the attitude that there must be so much less to truth. One of the most important consequences of the debate over Tarski's "theory" has been, says the scholar Robert Solomon, "the loss of interest in the very concept of Truth with a capital 'T.' In everyday contexts, of course, philosophers, like everyone else, will talk about statements and beliefs being 'true' and 'false' on the basis of a primitive correspondence notion, that is, correspondence to the facts. But philosophically, the power of the word 'Truth' has always dwelled in its strong metaphysical linkage to 'the way the world really is.' And having given up on that grandiose conception of Truth, many philosophers are sometimes inclined to give up the word 'truth' altogether."

Language becomes a source of knowledge in its own right and on its own terms. There is a sense that if we are only "telling the truth" we are not using language at its full stretch, as poets and imaginative liars do. We are squandering its resources, ignoring its higher dimensions, neglecting the potency of syntax to create situations that do not exist. It is as if we were to use a sophisticated, state-of-the-art computer as a typewriter.

Edmund Husserl, the founder of phenomenology, whose life spanned an era from Darwin to the eve of World War II, insisted that the only genuine speech is truthful speech. This was a revival of the "I think" philosophy of Descartes. Cartesian man is the individual in command, master of what he doubts and what he accepts as unquestionable knowledge, on the alert for the slightest hint of deception. He owns his language; it does not own him. There is a definite intention behind his utterances. Meaning is anchored in the firm rock of the conscious mind. A speaker is the supreme authority for the import of the words he uses. Truth resides in the interior of the "I," in that place without space where the mind communicates with itself in silence and is able to say "what it really means."

For Husserl, language is purged of the mendacity which flourishes in the rest of nature. Like Descartes, for whom the clarity and distinctness of an idea in the mind is a sign of its truth, Husserl thought the bedrock of language is "sincerity," the *arche* or bedrock principle from which any theory of it must begin. Lying is rigorously excluded, because it is contrary to that essential core of true belief.

In these days when language has lost its innocence, when it has been given its independence, like some breakaway colony at liberty to make its own laws and decide its own connections with the rest of the world; when the postmodern fashion is to deny the existence of a mental author responsible for the meaning of the sentences she utters or writes, Husserl's ideas seem quaint and hopelessly old-fashioned. "There is something glaringly wrong," decrees Richard Harland, "with a theory of language that has to prescribe 'honesty' as its first principle."

CHAPTER SIXTEEN

Playing the Truth Game

I am sitting with a philosopher in the garden. He says again and again, "I know that that's a tree," pointing to a tree that is near us. Someone else arrives and hears this, and I tell them: "This fellow isn't insane. We are only doing philosophy." —Ludwig Wittgenstein

I am willing to take life as a game of chess in which the first rules are not open to discussion. No one asks why the knight is allowed his eccentric hop, why the castle may only go straight and the bishop obliquely. These things are to be accepted, and with these rules the game must be played: it is foolish to complain of them.
—W. Somerset Maugham

N THE VICTORIAN ERA THERE WAS A marked tendency to treat language as divine, a supernatural gift Darwin's theory could not come close to explaining. As such, it gave access to truths that could be reached via no other vehicle. Max Müller, who quarreled with Darwin on this very point, believed that by using language, we wittingly or unwittingly utter eternal truths. The task of a philologist, which Müller was, is to recover the pristine origins of a language, its innocent, Garden of Eden purity, undistorted by millennia of accretions and modifications, and "bring that divinity to light."

The twentieth century brought the theory of language as godlike, as a hotline to ultimate truth, down to earth with a bump. One of its most unstinting deflaters was Ludwig Wittgenstein, who treated language as a social activity, and secular to the core. We take part in a variety of language "games," each with its own set of rules, and the "truth" of the words we use is determined by those rules. Lying would be equivalent to a soccer player who picks up the ball and runs with it. But that would be "truthful" behavior if the game were rugby or American football. We might note that rugby started with just such a flouting of the rules—how modernist an event!—and just such a conversion of wrong to right. There is a commemorative plaque at Rugby School applauding the "fine disregard for the rules" of the now heroic violator.

Throughout his life, Wittgenstein was mesmerized by the fact that lying comes so naturally to human beings. At the age of eight, he was struck by this question: Why speak the truth, if there is something to be gained by telling a lie? It was his earliest known encounter with philosophy. Unable to arrive at a good solution, he decided that one might as well be untruthful when it offers an advantage.

At that time, Wittgenstein was eager for the approval of others, and was inclined to say whatever would earn the applause of those around him. Later, he wrote of this early experience that if it was not decisive for his future way of life, it "was at any rate characteristic of my nature at that time." Wishing to please his father, he let his family think he was naturally fitted for a career in engineering, though in fact the subject did not appeal to him. As he grew up, however, Wittgenstein altered his attitude to become what he called "a truth seeker." He made a series of confessions about his own shortcomings as a truth-teller, early and late in life. As a schoolboy in Linz, he acknowledged his failings to his elder sister Hermine, an act he subsequently described as showing off.

Many years later, in the summer of 1937, Wittgenstein came back from a stay in Norway and announced abruptly to his friend Fania Pascal, a Russian-born student of philosophy who lived in Cambridge, England, that he had a confession to make. He informed her the matter was urgent and could not wait, which Pascal regarded as bothersome and inconvenient. Wittgenstein had prepared a written disclosure, singling out moments in his life when he had been dishonest, and was anxious to read it to his closest friends—more anxious than they were to hear it. Later, one of these, Rowland Hutt, recalls sitting in a Lyons café in London, in a state of acute embarrassment, across a table from Wittgenstein, who recited his sins in a loud, clear voice.

Fania Pascal, exasperated and busy, listening to the confession delivered in a "stiff and remote" manner, found the whole procedure irritating. During the recitation, she blurted out: "What is it? You want to be perfect?" Replied Wittgenstein: "Of *course* I want to be perfect." The sin which seemed to haunt him most painfully was that, as a young man, teaching in a village school in Austria, he hit a small girl for some misconduct in class and hurt her. When she ran to the headmaster to complain, Wittgenstein denied that he had struck her. "The event stood out as a crisis of his early manhood," Pascal confided to a friend. "It may have been this that made him give up teaching, perhaps made him realize that he ought to live as a solitary. On this occasion he did tell a lie, burdening his conscience for ever." Wittgenstein also confessed that he had more Jewish ancestry than people realized, and had done nothing to disabuse them of their error.

In a notebook entry of 1938, Wittgenstein wrote: "Lying to oneself about oneself, deceiving yourself about the pretence in your own state of will, must have a harmful effect on one's style; for the result will be that you cannot tell what is genuine in the style and what is false. This may explain the falsity of Mahler's style; and it is the same danger that I run myself."

Wittgenstein was born in 1889, the son of an immensely rich iron and steel magnate, at the *fin* of a very eventful *siècle*, which was ending in a period of decadence and doubt. European civilization was regarded by many artists and thinkers of the time as not being in the pink of health. But alongside this queasiness a strong wave of confidence was rising in the possibilities of science and logic. In 1904, Ernst Haeckel, the German biologist and philosopher, announced that the "astonishing" progress in technology, medicine, and other branches of science held out the hope of "a mighty, further elevation of culture in the twentieth century." If such advances were the norm, Darwinists, of whom Haeckel was one, conjectured that the human mind ought to reach a new evolutionary plateau of rationality and wisdom. And if human nature had actually changed, then such ruinous follies as wars and economic disasters might become obsolete. This kind of optimism was still afloat as the fateful steps were being taken toward World War I.

An impulse of scientifically minded thinkers at this time was to crush the pretensions of metaphysics. Idealism, a word first used in

philosophy by Leibniz in the eighteenth century as a description of
Plato's theory of the Forms, regarded mind, not matter, as the key to
understanding the universe. In its early twentieth-century form, idealism was viewed by many, including Wittgenstein, as pernicious, a
friend of authoritarian regimes and of muddled thinking. The
school of logical positivism wanted a return to clarity and simplicity, shunning any aspirations to a new theory of Being, or ultimate
reality.

There was a political ingredient to this project. Metaphysical nonsense in philosophy was mirrored by crazy notions in politics, an
upsurge of fanaticism and unreason, of cranks and extremists and
forebodings of unprecedented brutality. The logical positivists
hoped that by cooling the philosophical temperature, by sobering up
the dreamers, sanity could be restored on the political scene as well.
The supreme model of such reasonableness was science—the methods of science and the language of science.

By purging language of its bad habits, so the argument ran, the
decadence of society might be halted. As a young man, Wittgenstein
shared the view that the metaphysical idealism of the Victorian era
was in fact a mask for authoritarianism and suppression, abetted by
the obscurities that language makes possible. In order to eliminate
these falsehoods, he began to develop a new logic that would analyze
ordinary discourse.

In his early work, typified by the *Tractatus Logico-Philosophicus*, a
work rather traditional in its style and method, Wittgenstein took it
for granted that there is a preestablished correspondence between
the structure of a universal logical language and the structure of the
world. The Logos of the pre-Socratic Greeks was still in place,
though in a different form. Gottlob Frege, a logician with whom
Wittgenstein talked and corresponded, had abandoned a theory of
knowledge for a theory of language, a logical language cleansed of
those aspects of ordinary sentence structure that are not logical and
do not correspond to the way the world is organized. A basic,
unshakable principle for Frege was that logic is concerned with
truth, not with psychology, or the individual mind, nor with circumstances or culture. The laws of truth stay the same forever, in all

places, no matter how "human nature" evolves or regresses over time. The word "true," Frege thought, is the goal of logic, just as "good" is the goal of ethics and "beautiful" the goal of aesthetics. True thoughts are not invented by the mind, but discovered.

What all this comes down to, he decided, is that logic is unnatural, and we ought to accept it as such wholeheartedly, without any qualms or reservations.

One of the deficiencies of everyday discourse is that there are sentences that mean something, yet are neither true nor false. They do not refer to anything actual, though they may seem to refer. We can talk about an English-speaking rabbit, or a vanilla-flavored sunset, a ten-foot cockroach, without any insult to language itself. Ordinary speech can be witty, ironical, paradoxical, whimsical, guileful, enigmatic. It can tell lies just to avoid boring its audience, in the confidence that the audience knows perfectly well they are lies. A logically perfect language, on the other hand, would ensure that every well-formed expression has a reference and therefore a truth value: it is either true or false. Frege thought phrases like "the will of the people," which refer to nothing actual, were dangerous in the hands of demagogues, because they are a form of untruth that ordinary language typically permits.

Some thinkers, influenced by Frege, dreamed of a language so pure, "you could see right through it." There was a huge emphasis on language, in large part because it excused philosophers from messing with matters mental, getting bogged down in psychology. Anything that happened inside the human head was unscientific and must be ignored. The early Wittgenstein did imagine a purified form of language possessing a certain transparency, as if it were a window onto the truth about the world. Logical rules would ensure this pellucid accord between words and world and provide a preestablished harmony, no matter what Darwin thought.

In the end, however, Wittgenstein lost faith in the vision of such perfect compatibility, rather as Darwin cooled on the idea of perfect adaptation. After World War II, he came to regard the see-through theory of language as an actual obstacle to setting up a connection between sentences and what they picture. There had been an uncom-

fortable paradox in the work of the logical positivists, who treated
the *Tractatus* as a sort of Bible. Logic is a language without meaning,
without reference. It is completely general and we can manipulate its
symbols while remaining in complete ignorance of what the symbols
represent. That is part of its curious power. It is contentless,
unworldly, a universe of its own. Yet it is essential in logic that a
proposition be shown to be either true or false. And here reference
raises its importunate head. What is more, immense difficulties
arose over how a statement was to be made true by reference. Verifying a proposition involves experience, and experience is a tricky sort
of concept, later to be treated with great suspicion by Wittgenstein.
And if only those statements are acceptable that can be verified, we
at once eliminate the whole of ethics, religion, art, poetry, and music,
a rather breathtaking sweepout.

Wittgenstein grew disillusioned with his early theories before the
logical positivists did. He adopted a completely different view of language. In particular, he turned fiercely against the notion that philosophy should make scientific sorts of statements describing a state
of affairs. One should dirty up language a little, in a way that scientists would never dream of doing. If language is too chaste, too vir-
ginal, too pure and immaculately logical, Wittgenstein decided, it
provides no traction on which the mind can work. Instead of thinking of language as a vehicle for arriving at a truth external to itself,
he took a fresh look at the vehicle. Ordinary language might be too
"coarse and material" to give a clear window onto reality, but in that
case, how odd it is that we are able to do so much with it as it stands.
The closer we look at workaday language, the less it seems to conform to the Fregean ideal. The crystalline purity of logic, Wittgenstein said, was a requirement, "but the requirement is now in danger
of becoming empty. We have to go onto slippery ice where there is no
friction and so in a certain sense the conditions are ideal, but also,
just because of that, we are unable to walk. We want to walk: so we
need *friction*. Back to the rough ground!"

Now more than ever, the problems of philosophy become the
problems of language. The traditional concerns of philosophy, the
constitution of time and space, the nature of cause and effect, reali-

ty, free will, truth, are marginalized to make way for it. This is a quintessentially modernist step. Language is no longer simple, and its
frictional properties that make for ease of walking also render it
opaque; interestingly and provocatively so. "We prefer now to equate
language with thought," John Sturrock says, "and instead of looking
through it, at reality, we look at it, in an attempt to understand how
we first acquire it, and then use it."

Nietzsche had said that a person who finds language interesting
for its own sake has a mentality that is quite unlike that of someone
who treats it as a medium for thought. Part of the difference was that
both he and Wittgenstein believed the principles of language fix the
rules of truth, and not the other way round.

One of the crucial questions on which the early *Tractatus* and
Wittgenstein's later *Philosophical Investigations*, which appeared in
translation in 1953, go their separate ways, is whether there is a universal form of language. In the *Tractatus*, the answer is yes. For that
reason, "Truth" can be regarded as an absolute which holds across
the entire spectrum of sentences. A listener knows when someone is
lying or pretending or indulging in various types of irony. In
Wittgenstein's later work, truth is a much more elusive commodity,
because it plays different roles in different "language games." Paradoxically, as he became more intently possessed of a belief in strict
truthfulness as an essential component of an honorable life, truth
lost its status as an absolute in his philosophy. Much the same happened to Freud. In the *Tractatus*, a sentence presupposes the whole of
the rest of language, as it does in Saussure's structuralist theory. For
the later Wittgenstein, however, a sentence entails only a particular
language game, sufficient to itself, with its own rules and boundary
markers, and there are infinitely many different kinds of such games.

Lying is one type of language game, and so is pretending, bluffing,
feigning, putting the other person on, saying the opposite of what
we really believe. We are not born knowing these language games.
They must be acquired. In the *Investigations*, Wittgenstein says: "A
child has much to learn before it can pretend. (A dog cannot be a
hypocrite, but neither can he be sincere.)" If there is no insincerity,
even the transparent kind, the word "sincere" would have no mean-

ing. And he adds: "Lying is a language game that needs to be learned like any other."

Language games bear a certain resemblance to Kant's theory of the categories of the understanding, "truths" that are not given entirely by the world, but are partly constructed by the mind. The Kantian categories define the limits of the knowable. A language game, a situation in which the rules for the use of words are given more by social convention and custom than by anything else, defines the limits of the sayable. These rules are what Wittgenstein means when he talks about the "grammar" of sentences. Kant thought we can make sense of the world by not straying outside the confines of the categories. Wittgenstein warned of the perils of roving beyond the limits of a specific game. How "queer" it would be if somone said, out of the blue: "Shark is a five-letter word." The remark would sound bizarre, even crazy. But suppose it was in reply to a friend working a crossword puzzle, who asked: "Fish enforcing a high interest, five letters, any ideas?" Then it would make perfect sense. "If I make the same statement where there is some need for it," Wittgenstein said, "then, although I am not a jot more certain of its truth, it seems to me to be perfectly justified and everyday." Truth is a matter of being appropriate to the restricted microworld of the game. Speak the identical words outside that world and it "appears in a false light." There are things external to the language game of which God himself cannot say anything. In his late phase, Wittgenstein said: "The *truth* of certain empirical propositions belongs to our frame of reference."

As his ideas developed, Wittgenstein held to this Fregean notion of the public nature of meaning, but he could not accept that understanding is rooted in the concept of truth. Understanding was simply a matter of obeying the rules of the language game in question. That means truth cannot be a purely private affair. Truth is a matter of what the community accepts. Public usage determines the meaning of words and sentences. There is no such thing as a private language. The preeminence of culture elbows aside such staples of philosophy as logic, the preestablished harmony, the human mind's ceaseless hankering after the ineffable, Kant's *Naturlangen*. Wittgenstein gave culture pride of place. It became an *arche*, a first principle. The theory of language as a universal mirror of reality is now the enemy, a phantom beckoning us on in a deluded chase after the big, unanswerable questions of metaphysics. In its place is an open-ended array of language games, each autonomous, each with its own rules. There can be no such thing as an "absolute truth" under these circumstances. Something can be true in one game but false in another, because the rules are different, just as the rules of hockey are different from the rules of basketball.

As a result, no one language game is privileged above any other. There is a leveling out, a flattening and egalitarian espousal of the horizontal as opposed to the vertical dimension. The science game is no better and no worse than the poetry game, or the irony game.

In Wittgenstein's view, a language game is not "reasonable"—or unreasonable, for that matter. It does not have a definite foundation. It is just "there, like our life." He expounded on this theory in the early 1930s in a series of lectures which also took an iconoclastic stance toward the idea that mathematics is the discovery of truths, a question that had been debated for thousands of years. It is beside the point, he said, whether mathematics is true in itself or provides us with true statements about the physical world. Mathematics is just a technique, a tool. It is not "about" anything. Its propositions should not be seen as either true or false.

Wittgenstein's influence was huge, in part because of his mesmerizing, intense personality, which demanded utter loyalty. A Wittgenstein cult existed at Cambridge while he taught there. Students and some of the younger philosophers would affect his mannerisms, imitate his voice, his gestures, his walk. Gilbert Ryle wrote that at meetings of the Moral Science Club, "veneration for Wittgenstein was so incontinent that mentions, for example my mentions, of any other philosopher, were greeted with jeers." Desmond Lee, an undergraduate, likened Wittgenstein to Socrates in respect of the "numbing" effect he had on his youthful audience. There was a contempt for thoughts other than the Master's. Wittgenstein himself claimed with pride never to have read a word of Aristotle, a very modernist dismissal of history.

Criticism of him came to be just as vehement. Some of it centered on his antipathy to science, suggesting he had almost frivolously dismantled centuries of intellectual searching for a coherent and unified view of nature. Ernest Gellner was one of Wittgenstein's most formidable adversaries, complaining in particular that he subverted one of Western thought's most precious triumphs of the intellect, the belief that the world can be seen as a single idiom in which all facts cohere in some fashion. That, Gellner, said, "seems to me one of the most important and positive achievements of mankind. Science is not possible without it. The attainment of a single conceptual currency, in principle, is at least as important for intellectual advance as the attainment of monetary currency."

Such a worldview, Gellner thought, prepared mankind for the possibility of the notion of "Nature," a unitary and orderly system which could be investigated by observation and experiment. Wittgenstein sabotaged that movement by replacing unity of vision with differences, plurality, separate "language games" connected only within society, not by the necessity of logic, each game composing its own peculiar "truth." Gellner called this "a collective infantile regression for all mankind." Followers of Wittgenstein, ferocious in their allegiance, fostered the idea that the "spirit of the community" (Wittgenstein had called it a "form of life" constituted by a language game) is the only basis we have for the principles of human behavior, whether moral, artistic, scientific, or what have you. Cultures validate themselves and the "norms of conduct and sanity" they create.

The chief role of language in Wittgenstein's later philosophy is not to refer, name, describe, or make statements that are scientifically watertight. Language is not really an object at all. The meaning of a word is not an allusion to some thing or fact, but the use to which the word is put within the sentence, within the language game. All philosophical dilemmas are a result of using words according to the rules of the wrong language game, trying to make them do work they are not fitted to do, like using a screwdriver as a hammer.

There are countless different kinds of sentences, different kinds of *use*. Among them:

Giving orders and obeying them.
Reporting an event.
Speculating about an event.
Forming and testing a hypothesis.
Making up a story and reading it.
Play-acting.
Singing catches.
Guessing riddles.
Making a joke.
Solving a problem in practical arithmetic.
Translating from one language into another.
Asking, thanking, cursing, greeting, praying.

Wittgenstein seems to be saying that in a language game, words are responsible, not to what is real, what is "true," but to what has been agreed upon as real. The players of the game agree that they all mean the same thing when they use a word, but that is not because they would have meant it anyway. They are predisposed to mean the same thing by the fact of taking part in the game.

"In the beginning was the deed." Wittgenstein quotes Goethe's *Faust.* And later: "Words are deeds." It is the taking part, the playing of the game that produces meaning. And this puts truth and falsehood into a new kind of relationship. It is the difference between reading about a game of baseball and actually facing the pitcher, bat in hand, the crowd in a banshee howl, the outcome in doubt and tremendous things at stake. Something similar is the case with religion. Christianity is not based on a historical truth. Instead, it offers us a "historical" narrative and says: "Now, believe!" But wait a minute. You can't believe it as you would a history textbook or a newspaper report, on the spot, in a couple of hours and done with it. It takes a lifetime of believing, through thick and thin, for better or worse, for richer or poorer. It must occupy an entirely different place in your life.

In faith, moreover, there are various language games, and it is important to note which one you are playing. There are sundry levels of devoutness, and each has its proper form of expression. A doctrine might be right at one level but disastrously wrong at another.

For example, the Pauline doctrine of predestination is "ugly nonsense, irreligiousness" at the level at which Wittgenstein found himself. He could only understand it incorrectly, so it was null and void for him. The point is that a person can use a doctrine in her own life in a way that would be impossible for someone at a different level.

"Queer as it sounds," Wittgenstein said, "the historical accounts in the Gospels might, historically speaking, be demonstrably false, and yet belief would lose nothing by this: *not*, however, because it concerns 'universal truths of reason'! Rather, because historical proof (the historical proof game) is irrelevant to belief. This message (the Gospels) is seized on by men believingly (i.e. lovingly). *That* is the certainty characterizing this particular acceptance-as-true, not something *else*." We have different attitudes, he adds, even to different species of fiction.

There are those who deplore the choice of the term "language game." Bryan Magee, the Oxford philosopher, calls it "a disaster." "It makes it sound as if what he's doing, or what he's talking about, is somehow frivolous. And it feeds a very specific anti-philosophical prejudice that is quite widespread outside the subject, the idea that philosophy is all just playing with words, that it's all just a game, and that philosophers are people who are merely concerned superficially with language." Whereas in fact Wittgenstein had only meant that language is an activity that obeys certain rules already there in society. Words have meaning only to the extent that there are *public* criteria governing their use, criteria that are impersonal and social, which explains his curious preoccupation with the idea that a "private language," one unique to an individual and internal to him, is an impossibility.

Wittgenstein, like Kant, was not an implacable enemy of metaphysics. In the *Tractatus*, he simply shelved all metaphysical questions by ruling that they could not be spoken of, but only contemplated in silence. The later Wittgenstein refused to have any truck with the notion of an overarching metaphysical scheme, confining all such speculation to their appropriate language games. Meaning and truth are an internal function of language, but not of language as an entirety. "Truth" is simply the way we use the term "truth." "For the late Wittgenstein," says Hilary Lawson, "not only is there no objective reality, but there is no single meaning. Any sentence or proposition has as many meanings as there are contexts. Furthermore, anyone who desires to provide a final account is to be treated as if suffering from a philosophical disease. There are no answers in any ultimate sense, there are only responses within language."

Making a truthful life was one of Wittgenstein's perennial themes. It takes time and effort and the script is not written in advance. Unlike logic and mathematical theorems, this cannot be handed to anyone on a plate. "Often, it is only very slightly more disagreeable to tell the truth than to lie; about as difficult as drinking bitter rather than sweet coffee; and yet I still have a strong inclination to lie," he wrote in 1940. To speak the truth requires self-mastery, being comfortably at home in it. It cannot be done by someone who still lives in falsehood and reaches out from falsehood toward truth just now and then.

What makes truth so difficult is that language often tricks us, lures us into mistaking the kind of game we are playing. Philosophy spins its wheels, keeps poring over the same problems that Plato grappled with, because language has stayed the same and still seduces us into asking the same questions, century after century. "As long as there continues to be a verb 'to be' that looks as if it functions in the same way as 'to eat' and 'to drink,' as long as we still have the adjectives 'identical,' 'true,' 'false,' 'possible,' as long as we continue to talk of a river of time, of an expanse of space, etc. etc., people will keep stumbling over the same puzzling difficulties and find themselves staring at something which no explanation seems capable of clearing up."

The early Wittgenstein, the one who believed in a universal language whose structure matched up to the structure of the world, had said that in principle we can foresee any proposition, since it is just a new arrangement of the same old units. A new language game, by contrast, implies a new "form of life," where words are *used* in a different way. We can pretend, joke, say something that is blatantly false, knowing it will be taken as such, walk on all fours and growl like a lion if we please. To be at home in a language game, you need to have the equipment, the imagination, the worldly smarts, to understand what is going on and why everyone is not simply "telling the truth."

Truth and falsehood are thus radically destabilized. They are relative, local, conditioned by the rules of an autonomous language game, rules that are nothing like the laws of nature. There is no universal principle shared by all language games. Wittgenstein's postmodern successors assented to the notion of language games, but took them to be even more nugatory than their author may ever have intended. Not only is a game subject to the whims of social fashion and impromptu novelty. Now we cannot even be sure who is playing the game, whether they are playing in sober observance of the rules, or just fooling around.

Seriousness is not a ubiquitous rule of language games. Wittgenstein is apt to celebrate frivolity with unexpected bravura. "If people did not sometimes do silly things, nothing intelligent would ever get done." That is the aphoristic Wittgenstein of the notebooks. Certainly he had an intense dislike of pomposity, a horror of windbags and academic desiccation, a fondness for Hollywood Wild West movies and feeble jokes. He described his philosophical style as "poetry." All this presages the coming of frivolity and play in later, postmodern thought.

Lurking in the modernist core of Wittgenstein's mature philosophy is the postmodernist suspicion of anything sovereign, any supreme axiom that everything else must obey, any Big Truth to which smaller truths are subservient. Or any Big Falsehood, either. Around 1930, when his ideas were moving away from the "preestablished harmony" thesis of the *Tractatus*, he told a colleague that what he was doing in philosophy was quite different from physics, which is concerned with the truth or falsity of states of affairs. His business was to distinguish sense from nonsense. And a sentence does not have to be true to make sense. It simply has to *mean* something. Verifying the truth of a statement is simply one way among many others of getting clear about the *use* of a word or sentence.

There is a political dimension to the late twentieth-century hostility to truth as carrying the stigma of authority, élitism, hierarchy, tyranny, oppresssion, and totalitarianism. We have come a long way from the Enlightenment and the co-editor of the great *Encyclopédie*, Jean d'Alembert, whose central vision was the unity of truth, with each science simply the expansion of a single axiom and knowledge as a whole an unbroken chain of propositions. "The Universe," d'Alembert wrote, "for someone who was able to take it in as a whole from a single standpoint, would appear, if one may so put it, as a unitary fact and a single great truth." Twentieth-century deconstruction shows a contempt for any claim to have found definitive truth, value, or meaning, apart from and surpassing a given domain of discourse. Metatheories are out. And this, according to the fashion of the day, is reason for rejoicing. The dismantling of the single Truth, which caused anxiety in the Victorian era, is a necessary act of anti-élitism, good news and a reason to celebrate, to be lighthearted and playful. Have a good time, is the message of the millennial nihilists. Don't worry, be happy. A new perspective is as good as or better than something as solemn and grand as the secret of the universe, which would mean that knowledge had come to an end. "What a Copernicus or a Darwin really achieved," Wittgenstein said, "was not the discovery of a true theory, but of a fertile new point of view."

Yet this conflicts with Wittgenstein's own obsession with the importance of truth-telling, and his shame at the memory of lying. When he denied that he had struck a child in his school class, he was not "playing a language game," or adopting a fertile new point of view. He was saying that something which happened, which other children witnessed, that he knew to be the case, was not true. And it was a viper in his bosom. Ernest Gellner not only faults Wittgenstein for making the world harder to understand but also for elevating the autonomy of language and culture to such an extent as to "lead to a sad underrating of the regrettable, but only too blatantly real, *non-*semantic constraints in human history, springing from violence and poverty."

All the same, Wittgenstein democratizes truth, perhaps even socializes it. His is a philosophy of the bottom up. We do not have meaning, and then a way of expressing it. That would be far too aristocratic a thesis. What we have are words that do *work*, that labor to produce meaning, a blue-collar linguistic proletariat. Wittgenstein himself was a devotee of the ordinary, of the unpretentious, of other ranks rather than the officers' mess, of greasy spoon diners, not fancy restaurants, of furniture so simple it took months to obtain, of clothes chosen meticulously for their down-at-heel look, of pulp detective story magazines instead of the high masterpieces of literature. He took menial jobs, teaching poor children in a remote village, working as a gardener at the Klosteneuberg Monastery near Vienna, and as a hospital orderly.

Whether he was a socialist in the conventional sense is a complicated question. Certainly his encounter at Cambridge in 1929 with Piero Saffra, an Italian economist and Marxist, had a profound influence on his transformation as a philosopher. Saffra was a close friend of Antonio Gramsci, a Communist leader then in prison. There is a famous anecdote in which Wittgenstein insisted to Saffra that a proposition and what it describes must have the same logical form. Saffra did not reply, but simply brushed his chin with the tips of his fingers in a classic Italian gesture, taunting his interrogator: "What is the logical form of *that*?" That single incident helped to doom the preestablished harmony doctrine. Wittgenstein later told a friend that Saffra taught him to look at philosophical problems the way an anthropologist might, treating language not as something in splendid isolation but immersed in the flux and hurly-burly of life. No language game can be described without taking into account the way of life of the community that plays it.

In 1934, Wittgenstein took Russian lessons with Fania Pascal, who was married to a Marxist thinker, to prepare for a visit to the Soviet Union. He wanted to work there, preferably on a collective farm. His attitude to Marxism was that it was bad in theory but good in practice, and practice was the more important of the two. Theory was cold, gray, and untruthful. "I am a communist *at heart*," he told a friend. Many of his friends were Marxists; it was in 1935 that Anthony Blunt, much later unmasked as a spy for the Soviets, made his fateful trip to Moscow. Wittgenstein was not enchanted with Stalinist Russia and did not stay, but he admired the country for its lack of class distinctions, and, above all, because it provided *work* for the people. That, he considered, was better than all the theories in the world. It was all of a piece with his view that meaning is the result of the work words do and his attachment to the ordinary, the particular, the lowbrow. "It was," says Wittgenstein's biographer Ray Monk, "one more manifestation of his perennial desire to join the ranks."

CHAPTER SEVENTEEN

Giving Truth a Bad Name

Lies are usually attempts to make everything simpler—for the liar—than it really is, or ought to be. —Adrienne Rich

The last time we had a president who kept his promise never to lie to us—Jimmy Carter—we all fell asleep. —Charles McCarry

 COMMONSENSE VIEW OF LANGUAGE IS that a thought arises in the head and is then encoded in words, whose function it is to *reduce* the number of alternative readings of the messaage, to fix just a single meaning and close off all the others. The original thought is thus reliably preserved along the channel of language, and, like Montaigne's definition of truth, has "one face only." But what if this eminently simple picture is wrong, actually back to front? What if the whole process acts to multiply meanings, to produce the hydra-headed beast of falsehood?

What, exactly, is the relation of language to thought? That seemingly innocent question has given rise to a good deal of iconoclastic thinking about truth and falsehood which is not innocent in the least. In some cases it is politically motivated; in a few, downright mischievous. The received wisdom of postmodernism is that, absent language, thought does not exist, which puts words unconditionally in the driver's seat.

In the Enlightenment, speech and thought were two separate and dissimilar activities. Language, as a carrier or vehicle, communicated thoughts accurately from one person to another. Truth was its single, essential property. Locke had made much of the thesis that language, as communication, is a social practice, and therefore improvable. Language does not exist because man is a rational being, but because he is "a sociable creature and language is the great instrument and common tie of society."

Subversive of this belief, however, was the argument that language originated as an expression of the emotions and was not primarily a communications medium. This idea was advanced in 1735 by Thomas Blackwell, who suggested that early speech was akin to song. A few years later, in 1773, the gentleman polymath Lord Monboddo, in *Of the Origin and Progress of Language*, wrote that language was just a refinement of the "natural cries of the animal." Early Romantic theorists emphasized the kinship of words with animal vocalizing. They saw language, especially poetic language, as the expression of individual feeling, not a copying or mirroring of reality, or an invention by civilized people who had reached the age of reason. Kant's pupil Gottfried von Herder's prize essay *On the Origin of Language*, published in 1772, stressed the affinity with animal cries. For hard-core Romantics, language in the full sense was not a conveyor of information but the unbridled and only partly controllable outpouring of the artist's genius, and at that time genius was still equated with truth.

Conversely, there arose in the nineteenth century, based on a suspicion of words as words, the idea that truth is possible only by the medium of gesture, of body language. Hugo von Hoffmannsthal, Richard Strauss's librettist, planned to write a play in which a barefaced liar opts to train as a dancer "because he adores the truth, and dancing is the only profession in which there is *nothing but* truth."

Here were the seeds of a curious idea: that words are not properly or primarily communication. Darwin regarded the power of speech as a biological occurrence, originating in the primitive sounds made by nonhuman species: crying, yawning, laughing. Such ventings were only incidentally messages containing information. Language was also a mechanism for the association of ideas; a specific sound came to be linked to a certain type of event. Communication itself

does not loom large in Darwin's discussions of the evolution of artic-
ulate speech. He kept a diary of the activities of one of his children
from birth and decided that "instinctive cries" are later modified to
become a means of communication. Implicit in these speculations
was the idea that as an impromptu display of immediate emotion,
language in its origins was inherently truthful and candid.

Tying language closely to thought helped to promote the view,
mentioned by Leibniz as early as 1697, that words function not just
to convey the mind's products to other minds, but also to clarify and
organize them for the individual's personal benefit, in "inward conversation with himself." It was a means of organizing one's ideas.
That was congenial to the Romantic conception of language as a
kind of living entity in its own right, an organism, animate, not a useful contrivance for transporting information hither and thither. It
had a life of its own, a private truth of its own. The notion of truth
as meanings shared, demonstrable and intelligible to all, was an ideal
of the Enlightenment, but was uncongenial to the Romantic temperament. For the Romantics there were private truths, perhaps very
important and significant ones, that might become falsehoods if
translated into public form. One of the defining traits of the Romantic movement, the literary critic Tony Tanner suggests, is "the refusal
of the intensely feeling individual to have the meaning of his experience settled by other people's language. Indeed, there is a notion running through Romantic thought that all language is to some extent
a falsification, since it involves transposing unique inner feelings
into public terms and forms: there is even the feeling that, just as the
laws and taboos of a society determine how a man acts, so its language determines how he feels." Dictionaries were considered anti-
Romantic, at best no help at all and at worst killers of truth.

Noam Chomsky, arguably the twentieth century's most original
but hardly uncontroversial theorist of language, put a question
mark over the claim that language is "essentially" a vehicle of communication, and if it is, whether that is a help or a hindrance to
understanding its structure. Chomsky talks of language as if it were
a biological organ, analogous to the heart or lungs, and like them
coded into the genes. The heart pumps blood and the lungs provide

oxygen. That is their function in the body. What, then, is the "function" of language? A scientist studying the heart would certainly take into account the fact that it is the engine of circulation. Yet he or she would also take a look at the structure of the heart and its history, keeping an open mind as to how to explain the structure in terms of purpose.

The same applies to language, which has disconcerting properties not accounted for in terms of their role as message carriers. Just as Darwin had noted the appearance of "useless" organs in the anatomy of various species, Chomsky maintains that only parts of language are usable. At times, the way language is designed makes it difficult for us to say what we mean. "Language design," Chomsky says, "appears to be dysfunctional in certain respects, some rather basic." It is elegant, certainly, but only if we think of it apart from its utility, which is a very odd thing to do if we are treating it as biology, as a product of natural selection. Other biological organs are famous for their large amounts of redundancy, which protect them from injury and perhaps avoid difficult feats of computation by providing alternative modes of operation. But one of the surprises of modern linguistics is to discover that, in principle, language does not work that way. Theories that assume language possesses plentiful redundancy, asymmetries, and formal inelegance have very often turned out to be quite wrong. In one of his naughty-boy moods, Chomsky calls language design "beautiful but not usable."

One of the cardinal properties of language, "structure dependence," which Chomsky regards as hard-wired into the mind at birth, and thus a general feature of an interesting class of grammatical rules, cannot be explained if we look at it just as a tool for communication. Structure dependence means that language rules do not concern themselves with the order of words in a sentence, but with the structure of the sentence as a whole, even when there is no obvious need to do so. That is one reason why a theory of syntax is so complicated. As a communications device, language would work just as well without structure dependence. In fact, much better, since there would be no need to analyze all parts of a sentence simultaneously. Every known language has grammatical rules which are not logically necessary for communication, and, conversely, all that is known about comparative linguistics suggests that languages did not evolve from some kind of primitive communication system that lacked a grammar.

Unhelpful too, on this account, is the argument that the "meaning" of a sentence can be fully explained in terms of what a speaker intends the listener to believe or do. A leading sponsor of this view is the philosopher Paul Grice, who defined communication as the recognition by a listener of a speaker's intention. Communication is a cooperative effort, and as such should conform to certain definite rules, or maxims of conversation, which Grice enumerates. The maxims presuppose an almost Utopian level of gentlemanly conduct on the part of a speaker and an old-fashioned standard of truthfulness that George Washington might have found irksome. They remind one of the early Puritanism of the Royal Society. A speaker should give not too much but just enough information, hold his tongue about what he believes to be false, or for which he has insufficient evidence, be relevant, be brief and orderly, avoid obscurity of expression and ambiguity. Tell that to Henry James. Would we want to have dinner with such a person, such an impeccably polite maxim observer? And is that the *purpose* of language?

Says Chomsky, language can be meaningful in the absence of so much as an attempt to communicate, "as when I use language to express or clarify my thoughts, *with the intent to deceive*, to avoid an embarrassing silence or in a dozen other ways" (my italics).

Jean-Paul Sartre pinpointed 1848 as the watershed year when the Enlightenment ideal of liberating people from the "spell of words," the verbal mare's nest of medieval argumentation, faded, and literature turned in on itself. Until then, language had been treated for the most part as a centrifugal force, its trajectory aimed outward, at public life, its role to subvert supersitition, ignorance, fear, the thrall of priests and absolute rulers who use language to confuse and oppress the masses, "bladders blown up by wind." Writing a century later than that hinge year, Sartre in *What Is Literature?* vehemently opposed the aesthetic mode of writing as wordplay, arguing that language must function as communication, something useful and public.

"The function of a writer is to call a spade a spade," Sartre said. "There is nothing more deplorable than the literary practice which, I believe, is called poetic prose and which consists of using words for the obscure harmonics which resound about them and which are made up of vague meanings which are in contradiction with clear signification." Sartre went on to say: "Our first duty is to reestablish language in its dignity. After all, we think with words. We would have to be quite vain to believe that we are concealing ineffable beauties which the word is unworthy of expressing. And then, I distrust the incommunicable. It is the source of all violence."

Iris Murdoch, commenting on this statement by Sartre, notes that "We can no longer take language for granted as a medium of communication. Its transparency has gone. We are like people who for a long time looked out of a window without noticing the glass—and then one day began to notice this too." Such a transformation of language from a means of transmission to an object in its own right began as early as Thomas Hobbes in England, but, as Murdoch says, "it is only within the last century that it has taken the form of a blinding enlightenment or a devouring obsession." The advance of scientific discovery in the Victorian age, spurred on by new discoveries in mathematics, turned upside down the view of words as an instrument. Language no longer named things, but, like mathematical formulae, interpreted and predicted what impinges on the senses. Words decide the contours of reality. The search for "strange objects" lurking in the dictionary was stopped, the meaning of poetic and religious statements became questionable. The immediate result of this move, says Murdoch, "was a loss of confidence in the communicative power of language in these spheres. Language as exact communication seems possible only against the background of a common world." Nowadays we cannot even imagine an environment in which all thinking people have a common purpose and common values, a decidedly unfashionable idea. This was a perhaps inevitable "surrender to the incommunicable."

In the postmodern era, Roland Barthes, an admirer of the poems of Mallarmé, champion of a literature of noncommitment, who regarded it as a sort of lie to claim that a word stands for the truth of things in the world, insisted that literature is not a collection of messages but an encounter with language per se, and is made all the more so by virtue of the discontinuity between language and the world. Thus it marginalizes truth by demolishing its opposition to falsehood. Barthes called this flattening out of truth and untruth "writing degree zero." In a manifesto published in the 1960s which took a jab at Sartre, he said of the role of the writer: "By identifying himself with language, the author loses all claim to truth, for language is precisely that structure whose very goal (at least historically, since the Sophists), once it is no longer rigorously transitive, is to neutralize the true and the false. But what he obviously gains is the power to disturb the world, to afford it the dizzying spectacle of *praxis* without sanction. That is why it is absurd to ask an author for 'commitment.' "

Barthes was a great defender of the pleasures of reading, and in particular the pleasure a reader obtains by ignoring the intentions, the messages and communications originating with the author, inventing his own unique rendition of the text. Marcel Proust had hinted at such a position when he charged Ruskin with "idolatry" for writing as if "truth were a material object that could be inserted by a writer into a book and taken out intact by the reader." Proust knew that sentences on a page are more valuable when taken "not as a substitute for the experiences they describe but as a stimulus to related mental experiences" in the mind of the reader. Barthes, whose favorite literary figure was Proust, aimed to dislodge the author from his place of privilege. He talked about the "death of the author" and wrote in the year of upheaval 1968: "We now know that a text is not a line of words releasing a single 'theological' meaning (the 'message' of an Author-God) but a multidimensional space in which a variety of writings, none of them original, blend and clash." In a provocative phrase, Barthes held that the function of literature is most fully satisfied by "unreadable" works that fly in the face of normal canons of intelligibility.

Diametrically opposed to such postmodern orothodoxy, with its built-in presumption that the Enlightenment agenda is exhausted, is the somewhat forbidding figure of Jurgen Habermas, who insists that modernity, with reason as its central instrument, is not *passé* or obsolete; its potential has simply not been developed. Habermas was in his teens when World War II ended, and was aghast to discover that the adults around him were able to shut out the horror of Nazi atrocities, discussing the Nuremberg Trials in terms of procedural questions and whether or not the trials were fair, instead of being "struck silent" by the abomination of the crimes. It flew in the face of reason, suggested an insularity, a total breakdown in the communication of what the trials were all about. Habermas was attracted to the work of Dewey, with its sense of the importance of a critical community, imperfect and for that very reason radically open, arguing and debating in the public arena. Habermas talks about an "ideal speech situation" in which what is said or written is not based on individual desires, but on a general reasonableness, a consensus of all the parties. An assertion is not justified by the intention of the author, but by whether it has the status of a universal truth.

Habermas uses the startlingly unfashionable phrase "the cooperative search for truth." That is a Utopian concept, but it operates like a Kantian regulative principle, pointing an imperfect society in the direction of a perfect one, in which a speaker would communicate the pure truth, and enable his listeners to share it, by virtue of the fact that the intention "to deceive, to manipulate, to persuade" had been eliminated. Ideal speech is different from all other kinds of social encounter, which are geared to success and the attainment of a specific purpose. Sincerity is a key component, which Habermas controversially contends is built into our ordinary everyday conversations. The means to the discovery of truth is already there in common speech; we "talk ourselves into" a consensus. Language is not an art object, but a means of converting private knowledge into mutual understanding. Philosophy is no longer the bailiwick of solitary geniuses of sometimes odd eccentricities, but a cooperative enterprise not unlike physics or astronomy.

Truth in this scheme is cumulative, always increasing, always leading to more freedom, as long as the openness of human communication is preserved. Anyone who speaks a language is by that very fact a member of the community of the potentially enlightened, united by the agreement that comes with communication. But Habermas is not popular with some postmodernists; they suspect he has his own political agenda, which is not theirs.

If language is not primarily communication, its obligation to sincerity and truthfulness is relaxed. Instead, its chief role might be as a producer of possibilities, the more the merrier. The notion that falsehood increases the scope of differences and so contributes to the richness of life, especially if you regard life as a form of art, is behind the argument, epidemic in the postmodern era, that strict truth-telling is a sign of depleted resources, a psychological disorder, a character defect, a kind of linguistic anorexia. Without at least the capacity to lie, a person is not fully human and may even require professional help.

One of the most telling examples of this seemingly perverse theory occurs in the study of autistic children. A reliable indicator of autism seems to be an incompetence in the arts of hiding, pretending, dissembling, and lying. It is thought that autism is the absence of the normal ability to make sense of what another person is up to. An autistic child lacks a "theory of mind," essential for proper social relations. Language is deviant. There is an "insistence on sameness," and an avoidance of difference. An autistic child is likely to be deficient in understanding false belief, not knowing whether another person is under a mistaken impression or can be tricked into acquiring it.

Chimpanzees can be trained to point to an empty container, leading another chimp to assume, erroneously, that there is food inside it. Does that show that chimps have a theory of mind, missing in autistic children, on the evidence that they are able to lie, to plant a false idea in another mind? Perhaps not. A better test with humans is to hide a treasure in one of four boxes, leaving footprints which lead to the chosen box. A child is instructed to "make it difficult" for another person to find the treasure. A person who had a theory of mind would wipe out the telltale tracks. The results of this simple test show that there is a "cognitive watershed" in a child's understanding of the mind. At about the age of four, the child begins to understand that the other person believes to be true what she knows to be false. Before that age, children tend to assume that another person will believe what they themselves know to be true. Autistic children with a mental age well over four, however, are not able to grasp that others have false beliefs, and do not attempt to manipulate those beliefs to their own advantage.

It is touching, and tragic, to find that parents will sometimes express great relief when their autistic child, otherwise intellectually able, tells his first clumsy lie in his teens. One mother, intensely concerned about her sixteen-year-old autistic son, who attacked her physically and threw food and furniture about, was most alarmed at his social ineptitude, describing him as "too good, totally honest and unable to lie." So literal-minded was the child that if told to go to bed at ten o'clock, he would do so whether or not there was anyone in the house to check up on him. Most baffling to these children is the double-bluff deception, offering truth as a decoy. They would be hopelessly uncomprehending if told the joke about the man in the Polish train, lying to his companion by telling the truth that he was going to Krakow.

In the case of a boy suffering from aphasia, who could speak but could not tell a lie, he was described as losing "all notion of the possible." The boy could refer only to the actual, as if using one of those artificial languages, all the rage in the seventeenth century, designed to match one and only one word to one thing, and for that reason totally inadequate to the requirements of everyday existence. John Forrester tells the story of an elderly lady who, as a little girl, was told by her mother that she could always tell when someone was lying by looking into their eyes. The girl lived in fear of this awesome power until one day at the age of five or six, coming home from school, she lied to her mother about some delicate matter. Her mother searched the girl's eyes, but seemed to notice nothing amiss. The girl felt a sensation of immense relief, as if she had at last established her independence. It showed her that she possessed a mind different from her mother's mind. "This creative function of the lie, linked to the possibility of otherness, the very possibility of possibility, appears to be a natural function, one whose absence is viewed as pathology," Forrester comments. Thinking against the real is one of the faculties that mark the human species as human, as different, and it is abetted by language.

Henry James explored that idea in a short story, "The Liar," written after meeting, at a London dinner party, a guest who regaled the company with a string of tall tales that were manifest inventions. "The Liar" concerns a certain Colonel Capadose, encountered at a country house party by the narrator, Oliver Lyon, a gifted young artist who is invited to paint the portrait of the master of the house, Sir David Ashmore. Colonel Capadose is at first meeting very handsome, charming, with perfect manners and plentiful curly mustaches. His personality is "as pleasant as the September sun—as if he could make grapes and pears or even human affection ripen by looking at them."

Into the narrator's innocent ear the Colonel imparts the most astounding information. That once, in Ireland, he fell out of a dogcart onto his head, was unconscious for three entire months and nearly buried alive. That in India a friend, supposed to have died of jungle fever, was actually put in a coffin and interred, only to be rescued by the redoubtable Colonel himself, who had had a dream in which the prematurely sepulchered man called out to him. Also, that a certain room in the older part of the house in which they are staying is haunted by ghosts, making nervous wrecks of otherwise strapping and mentally robust young men who slept the night there. The shattered guests had departed the house the next morning under cover of fictitious "letters of importance" that arrived at breakfast to summon them home.

Finally, Lyon tumbles to the fact that all this is make-believe, that his agreeable dinner companion is caught in a compulsion to lie that is as "natural" as being afflicted with a stutter or a limp. "It's quite disinterested," Sir David informs the disillusioned young portraitist. "He'll lie about the time of day, about the name of his hatter." There is no harm in the Colonel, no bad intention. "He doesn't steal or cheat nor gamble nor drink; he's very kind—he sticks to his wife, is fond of his children. He simply can't give you a straight answer."

Oliver Lyon is stuck with a dilemma. He considers lying to be despicable, the least heroic of vices. Yet here is the Colonel, a virtuoso of falsehood, married to a wonderful woman Lyon admires as honest and straightforward to the core. This peerless spouse had to be aware of her husband's flair for mendacity, unless she is deeply obtuse, which she is not. That being the case, how can she bring herself to aid and abet, day in and day out, such systematic deception? The answer is, of course, that she loves him. Lyon consoles himself with the thought that the Colonel is an abundant but not a malignant liar, confining himself to matters of small importance. He is a "Platonic" liar, with no intention to profit or injure. His falsehoods are art for art's sake, a law unto themselves. In Kant's term, they are purpose without purposefulness. "It's art for art," Lyon the artist decides. "He's prompted by some love of beauty. He has an inner vision of what might have been, of what ought to be, and he helps on the good cause by the simple substitution of a shade. He lays on color, as it were, and what less do I do myself?" As a female guest at the house party remarks of Mrs. Capadose: "I must say I like her husband better: he *gives* so much."

Here the old connection of truth with goodness is strained to the breaking point. Makers of possibility are more generous, more giving, than those who stick to the pedestrian facts. Bare truth-telling is a blemish, an inadequacy, a sort of miserliness, a species of Philistinism. It is a sign of a stunted mentality. It offers no improvement on what is actually the case. It is black and white, when what people crave is color. An uneasy relation has come to exist between imagination and falsehood, never quite resolved since the early Romantics. The Age of Reason, with notable exceptions, looked askance at imagination as being perilously associated with trickery and unsound thinking, even madness. In a complete reversal, the Romantics saw it as a symptom of mental health. In 1826, Charles Lamb wrote *The Sanity of True Genius*. Imagination was the new Logos, the bridge between the mind and the world and the key to understanding other minds. Interestingly, the word "artist" originally referred to a painter, a craftsman, or a scientist. It was only in the middle of the nineteenth century that it acquired the meaning of someone who creates with the imagination. Thanks in part to Ruskin, who championed the importance of the imagination as opposed to the domain of the merely social, it began to be given a heightened respect. It became an absolute. Graham Hough has noted the tendency for the strong ethical and social bent of high Victorianism to engender its own opposite, an asocial aesthetic based on the individual imagination. This led to "a gradual severance, increasingly apparent from Ruskin onwards, of art from the interests of common life, and a constant tendency to turn art itself into the highest value, to assimilate aesthetic to religious experience."

All this tends to give truth a bad name. That is the curious situation that Romanticism bequeathed to us, thanks to the powerful pull of its poetic vision. Meaning has become more valuable, more *useful* than truth. And because meaning has been separated off from truth, increasingly, since Kant, it becomes a sovereign eminence. It can make truth false. Vaclav Havel has pointed out, in the spirit of a warning, how easily language enables us to shade the truth, how a context of meaning can subtly alter the integrity of what we say. How words are placed, what surrounds them, who interprets them, the hidden intentions that lurk behind the words, can transform truth into something else entirely. In his plays, Havel sometimes writes speeches in which sheer nonsense is justified with impeccable logic, pure truths asserted "which are pure lies from beginning to end." There are passages containing truths that an audience can identify with, yet uneasily senses a barely perceptible whiff of mendacity, due to the context of meaning in which the "truths" are made. In *Temptation*, a character, Foustka, explains his view on the basic questions of existence to a woman, Marketa—opinions that Havel himself sincerely holds, and has written in his letters from prison. Yet there is something artfully false in what Foustka says. He is saying it, in part, because he wants Marketa to fall in love with him.

Relentless sincerity, "being yourself" and never shading the truth, is too simple, too easy a formula to do justice to a complicated, tricky, platitude-averse thing like modern society. It is unsophisticated and may even be uncivilized. That is the paradox in an age which has steeped itself in the notion of life as art. "As practical intelligence has become more and more refined," says the moral philosopher David Nyberg, "deception has come to play a central and complex role in social life." In his very influential book *The Presentation of Self in Everyday Life*, the social scientist Ervin Goffman argued that in social situations the individual is a performer, an actor playing a role in which he or she may or may not believe. The very word "person" once meant a mask. The mask, however, is not a "pure" lie. Goffman sees it as a different kind of truth. "In a sense, and in so far as this mask represents the conceptions we have formed of ourselves—the role we are striving to live up to—this mask is our truer self, the self we would like to be. In the end, our conception of our role becomes second nature and an integral part of our personality." The actor becomes the part he or she is playing.

It is not a very long step from saying that our "truer" self is the one we would like to be to asserting that the version of reality we prefer can be substituted for the historically accurate one because it is more interesting. Once it is accepted that there are "different kinds" of truth, some superior to others, then truth acquires the advantages of falsehood in being multiple, not single. It is hard to distinguish one from the other.

In reality, a society in which untruth is the norm would be unworkable. Human nature is such that the more lies we encounter, the more strenuously we reach for truth, the truth of correspondence to facts, just as in the absence of meaning and the presence of the inane, we struggle all the more desperately for meaning. Alasdair McIntyre thinks that we define our relationships with others in terms of certain virtues, among them truthfulness, and this is the case no matter what the codes of a particular society may be. Lutheran Pietists were taught from childhood to tell the truth to everyone at all times, whatever the circumstances or context, a tradition that Kant inherited. At the other extreme, Bantu parents instruct their children not to tell the truth to perfect strangers, exposing the family to witchcraft. "In our culture," says McIntyre, "many of us have been brought up not to tell the truth to elderly great-aunts who invite us to admire their new hats. But each of these codes embodies an acknowledgement of the virtue of truthfulness." Liars, in the last analysis, depend on the truthfulness of others to pass their stories off as God's truth.

CHAPTER EIGHTEEN

Language Made Me Do It

As a tactic of liberation, and a mode of discovery, deconstruction is bracing; but made permanent, it is akin to cerebral fibrillation. Odysseus presumed he had a home to go to, where he would not have to look the Cyclops in the eye every day; but when deconstruction is institutionalized, it resembles a decision to stay in the cave of Polyphemus and engage in an endless battle of wits with a very large and ill-tempered idiot. —Leroy Searle

 LONG TRADITION STANDS BEHIND THE notion that a person is author of his or her own thoughts, that the mind, as a creative instrument, can arrive at new truths, and that these truths are powerful in their ability to make some sense of what would otherwise be a senseless universe. That tradition is known as humanism. Language and literature are among its key components, as is also the belief that the individual is in control of those media. Imagination is prized, as a producer of possibilities, but the thrust of the humanist position is that possibilities cannot be allowed to multiply beyond all reason, or escape into a kind of nonsense in which the mind may not feel at home, as in the early twentieth-century cult of surrealism, which developed "a scorn not only for reason but for humanity."

Yet clever thinkers in our own time have argued that possibilities are out of control and that this is due in large part to the hitherto underestimated element of the arbitrary in the language we use—or, as they suggest, are used by.

Ferdinand de Saussure, who made modern linguistics possible, laid down as the first principle of his theory that the sign is arbitrary. He regarded this as the central fact of language. There is no natural, given connection between the sign, the word, and the signified, the idea in the mind. The sign is "unmotivated." How trite to say so. Yet from this modest principle surprisingly unobvious, even subversive consequences ensue. They are not immediately apparent, but are discovered "after many detours."

A word has no instrinsic connection with the thing it denotes. A tree might just as well have been called a shree, or a bree. Convention sees to it that when we use the word "tree," everyone knows what we are talking about. But life and language are far from simple. A signified is a mental concept, but it may not be a universal concept. It, too, can be as arbitrary as the sign. Signifieds may differ from one language to another. The French have a word for a dog, *chien*, but there is no proper concept for "pet." What is more, the ideas in the mind tend to shift and break out of their frames as time goes on. The signified slices up and organizes the world in its own particular way, and that way can change. There is no fixed, immutable dictionary definition the concept must retain through all eternity in order to be regarded as the correct signified for a given signifier. "Propriety," for example, once carried the sense of ownership of property, hence conferring a measure of respectability. Later, all traces of the primary meaning fell away. Language, said Saussure, has "no positive terms," by which he meant it contains no freestanding words with a unique, permanent reference.

It is easy to see which way the philosophical winds are blowing. They are squalling away our trust in universal concepts, in truths that can stand fast in the teeth of the modernist gale, in words that have stable meanings. The fact that concepts as well as words are arbitrary robs them of their sovereignty. It means they are not held in place by some sturdy inner core of meaning, but only by their unsteady couplings with other, equally wobbly concepts. An example is the English word "river," which differs from "stream" only in respect of its size. In French, a *fleuve* is distinct from a *rivière* not primarily because it is the larger of the two, but because it flows into the sea, whereas a *rivière* does not.

In one respect, the arbitrary nature of the sign protects language from deliberate efforts to modify it. If there is no logical, natural, or theological reason for a word to be as it is, it is pointless to produce rational arguments for altering it to a different word. There is no basis for debate. We can argue that having one wife is more reasonable, more economical, and even more moral than having half a dozen, but can the same be said for the existence of a whole lexicon of terms for "hat"? Conversely, the arbitrariness of language means that it mutates over time in its own languagey fashion, willy-nilly, as the failure of hundreds of schemes for artificial languages shows. It is a hallmark of artificial languages, which began to be invented in the seventeenth century, that they were either too logical or too simple to be universally accepted. From that insight comes the postmodern view that we are helpless in the grip of language. We are captured by it. It "speaks us," we do not speak it. That is a fair specimen of the late twentieth century's brand of anti-humanism.

Such changes as do take place in a natural language result in a shift, not just in the sign by itself, or in the concept by itself, but in the relationship between the two. Latin *necare*, meaning "to kill," became *noyer*, "to drown," in French. Both the word and the idea, the signifier and the signified, underwent an alteration. It is a hopeless task trying to separate the two. It would be like trying to uncouple the two sides of a single sheet of paper. "Language is radically powerless to defend itself against the forces which from one moment to the next are shifting the relationship between the signifier and the signified," Saussure said. And of all institutions—politics, economics, law, manners, even fashion—where certain basic constraints of social order, subsistence, justice must be observed, none is more free to be arbitrary than language.

Except perhaps art. Cubist painting, the epitome of modernist art, requires the viewer, if he is to have any rapport with the work at all, to accept that the so-called natural ways of seeing the world are actually quite arbitrary, as indeed is the painting he is looking at. That is shocking, but no more so than the modernist realization that Euclidean space is not the only possible geometry of the physical world. The non-Euclidean geometries high-handedly introduced in the nineteenth century, an affront to common sense and seemingly capricious, which contradicted the utterly obvious rule that parallel lines never meet, were mirrored in the subversion of realistic space in the work of such artists as Georges Braque and Picasso early in the twentieth century. In both cases, it was risky to decide *ex cathedra* which spaces were natural and which artificial. A non-Euclidean geometry in which light rays are curved became an important component of Einstein's theory of relativity, which describes the physical universe.

Since the fifteenth century, painters had represented the world as if from the viewpoint of a single observer in three-dimensional space. They called this realism, but Cubists took pleasure in pointing out that the method was not at all realistic, but actually a deception, an elaborate artificial illusion. Hints of this seditious idea appeared in the work of nineteenth-century Post-Impressionist painters like Van Gogh, Cézanne, and Gauguin, who began to rebel against the notion that the world is the same for all observers. The single eye was to go the way of the single Truth. These artists played havoc with the rules of perspective, defrauding, stretching them to the utmost, and in the end transgressing them entirely. As long ago as 1880, Cézanne had introduced breaks and dislocations into his paintings, unevenness in the realistic spaces. Distortion of the single perspective was for him not another sort of optical gimmick, but a "necessary truth to nature." In his *Nature morte au panier*, painted in 1888, each end of a kitchen table laid with fruit is depicted as if seen by a different observer, one taller than the other. Cézanne concealed the disparity with a rumpled tablecloth. In the world of his picture, gravity seems to be of a Martian lightness. One critic claimed to detect not two but three perspectives in this picture.

Cubism took the technique of multiple observers to brazen extremes. One part of a face might be seen head-on, another part shown in profile. The human anatomy was taken apart and reassembled in discontinuous bits. A 1912 account of Cubism justified this deprivileging of the "natural" rules of painting by declaring that the rules were not natural at all, but a mere convention, *nomos*, not *physis*. They were arbitrary. In order to display a true relation, a modernist painter had to sacrifice a thousand apparent truths: "the visible world can become the real world only by the operation of the intellect." A Cubist painting represents not reality as we define it in everyday life, but the artist's *concept* of what reality might be if it were rearranged to his specifications, and that concept, as in the theory of Saussure, is not universal, not fixed and part of the given order of things. To understand a Cubist painting, we need to recognize that our way of organizing the world is not the "right" way. In fact, there may be no right way. "If we achieve this realization, that our traditional, realist assumptions are themselves arbitrary," say the scholars of modernism Thomas Vargish and Delo Mook, "as arbitrary as the Cubist techniques before us, then the visual trauma and the consequent effort of recovery that characterize the experience are justified."

Science is not exempt from the same sort of caprice. New theories of the structure of matter stretched common sense to outlandish extremes, to the point where it was not unusual to hear a scientist insist that theories "had" to be strange, that a certain theory was "crazy, but not crazy enough to have a chance of being true." Physics defamiliarized nature as modernist art estranged the world of normal experience. Gunther Stent, a molecular biologist at Berkeley, suggests that the terms physicists use to describe the elementary bits of matter that show up on their instruments are now so purely arbitrary they do not touch our ordinary understanding, even in its "poetic" dimension. What does it mean to refer to properties of elementary particles by such words as "flavor" and "color," which are totally unrelated to the dictionary definitions and in that sense meaningless? The natural concepts that develop in us from childhood, says Dr. Stent, have built the vast enterprise of science. But concepts such as space, time, object, and cause, also form the boundary marks, the limits beyond which our normal intuitions fail. We are in the position of visitors to a foreign country who do not speak the language. The particles of quantum mechanics, electrons, protons, and neutrons, violate our commonsense insights, but the technical terms scientists used to describe their behavior were couched in the sort of language anyone could understand: mass, charge, spin. Once the quark doctrine of matter came into fashion, however, expressed in the theory of chromodynamics, all connection, even a metaphorical one, with everyday parlance was broken. Words like "charm," "strangeness," "up," "down," are semantically barren. There is no reason why "vanilla," "liquorice," "red," and "yellow" could not just as well have been selected.

Arbitrariness was a spur to the development of deconstruction, a set of ideas that separated language from truth altogether. Jacques Derrida, the leading figure of the movement (a term he resists), seized on the work of Saussure to develop a much more radical theory of the unmotivated character of language. If mental concepts do not exist independently of signifiers, then thoughts, ideas, can no longer be privileged carriers of a non-arbitrary "truth," while words, signs, are relegated to an inferior status. The ancient, metaphysical lore of the "transcendental signifier" had to go. Derrida emphasized the role of differences in a quite uninhibited fashion, though it was still part of the arbitrariness of language in its Saussurian form. A word is always surrounded by the ghostly "absence" of other words from which it differs. Such an absence is also a wraithlike kind of presence. Every sign in a system of signs is what it is by virtue of not being the others.

The catch is that by not being the others, a sign must also imply them. Meaning is always sliding off, scattering across the length and breadth of the entire language. The restless shuttling between presence and absence is an inherent instability, a permanent condition of language, making words wobbly, treacherous, never quite securely within our grasp. There are no exceptions, even for words consecrated and hallowed by centuries of philosophy. Not the least of them is the word "truth." Truth can no longer be regarded as a definite something always present, hiding behind appearances, or a fixed star to steer by. Gone glimmering is the pre-Socratic Logos, which harmonized world and mind and made ultimate truth accessible to human reason. And all this owes a great deal to the drawing out by Saussure of the "obvious" fact that words are arbitrary.

In the Derridean universe, there is a glut, a superfluity of meaning, too much for a sentence to simply "mean what it says." This inevitably opens the floodgates of suspicion, misgiving, and distrust. Language acquires a life of its own, a dynamic of its own. Let off the leash, it is irresponsible, anarchic, and undermines the accepted

meanings that society has approved. The sign is restless, promiscuous, untethered, chasing after novelty, cruising the surface of things
because there is no depth; never still, never satisfied, a fairly typical
representative of its time and generation.

Derrida, born in Algeria, studied philosophy at the Ecole Normale
Supérieure and was much taken with the three H's: Hegel, Husserl,
and Heidegger. His attraction to literature, however, led him to
detect in the work of these and other philosophers the same literary
devices and figures of speech used by writers of fiction. He came to
regard the texts he read as deceptive, the language masquerading as
transparent, sheer and lucid, austerely logical, when in reality it oper-
ated with images and metaphors and harbored various metaphysical
assumptions. Take these away, and the potency of the bare argument
by itself would be severely weakened. Plato himself used such contrivances while in the same breath criticizing the Sophists for doing
the very same thing. All this made Derrida deeply suspicious of the
philosophical tradition. While some philosophers regarded him
as a charlatan, he obtained a considerable following among literary
critics.

Useless to try to unpack the work of a philosopher, to "do philosophy" by dissecting and analyzing a text in the hope of finding something "true" beneath the author's literary bag of tricks. Derrida
echoed Wittgenstein in asserting that there is no such thing as a hidden truth. Better to treat the writings of philosophers as a form of
literature, where truth and falsehood have an entirely different status, and the "meaning" depends as much on the force of images,
tropes, and other literary contraptions as on the soundness of a tex-
t's logical structure. And a work of literature, as anyone would agree,
is open to more than one, perhaps a myriad of different interpretations. Derrida has said that literature is "the right to say everything."
It is an axiom of his thought that even "literal" sentences have
metaphors skulking inside them. A deconstructor pries metaphors
out of hiding as classical philosophers used to flush out truths. In
Margins of Philosophy, Derrida writes about the poet Valéry, who put
philosophy firmly into the category of literature. Valéry maintained
that a poet is not always incapable of solving a problem in logic, and

a logician can sometimes see in words something other than pretexts for syllogisms. In fact, the poet is more apt to engage in reason and logic than the philosopher, since his mind is "terribly variable, deceptive and self-deceiving, fertile in insoluble problems and illusory solutions."

We must situate philosophy quite close to poetry. That means recognizing philosophy as a kind of writing that organizes figures of speech, similes and metaphors, metonyms and personifications, all of which are far older than philosophy. We upend the commonsense idea that literal language came first and metaphor was a later embellishment. Figurative speech is not something that arose out of language, but "the emergence of language itself." Thus any text posing as literal is immediately under suspicion of sheltering devices of rhetoric under its cloak. Serious language is a special case of the nonserious, and "truths are fictions whose fictionality has been forgotten."

Deconstruction delights in such subversion of the normal in favor of what the ordinary person would regard as deviant or marginal. There is an echo here of surrealism, the movement which flourished in the 1920s and was much concerned with "polarities," or oppositions, aspects of life which seem contradictory and exclusive, but by an act of intellectual originality can be seen as part of a larger whole. The real and the imaginary, the past and the future, what can be said and what cannot, the elevated and the base, man and nature, cease to oppose each other under the synthetic embrace of surrealism. Similarly, deconstruction claims to dissolve the antagonisms between the natural and the artificial, male and female, high art and pop culture, truth and falsehood. As surrealism was an acute reaction to the senseless slaughter and waste of World War I, an expression of rage by returning soldiers at the loss, not just of human life, but also of that part of young manhood which in peacetime would be given over to art and philosophy, deconstruction came from the epoch of the Vietnam War, another conflict hugely profligate of human life, leading to widespread social upheaval.

If the normal, the consensual, the commonly accepted is the criterion of truth, as in American pragmatism, then deconstruction is about as far from pragmatism as you can get. Would you include a poet in your pragmatic consensus, or a secondhand car salesman, a spin doctor, a White House speechwriter? Deconstruction's complaint is that "truth" is produced by forcibly excluding such fringe elements. Deconstruction "tries to keep alive the possibility that the eccentricity of women, poets, prophets and madmen, might yield truths about the system to which they are marginal—truths contradicting the consensus and not demonstrable with a framework yet developed."

Derrida regards figures of speech not just as the basis for the emergence of language, but as inherent in all language. "Poetry swallows everything in sight." All texts are treated as part of the genre of literature, including scientific ones. We can talk about the "flavor" of a quark because poetry grants such license, and deconstruction says words are not for referring to things, or even, stably, to concepts in the head. "The need for a theory of aesthetic autonomy as a defense of poetry disappears, because everything being linguistic and all language being fundamentally 'poetic,'" says Hazard Adams, "there remains nothing for poetry to be distinguished *from*. It is no wonder that with this movement come declarations either of the death of literature or of the breakdown of distinctions between literature and other things, including criticism itself." We lose also the distinction between the singularity of truth and the multiplicity of falsehood, since all is multiplicity, all is difference.

In deconstruction, meaning leaks, spills, overflows, seeps from one text into a profusion of others. There is no such thing as interpreting a text on its own. In his eccentric work *Glas*, Derrida celebrates the coalescing of philosophy and literature. The pages of this book are divided into vertical columns interspersed with passages from different authors in diverse type fonts, languages, and layouts. Hegel takes up space on the left, while the right-hand column gives room to the French homosexual thief and transvestite turned writer Jean Genet. The effect, as cheeky as graffiti on a subway train, is to merge the anarchic effusions of *Journal of a Thief* with the great nineteenth-century prophet of reason, the authority of the family and the state, the sovereignty of truth. Meanwhile a commentary by Derrida

muses on such matters as whether the rules of metaphoric versus literal language are able to contain the seepage of meaning from text
to text.

The ghost of another debate, another quarrel, hovers over such
postmodern channel surfing. At the very birth of Western philosophy, in the sixth century B.C., a divorce took place between poetry and
rational thought about the universe. Thales of Miletus, who said the
world is made of water, broke free of the older ways of explaining
things by means of storytelling and myth. Thales is often described
in terms of what he was not: not a poet, not a teller of tales or a maker
of fictions. In that respect he was quite different from earlier, gifted
individuals who put their stamp on Greek culture. Hesiod, the shepherd poet who flourished around 700 B.C., told stories about the
affairs of the gods and the emergence of the world, its transition
from chaos to a complex order. Whereas Thales drew on observation
and argument, Hesiod wrote at the inspiration of the Muses, and he
acknowledged that these ladies, divine daughters of Zeus and
Mnemosyne, were not one hundred percent reliable. They "know
how to speak many false things as though they were true." Yet, when
the Muses feel inclined, they can speak things which are actually
true. Under the spell of the Muses, Hesiod the poet cannot conduct
a rational argument; that is not part of their gift to him.

The classical scholar David Roochnik thinks Hesiod and Derrida
have quite a bit in common. In Hesiod, there is a fundamental mismatch between the shapelessness of primeval Chaos and the mind
that aspires to think it. In order to bridge that gap, Hesiod must find
some other vehicle, and that vehicle is the Muses. He could not use
reasoned argument and logic to make the connection. In that enterprise he would have been defeated by the contradiction between
rational thought and something that is inimical to rational thought.
The invocation of the Muses is an admission of the intellectual limits of the poetic genre. By surrendering "authorship" to Zeus' daughters, the poet loses control of truth. Hesiod playfully undercuts his
own assertions while in the act of making them. Derrida, too, adopts
playfulness as a device to avoid privileging one concept over any
other. Playfulness, Roochnik suggests, is a postmodern version of

archaic Chaos. Both put truth out of reach. Just try translating Hesiod into propositions that are either true or false. Wittgenstein had also recommended recourse to the nonserious. "Never stay upon the barren height of cleverness," he wrote, "but come down into the green valleys of silliness."

In the heyday of the Greek Enlightenment, there was a certain amount of suspicion where poets were concerned. Socrates, in the *Apology,* reaffirmed that when a bard is in the grip of the Muses, he produces many beautiful effects, but is never sure what he says is true. As for what a poem "means," any old passerby on the street could give a better explanation than the poet himself. In Plato's *Protagoras,* a character remarks that arguments about poetry remind him of provincial drinking parties, where the imbibers, "because they are not able to converse with or amuse one another while they are drinking, by reason of stupidity, raise the price of flute girls, hiring for a great sum the voice of a flute instead of their own breath." Plato would ban poets from his ideal Republic if they did not cultivate the "beautiful and fitting," and lead people to see the splendor of reason. If any other sort came along, "We would pour myrrh on his head and crown him with wreaths and send him away to another country." In other words, run him out of town on a rail. All poets since Homer were to consider themselves uninvited, and even Homer was not thought all that much of a catch. In his Dialogues, Plato betrays a deep uneasiness about the nature of language and its resources. Art is specious. It aims at plausibility, not truth. The danger is that naive people might mistake the lies of art for the literal truth.

Derrida would certainly not have been welcome in Plato's Republic. He might have made congenial company for the Sophists, but probably would have been given short shrift by Aristotle, who took the simple view that truth occurs when what is said coincides with what is, and falsehood is a mismatch between the two. Aristotle took it for granted that nature has priority over language, and over culture and history as well, a ranking Derrida takes pleasure in turning upside down.

Freud, someone Derrida admires tremendously, had set himself free from the Romantic thrall. He insisted on a clear distinction between dreams and fantasies on the one hand and real life on the other. He would have no truck with the idea that everything is art. Believing in the importance of reality, he did not want it to lose its seriousness, to be made into a game, a recreation, or an aesthetic object. Some of Freud's successors, however, thought differently. Philip Rieff, author of one of the best books on Freud, warned of the nightmarish consequences that might ensue from making life into art. "That aestheticizing reality, as a thing of lightness and play: it will make murder and incest, too, acts of lightness and play," Rieff cautioned. Early on, Freud subscribed to the Romantic view that art provides a vehicle for expressing emotions that are otherwise stifled. It can release "the rebel and the blasphemer or the pietist in us all." In that sense, every individual is a born artist, and psychiatry an aesthetic activity. Later, however, he came to regard a work of art as a means of achieving mastery over oneself, organizing and stabilizing otherwise chaotic desires. That was part of Freud's belief that everything in the psyche has some use, some function, a most un-Darwinian notion. There was no room for a theory of spontaneous, impromptu play that is in excess of what is needed for the serious business of life.

Derrida aims to break down the prohibitive Freudian barrier between the aesthetic and the real, between poetry and truth. He puts in question the frame that separates art from non-art. In his *First Essay in Truth in Painting*, he suggests there should be no frame around art as there is around a painting. "Just try to frame a perfume," he flings out, typically in a parenthesis. A moment later he seems to repent of saying anything so straightforward: "Deconstruction must neither reframe nor dream of the pure and simple absence of the frame." Instead, he favors "a regulated, irrepressible dislocation, which makes the frame in general crack, undoes it at the corners in its quoins and joints, turns its internal limit into an external limit." Only a "certain practice of theoretical fiction" can work against the frame.

Noticeable in Derrida's writings is the influence of one of the patron saints of modernism, Mallarmé, who held as an article of faith that literary language is autonomous, an independent reality.

Derrida commended Mallarmé's poems as "standing in the air, all alone, separated from being." Mallarmé had seen language as so unstable, transitory and fluctuating, like a diaphanous spray of mist on the surface of churning waters, that a colleague once jokingly wondered why the words in a book did not become all muddled and mixed up during the night when the book was closed. In Mallarmé can be glimpsed the doctrine of the death of the author which was to follow the death of God in the ensuing century. A poem tends to erase vestiges of the poet's personality and become pure language. Words make no reference to anything but other words in the poem. "Everything in the world tends to end up in a book," Mallarmé said. A painting exists to exhibit the material properties of paint; a poem to show off the effects of language. Mallarmé described as his chief aim "to make the words of a poem self-mirroring." Paul Valéry, one of a captive audience at Mallarmé's one-man evening dissertations on aesthetic theory, once said that Mallarmé talked and behaved as if he had invented language all on his own.

Derrida approved of the importance given to the materiality of words, the impossibility of verifying anything in a poem, the dispersal of meaning, the absence of referents, the concern, not with the delivery of truth but with the operation of writing. In a literal sense, he thought, "writing does not wish to say/mean anything." But he differs from his iconoclastic predecessor by refusing to agree that a poem is an isolated entity. In Saussure, language is like a game of chess, and nothing matters outside the little world of the chessboard. Derrida sweeps aside such limitations. There is nothing outside the text. That is a Derridean first commandment. On the other hand, all of culture is a text, and because there is nothing else but culture, there is no end to textuality. All reality has the structure of a differential trace. We are permanently embedded in various networks: historical, linguistic, political. Saussure's concern for objectivity, for scientific truth, goes out the window.

Once, at a conference in Cambridge, England, Derrida was asked by a journalist to describe deconstrucution "in a nutshell." One of his colleagues, John Caputo, took it upon himself to demolish the metaphor as being almost comically inept. "Nutshells enclose and encapsulate, shelter and protect, reduce and simplify, while everything in deconstruction is turned towards opening, exposure, expansion and complexification, toward releasing unheard-of, undreamt-of possibilities *to come*, toward cracking nutshells wherever they appear," Caputo said. Deconstruction is about breaking through boundaries, transgressing confines, bursting out of hard outer casings.

That sort of thinking in philosophy shares much in common with fiction and poetry. They both press up hard against the impossible. Literature is an institution which tends to overflow the institution, even to destabilize the distinction between nature and the institution. Writing and reading have unlimited rights to resist laws and taboos. We are advised that Derrida is not recommending that "anything goes," nor does he want to substitute caprice for truth, though he sometimes gives the impression that he is blithely doing both. What he is up to is arguing "for a democratic open-endedness that makes those who have appointed themselves the Guardians of Truth nervous."

A consequence of dissemination, of unlimited textuality, however, is the vanishing even of the truth of art, never mind the truth of fact. Autonomy gives a poem, a painting, a certain integrity that is an aspect, perhaps the most important one, of aesthetic truth. The Romantics regarded poetic truth as internal and contextual. But if everything is literature, and if literature is everything, then it is nothing. We are left with play, interpretation, and sign. Derrida celebrates the "Nietzschean *affirmation*, that is the joyous affirmation of the play of the world and of the innocence of becoming, the affirmation of a world of signs without fault, without truth and without origin." Throughout history, mankind has dreamed of the end of play, the end of uncertainty, the arrival of the truth, the security of knowing that truth is present. By contrast, deconstruction aims to pass beyond mankind, beyond humanism, toward a radical, foundationless insecurity of absence. All this may seem disturbing, and Derrida makes it clear that it is. We are faced, he says, "by the yet unnameable which is proclaiming itself and which can do so, as is necessary whenever a birth is in the offing, only under the species of the nonspecies, the formless, mute, infant and terrifying form of monstrosity."

It has been said that Derrida's intention was to take Saussure's ideas to their logical conclusion. To take anything to its logical conclusion, of course, almost guarantees it will become a species of monstrosity, in the sense that it no longer has any connection with or bearing on human needs, affections, or interests. It is like a freak of nature, unfitted to the environment in which it must flourish or become extinct. Mathematics and other abstract forms of knowledge can be stimulated to make new discoveries under the impact of logical extremes that part company violently with common sense, but quotidian human existence is not like mathematics. That is one reason why deconstruction is a profoundly anti-humanist philosophy.

There is an element of Romanticism, certainly, in deconstruction, if only by virtue of its antipathy to certain pieties of the Romantic sensibility. In America, it was welcomed by literary scholars noted for their studies of Romantic and post-Romantic poetry. The Romantics had both celebrated and thrown doubt on the Enlightenment belief in the attunement of mind and nature. But they were strongly inclined to regard a work of art as providing a unique kind of security and control in a chaotic universe. That ordering function was art's own special kind of truth, quite different from the truth which corresponds to an external, verifiable fact. It was akin to the insight of Spinoza, that religious truth does not disclose knowledge of the nature of reality, but produces an attitude, brings about an alteration of the mind, by an immediate appeal to the heart. Faith, said Spinoza, "does not demand that dogmas should be true as that they should be pious—that is, such as will stir up the heart to obey." The idea is not to know the truth about things, but to undergo a reorganization of one's mental economy. Matthew Arnold, writing at a time when Romanticism still cast a long shadow, talked about the Victorian craving for "intellectual deliverance," by which he meant, not a longing for the ultimate key to the universe, but rather the "satisfaction of a need, felt instinctively or emotionally, for rational order." For this, any consistent "idea of the world" will suffice, and art or literature can provide it. Dante might supply such an idea, but so could Shakespeare or Milton. Arnold, who repeatedly mentions the complexity of modern society, thought the need for order was an instinct, a built-in propensity, like the tendency to self-preservation or the reproduction of the species. He suggested that while the illusions of art are not true in the sense of being factually correct, they are genuine because their existence is a meaningful fact in our lives. "More and more," said Arnold, "mankind will discover that we have to turn to poetry to interpret life for us, to console us, to sustain us. Without poetry, our science will appear incomplete; and most of what now passes with us for religion and philosophy will be replaced by poetry."

In Derrida's deconstruction, however, we have arrived at a curious state of affairs. Writing acquires a preeminence and importance that in philosophy or literary theory is quite different from anything that has gone before. Philosophers like to think they are engaged in pure argument, which they hope will culminate in a final truth. In argument, it is often the case that one person has the last word. That is because meaning is basically stable and can be understood in its entirety. Philosophers have been called natural enemies of writing, since they are on the side of reason and truth, and these tend to be contaminated and distorted by the rhetorical devices and built-in imprecisions of the written word. Is an argument more authentic, closer to the original thought, when it is spoken as opposed to being put down on paper? Derrida explodes this commonsense idea. For him, everything is writing, including speech. And writing produces more writing, and still more, and so on ad infinitum.

It is a fundamental axiom of Derridaism that speech, conversation, one person talking intimately to another, is not privileged as being more truthful than writing, in the sense that if we are face to face with the "author" of what is said we can confirm its accuracy firsthand, make sure we understand his or her real intentions. Saussure, aiming to create a science of language, had ignored the author and the referent, much as a physicist would disregard friction and atmospheric conditions in a study of the laws of motion. "My definition of language presupposes the exclusion of everything that is outside its organization or system," Saussure said.

Derrida wants to persuade us that speech displays the crucial features of all language, written or spoken. That means the spoken word, even in its immediacy, contains "distance, absence, misunderstanding, insincerity and ambiguity." It is part and parcel of his provocative suggestion that the artificial is prior to the natural, that what came first in time may not be "truer" than what comes later. It is recognized now, for example, that Einstein's relativity theory is basic and primary, while Newton's work is a special case of that theory and subsidiary to it, even though it preceded Einstein by more than two centuries. Writing is the most complete manifestation of the key properties of language, namely, that the sign is arbitrary and operates by means of differences, that words can be repeated and be the same in different situations. It is the universal system of which speech is a subsystem. Writing, Derrida decided, covers the entire domain of linguistic signs. The idea of the arbitrariness of the sign, which applies with equal force to speech, is unthinkable outside the horizon of writing. What Derrida calls *archi-ectriture*, or primary writing, writing in general, is the *arche* of language, prior to speech and prior to writing in the ordinary sense. It implies that in all forms of language, meaning does not exist before words are spoken or written. Language is not the vehicle of meaning, but its producer.

"By a slow movement whose necessity is hardly perceptible," Derrida wrote, "everything that for at least some twenty centuries tended toward and finally succeeded in being gathered under the name of language is beginning to let itself be transferred to, or at least summarized under, the name of writing." Writing comprehends language. A thought, a mental concept, cannot escape the play of signifiers that constitutes language. There is no stronghold, no out-of-bounds shelter for it.

We have come a long way from the situation that arose when, in the pivotal period of the late fourteenth century in England, there began to emerge an increasing emphasis on the written over the spoken word. This was accompanied by important changes in legal theory and practice. Simultaneously, the word "trouthe" underwent a mutation that was to have momentous consequences. Its Middle English meaning of personal integrity, loyalty, steadfastness, the opposite of treason, shifted to the modern, impersonal sense of correspondence to fact, accuracy, correctness. That was the result in part of the spread of literacy in the England of Richard II, and the explosion of lawyerly paperwork under an authoritarian regime. In oral cultures, says Richard Green, "truth" often means loyalty to a particular social order or tradition. It does not consist primarily of statements that are either true or false. In Islamic society, for example, the word for propositional truth, *sahha*, is not privileged over *sadaqa*, being trustworthy, being true to oneself, to others, and to the particular situation. Arabic makes no firm distinction between reference to nature and and loyalty to the social order. Among the Tiv of Nigeria there are two kinds of truth in courts of law, *mimi* and *vough*. The first means the morally good and socially correct thing, but not the factually correct thing. The word *vough*, meaning "straight" or "precise," is used for that. Good social relationships are given precedence over simple agreement with the facts. The anthropologist Michelle Rosaldo reports that in disputes among Philippine headhunters, the parties "were not concerned with telling lies or telling truths. As always, what they claimed was that 'true' depended less on 'what took place' than on the quality of an interaction where what mattered most was who spoke out."

How odd that, at the turn of the millennium, deconstruction, by making everything, including speech, into writing, should have the entirely different result of putting truth out of reach, of deferring it in a proliferation of endless games, where writing begets more writing and interpretation more interpretations. We live in a world of hyperliteracy where "there is nothing outside the text," and yet there is a large body of opinion holding that literal truth, truth to the facts, is socially disruptive, naive, betokening a deficit of imagination and sensitivity, a "disloyalty" to the codes of acceptable behavior, bearing a remarkable resemblance to the traditions of oral cultures and to the "trouthe" of an England that was still medieval.

Not that Derrida is studied with close attention by the average person. His writings are abstruse, alien, intimidating, and even barbarous to the common reader. But his ideas filter down in popular and highly simplified and predigested form, "in a nutshell." Down from that unscalable Mount Sinai of deconstruction comes the message that truth as well as falsehood are as dead as God, as extinct as humanism, as obsolete as the individual self. Truth-telling is devalued even though the arguments behind the devaluing are not respected, not taken apart and examined, not fully understood. The imprimatur of philosophy is used to sanction a new kind of Sophistry that elevates lying to the status of an art and neutralizes untruth by proclaiming that all language is inherently untrustworthy, that it produces meaning rather than being produced by meaning, that it speaks us rather than we speaking it, not only absolving us from various kinds of plagiarism but also giving us the perfect alibi for mendacity: "Language made me do it."

CHAPTER NINETEEN

A Certain Kind of Madness

I mistrust those hopes which can give murderers a clear conscience.
    —Raymond Aron

Man's foundation is mendacious because it is optimistic.
    —Friedrich Nietzsche

HE GREEK SOPHISTS HELD THAT PLAYING games with language, presenting falsehood in the guise of truth, was a key to power, to winning. They "threw" true statements upside down, as a wrestler floors an opponent in the ring. By contrast, Descartes, pioneer of modern thought, asserted that anything tainted with falsehood is a mark of feebleness, of neediness, while truth is manly and strong.

The Sophists separated culture from nature in pursuit of the power words wield. In our own time, elaborate theories have been spun around the idea that language is autonomous, disengaged not only from nature and material existence but from everything that is not language. Does that enable it to exercise a power commensurate with its vastly privileged status?

In George Orwell's anti-bureaucratic fantasy *1984*, a totalitarian regime maintains its hegemony over its people by the simple expedient of denying that truth has any independent existence outside the mind. Insisting that truth is not in the world, not in external facts or things, but only in the head, the Party is able to procure the acceptance of the most outrageous lies as eternal verities. By exerting mastery over minds, it can decide what is true and what is false. "In the end, the Party would announce that two and two make five, and you would have to believe it. The heresy of heresies was common sense. And what was terrifying was not that they would kill you for thinking otherwise, but that they might be right. For, after all, how do we know that two and two make four? Or that the force of gravity works? Or that the past is unchangeable? If both the past and the external world exist only in the mind, and if the mind itself is controllable—what then?" In Orwell's monstrous superstate, Oceania, inconvenient truths are flushed away by systematically deleting words from the dictionary: without language, thoughts cannot exist.

Orwell's parable is about power. The ruling elite has one and only one goal: to stay on top. Ideology is a mere device, a rational underpinning to the desire to hold onto power. Nazi Germany and the Soviet Union were alike in using the "philosophy" of their regimes as a prop to the job security of the leaders. The point, for totalitarian systems, is to use the ruling doctrines to preempt the emergence of ideas that might destabilize the status quo. Power is able to create truth, as it creates a fictional past, by rewriting history. That is the function of Orwell's Ministry of Truth, which exists to decide what is true and what is false. One person alone, by himself, is unequipped to do so. Like Wittgenstein, Orwellian society mistrusts the accuracy of personal memory. That makes it possible to play fast and loose with memory, hoodwink it with fake documents and consign the genuine ones to oblivion. In any case, "the truth is always mediated through human consciousness, and the principles which determine human consciousness are quite other than truth." This is the pragmatic theory of truth taken to bizarre extremes. Big Brother, the omnipresent but unseen master of Oceania, sees to it that whatever serves his purposes and secures his total ascendancy is truth. "It is one of the most characteristic and destructive developments of our own society," wrote Erich Fromm in an essay on Orwell's novel, "that man, becoming more and more of an instrument, transforms reality more and more into something relative to his own interests and functions."

The useful lie, available thanks to the lingering demise of the concept of timeless truth, has been adopted by regimes of the right and the left indiscriminately. Benito Mussolini, for example, welcomed the disappearance of absolutes with open arms. "If relativism signifies contempt for fixed categories and men who claim to be the bearers of an objective, immortal truth," Mussolini wrote at the opening of the confident decade of the 1920s, "then there is nothing more relativistic than Fascist attitudes and activity." He went on to say that if all ideologies are of equal value, if all of them are fictions, "the modern relativist infers that everybody has the right to create for himself his own ideology and to attempt to enforce it with all the energy of which he is capable."

As for the Soviet regime, it needed a vast supply of lies in order to maintain the "truth" of its holy scripture. Galina Vishnevskaya, the soprano whose career began at the Bolshoi Opera, remembers as a young woman being enveloped in untruth continually, at every moment. Being recruited to spy on her colleagues at the Bolshoi by the KGB, Galina knew from the start that mendacity was her only hope. In her memoirs, published in the United States in the actual year 1984, she said: "I had to be tricky, lie and pretend I was a naive featherbrain." After all, she was only too familiar with the blatant official falsehoods and distortions inserted into Soviet operas dealing with contemporary or revolutionary themes. Walking the streets of Moscow after a particularly unnerving encounter with her KGB handlers, Galina thought to herself: "Lies, lies, lies everywhere. Like a sticky spider web they entangle one's consciousness, they twist the soul, they hang over you from cradle to grave."

The relativity of truth, the theory that truth is "produced" rather than discovered, that it may be a creature of political or other kinds of power, is a central theme of postmodernist thought. But it favors no single ideology, whether Socialist or National Socialist. It is as likely to result in anarchy as in totalitarian repression. When "objective, immortal" truths are abolished and replaced by pure inventions, obedience to them is not secured by the traditional popular beliefs. Keeping these artifacts in business entails some form of coercion, whether the mild device of political correctness and social shaming or the more sinister apparatus of the police state.

Deconstruction became high fashion after the student demonstrations in Paris in May 1968, and was therefore seen as an adjunct of the political left. There was an atmosphere of political claustrophobia prevailing at the time, thanks in part to the stability of the French establishment, rooted in the robustness of institutions put in place by the Fifth Republic. Charles de Gaulle had been in office for a decade, and there was no plausible alternative to him. The entrenched solidity of the government simply intensified the rage in the streets and fed a new kind of extremism.

For thirty years after World War II, much of cutting-edge Parisian culture was ruled by the left. The University of Paris boasted an especially large share of Marxist professors in all departments and the upheavals of the sixties increased such penetration. Before the big event on the night of May 10, 1968, colleges all over France were shaken by student demonstrations; their intensity was shocking to many officials and student leaders. On that night, some twenty thousand young people massed in the streets of the Latin Quarter as a mark of outrage at the government decision to shut down the Sorbonne. The police had clubbed several innocent people who just happened to be passing by. There was also anger at the despotic character of French schooling. Barricades were set up, sixty of them. Billboards were destroyed, cars overturned. Then police in gas masks threw incendiary grenades. Protesters retaliated with cobblestones and Molotov cocktails. When it was all over, some two hundred cars had been incinerated and more than three hundred and fifty people injured. A general strike the next Monday drew more than a million people into the streets to oppose "the very order of things in the modern world generally."

Yet there was a "virtual" aspect to the May upheavals. If they could not overthrow a government, the protesters might at least destroy the tyranny of fixed truths and single meanings. Among the graffiti at the Sorbonne were the scrawled statements: "Actions, no! Words, yes!" And, "I take my desires for reality, because I believe in the reality of my desires." Another mantra was "There are no facts." The slogan: "It is forbidden to forbid," began to appear on the walls of the Sorbonne.

Roland Barthes, a central figure in the literary vanguard of Paris at the time, decided to organize a seminar on the connection between "language and the student movement." This was greeted with cat-calls by students as being too inert and cerebral at a moment of such pivotal crisis. Perhaps they also sensed that Barthes regarded them as narcissists, and *petit bourgeois* to boot. In a famous incident during one of these seminars, at which Saussure's structuralism was often pilloried and language theories ransacked for hidden political bias-es, a philosophy teacher, Catherine Backes-Clement, arrived and announced: "I've just come from the general assembly of the philos-ophy department. We have just passed a motion which concludes, 'It is obvious that structures do not take to the streets.'"

Next day an enormous poster was affixed to the wall of a corridor on the first floor of the Sorbonne which read: "Barthes says struc-tures do not take to the streets. We say, neither does Barthes." In fact, Barthes was not the author of the phrase, which became famous not only in Europe but in America as well. It summarized an uneasy feel-ing that actual revolution, the total transformation of institutions, was no longer feasible after the failure of the Soviet experiment; the only insurrections left were those that tilted against ideas, revolu-tions in the head. Ironically, a dozen years before the May barricades, Simone de Beauvoir had written in the journal *Les Temps Modernes*: "The truth is one, only error is multiple; it is no accident that the right professes pluralism." Now here was the left lurching into the most extreme pluralism, storming the Bastille of the old Enlighten-ment tradition of the single Truth.

One of the basic quarrels deconstruction had with structuralism was that it suspected the latter of sheltering a form of the hated phi-losophy of idealism. A theory that says all languages, cultures, minds, societies participate in a system of structures, a common code, is not likely to recommend tampering with these things in the hope of making a better world. It suggests that what we have is "given," not made. We are stuck with the world as it is. And that is a conservative point of view.

Of the Parisian intellectuals of the time, John Ardagh has written that they showed more respect for ideas than for facts. They har-bored a "contempt for the authenticity of information," and tended

to select or even distort facts to suit their purposes. That was especially the case for Marxists and other supporters of the left. Marx
himself was no admirer of anarchism, Romanticism, or the irrational. His theories were intended to be scientific and rigorous, and
were quite restricted in their scope. He believed in such Enlightenment ideas as the existence of an "authentic" human nature; he saw
it as being estranged by the dehumanizing squalor of working conditions in factories. Truth existed, but the masses, duped by false
consciousness, were blind to it and did not know what was best for
them. That gave a free hand to the élite, who were in possession of
the truth, to seize power arbitrarily, as Lenin's minority faction did
in the Russian Revolution of 1917.

In that respect, Marxism was a philosophy of universal truth.
There is a single universe, and it is rational through and through.
Everything made by human art, all that is given by nature, can be
explained in terms of one overarching nexus of laws that makes both
worlds intelligible. Marx believed such laws explain not only the
advances and successes of history but its mistakes as well, its accidents, wrong turns, and blunders. When all is understood in this scientific fashion, the world will be a place of harmony and concord, of
unity, where all differences are smoothed away, because that is the
natural, undistorted condition of the human species.

Theory had its place in this scheme, certainly. But so did action,
the confrontation with brute fact. Marx recognized the importance
of philosophy, but he also believed that at certain hinge moments in
history, theory must be set aside to make way for political practice,
based on the truth of what philosophy had revealed. Philosophy
throws off its mantle of lofty speculation and takes part in history as
"a practical person hatching intrigues with the world." There was
always a certain ambiguity between Marx's doctrine of historical
inevitablity, which he wrote about as if it were a great force of nature,
and his acknowledgment of the need for action. He seems to agree
with those Greek philosophers for whom it was a truism that as long
as a person knows what is good, he or she will do the good thing.
There is no firm distinction between knowing and acting on that
knowledge.

Western Marxists in the modernist period tended to throw Marx into reverse. He started with philosophy, then proceeded to the more worldly questions of the means of production and the ownership of capital. His successors and followers in Europe moved in the opposite direction, from economics back to ideas. The historian Perry Anderson thinks the Marxian unity between theory and practice was destroyed when Stalin's political apparatus stamped out revolutionary mass actions in Russia and sabotaged them in other countries. All serious theoretical work came to an end in the Soviet Union after collectivization. In the West, Socialist thought became Utopian, cut off from the reality of working-class life. The failure of the Socialist Revolution to take fire outside Russia bred a generation of Marxist intellectuals remote from those gritty facts of material existence which Marx had put at the top of his agenda.

This had two effects on the writings of Western Marxists between the end of World War I and the tumult in the streets of Paris in May 1968. One was that, in Anderson's words, "Theory became, for a whole historical period, an esoteric discipline whose highly technical idiom measured its distance from politics." After 1848, Marx had wanted his work to be accessible to the working class, deliberately making his writing simple and lucid. His twentieth-century followers in Europe did exactly the opposite. They adopted the most abstruse, alien, and inhospitable literary manner, needlessly complex, enigmatic, and obscure. This strategy has survived in the work of postmoderns like Lacan and Julia Kristeva, of whose writings it has been said that they resist meaning so powerfully that "the very process of failing to comprehend the text is part of what it has to offer."

As in Orwell's Oceania, common sense is the great heresy, but so too is the slightest impulse to make the ordinary intelligent reader at home; the idea is to enmesh him or her in dense thickets of prose, which strangle understanding in the cradle. It is as if all these writers imitated and then raised to eccentric levels of intricacy the cryptic style of Antonio Gramsci, founder of the Italian Communist Party, who as an inmate of the prison system was forced by a brutal censorship to make his meanings opaque. Their language, says

Anderson, "was subject to a wider historical censor: the gulf for nearly fifty years between socialist thought and the soil of popular revolution." One of them, Theodor Adorno, deliberately tried to inflict
pain on his readers, taking care never to make them comfortable.
"The splinter in your eye is the best magnifying glass," was one of his
harsher maxims. When his friend Siegfried Kracauer complained of
dizzy spells while reading one of Adorno's books, he was told by the
testy author he could not hope to comprehend a single work until he
had read the entire *oeuvre*. The editor of an American journal altered
one of Adorno's essays to make the argument clear, whereupon
Adorno "decided it was time to return to his native Germany."

A second consequence of the divorce between theory and revolutionary practice was that Western Marxism adopted a strikingly aesthetic posture. The status of art and literature in a Marxist Utopia
had always been a ticklish question. In principle, the arts ought to
help in the work of educating the masses in the correct ideology, sup-
plying their needs according to what the state defines as needs.
Newly installed Communist regimes do not like abstract art any
more than the experimental novel, which constructs its own idiosyncratic version of reality. Paintings and books that refer only to
themselves are frowned upon, as is the notion that the artist or writer
is an autonomous being answering only to the voice of his or her own
genius. Modernism was considered anti-Soviet and modernists were
classified by Stalin as enemies of the people, though this attitude
eased somewhat under Mikhail Gorbachev.

In the West, during the twenties and thirties, some socialist figures
who did not take their cue from Lenin but from the early, "humanist" Marx began to emphasize culture rather than politics as the path
to the desirable socialist future. Art, music, poetry have a measure of
independence from the economic and political establishment and
can therefore be used to disturb and destabilize it, perhaps even overthrow it, who knows? Gramsci theorized that the arts acquire a life
of their own and are partly out of control in capitalist societies.

Many neo-Marxists wrote books on aesthetics. Adorno, a leader of
the Frankfurt School, was far too prickly and independent to ally
himself with any organization having a specific program for social

reform. It has been said of him that "his refusal to compromise grew out of a characteristically Western Marxist insistence on the Utopian potential of modern society, which prevented him from ever confusing any actually existing socialist regime with the genuine realization of the socialist dream." Adorno was also a gifted musician and composer in the atonal mode (his writing is also "atonal") and a strenuous champion of modern art. His final, unfinished book, *Aesthetic Theory*, was intended to be dedicated to Samuel Beckett, patron saint of the modernist theater. Yet, paradoxically, he was also a cultural conservative, disdainful of popular music and literature, hostile to the kind of instrumental reason that produces more and better technology. In fact, he thought one of the wellsprings of fascism might be our "mythic" past, breaking out of its home in the unconscious; also that it was a turning of the tables, a kind of retribution on the part of nature for our ruthless mastery of her. In 1967, Adorno made it clear that he valued aesthetics over politics when he refused to change the subject of a lecture, "The Classicism of Goethe's Iphegenia," in Berlin soon after a student, Benno Ohnesorg, had been killed by the police during a visit by the Shah of Iran. He believed that true art could show the way to social change. Ideology, he said, is untruth, a lie. "The greatness of works of art lies solely in their power to let those things be heard which ideology conceals." They point toward the truth, including the vision of a future "true" society. Only in the utter uselessness of art can the utilitarianism of today's civilization be resisted.

Another theorist who considered Marxism in need of thorough review if it was to survive was Herbert Marcuse, a colleague of Adorno's, whose sayings were painted on the walls of the Sorbonne during the May 1968 uprisings. Marcuse, like Adorno, believed that art, literature, and music can express truths impossible to capture in any other form. Art is a "rupture with the established reality system" and therefore an avenue of liberation. "The message of art and literature is that the world really is as the lovers of all times experienced it, as King Lear experienced it, as Anthony and Cleopatra experienced it." Marcuse adopted Schiller's theory of aesthetics, which emphasized art as a "play impulse," a frolic without any other purpose. The inclination to play is a "third way" of explaining the world, apart from the operations of sense and reason. Human beings are free only when "reality loses its seriousness." It was this conception that evolved into the late nineteenth-century cult of art for art's sake. Marcuse also agreed that philosophical writing ought to verge on the unintelligible and acknowledged that quite a bit of Adorno's work was over his head, which was presumably all to the good. As he explained: "Ordinary language, ordinary prose, even a sophisticated one, has been so much permeated by the Establishment, expresses so much the control and manipulation of the individual by the power structure, that in order to counteract this process you have to indicate already in the language you use the necessary rupture with conformity. Hence the attempt to convey this rupture in the syntax, the grammar, the vocabulary, even the punctuation." Commas can start a revolution.

The retreat into aesthetics and the adoption of what is virtually a private code in these neo-Marxist thinkers anticipated the postmodern evasion of hard truths and stubborn facts. For Marx, capital was a substantial thing, following trajectories of development that are unpredictable and sui generis. It took on a life of its own. Capital was a living force that, once sufficiently enlarged, once embarked on a certain course, is unstoppable until it breaks down in its own fashion. In Western post-Marxist thought, by contrast, it is language, the signifier, that emulates the role of capital in Marx's theory: something idiosyncratic, self-sufficient, out of control. Traditional leftists complain that deconstruction, with its emphasis on words not deeds, signs not beliefs, is a philosophy of inertia and passivity. Robert Fitch, for example, a professor of urban economics at New York University, believes that an "unhealthy fixation" on such cultural issues as feminism, racism, and sexual orientation tends to relegate ordinary truthfulness to a secondary role. "There is a sense that objective conditions don't matter at all," Professor Fitch observes. "They don't believe in facts." The recourse to aesthetics, Christopher Norris thinks, appears to be "little more than a desperate holding operation, a means of continuing to talk, think and theorize about issues of a vaguely political import while serenely ignoring the manifest 'fact' that socialism is everywhere in a state of terminal decline."

Strange things happen when language and culture are given a privileged status, above nature, above "what is," superior to hard reality. It is then and only then that the question of truth becomes a difficult and perplexing one, inviting heretical answers, making it possible to doubt the value of plain speaking, to look for exotic new sources of truth, new reasons to make it subordinate to other, more immediately felt interests. Truth is not sacred any more. That shift of accent is nowhere more apparent than in the work of the post-Marxist thinker Michel Foucault, who along with other French intellectuals in the aftermath of the 1968 tumult shared a deep distrust of the power of institutions to control individual thought and behavior.

Foucault, obsessed for much of his life with death, suicide, drugs, and various forms of eroticism, held that language, in the broadest sense of the word, determines what reality is. Language is the world. And truth is wholly a matter of language. It is a creature of that world, generated by its many kinds of limits and coercions, by its "power." Contrary to a myth whose history would repay further study, Foucault said that "truth isn't the reward of free spirits, the child of protracted solitude, not the privilege of those who have succeeded in liberation themselves. Truth is a thing of this world: it is produced only by virtue of multiple forms of constraint. And it induces regular effects of power."

For Foucault, truth, like the self, is not given but made. A vast array of humanly invented rules, ordinances, laws, social norms, institutions press in upon each person, shaping his or her identity. The Marxist idea of a human essence, he rejected totally. And in thus casting aside the traditional theory of a fixed and innate core of human being, in ushering in the seemingly perverse notion of the "death of man," he was able to envisage the emergence of something quite new and different, something that never existed before and about which we are entirely ignorant. Foucault embodied some of the chief features of the postmodern: novelty, obscurity, and play. The concept of a perfectly transparent communication between people was something almost abhorrent. "The thought that there could be a state of communication which would be such that the games of truth could circulate freely, without obstacles, without constraint, and without coercive effects, seems to me to be Utopia." Foucault did not believe in Utopia.

As the chairman of a new philosophy department at the University of Paris at Vincennes, Foucault indulged his impulse for play. One of his colleagues, Judith Miller, the daughter of Jacques Lacan, dispensed certificates of course credit to total strangers on a bus, explaining later that if the credits were imaginary, so was the university. It was nothing but "a figment of capitalist society." In the same vein, Foucault told an interviewer: "I am not sure, you know, if philosophy really exists." The "games of truth" really ought to be games, not something sober and serious and purposeful. They are rituals, "completely arbitrary things, tied to our bourgeois way of life; it is good—and that is the real theater—to transcend them in the manner of play, by means of games and irony; it is good to be dirty and bearded, to have long hair, to look like a girl when one is a boy (and vice versa); one must 'put in play,' show up, transform, and reverse the systems which quietly order us about. As far as I am concerned, that is what I try to do in my work."

Foucault insisted that truth is produced by power, that every society has a "regime" of truth special to it, which is an entirely idiosyncratic distortion of the classical concept of truth. He also talked about the art of not being governed as a key to the discovery of truth, detaching oneself from the jurisdiction of power, as dissenting sects did during the Reformation, by "thoughtful disobedience." We can make our own history, sifting through the ideas inherited from the past, replacing them with new ones, "fabricated as in a fiction." Foucault did not even try to determine what is true and what is false, but only studied the fictions themselves, the various ways in which people have thought about madness, crime, sexual identity. What this method discovers, he said, is the "arbitrariness" of understanding, of what one takes to be the truth. Games of truth are always variable and uncertain. We can always think differently about what seems to be self-evident, and the starting point is a decision not to be governed.

Foucault was anti-humanist, if humanism is taken to involve the disovery of universal truths about human nature, which, being the same at all times and in all places, fix the perimeters, the boundaries, of what individuals can be and do. Eternal truths will never be anything other than what is the case. Foucault was interested in what has never been the case. His special brand of anti-humanism is intended to release unsuspected potential in us, launch us from the cramped familiar into the ample unknown. The insistence that truth and falsehood are products of a particular "regime," that truth is a game in Wittgenstein's sense, is part of the work of liberation. Nothing is absolutely true, and that includes humanism. No theory—and by definition a theory imposes certain constraints on what it theorizes about—can constrain the possibilities inherent in us. Foucault aimed to identify the accidental limits thrust on us by the conditions of our particular time and place in history; becoming aware of these largely unconscious curbs, we may escape them and embrace the prospect of "no longer being, doing or thinking what we are, or do, think."

Another kind of "truth" Foucault explored is the insight that comes from a particularly difficult or harrowing experience. Such a truth "does not belong to the order of that which is, but rather of that which happens." An experience of this sort can range from the actual torture of a heretic to a crisis of religious faith, when someone is forced to question everything he or she believes. Foucault called this a "limit experience." The whole point of a limit experience is its novelty, its unpredictability, its capacity to produce mental agitation. Only if it is strange and different will it give rise to the necessary inner turmoil. Thus, one should go out of one's way to invite such a crisis. Perhaps this was a motivation for Foucault's notorious experiments with sex, sadomasochism, and drugs. In July 1978, a biographer reports, he "enjoyed one of the most important mystical experiences of his life" when he smoked opium for the first time. A limit experience, for sure.

Newness, first-time encounters, became a kind of obsession with Foucault. It was anathema to him to think or write anything he had thought or written before. He pursued novelty "with a hint of desperation." The work of the intellectual, he said, is "to shake up habitual ways of working and thinking, to dissipate conventional famliarities, to reevaluate rules and institutions."

He flirted with limit experiences of many kinds, a postmodern Dorian Gray, finding that pleasure became more and more difficult to obtain. "I would like and I hope to die of an overdose," he told an interviewer. Hit by a car in the street outside his Paris apartment, he had the brief impression he was dying, and found it "really a very, very intense pleasure." Extremist politics also became a stimulant. As a journalist in Iran during the revolution against the Shah in 1978, his dispatches seemed self-intoxicated, describing the aim of setting up an Islamic government as a new kind of "political spirituality" holding out the prospect of a "total transfiguration of this world." In the bloodbath that ensued, however, Foucault drastically moderated his enthusiasm for revolution, speaking out for human rights and championing the cause of refugees.

In the early eighties, Foucault sought limit experiences in the gay culture of San Francisco. He was teaching at Berkeley two months out of every year. Hans Sluga, chairman of the philosophy department, remembers telling Foucault, while driving across the Bay Bridge, about a strange disease that was appearing, so new it did not even have a name. "You'd better be careful," he warned his colleague. But Foucault refused to believe what he was being told. True to his theory that "discourse makes truth," he replied that it was all an effusion of words, that the prudish and anti-sexual forces in the American psyche were finding an outlet in the form of mass hysteria and exaggeration about a disease nobody understood. Even when the terrible truth about AIDS became common knowledge, and Foucault had every reason to believe he had contracted the disease, he still frequented the bathhouses of San Francisco, "accepting the new level of risk," as his biographer James Miller puts it. But of course the risk was for his partners, who might not yet have succumbed. The grotesque possibility emerges that Foucault, in search of the "truth" that comes from limit experiences, from the "overwhelming, the unspeakable, the creepy, the stupefying, the ecstatic," did not communicate to his partners the life-or-death-dealing truth that he had AIDS.

George Orwell believed that the most ominous peril in the future was that "the very concept of truth is fading out of this world." He argued that a surrender to mere words leads to the idea that all truth is relative, which in the end results in the debauching of "every department of thought." If truth is relative, so is oppression, injustice, coercion, and dictatorship. Abortion can be equated with homicide, the U.S. combat role in Vietnam with Nazi terror. Orwell came to have an abhorrence for the power of political orthodoxy, especially its effects on intellectuals, and in particular the orthodoxy of communism, which in some cases provided English thinkers with a substitute for an authoritarian religion, a superstition disguised as a political fact. At the BBC, where he worked for a time, the name of Stalin was "completely sacrosanct." Orwell regarded left orthodoxy as "poisonous" to literature. In fact, he considered that leftist writers had acted most poorly, most dishonestly, in respect to the Spanish Civil War, omitting to mention that the Communists were among the worst offenders in suppressing revolution. They were simply hewing to the party line. And they were dealers in words, not deeds. They were "people to whom war is fought on paper—without any more personal danger than was entailed in a move at chess." Of W. H. Auden, who in a poem about the Civil War used the phrase "necessary murder," Orwell said this could only have been written by a person for whom "murder is at most a *word*."

Orwell specifically rejected the excuse that lying is a necessary form of politeness or the preservation of values more important than truth. He called the idea that intellectual honesty is a form of antisocial selfishness a "dangerous proposition." Lying for a worthy cause, say to deceive the enemy in wartime, might justify lying for much less worthy causes when the war is over. "Lying becomes the norm, and one cannot, even by an act of will, confine it to just military matters."

In *1984*, language is the key to either mental serfdom or decency and freedom. Big Brother can exercise total control over the thoughts of all in Oceania if language is detached from nature, if it becomes completely autonomous. The only hope for an end to this totalitarian bad dream lies with the proles, the uneducated masses working at menial tasks, because their daily, direct contact with the physical world through manual labor gives them a handhold on reality that brain workers lack. It helps them to resist the effects of the Party's main instrument of deception, Newspeak, the official language of Oceania.

Only by reconnecting language back to actual felt existence and thought, to simple, objective truth, could a sane and decent society be restored, Orwell suggested. No intellectual, no Party hack or bureaucrat would be equippped to perform that feat. The people likeliest to use simple concrete language, and to think of metaphors that really call up a visual image, are those in contact with physical reality. One of the characters in *1984* of whom Orwell clearly approves is a young woman of lurid profanity who is unable to mention the Party "without using the kind of words that you saw chalked up in dripping alleyways."

In one respect, the operating principles behind Newspeak are quite different from those deconstructionists tell us reside in ordinary language. Here meaning contracts. It is tightly constrained so that one word signifies one thing and excludes everything else, as in the artificial languages of the seventeenth century, which failed for the very reason that they lacked the rich ambiguity and depth of ordinary English. In deconstruction, by contrast, a word is surrounded by a spectral aura of other words whose absence constitutes a sort of presence. Meaning is unstable, off the leash, always on the move. Yet in both cases, language has been disengaged from the mind that produces it, taking on a life of its own, having no anchor in objective reality, divorced from any author's intentions. The separation of nature, the hard concrete world of facts and things, from culture, is radically extended.

For Newspeak, as for deconstruction, language is all there is. In the first case, this acts to suppress possibilities; in the second, to open up so many possibilities speakers may never settle on the best one. There is no way of deciding which is best. George Steiner said the unboundedness of falsehood, which words permit, "is crucial both to human liberty and to the genius of language." But whereas Orwell's nightmare state shrinks all expression to a single, bogus "truth," deconstruction throws open the gates to endless equivocation, never terminating, because there is nothing external to language that might resist its flighty acrobatics. Words have nothing to push against. There is only the principle of "endlessly aiming at generating the new." Everything is suspect, because in everything lurks its opposite. Postmodernism refuses to admit any difference between the imaginary and the symbolic, the true and the false, reality and imitations of reality. Derrida does not believe that what is said or written is without meaning, or that anything goes, but rather that discourse "has too many meanings so that we can fix meaning only tentatively and only so far." That is why postmodernism can be made to serve the interests not only of the permanent revolution but also of the status quo. For that reason, Jurgen Habermas called the French intellectuals of the post-1968 period the "Young Conservatives."

The retreat into language, the idea that the genuine and the fake are now so thoroughly merged that everything is simulation, that the sign is sovereign, that there is no need to make contact with anything actual—real suffering, real happiness—has bred a certain disengagement, what Don Cupitt, the English theologian, approvingly describes as an antipathy to "stupid seriousness," and the extreme anthropocentrism that comes from the belief that everything that matters, everything that has meaning, is a human creation. Before postmodernism was a glimmer on the horizon, Bertrand Russell warned of the risks inherent in a set of ideas that diminish the "real world" to nothing more than an effect of language. "The concept of 'truth' as something dependent upon facts largely outside human control has been one of the ways in which philosophy hitherto has inculcated the necessary element of humility," Russell wrote. "When this check upon pride is removed, a further step is taken along the road towards a certain kind of madness—the intoxication with power which invaded philosophy with Fichte, and to which modern men, whether philosophers or not, are prone. I am persuaded that this intoxication is the greatest danger of our time, and that any philosophy which, however unintentionally, contributes to it is increasing the danger of vast social disaster."

CHAPTER TWENTY

Good at Being Human

"In the same novel," said the Dean, "somebody deliberately falsifies a result—later on, I mean—in order to get a job. And the man who made the original mistake finds it out. But he says nothing, because the other man is very badly off and has a wife and family to keep."
"These wives and families!" said Peter.
—Dorothy L. Sayers, *Gaudy Night*

To pursue truth with such astonishing lack of consideration for other people's feelings, to rend the thin veils of civilization so wantonly, so brutally, was to her so horrible an outrage of human decency that, without replying, dazed and blinded, she bent her head as if to let the pelt of jagged hail, the drench of dirty water, bespatter her unrebuked. There was nothing to be said.
—Virginia Woolf, *To the Lighthouse*

S HE GREW MORE ARTIFICIAL, HE BECAME more genuine." That masterpiece of paradox is a description of the entertainer Liberace, but it might stand for the way in which the Wildean substitution of the counterfeit for the real has become common currency in the thinking of our twenty-first century. In a biography of Liberace, Darden Pyron narrates the episode in which the rhinestone-studded pianist sued a London newspaper for hinting that he was homosexual. Liberace's whole persona, behind the outrageous gaudiness of his dress and manner, was calculated to appeal to the conservative, the middle class, the normal and the square. His act would have been seriously compromised by such innuendoes as the newspaper circulated. When asked in court, "Have you ever indulged in homosexual practices?" he replied: "No, sir, never in my life." Liberace died of AIDS in 1987, but never let on that he had contracted the disease. He won the libel suit. Was he guilty of outright lying? It seems not, at least in the presently accepted use of the word. Being someone who held an egregiously old-fashioned, almost prim view of what sort of audience he should appeal to, a critic noted, "a lie like that was a curious, backhanded way of telling some larger truth."

The "some larger truth" presumably was the image Liberace culti-vated, the belief he harbored that he must gratify the tastes of the vast median multitude who would be offended by any inkling of the not quite straight and wholesome. He held a mental picture of an America essentially conventional and regular in its average com-portment; such ordinariness made all the more keen a desire for the illusion of wealth and glamour that was Liberace's trademark. Pre-serving the illusion was more important by far than owning up to some inconvenient historical data relating to his actual sexual ori-entation that might taint it beyond redemption. The artificial is "truer" than the natural, because the artificial is what we would pre-fer ourselves, our world, to be; what it *is*, in imagination.

This view of things puts human needs and interests first, and mat-ters of known fact which may conflict with them a long way second. By contrast, the Greeks of the classical period observed a hard and principled separation between what something is and how it con-nects with what human beings desire. The American philosopher Richard Rorty has now declared this ancient distinction obsolete.

The millennia-old conundrums of philosophy, Rorty thinks, are artifacts in the sense that they were made by a language which has now lost its usefulness, and should be unmade by using a different language, better adapted to our interests. We need not talk about "reality and appearance" or "absolute and relative" any more. Plato's theory of the Forms as being the true reality, of which mundane things are mere imitations, was not the last word on this matter. It was merely useful for his purposes, for his "needs," at a particular stage of the Greek Enlightenment. We today have different needs, other kinds of interests, and therefore we use a different vocabulary, in which the Forms are conspicuously absent. Our requirements do not stay the same century after century.

Today's breed of pragmatists, of whom Rorty is a leading repre-sentative, begin their project with Darwin. According to this account, human beings share with the rest of the animal kingdom a need to come to grips with their surroundings, "doing their best to develop tools which will enable them to enjoy more pleasure and less pain."

Darwin, says Rorty, made it difficult for us to think of the higher anthropoids as having suddenly become a different sort of creature by evolving a brand-new faculty called "reason" or "intelligence." Better to see reason as a more complex form of the cunning which the lower anthropoids already possessed in abundance, before mankind came along. The truth-seeking aspect of human character is merely a later, more sophisticated form of animal cunning, and that includes the tricky, "Machiavellian" strategies deployed by non-human creatures who are up against it in the competition for survival. The theory of evolution might not have become accepted so quickly by large numbers of people were it not for the lessons learned from the advance of democracy and the rise of technology, which showed that mankind, by effort and brain power, by cleverness, can be master of its fate, can win against the forces of nature and accident. It became clear that this superior kind of cunning, descendant of pre-human craftiness, could alter reality so as to make it provide more happiness, whereas the early modern philosophers, notably Descartes, thought we should adapt to reality and find happiness in doing so, "trimming the sails of our desires to the prevailing winds." But as the age of Darwin merged into the age of Freud, human "desires and interests" became more problematic, grew suspect and not a little murky. Can we be truthful about what we *really* want, given the fact that much of what goes on in the mind is locked up in the unconscious, like a mad wife in the attic? "Our conscious mind," said Ernest Gellner, "seems to be rather like the public relations department of a large, complex and turbulent firm, dominated by a secretive and divided management, which never allows the PR officer to be privy to its secrets."

If truth is connected to our desires and interests, if those interests are ephemeral, if, in an important sense, we do not know what they are, then truth itself is built on shifting sands. Rorty recommends that we give up the quest for truth altogether, throw overboard the idea that there is some grand secret at the heart of things. Instead, he wants us simply "to be good at being human." Like Darwin, Rorty is averse to metaphysics. But Darwin, though inclined to materialism, was never in haste to relinquish his belief in God, feeling "compelled to look to a First Cause having an intelligent mind in some degree analogous to that of man; and I deserve to be called a Theist." That was Darwin's version of the Logos. It is anathema to many of today's philosophers. They claim to detect religious concepts still lurking in our modern worldly theories, and mercilessly root them out. The idea that there is a universal human nature is suspected of concealing the unwanted assumption that if we were all made by God, then we must share a common core of attributes. Similarly, the insistence that there can be no thoughts without language, an axiom of postmodern doctrine, is emphasized because "thoughts" by themselves smack of the disembodied Ideas of Plato, with their otherworldly status and link to the divine. "We will be wary," writes the University of Paris linguist and feminist Julia Kristeva, "of affirming that language is the *instrument* of thought. Such a conception leads one to believe that language *expresses*, as if it were a *tool*, something—an idea—external to it. But what is this idea? Does it exist other than in the form of language? To claim that it may exist in that way would amount to an idealism whose metaphysical roots are only too visible. One can thus see how an instrumentalist conception of language, whose basis presupposes the existence of thought or symbolic activity without language, by its philosophical implications leads to theology." Heaven forbid!

The suggestion Kristeva is anxious to discredit is that thoughts are somehow "truer" than language because they are nearer the source of metaphysical truth, closer to the Cartesian God who because he is perfect never deceives. And this is a God who, because he has no "needs and interests," no desires or wants; because he is a deity entirely remote from the arena of struggle and cunning that is Darwin's world, can know truth in all its pristine splendor. The death of God, to the new pragmatists, must also mean the death of truth, the decease of anything that stands outside the human, beyond human concerns, exterior to language. Truth, like morality and religion, is made for us and by us. We are not made for it. Rorty turns the sentiment, "Nothing human is alien to me," into the doctrine, "Everything that is placed above and beyond the human is unacceptable to me." Truth is one of the last points at which human beings are responsible to something nonhuman. So crush the infamous thing.

For the eighteenth century, "rational" meant being careful not to entertain ideas that had not been put through the wringer of critical scrutiny. Rorty defines it more as an attitude, an outlook of open-mindedness, a readiness to pay attention to different opinions, with a dash of the virtues the Greek Sophists adhered to: the sweet lubricant of persuasion as opposed to the brute force of logic. Again, he sniffs out a residue of theology in the notion that by intellectual sweat we can hope one day to arrive at a unique point of convergence where the truth, the Great Secret, is at last unveiled. This belief, he thinks, "seems to us an unfortunate attempt to carry a religious conception over into a secular culture." He does not want inquiries to converge, but to multiply, to propagate: "The end of human activity is not rest, but rather richer and better human activity." Progress consists in making it possible for us humans to "do more interesting things and be more interesting people."

In traditional philosophy, there were pairs of concepts in opposition to one another, and it was the job of philosophers to sort them out. These included mind and world, appearance and reality, subject and object. What is truth opposed to? Not falsehood, according to Rorty, but pleasure. And pleasure includes taking a delight in the original, the new, the surprising, the never before imagined. In an ideal Rortyan community, the image of the great scientist would not be of someone who "got it right," but of somebody who "made it new."

If language is just the correspondence of words to facts, then it is severely limited in the power of making new. If it must express only "true" thoughts, confine itself to getting it right, where is the pleasure then? Darwin, like Rousseau, speculated that language evolved out of the emotional cries of animals, and that the original human language was in the form of song and poetry. It was tightly linked to feelings and moods. (Rorty says the new rhetoric in his ideal community would draw on the lexicon of Romantic poetry and socialist politics rather than on that of Enlightenment rationalism.)

Today, there is an opposite tendency to view language as something quite arbitrary, abstract, a theory built into the mind, according to Chomsky, elegant but not designed for usefulness alone. It is not an "adaptation" in the usual sense. It has nothing to do with feelings. Being arbitrary, it has no natural correspondence with external reality or internal needs and desires. "Syntactic behavior," says Paul Heyer, "the increasing separation of conceptual activity from the sensory environment, now appears to be a more revealing place to look for language origins than in the emotional and imitative domain that Darwin focused on." Disconnected from the actual, language is thus free to fabricate the never was, the never is, the never will be. It enables smart-alecs to ask such questions as what the meaning of the word "is" is.

Celebrating the new means devaluing the familiar, the generally accepted, the widely agreed. And originality is uncomfortable in the presence of common sense, Darwin's great virtue and trademark habit of mind, which for the ordinary person embodies the workable truths of everyday existence. Iris Murdoch noted that today's literature tends to be involuted and obscure because the idea is to play with the language in a puzzling, "exciting" manner, to confound common sense. The idea that words refer to something outside themselves is simple-minded. "Literature must therefore be full of novelties, and obstacles and obscurities." And science too has succeeded in making what once seemed comfortable and familiar problematic and disconcerting. New, specialized languages of physics and biology refer only to themselves, elucidate nature in codes that are highly artificial and unnatural. This is a distant remove from the medieval concept of natural reason, which for the most part was glorified common sense. Murdoch talked of the "recurrent anti-rational and anti-intellectual reaction of intellectuals against what seems to them an old, tired tradition, heavy with unavailing thoughts which have been worked over innumerable times, an exasperated weariness with the old metaphysical world." The new anti-metaphysical metaphysic sets the intellectuals free to play, and such a license suits the humor of a culture captivated by the dizzying pace of technological change. But the suspicion held by the rest of humanity, the commonsensical ones, that the intellectuals "are merely playing about instead of serving society" can stabilize a tyranny as well as prompting a revolution. Here the severance of meaning from truth, and language from the world, can be seen not only as philosophically baseless and morally intolerable but as politically suicidal. The fundamental value which is obscured by this sort of outlook, Murdoch goes on, "is truth, language as truthful, where 'truthful' means faithful to, engaging intelligently and responsibly with, a reality which is beyond us."

For much of the nineteenth century, common sense was something like an official philosophy in America. As developed by such thinkers as Thomas Reid, eighteenth-century founder of the Scottish School of Common Sense, Dugald Stewart, his pupil, and Lord Kames, it was taught at universities, being regarded as a useful damper on the tendency of imagination to overheat, run riot, something the Puritans kept a wary eye on. Stability was an important requirement for the fledgling republic. At Princeton, the common-sense metaphysic was very much in vogue, and it was taught at Harvard and at Yale. It tended to inhibit writers of fiction, some of whom sought escape through the genre of the romance. Thomas Jefferson, who said that in the Declaration of Independence he had not tried to discover new principles, but simply "to place before mankind the common sense of the subject," deplored the popular taste for novels, which he felt destroyed a person's natural respect for "reason and fact, plain and unadorned." We may have got our ideas of anti-intellectualism in America back to front. Anti-intellectualism was not the reason for a distrust of the imagination, which multiplies possibilities; rather, Terence Martin thinks, it was part of a larger, all-embracing suspicion of the imaginative mind. College professors liked the Scottish School because it made no bones about the existence of right and wrong, and the reality of the world outside language and our minds. It was the kind of no-nonsense standpoint that suited a country on the move, one that had no time for frills. Philosophers like Bishop Berkeley, who championed common sense but produced theories that flew in the face of it, were pushed aside to make room for something more practical and conservative, more down to earth, more natural. Common sense was a sort of instinct, a compulsion like breathing and walking. Oliver Wendell Holmes remarked to his friend Sir Frederick Pollock: "As I have said so often, all I mean by truth is what I can't help believing." Holmes also said that philosophers were people hired by the comfortable class to prove that everything is all right. He added that he thought everything *was* all right, "but on very different grounds."

Thomas Reid held the view that common sense, like the Logos of Heraclitus, is shared by everyone, but not through reading and study. Philosophers like Descartes, Berkeley, and Hume had tended to make familiar knowledge strange, alien and difficult, limited to a handful of ingenious thinkers. Berkeley had made the world disappear and Descartes doubted everything. Commonsense philosophy said the world does exist, but we can't prove it. In Reid's account, we don't *need* to prove it. Someone well versed in the theory of optics does not see any better than a person to whom that theory is a closed book. It is exactly for this reason that our powers of common sense are shrouded and inexplicable. Philosophers are free to ferment distrust in their ability to give us genuine knowledge. Reid suggests such knowledge is God-given, a kind of miracle. We take it for granted. Philosophy can give no firm reason why we are the same person today that we were yesterday, but somehow we *know* we are the same person.

The Scottish School was popular with the clergy because it was seen to promote good morals, was compatible with liberal politics, and kept heterodox ideas at bay. It suited the "defensive" character of the American Revolution as opposed to the reckless trashing and overthrowing of the French one. Benjamin Franklin met Lord Kames in Scotland in 1759 and the two men exchanged letters. Jefferson read Kames, and found in his writings the theory of natural rights. But the reign of common sense in the new republic was not permanent; it was overtaken by the flowering of transcendentalism, which placed imagination firmly ahead of reason. The "commonsense" axioms of the Declaration of Independence came to be regarded by some as not common at all. In the nineteenth century they were seen as a possible incitement to revolutions of a less sane and reasonable kind. "What seems but common sense in one age often seems but nonsense in another." Jefferson moved on from the Scottish thinkers to an "operative" theory of democracy. James Marsh, president of the University of Vermont, in a letter to Coleridge in 1829, blasted the entire cast of the school of common sense for their "pages of inanity" and scoffed at their numerous readers "who are content to read without thinking."

Today, common sense is regarded in some quarters as a sort of Cartesian imp of deceit, a plausible falsifier and storyteller, while language is a device for unsettling and confounding the malign incubus. Lacan saw the unconscious as operating like a language unhooked from common sense and free to go its own way. It can lie to itself about such a basic thing as that a lemon tastes not like a lemon but like a vanilla ice cream. Philosophers must not commit the crime of being transparently easy to understand or summarize. In the war on common sense, intelligibility is a retrograde step, as good as a surrender to the enemy. Judith Butler, a professor of rhetoric at Berkeley, set off a flurry of correspondence in *The New York Times* with a defense of what she called "difficult sentences" in academic writing, but which others regarded as bad, pretentious, and impenetrable. Professor Butler wrote that it is necessary to couch one's arguments in language that seems deliberately perverse, refusing to make words mean what they customarily mean, exploding the notion that there is a "natural" way of understanding social and political realities, in order to dismantle commonsense ways of looking at the world. "If common sense sometimes preserves the social status quo and that status quo sometimes treats unjust social hierarchies as natural, it makes good sense on such occasions to find ways of challenging common sense. Language that takes up this challenge can help point to the way to a more socially just world."

One twentieth-century philosopher who despised such obfuscations was G. E. Moore. He cultivated a lucid, plain style and championed certain simple commonsense statements as true: absolutely, positively, manifestly true. Defying centuries of philosophical speculation that time and space are mental fictions, that we cannot prove there are other minds apart from our own, Moore expressed amazement that anyone could entertain such bizarre and outlandish ideas. Today, it is Moore who arouses the antipathy of thinkers who insist that only the bizarre does justice to the oddness of the world. In deploring Moore's influence, which he considers an intellectual catastrophe, Bryan Magee believes that the "greatest tragedy" of philosophy in the twentieth century was that it was dominated largely by thinkers who had no appreciation for the *strangeness* of things, who simply analyzed statements asserted by others instead of putting forward ideas of their own. They did not "make it new" because they were people for whom the world was not a problem. Quite apart from philosophy, modern science has shown that behind the surface ordinariness of things "teem truths and realities that common sense is totally unaware of, that are frequently astounding and often counter-intuitive, and sometimes deeply difficult to grasp even when we know them to be true." Only a few hundred years ago, people who dared to flout common sense by suggesting we are living on the surface of a huge sphere that is whirling on its axis and hurtling through space "were denounced as either ludicrous fantasists or dangerous liars whose wild falsehoods would, if believed, undermine all true religion and (therefore) true morality."

The overturning of common sense, the desire to escape from the familiar and the obvious, so necessary in science, one of the "unnatural" branches of knowledge, has been conspicuously at work during the past several decades in the formulation of social policy. If it is common sense to deny that all are born equal, to assume that boys are more intellectually robust than girls, to regard homosexuality as a removable kind of pathology, to define as "murder" the termination of a pregnancy, to treat animals as having no rights and no capacity for suffering, then common sense has to be abandoned and something new and different brought in to take its place. That may lead to the creation of double standards, and, judged by normal criteria, double standards are a sort of lie. They punish outbursts of hate on the part of the right more severely than those emanating from the left. They are harder on men who create an uncomfortable atmosphere for female workers than on women who do the same for their male colleagues. They tolerate untruths, if those untruths have

useful social consequences, whereas mendacity of other, less beneficial kinds is given short shrift.

The targeting of social inequality as the single greatest threat to
the moral authority, even the legitimacy of American democracy,
says Shelby Steele, "transformed our culture in a way that we are just
beginning to understand. It made social morality, more than personal morality, the test of moral authority in public life."

Lying, misleading, letting silences be misinterpreted, using language to confuse and misdirect, are grievous lapses when seen from
the viewpoint of personal morality. They may be less damning if, like
Nietzsche's lies of life, they bolster the advance of social decency,
especially the task of making every American equal. That is why President Bill Clinton, as a Democrat wedded to the concept of equality,
was so rapidly, against the best predictions of political experts, forgiven for lying about his relations with Monica Lewinsky. Common
sense told those experts that a president who behaved like that,
whose personal morality was deplorable, could not stay in office. But
social morality, the "needs and interests" of the majority, which
approved of the direction in which he was taking the country, tran-
scended the principle that a president should always tell the nation
the truth.

The new pragmatists see truth as a dead end when it comes to
remaking society. Rorty asserts flat out that the trouble with aiming
at truth is that you would not know when you had reached it, even
supposing you could reach it. The same goes for morality. You may
think you have done "what is right," but who knows, a hundred, two
hundred years from now, it may all turn out to be a ghastly mistake.
All you can confidently hope for is the "greater satisfaction of ever
more various needs," and this is accomplished by taking the desires
and interests and views of more and more diverse human beings into
account. Above all, you must think of something new. "We see both
intellectual and moral progress not as a matter of getting closer to
the True or the Good or the Right, but as an increase in imaginative
power," Rorty writes. "We see imagination as the cutting edge of cultural evolution, the power which—given peace and prosperity—
constantly operates so as to make the human future richer than the

human past. Imagination is the source both of new scientific pictures of the physical universe and of new conceptions of possible communities. It is what Newton and Christ, Freud and Marx, had in common: the ability to redescribe the familiar in unfamiliar terms."

The trouble is of course that when philosophers develop a theory that entails abandoning the True, the Good, and the Right, for seemingly admirable reasons, people are apt to be vaguely receptive to the abandonment without making an effort to understand the theory in any depth. Trickle-down wisdom is as iffy as trickle-down economics. That is clear from the devastating exposé by Alan Sokal of the use of mathematical concepts and jargon by so-called experts on the humanities in a hoax paper published in the journal *Social Text,* whose editors mistook it for a serious academic project. The paper argued that physical reality, no less than social reality, is at bottom just a social and linguistic construct: "the pi of Euclid and the G of Newton, formerly thought to be constant and universal, are now perceived in their ineluctable historicity; and the putative observer becomes fatally de-centered, disconnected from any epistemic link to a space-time point that can no longer be defined by geometry alone." The point of the hoax was to bring home the fact that even professional scholars will accept gross insults to common sense, such as the idea that physical reality is made of language, if they are dressed up in the seductive apparel of ideas drawn from the discoveries of science which, since Galileo and Newton, have confounded our expectations of how the world works. The intention is to make the study of society as counterintuitive as the theories of science which first struck the commonsense public as "wild falsehoods." Cynicism, as Iris Murdoch said, is often bred from a superficial acquaintance with theories. It may at first be an affectation, but later it can develop into a deadly disease.

The Age of Theory and the Age of Suspicion converge at a time when culture, not nature, is the medium to be manipulated and toyed with for our pleasure and benefit, for the sake of our desires and needs. In a sense, Darwin brought human beings closer to nature by showing that they evolved from simpler and older species. But in another way he estranged us from nature by his hardheaded conviction that nature was not created to satisfy our needs. Culture took on that role, and culture, unlike nature, is infinitely malleable, endlessly subversible. It has no fixed relation to "the Truth" or to the physically real. That was the reason why the theologian Karl Barth waged such a vehement war of words against the idea that theology is a creation of culture, which he recognized as primarily a need-supplying vehicle, not a truth-preserving one. Barth's intemperate onslaughts on the liberal theology fashionable at the time were motivated by a belief that what is in fashion today can easily pass out of it tomorrow. He set great store by the prophetic role of the church, which he feared would be lost if it attached itself to something as self-legitimating, as keyed to the ideal, not of truth but of the "more important" considerations of human well-being and social progress, as culture.

A history of falsehood may start with the world of Darwin, with the surprisingly "natural" evolution of cunning and chicanery in the animal kingdom, but it ends with the triumph of culture; of language, art, politics, social theory, all now regarded as founts of meaning, as vehicles for multiplying possibilities, for sustaining and justifying beneficial untruths, for making human life more interesting by removing the traditional anchors, dissolving the foundations. Society is not simple enough for its members to survive by always telling the truth, but one result of the decline of the concept of truth has been to make the culture more complex than ever, which in turn promotes the sort of falsehood an in-fashion critic can dignify by calling it "a curious, backhanded way of telling some larger truth."

Notes

INTRODUCTION

p. 11   *The Kaiser Family Foundation*: "Doctoring the Truth, " *New Republic*, November 15, 1999, p. 13.

p. 11   *"There are things much more important than civility"*: See Benjamin De Mott, "Seduced by Civility, " *The Nation*, December 9, 1996, pp. 11–19.

p. 12   *"Socrates was told as much"*: Aristophanes, *The Clouds*, trans. Benjamin Bickley Rogers (Cambridge, MA: Harvard University Press, 1978). Aristophanes gives a wildly unfair picture of Socrates as a purveyor of sophistry, but the drift of the play is that philosophy and abstract thought generally tend to disrupt the ordinary decencies of civilized life. "Socrates is portrayed as one who investigates and teaches without bothering to think about the effects of his teaching on other people. He loves the truth but has not given any thought to the possibility that others may love some things more than truth"—John W. Danford, *David Hume and the Problem of Reason* (New Haven: Yale University Press, 1990), p. 4.

p. 12   *David Stoll . . . examined*: Kenneth Lee, "Untruth in Academe," *The American Enterprise* (May–June 1999), pp. 43–47.

p. 12   *While there are an infinite number*: *The Essays of Michel Montaigne*, ed. W. Carew Hazlitt, trans. Charles Cotton II (Chicago & New York: A. L. Burt Company, 1892), Vol. I. p. 33.

p. 12   *A new dramatic genre*: Ben Brantley, "Extracting the Essence of Real Lives Onstage," *New York Times*, January 27, 2000, pp. B1, 9.

p. 13   *"lives are transformed"*: Peter Nicholls, *Modernism: A Literary Guide* (Berkeley: University of California Press, 1995), p. 8.

p. 13   *"Art is the lie that makes us realize"*: Pablo Picasso, "Art as Individual Idea," in Richard Ellman and Charles Feidelson, Jr. eds. *The Modern Tradition* (New York: Oxford University Press, 1965), p. 25.

p. 14   *the "Demon of Originality"*: Roger Shattuck, *The Innocent Eye* (New York: Farrar, Straus & Giroux, 1984), p. 62.

p. 14   only "absolute newness": See Roland Barthes, The Pleasure of the Text, trans. Richard Miller (New York: Hill & Wang, 1975).

p. 15   as "born psychologists": Nicholas Humphrey, Consciousness Regained (New York: Oxford University Press, 1983).

p. 15   "We secrete from within ourselves": George Steiner, After Babel (New York: Oxford University Press, 1998), p. 238.

p. 16   lies are all the more effective: John Kucich, The Power of Lies (Ithaca & London: Cornell University Press, 1994), p. 22.

CHAPTER ONE

p. 17   "If, as Western ethics and theology": Emil Wenzel in Robert W. Mitchell and Nicholas S. Thompson, eds., Deception: Perspectives on Human and Nonhuman Deceit (Albany: State University of New York Press, 1986), p. xv.

p. 17   "from the war of nature": Charles Darwin, Origin of Species (New York: Modern Library, n.d.), p. 374.

p. 18   he commended as "admirable": Charles Darwin, The Descent of Man (New York: Modern Library, n.d.), p. 666.

p. 18   of course no intelligence would be involved: Cf. History of Biology, 15 (1982), pp. 163–89.

p. 18   Spencer considered basic to all ethical progress: Darwin: A Norton Critical Edition, ed. Philip Appleman (New York & London: W. W. Norton, 1970), p. 393.

p. 19   rips off pieces of their flesh: Mitchell and Thompson, eds., Deception: Perspectives on Human and Nonhuman Deceit, p. 61.

p. 19   who never tumble to the fact: Howard Topoff, "The Ant Who Would be Queen," Natural History, vol. 103, no. 8 (August 1994), pp. 41–46.

p. 19   a certain genus of beetle: Deborah Letourneau, "Ants That Pay the Piper," Natural History, vol. 102, no. 10 (October 1993), pp. 4–8.

p. 20   Certain fireflies have become: Mitchell and Thompson, eds., Deception: Perspectives on Human and Nonhuman Deceit, p. 113.

p. 20   These deplorable ruses probably explain: James Lloyd in ibid., p. 124.

p. 21   It may be that the silk tufts: Catherine Craig, "Webs of Deceit," Natural History, vol. 104, no. 3, (March 1995), pp. 33–35.

p. 21   "may be said to have taken pains": Darwin, Origin of Species, p. 367.

p. 23   "Lying is not permitted in this universe": Quoted in Gertrude Himmelfarb, Darwin and the Darwinian Revolution (New York: W. W. Norton, 1968), p. 239.

p. 23   "a human being cannot tell": See Lewis Thomas, Late Night Thoughts on Listening to Mahler's Ninth Symphony (New York: Viking Press, 1983), pp. 127–32.

p. 24   "a great feigner and fraud": Machiavelli, The Prince, trans. Bruce Penman (London: J. M. Dent, 1981), p. 104.

p. 25   "an endless process of cut-throat competition": Isaiah Berlin, The Crooked Timber of Humanity (New York: Knopf, 1991), p. 73.

p. 25   "truer than every other truth": Quoted in Leo Strauss, Thoughts on Machiavelli (Glencoe, IL: The Free Press, 1959), p. 178.

p. 25   "*Many instances could be given*": Darwin, *The Descent of Man*, p. 488.

p. 27   *Why, for instance, is the eye*: William Paley, *Natural Theology*, ed. Frederick Ferre (Indianapolis: Bobbs-Merrill, 1963), p. 18.

p. 27   *The eye is ingenious, certainly*: Darwin, *Origin of Species*, p. 135.

p. 27   "*One might say that nature has taken*": Ibid., p. 149.

p. 28   "*with me the horrid doubt*": Francis Darwin, ed., *The Autobiography of Charles Darwin and Selected Letters* (New York: Dover Publications, 1958), p. 68.

p. 28   "*Natural selection simply does not care*": Michael Ruse, *Taking Darwin Seriously* (Oxford & New York: Basil Blackwell, 1986), p. 172.

p. 29   "*Masters of Suspicion*": Paul Ricoeur, *Freud and Philosophy*, trans. Denis Savage (New Haven: Yale University Press, 1970), p. 33.

p. 29   "*Socrates was the first person*": Cicero, *Academica*, trans. H. Rackham William (New York: G. P. Putnam & Sons, 1933), p. 425.

p. 29   "*A dog might as well speculate*": Charles Darwin, Letter to Asa Gray in *The Autobiography of Charles Darwin*, p. 249.

CHAPTER TWO

p. 31   "*One of the most important things*": Robert Trivers, *Social Evolution* (Menlo Park, CA: Benjamin Cummings Publishing Co., 1985), p. 395.

p. 31   "*God is sophisticated*": Ronald Clark, *Einstein: The Life and Times* (New York: Avon Books, 1971), p. 19.

p. 33   *It has been suggested that the revival*: Peter J. Bowler, *Evolution the History of an Idea* (Berkeley: University of California Press, 1989), p. 258.

p. 34   "*a rope of sand*": Peter Raby, *Samuel Butler: A Biography* (Iowa City: University of Iowa Press, 1991), p. 164.

p. 34   *an esoteric doctrine*: Ibid., p. 176.

p. 34   *cunning as opposed to "strokes of luck"*: Ibid., p. 166.

p. 34   *Cunning does exist in nature*: Karl Popper, *Unended Quest: An Intellectual Biography* (London: Fontana Paperbacks, 1976), p. 179.

p. 34   *a "mind and intelligence throughout the universe"*: Raby, *Samuel Butler*, p. 176.

p. 34   "*to see every atom*": Samuel Butler, *Unconscious Memory* (New York: AMS Press, 1968), pp. 194, 196.

p. 34   "*The theory that luck*": Samuel Butler, *Luck or Cunning?* (New York: AMS Press, 1968), p. 235.

p. 34   "*Darwin Denounced!:*" Raby, *Samuel Butler*, pp. 176, 244.

p. 35   "*a chaotic loss of control*": Sally Peters, *Bernard Shaw: The Ascent of the Superman* (New Haven: Yale University Press, 1996), p. 192.

p. 35   *a philosophy of the Life Force*: Richard M. Ohmann, "Born to Set It Right," in R. J. Kaufmann, ed., *G. B. Shaw: A Collection of Critical Essays* (Englewood Cliffs, NJ: Prentice-Hall, 1965), p. 40.

p. 35   "*higher and higher individuals*": G. B. Shaw, *Man and Superman: A Comedy and a Philosophy* (New York, 1911), pp. 113–14.

p. 36   *the "meaning" of the colors of animals*: Bowler, *Evolution*, p. 250.

p. 36   its nasty habit of squirting: Wolfgang Wickler, *Mimicry in Plants and Animals* (New York: McGraw Hill, 1968), p. 14.

p. 36   "overactive Darwinian imaginations": Peter J. Bowler, *The Eclipse of Darwinism* (Baltimore: Johns Hopkins University Press, 1983), pp. 30, 151.

p. 37   keeping numbers down to manageable size: Michael Ruse, *The Darwinian Revolution* (Chicago: University of Chicago Press, 1979), p. 12.

p. 37   quite free in using the language: See Eileen Crist, *Images of Animals* (Philadelphia: Temple University Press, 1999), pp. 128–43.

p. 38   the case of the ten-spined stickleback: Trivers, *Social Evolution*, p. 406.

p. 38   "Something priceless was lost": Mitchell and Thompson, eds., *Deception: Perspectives on Human and Nonhuman Deceit*, pp. xxiv–xxv.

p. 38   an animal posing as another sort: Ibid., p. 25.

p. 39   Mitchell sees four levels of deception: Ibid., p. 25.

p. 39   "a pervasive distortion of information": Francis de Waal, "Emotional Control," *The Behavioral and Brain Sciences* (Cambridge: University Press, 1988), Vol. 11, No. 2, p. 254.

p. 40   " . . . they cannot have beliefs about Friday": Daniel Dennett, *Brainstorms* (Montgomery, VT: Bradford Books, 1978), p. 274.

p. 40   the case of Austin: Sue Savage-Rumbaugh and Kelly McDonald, "Deception and Social Manipulation in Symbol-using Apes" in Richard W. Byrne and Andrew Whiten, eds., *Machiavellian Intelligence* (Oxford: Clarendon Press; New York: Oxford University Press, 1988), pp. 224–37.

p. 41   the chimp can understand only rather simple: David Premack, "Does the Chimpanzee Have a Theory of Mind?" in Byrne and Whiten, eds., *Machiavellian Intelligence*, p. 175.

p. 41   "Within little more than a week": Humphrey, *Consciousness Regained*, p. 3.

p. 42   "At every level": Steiner, *After Babel*, p. 239.

CHAPTER THREE

p. 43   "It is much easier to recognize error": Johann Wolfgang von Goethe, *Maxims and Reflections*, trans. Elisabeth Stopp, edited with an Introduction and Notes by Peter Hutchinson (London & New York: Penguin Books, 1988), p. 19.

p. 44   When Odysseus cooks up a piece of fiction: Homer, *The Odyssey*, trans. Robert Fitzgerald (New York: Farrar, Straus & Giroux, 1988), p. 239.

p. 45   He is an expert in the use of words: Simon Goldhill, *The Poet's Voice* (Cambridge & New York: Cambridge University Press, 1991), p. 4.

p. 45   "Were we to trace": Paolo Vivante, *Homer* (New Haven: Yale University Press, 1985), p. 98.

p. 45   "the truth about physical objects": Bertrand Russell, *Problems of Philosophy* (London: Thornton Butterworth, 1936), p. 59.

p. 46   they "were not simply trying to explain": G. S. Kirk, "Greek Science," in Hugh Lloyd-Jones, ed., *The Greek World* (Baltimore: Penguin Books, 1965), p. 118.

p. 46 *corner the market in olive oil presses*: Aristotle, *Politics* , trans. H. Rackham (Cambridge, MA: Harvard University Press, 1977), p. 55.

p. 46 *When people say that it "quakes"*: Quoted in G. S. Kirk and J. E. Raven, *The Presocratic Philosophers* (London & New York: Cambridge University Press, 1963), p. 92.

p. 47 *Anaximander, one scholar speculates*: Drew A. Hyland, *The Origins of Philosophy* (New York: G. P. Putnam's Sons, 1973), p. 106.

p. 48 *"move around the earth"*: Quoted in Kirk and Raven, *The Presocratic Philosophers*, p. 154.

p. 48 *"flat like a leaf"*: Quoted in *ibid*.

p. 49 *"He was fond of concealing"*: Philip Wheelwright, *The Presocratics* (Indianapolis: Bobbs-Merrill, 1966), p. 65.

p. 49 *"There comes a stage"*: Ibid., p. 66.

p. 50 *Logos was first given metaphysical status*: See Granville C. Henry, *Logos: Mathematics and Christian Theology* (Lewisberg, PA: Bucknell University Press, 1976).

p. 50 *In the prologue to the Gospel of St. John*: C. H. Dodd, *The Interpretation of the Fourth Gospel* (Cambridge: University Press, 1958), p. 277.

p. 51 *simply blowing hot air*: Aristotle, *Metaphysics*, trans. Hugh Tredennick (Cambridge, MA: Harvard University Press, 1980), p. 163.

p. 51 *"Eyes and ears are bad witnesses"*: Wheelwright, *The Presocratics*, p. 70.

p. 52 *"Nature loves to hide"*: Ibid.

p. 52 *"admirable laws"*: Quoted in Kirk and Raven, *The Presocratic Philosophers*, p. 263.

p. 53 *"It is an intelligence"*: Marcel Detienne and Jean-Pierre Vernant, *Cunning Intelligence in Greek Culture and Society*, trans. Janet Lloyd (Totowa, NJ: Humanities Press; Brighton, UK: Harvester Press, 1978), p. 44.

p. 54 *Thanks to the Metis within him*: Ibid., p. 14.

p. 54 *"the ancient of the salt sea"*: Homer, *The Odyssey*, p. 64.

p. 54 *"The many-colored, shimmering nature"*: Detienne and Vernant, *Cunning Intelligence*, p. 21.

p. 55 *a "glossomorph"*: Felix Cleve, *The Giants of Pre-Socratic Philosophy* (The Hague: Martin Nijhoff, 1965), Vol. 2, p. 538.

p. 55 *"Mortals are immortals"*: Kirk and Raven, *The Presocratic Philosophers*, p. 210.

p. 55 *God undergoes alteration*: Ibid., p. 199.

p. 55 *Heraclitus, like many a modern bard*: Myles Burnyeat, "Message from Heraclitus," *New York Review of Books*, May 13, 1982, pp. 44–47.

p. 55 *One scholar maintains*: William Jordan, *Ancient Concepts of Philosophy* (London & New York: Routledge, 1992), p. 27.

p. 56 *the whole system rests on a "sandy" foundation*: Jonathan Barnes, *The Presocratic Philosophers* (London & New York: Routledge, 1993), p. 167.

p. 56 *treating Parmenides as if he were*: Ibid., p. 172.

p. 57 *to think in that way*: Aristotle, *On Coming to Be and Passing Away*, trans. E. S. Forster (Cambridge, MA: Harvard University Press, 1965), p. 238.

p. 57 "an exploration of the field of possibilities": Morris R. Cohen, A Preface to Logic (New York: Dover Publications, 1944), p. 181.

p. 57 "the aesthetic view of being": Karl Jaspers, The Great Philosophers, Vol. 2, ed. Hannah Arendt, trans. Ralph Manheim (New York: Harcourt Brace & World, 1962), p. 25.

CHAPTER FOUR

p. 58 "We have to mix a little falsehood": Iris Murdoch, Metaphysics as a Guide to Morals (London: Penguin Books, 1995), p. 105.

p. 58 provoked ingenious speculations: Nicholas Denyer, Language, Thought and Falsehood in Ancient Greek Philosophy (London & New York: Routledge, 1993), p. 1.

p. 58 Plato's Dialogue: Plato, Euthydemus, trans. W. R. M. Lamb (Cambridge, MA: Harvard University Press; London: William Heinemann Ltd., 1977), pp. 393–97.

p. 62 Known at a later time as the "Throws": W. K. C. Guthrie, The Sophists (Cambridge & New York: Cambridge University Press, 1971), p. 264.

p. 62 Protagoras invented the shoulder strap: Diogenes Laertius, Lives of Eminent Philosophers, Vol. 2, trans. R. D. Hicks (Cambridge, MA: Harvard University Press, 1970), p. 465.

p. 63 "Man is the measure of all things": Plato, Theaetetus, trans. Harold North Fowler (Cambridge, MA: Harvard University Press, 1987), 152A.

p. 64 "instead of comparing us Sophists": Ibid., 167B.

p. 65 "Nature, we assert, does nothing in vain": See, for example, Aristotle, De Caelo, trans. W. K. C. Guthrie (Cambridge, MA: Harvard University Press, 1971), p. 201.

p. 66 in a scene where an obnoxious young man: Aristophanes, The Clouds, p. 137.

p. 67 "a spiritual revolution": Louis Dupré, Passage to Modernity (New Haven & London: Yale University Press, 1993), p. 23.

p. 67 "the beginning of a division between mind": Lawrence Hatab, Myth and Philosophy (La Salle, IL: Open Court Publishing, 1990), p. 159.

p. 67 "started from the premise that": Albert Borgmann, The Philosophy of Language (The Hague: Martin Nijhoff, 1974), pp. 16–17.

p. 67 "how to win in the game of life": Robert Brumbaugh, Plato for the Modern Age (New York: Crowell-Collier, 1962), p. 22.

p. 68 "about the surface of human conflicts": John Herman Randall, Plato, Dramatist of the Life of Reason (New York: Columbia University Press, 1970), p. 82.

p. 69 "Not only success, but sometimes effective survival": Brumbaugh, Plato for the Modern Age, p. 24.

p. 70 "the Absolute Talker": Randall, Plato, p. 2.

p. 70 "the most persuasive orator": Robert W. Hall, Plato (London: Allen & Unwin, 1981), p. 7.

p. 70 "upon those who hear it": Barnes, The Presocratic Philosophers, p. 463.

p. 71   *"the proper way of telling lies"*: Aristotle, *Poetics*, trans. W. Hamilton Fyfe (Cambridge, MA: Harvard University Press, 1973), p. 99.

p. 71   *"Any fool can tell a lie"*: Dorothy L. Sayers, "Aristotle on Detective Fiction," in Sayers, *Unpopular Opinions* (New York: Harcourt Brace & Co., 1947), pp. 231–32 (italics in the original).

p. 71   *"The power of speech"*: Wheelwright, *The Presocratics*, p. 250.

p. 71   *"the charmer to whom nothing is denied"*: Guthrie, *The Sophists*, p. 50.

p. 72   *And the absence of a sense of fun*: Ibid., p. 194.

p. 72   *"Shame on you, Philomena!"*: Aristotle, *Rhetoric*, trans. John Henry Freese (Cambridge, MA: Harvard University Press, 1975), p. 367.

p. 72   *Socrates is not a "real man"*: Plato, *Gorgias*, trans. W. R. M. Lamb (Cambridge MA: Harvard University Press, 1983), p. 389.

p. 72   *"For while men believe"*: Francis Bacon, *Novum Organum*, trans. and ed. Peter Urbach and John Gibson (La Salle, IL: Open Court Publishing, 1994), p. 64.

p. 73   *"The true end, scope"*: Francis Bacon, *Valerius Terminus or the Interpretation of Nature*, in Basil Montague, ed., *Works of Francis Bacon* (London, 1825), Vol. I, p. 281.

p. 73   *"representatives of falsehood"*: Benjamin Jowett, ed. and trans., *The Republic of Plato* (Oxford: Clarendon Press, 1925), p. clxi.

p. 73   *"A principle requiring all beliefs"*: Denyer, *Language, Thought and Falsehood* . . . , p. 46.

CHAPTER FIVE

p. 74   *"Theories usually result"*: Goethe, *Maxims and Reflections*, p. 54.

p. 74   *Consciousness is not an artifact*: Norman Cantor, *Civilization in the Middle Ages* (New York: HarperPerennial, 1993), p. 17.

p. 75   *"the first nominalist"*: Guthrie , *The Sophists*, p. 214.

p. 77   *comparable to the secret journey*: David Knowles, *The Evolution of Medieval Thought* (Baltimore: Helicon Press, 1962), p. 320.

p. 77   *likened to a nineteenth-century liberal*: John Kilcullen, "The Political Writings," in Paul Vincent Spade, ed., *The Cambridge Companion to Ockham* (New York: Cambridge University Press, 1999), p. 319.

p. 77   *"Ockham's name continued to carry"*: Ibid., p. 3.

p. 78   *the task of redeeming a language*: See Mary Carruthers, *The Search for St. Truth* (Evanston, IL: Northwestern University Press, 1973).

p. 78   *a philosophical poet fascinated with nominalism*: John Gardner, *The Life and Times of Chaucer* (New York: Knopf, 1977), p. 224.

p. 79   *"No fourteenth century nominalist"*: Ibid., p. 292.

p. 79   *"There is hardly a day"*: Paul Tillich, *A History of Christian Thought*, ed. Carl E. Braaten (New York: Simon & Schuster, 1968), pp. 142–44.

p. 80   *"The separation of the sign"*: Dupré, *Passage to Modernity*, p. 104.

p. 82   *"Among those who labor in philosophy"*: Josef Pieper, *Scholasticism* (New York: McGraw-Hill Book Co., 1960), p. 122.

p. 82   that "any sure and pure truth": Bertrand Russell, *A History of Western Philosophy* (New York: Simon & Shuster, 1945), p. 466.

p. 83   That condemnation was a hinge event: Francis Oakley, *The Medieval Experience: Foundations of Western Cultural Singularity* (New York: Scribner, 1974), pp. 164–65.

p. 85   Nominalism has been blamed: John Herman Randall, Jr., *The Making of the Modern Mind* (Boston: Houghton Mifflin, 1940), p. 103.

p. 85   "though some poet's dream might be": Noel Annan, *Leslie Stephen, The Godless Victorian* (New York: Random House, 1984), pp. 200–01.

p. 86   the speech fell flat: *Ibid.*, p. 208.

p. 86   true "for certain practical purposes": *Ibid.*, p. 220.

p. 87   not one of the "theological" virtues: Hans Küng, *Truthfulness: The Future of the Church* (New York: Sheed & Ward, 1968), p. 22.

p. 87   "Since truthfulness does not concern": *Ibid.*, p. 73.

CHAPTER SIX

p. 89   "The human world flourishes best": Roger Scruton, *Modern Philosophy: A Survey* (London: Sinclair-Stevenson, 1994), pp. 245–46.

p. 89   "If everything is possible": Alexandre Koyre, in *Descartes's Philosophical Writings*, selected and trans. by Norman Kemp Smith (New York: Modern Library, 1958), p. ix.

p. 90   the epitome of "malice or feebleness": René Descartes: *Meditations on First Philosophy*, Margaret D. Wilson, ed., in *The Essential Descartes* (New York: Penguin Books, 1983), p. 194.

p. 90   he talks about "my lying memory": *Ibid.*, p. 6.

p. 90   "I will suppose, then": Elizabeth Anscombe and Peter Geach, eds., *Descartes: Philosophical Writings* (London: Nelson Paperbacks, The Open University, 1972), p. 65.

p. 92   math by itself cannot be used to legitimate: *Ibid.*, p. 209.

p. 92   thinks the demon is arguably: Scruton, *Modern Philosophy*, p. 20.

p. 93   "carts, precipices, dogs and whatnot": Diogenes Laertius, *Lives of Eminent Philosophers*, Vol. 2, trans. R. D. Hicks (Cambridge, MA: Harvard University Press, 1970), p. 475.

p. 93   "We differ in our constitutional peculiarities": Philip P. Hallie, ed., *Sextus Empiricus: Selections from the Major Writings on Skepticism, Man and God* (Cambridge, MA: Hackett Publishing Co., 1985), pp. 54–55.

p. 94   "every place swarms" . . . "does nothing but ferret": *The Essays of Michel de Montaigne*, Vol. II, pp. 566, 564.

p. 94   "ignorantly and negligently led": *Ibid.*, Vol. II, p. 570.

p. 94   "would put themselves out of themselves": *Ibid.*, Vol. II, p. 621–22.

p. 95   "Presumption is our natural and original disease": *Ibid.*, Vol. I, p. 436.

p. 95   capable of "subtleties and inventions": *Ibid.*, Vol. I, p. 460.

p. 96   "By extending the implicit skeptical tendencies": Richard H. Popkin, *The His-*

tory of Skepticism from Erasmus to Spinoza (Berkeley: University of California Press, 1979), p. 54.

p. 96 "I cannot imagine": Letter to Marin Mersenne quoted in Jack R. Vrooman, René Descartes: A Biography (New York: G. P. Putnam's Sons, 1970), p. 84.

p. 97 "Skepticism was simply a means to an end": Stephen Gaukroger, Descartes: An Intellectual Biography (New York & Oxford: Clarendon Press, 1977), p. 12.

p. 97 One answer . . . was to insist: Ibid., p. 149.

p. 98 for being "profoundly bourgeois": Ernest Gellner, Reason and Culture (Oxford & Cambridge, MA: Basil Blackwell, 1992), pp. 5, 13.

p. 98 "a yearning for freedom": Ibid., pp. 5–6.

p. 98 "'Tis the misery of our condition": The Essays of Michel de Montaigne, Vol. I, p. 508.

p. 98 "Descartes lived an unhappy": Gaukroger, Descartes: An Intellectual Biography, p. 9.

p. 98 "I always had an excessive desire": Descartes's Philosophical Writings, p. 13.

p. 99 "the constitution of true Religion": Ibid., p. 16.

p. 100 "When we no longer look": Darwin, Origin of Species, p. 371.

CHAPTER SEVEN

p. 102 "There is no a priori reason": C. I. Lewis quoted in Isaiah Berlin, The Sense of Reality (New York: Farrar, Straus & Giroux, 1966), p. 266.

p. 102 "I have come to think": Quoted in Lancelyn Green and Walter Hooper, C. S. Lewis, A Biography (New York & London: Harcourt Brace Jovanovich, 1974), p. 83.

p. 102 "opinions most dubious": Descartes, Discourse on the Method, ed. Wilson, p. 122.

p. 104 "affrighted and confounded": David Hume, A Treatise of Human Nature, ed. Ernest C. Mossner (London & New York: Penguin Books, 1985), pp. 311–12.

p. 104 The most natural life for humans: David Hume, An Enquiry Concerning Human Understanding, ed. Eric Steinberg (Indianapolis: Hackett Publishing Co., 1977), p. 3.

p. 104 "fell deadborn from the press": "My Own Life," in V. C. Chappell, ed., The Philosophy of David Hume (New York: Modern Library, 1963), p. 4.

p. 104 Socializing "cures me of this": David Hume, A Treatise of Human Nature, p. 316.

p. 105 "The world plainly resembles" . . . "If we survey a ship": David Hume, "Dialogues Concerning Natural Religion" in The Philosophy of David Hume, ed. V. C. Chappell (New York: The Modern Library, 1963), p. 548, 539–40.

p. 106 "The feelings of our heart": David Hume, An Enquiry Concerning Human Understanding, p. 2.

p. 107 It is "the great guide": Ibid., p. 29.

p. 108 "professionally disinterested in the difference": John Forrester, Truth Games (Cambridge, MA: Harvard University Press, 1997), p. 70.

p. 108   *indolently subscribe to the "general maxims of the world"*: Hume, *A Treatise of Human Nature*, p. 316.

p. 108   *"The mind is such"*: Ruse, *Taking Darwin Seriously*, p. 188.

p. 109   *a person who "loves the truth"*: John Danford, *David Hume and the Problem of Reason* (New Haven & London: Yale University Press, 1990), p. 4.

p. 109   *"immoderate" ambitions of early modern philosophers*: Ibid., p. 3.

p. 109   *"I believe the disappearance"*: Ibid., p. 24.

p. 110   *"Philosophicaly, the power of the word"*: Robert C. Solomon, *Introducing Philosophy, 2nd ed.* (New York & London: Harcourt Brace Jovanovich, 1981), p. 185.

p. 110   *"habit may lead us to belief"*: Albert Einstein, *Ideas and Opinions* (New York: Modern Library, 1994), p. 23.

p. 110   *"I studied it with fervor"*: Denis Brian, *Einstein: A Life* (New York: John Wiley & Sons, 1996), p. 61.

p. 111   *"Nothing is more dangerous"*: Hume, *A Treatise of Human Nature*, pp. 267–68.

p. 111   *"one of the most fascinating and disquieting"*: John Passmore, "Hume," in Bryan Magee, ed., *The Great Philosophers* (Oxford & New York: Oxford University Press, 1987), p. 167.

CHAPTER EIGHT

p. 112   *"The truth is too simple"*: George Sand quoted in Bruce Krajewski, *Traveling with Hermes* (Amherst, MA: University of Massachusetts Press, 1992), p. 32.

p. 112   *"There is no 'the truth' "*: Adrienne Rich, *On Lies, Secrets and Silence: Selected Prose 1966–1978* (New York & London: W. W. Norton, 1979), p. 187.

p. 112   *"Simplicity! He's as simple as the truth"*: Maxim Gorky, *Collected Works, Vol. 17,* trans. Yuri Barabash (Moscow: Aesthetics and Poetics Moscow Progress Publishers, 1977), p. 168.

p. 113   *"scorned the value of evidences"* . . . *"By the very simplicity"*: Noel Annan in Richard A. Levine, ed., *Backgrounds to Victorian Literature* (San Francisco: Chandler Publishing Co., 1967), p. 103.

p. 114   *"God does many things"*: Quoted in Julius Weinberg, *A Short History of Medieval Philosophy* (Princeton: Princeton University Press, 1964), p. 239.

p. 115   *a cult of the "Christian gentleman"*: Steven Shapin, *A Social History of Truth* (Chicago & London: University of Chicago Press, 1994), pp. 81–83.

p. 115   *"a lie is useless to the gods"*: Jowett, *The Republic of Plato*, p. 72.

p. 115   *"no occasion to deceive"*: Ibid., p. 331.

p. 115   *"seems a notion so transcendantly clear"*: Gaukroger, *Descartes*, p. 327.

p. 115   *writing in the "vulgar tongue"*: Vrooman, *René Descartes*, p. 93.

p. 115   *"If falsehood had"*: *The Essays of Michel De Montaigne*, trans. Charles Cotton, ed. W. Caren Hazlitt (New York, Chicago: A. L. Burt Company, n.d.), Vol. 1, p. 33.

p. 116   *"My whole physics"*: Keeling, *Descartes*, p. 132.

p. 116   *"Nature does nothing in vain"*: Sir Isaac Newton, *Principia*, trans. Andrew Motte, rev. Florian Cajori, Vol. II, *The System of the World* (Berkeley & Los Angeles: University of California Press, 1966), p. 398.

p. 116 nature *"had been covered by an ugly veil"*: Quoted in Thomas A. Spragens, Jr., *The Irony of Liberal Reason* (Chicago & London: University of Chicago Press, 1981), p. 85.

p. 116 *"Puritanism allowed men"*: Perry Miller, *The New England Mind* (Cambridge, MA: Harvard University Press, 1953), p. 45.

p. 117 *"doth more cleerely appeare"*: *Ibid.*, p. 349.

p. 117 *"Science had a new charm"*: Jacob Bronowski and Bruce Mazlish, *The Western Intellectual Tradition from Leonardo to Hegel* (New York: Harper, 1960), p. 183.

p. 118 Cicero, not Aristotle, was the model: See Rosamund Tuve, *Elizabethan and Metaphysical Imagery* (Chicago: University of Chicago Press, 1947).

p. 118 warned against the sort of excellence in speaking: Quoted in W. Ross Winterowd, *Rhetoric: A Synthesis* (New York: Rinehart & Winston, 1968), p. 40.

p. 118 *"nothing may be sooner obtain'd"*: *Ibid.*, p. 65.

p. 119 *"It was now obvious"*: Norman Hampson, *The Enlightenment* (New York: Penguin Books, 1990), p. 73.

p. 119 shun all *"fabulous relations"*: Shapin, *A Social History of Truth*, p. 74.

p. 120 The Society tended to resist: Jacob Bronowski, *The Common Sense of Science* (Harmondsworth, UK: Penguin Books, 1960), pp. 50–51.

p. 120 *"All knowledge is of the same nature"*: René Descartes, "Rules for the Direction of the Mind," in Margaret D. Wilson, ed., *The Essential Descartes* (New York: Penguin Books, 1976), p. 85.

p. 120 *"A work of morals"*: Quoted in Randall, *The Making of the Modern Mind*, p. 254.

p. 121 *"always starting from a quite inadequate knowledge"*: *Ibid.*, p. 318.

p. 122 *"With each freshman class"*: Alan Cromer, *Uncommon Sense: The Heretical Nature of Science* (New York & Oxford: Oxford University Press, 1993), p. 23.

p. 122 *"There can be no doubt"*: Rom Harré, *The Philosophy of Science* (New York & Oxford: Oxford University Press, 1972), p. 45.

p. 123 *"I know of no other reason"*: Ian Hacking "Disunited Sciences" in Richard Q. Elvee, ed., Nobel Conference XXV, *The End of Science? Attack and Defense* (University Press of America, Inc., 1992), pp. 42.

p. 123 *"Man tries to make"*: Yehuda Elkana, "The Myth of Simplicity," in Gerald Holton and Yehuda Elkana, eds., *Albert Einstein: Historical and Cultural Perspectives* (Princeton: Princeton University Press, 1982), p. 214.

p. 123 Einstein's is the more aesthetically pleasing: Cf. Steven Weinberg, *Dreams of a Final Theory* (New York: Pantheon Books, 1992), p. 106.

p. 123 *"How unfashionable Einstein was"*: Elkana, "The Myth of Simplicity," p. 243.

p. 124 *"a revolt against simplicity"*: Anthony Wilden, *System and Structure: Essays in Communication and Exchange* (London & New York: Tavistock Publications, 1980), p. 303.

p. 124 a *"complicated simplicity"*: Jack Cohen and Ian Stewart, *The Collapse of Chaos* (New York: Viking Press, 1994), p. 399.

p. 125   *A rock-bottom unifying principle: Ibid.*, p. 284.

p. 125   *"The idea of simplicity is falling apart"*: John Briggs and F. David Peat, *Turbulent Mirror* (New York: Harper & Row, 1989), p. 147.

CHAPTER NINE

p. 127   *"When people invited the Duchesse de Guermantes"*: Marcel Proust, *Remembrance of Things Past*, Vol. 2, trans. C. K. Scott Moncrieff and Terence Kilmartin (New York: Vintage Books, 1982), p. 495.

p. 127   *"What a strange contrast"*: Heinrich Heine, *Religion and Philosophy in Germany*, trans. John Snodgrass (Boston: Beacon Press, 1959), p. 109.

p. 127   *"the tremor of a coming earthquake"*: Berlin, *The Sense of Reality*, p. 176.

p. 128   *"the destruction of the notion of truth"*: *Ibid.*, p. 170.

p. 128   *"set me straight"*: Ernst Cassirer, *Kant's Life and Thought* (New Haven: Yale University Press, 1981), p. 89.

p. 128   *"Newton first saw order and lawfulness"*: *Ibid.*, p. 89.

p. 129   *When Kant was thrust willy-nilly*: David Masson, *The Collected Writings of Thomas de Quincey* (New York: AMS Press, 1968), Vol. IV, pp. 323–79.

p. 129   *It is said that Kant made room*: Heine, *Religion and Philosophy in Germany*, p. 119.

p. 129   *"presuming upon his own indispensableness"*: Masson, *The Collected Writings of Thomas de Quincey*, pp. 378–79.

p. 130   *"Kant's well-known reverence for truth"*: *Ibid.*

p. 130   *The epithet "prig"*: Robert Solomon, *Continental Philosophy* (New York & Oxford: Oxford University Press, 1988), p. 39.

p. 131   *his "dogmatic slumber"*: Immanuel Kant, *Prolegomena to Any Future Metaphsyics*, Introduction by Lewis Beck (New York: Liberal Arts Press, 1951), p. 8.

p. 133   *the same "talent of suspicion"*: Heine, *Religion and Philosophy in Germany*, p. 109.

p. 133   *"God, according to Kant"*: Kant, *Prolegomena*, p. 115.

p. 133   *"packing-paper" prose style*: *Ibid.*, p. 121.

p. 134   *"This domain is an island"*: Immanuel Kant, *Critique of Pure Reason*, trans. Norman Kemp Smith (New York: St. Martin's Press, 1965), p. 257.

p. 134   *"That the human mind will ever"*: Kant, *Prolegomena*, p. 367.

p. 135   *"will not cease to play tricks"*: Kant, *Critique of Pure Reason*, p. 300.

p. 135   *the word "neurosis"*: Susan Neiman, *The Unity of Reason* (New York & Oxford: Oxford University Press, 1994), p. 189.

p. 135   *he had taken reason off the leash*: Hannah Arendt, *The Life of the Mind* (New York: Harcourt Brace Jovanovich, 1978), p. 15.

p. 135   *"The need of reason"*: *Ibid.*

p. 136   *In the later Middle Ages, meaning had been given*: Randall, *The Making of the Modern Mind*, p. 28.

p. 137   *"To the mind of the scholar"*: *Ibid.*, p. 35.

p. 137   *Only by virtue of practical reason*: Kant, *Critique of Practical Reason*, trans. and ed. Mary Gregory (Cambridge: University Press, 1956), p. 55.

p. 139 "*the world would be devoid of meaning*": Richard Kroner, *Kant's Weltan-schauung*, trans. John E. Smith (Chicago: University of Chicago Press, 1956), p. 55.

p. 140 "*Unfortunately, this encourages moral*": Solomon, *Continental Philosophy*, p. 41.

p. 140 "*the great mystery of ethics*": Murdoch, *Metaphysics as a Guide to Morals*, p. 64.

CHAPTER TEN

p. 141 "*An ironic person*": Jacob Golomb, *In Search of Authenticity* (London & New York: Routledge, 1995), p. 8.

p. 141 "*Irony removes the security*": Linda Hutcheon, *Irony's Edge* (London & New York: Routledge, 1994), p. 14.

p. 141 "*There is no possibility*": Immanuel Kant, *Grounding for the Metaphysics of Morals*, trans. James W. Ellington (Indianapolis & Cambridge: Hackett Publishing Co., 1981), p. 7.

p. 143 "*Autonomy is the ground of the dignity*": *Ibid.*, p. 41.

p. 143 "*Perhaps Kant did not, like Hume*": Berlin, *The Sense of Reality*, p. 178.

p. 145 a "*shattering mystical experience*": Frederick Beiser, *The Fate of Reason: German Philosophy from Kant to Fichte* (Cambridge, MA: Harvard University Press, 1987), p. 20.

p. 145 "*The breath of life in our nose*": *Ibid.*, p. 21.

p. 146 "*we need faith to eat an egg*": *Ibid.*, p. 24.

p. 146 "*personal relations, inner life*": Isaiah Berlin, *The Magus of the North* (London: Fontana Paperbacks, 1994), p. 12.

p. 146 *Irony in the Romantic era*: See D. C. Muecke, *Irony and the Ironic* (London & New York: Methuen, 1982), p. 22.

p. 147 *a post-Enlightenment distrust*: Anne K. Mellor, *English Romantic Irony* (Cambridge, MA: Harvard University Press, 1980), p. 4.

p. 147 *eironia meant a devious way of fooling*: Muecke, *Irony and the Ironic*, p. 16.

p. 147 "*it may perhaps be that nature*": See William K. Wimsatt, Jr., and Cleanth Brooks, *Literary Criticism: A Short History* (New York: Knopf, 1962), p. 45.

p. 148 "*Ironia est tropus*": Quoted in Earle Birney, *Essays on Chaucerian Irony* (Toronto: University of Toronto Press, 1985), p. xvi.

p. 148 "*It is an outward casing he wears*": Plato, *Symposium*, trans. W. R. M. Lamb (Cambridge, MA: Harvard University Press, 1983), p. 222.

p. 148 "*praise, but facetiously*": Birney, *Essays on Chaucerian Irony*, p. xvii.

p. 148 "*An irony hath the honey*": *Ibid.*, p. xviii.

p. 149 "*implies and projects other possible cases*": Preface to *The Lesson of the Master*, in Henry James, *The Art of the Novel: Critical Prefaces* (New York & London: Charles Scribner's Sons, 1934), p. 222.

p. 149 "*language drawing attention to its own limitations*": Mellor, *English Romantic Irony*, p. 24.

p. 149   *post-Kantian irony "is not used"*: Lilian Furst, *Fictions of Romantic Irony* (Cambridge, MA: Harvard University Press, 1984), p. 228.

p. 149   *"The habit of irony"*: Friedrich Nietzsche, *Human, All Too Human*, trans. Helen Zimmern (Edinburgh & London: T. N. Foulis, 1910), p. 289.

p. 149   *A poet "nothing affirmeth"*: Sir Philip Sidney, *The Defence of Poesy*, in *Sir Philip Sidney: Selected Prose and Poetry*, ed. Robert Kimbrough (New York & London: Holt, Rinehart & Winston, 1969), p. 136.

p. 150   *"After centuries of abuse"*: Robert C. Solomon, *From Hegel to Existentialism* (New York & Oxford: Oxford University Press, 1987), p. 43.

p. 150   *"In proportion as the Will"*: Russell, *A History of Western Philosophy*, p. 759.

p. 150   *"preoccupied to an extreme degree"*: Lionel Trilling, *Sincerity and Authenticity* (Cambridge, MA: Harvard University Press, 1972), p. 13.

p. 150   the *"ruthless and suspicious character"*: Quoted in Joseph Mazzeo, *Renaissance and Revolution* (New York: Pantheon Books, 1967), p. 124.

p. 151   *"misrepresented the Critique of Pure Reason"*: Berlin, *The Magus of the North*, p. 47.

p. 152   *"Himself as everything!"*: Quoted in Solomon, *Continental Philosophy*, p. 53.

p. 152   *"a great attachment to life"*: Arthur Schopenhauer, *The World as Will and Representation*, trans. E. F. J. Payne (New York: Dover Publications, 1966), Vol. II, p. 206.

p. 153   *Suppose I have devised a plan*: Ibid., Vol. II, p. 209.

p. 153   *"come close to calling into question"*: Robert Wright, *The Moral Animal* (New York: Vintage Books, 1994), p. 325.

p. 153   *"soapsud or barber" book*: Himmelfarb, *Darwin and the Darwinian Revolution*, p. 304.

p. 155   *"roundabout ways and bypaths"*: Hans Vahinger, *The Philosophy of 'as-if'* (New York: Brace & Co., 1925), p. xvii.

p. 155   *"what Darwinism calls useful illusions"*: Ibid., p. 48.

p. 156   *"We have seen instead of pessimistic"*: Thomas Mann, "Schopenhauer," in *Essays of Three Decades*, trans. H. T. Lowe-Porter (New York: Knopf, 1947), p. 409.

CHAPTER ELEVEN

p. 157   *"Truth is contrary to our nature"*: Goethe, *Maxims and Reflections*, p. 37.

p. 157   *"Anything that raises"*: Joe Queenan in *The Washington Post*, June 26, 2000, p. C3.

p. 157   *"ruthlessness, cruelty, and suffering"*: Arthur Danto, "Nietzsche," in O'Connor, ed., *A Critical History of Western Philosophy*, p. 385.

p. 159   *"That celebrated veracity"*: Friedrich Nietzsche, *Beyond Good and Evil*, trans. R. J. Hollingdale (London & New York: Penguin Books, 1990), p. 33.

p. 160   *"Those who can breathe the air"*: Friedrich Nietzsche, *Ecce Homo*, trans. Walter Kaufmann (New York: Vintage Books, 1969), p. 218.

p. 160   *"Only great pain"*: Nietzsche, *The Gay Science*, p. 36.

p. 160   *"The philosopher, as the creature"*: Nietzsche, *Beyond Good and Evil*, p. 65.

p. 161   *"All our so-called consciousness"*: Friedrich Nietzsche, *Daybreak Thoughts on the Prejudices of Morality*, trans. R. J. Hollingdale (Cambridge: University Press, 1982), p. 76.

p. 161   *"My writings have been called"*: Nietzsche, *Human, All Too Human*, pp. 1–2.

p. 162   *"chills and anxieties of loneliness"*: *Ibid.*, p. 2.

p. 162   *"masters of cunning"*: Ernst Behler, *Irony and the Discourse of Modernity*, (Seattle: University of Washington Press, 1990), p. 93.

p. 162   *"Oh, the fatal curiosity"*: Friedrich Nietzsche, "On the Pathos of Truth," in *Philosophy and Truth*, ed. & trans. Daniel Breazeale (Totowa, NJ: Humanities Press, 1997), p. 65.

p. 162   *"The man who does not believe"*: *Ibid.*, p. 57.

p. 162   *"The whole of English Darwinism"*: Nietzsche, *The Gay Science*, p. 292.

p. 163   *If "one wanted to abolish"*: Nietzsche, *Beyond Good and Evil*, p. 65.

p. 164   *"what if this belief"*: Friedrich Nietzsche, *The Genealogy of Morals*, trans. Walter Kaufmann and R. J. Hollingdale (New York: Vintage Books, 1969), p. 152.

p. 164   *"I cannot escape the ghastly suspicion"*: Quoted in Ronald Hayman, *Nietzsche: A Critical Life* (New York & Harmondsworth, UK: Penguin Books, 1982), p. 341.

p. 165   *"trying for once to be natural"*: Henry James, *The Europeans* (New York & Harmondsworth, UK: Penguin Books, 1984), p. 128.

p. 165   *"The Puritans' self-conceit"*: Tony Tanner, *Henry James the Writer and His Work* (Amherst, MA: University of Massachusetts Press, 1985), p. 27.

p. 166   *nature's "extraordinary monotony"*: Oscar Wilde, "The Decay of Lying," in Richard Ellman, ed., *The Artist as Critic* (New York: Random House, 1969), pp. 291, 313.

p. 166   *"a new kind of flatness"*: Frederic Jameson, "Postmodernism or the Cultural Logic of Capitalism," *New Left Review*, 146 (July–August 1984), p. 60. Cf. Behler, *Irony and the Discourse of Modernity*, p. 7.

p. 166   *a world without "causality, sequence or depth"*: Alan Wilde, *Horizons of Assent* (Baltimore: Johns Hopkins University Press, 1981), p. 108.

p. 167   *"The early modernist tendency"*: *Ibid.*, p. 108.

p. 167   *"This bad taste"*: Nietzsche, *The Gay Science*, p. 38.

p. 168   *"Lying, the telling of beautiful untrue things"*: Wilde, "The Decay of Lying," p. 320.

p. 168   *Odysseus polytropoi*: Nietzsche, *The Gay Science*, p. 282.

p. 168   *"Oh those Greeks!"*: Nietzsche, *The Gay Science*, p. 38.

p. 168   *"As hardworking and solitary animals"*: Hayman, *Nietzsche*, p. 289.

p. 169   *comes from a man in whom the instinct*: *Ibid.*, p. 289.

p. 169   *"grim hours, entire days and nights"*: *Ibid.*, pp. 314–15.

p. 169   *"in which the whole machine is worth nothing"*: *Ibid.*, p. 320.

p. 169   *to smash "with a hammer"* . . . *"make a mummy"*: Friedrich Nietzsche, *Twilight of the Idols*, trans. R. J. Hollingdale (Baltimore: Penguin Books, 1969), pp. 21, 36.

p. 169   The "real" world of hidden truth: Ibid., p. 36.

p. 169   "We have become cold": Nietzsche, The Gay Science, p. 286.

p. 170   "The pleasure of lying": Nietzsche, "Truth and Lies in a Nonmoral Sense," in Philosophy and Truth, p. 96.

p. 170   all the "metaphysical nausea": Henry Donato, Nietzsche, Henry James and the Artistic Will (New York: Oxford University Press, 1978), p. 223.

p. 170   "The Greek knew and felt": Friedrich Nietzsche, The Birth of Tragedy, trans. with a commentary by Walter Kaufmann (New York: Vintage Books, 1967), pp. 42–43.

p. 171   "Existence under the bright sunshine": Ibid., p. 43

p. 171   "One must have chaos in one": Friedrich Nietzsche, Thus Spake Zarathustra, trans. R. J. Hollingdale (London & New York: Penguin Books, 1969), p. 46.

p. 172   "Nietzsche stands as the founder": Alan Megill, Prophets of Extremity: Nietzsche, Heidegger, Foucault, Derrida (Berkeley: University of California Press, 1985), p. 31.

CHAPTER TWELVE

p. 173   "You must not be frightened by words": Oscar Wilde in Ellman, ed., The Artist as Critic, p. 393.

p. 173   "It was so sincere, that nineteenth century": Thomas Mann, Essays, trans. H. T. Lowe-Porter (New York: Vintage Books, 1958), pp. 308–09.

p. 174   Sorel is one of the fathers: Isaiah Berlin, Against the Current: Essays in the History of Ideas (New York: Viking Press, 1979), p. 328.

p. 174   "little and illusory divinity of Reason": Jack J. Roth, The Cult of Violence (Berkeley: University of California Press, 1980), p. 4

p. 175   "One cannot understand Sorel": Berlin, Against the Current, pp. 299–300.

p. 176   "When we act": Richard Humphrey, Georges Sorel, Prophet Without Honor (Cambridge, MA: Harvard University Press, 1951), p. 10.

p. 176   "the alpha and omega of socialism": Irving Louis Horowitz, Radicalism and the Revolt Against Reason (New York: Humanities Press, 1961), p. 72.

p. 176   "an economic tactic of the weak": Ibid., pp. 73, 75.

p. 177   "the entire structure of conventional falsehoods": Ibid., p. 91.

p. 177   "to fix dates for the arrival": Ibid.

p. 177   "It is to violence": Quoted in Gerhard Masur, Prophets of Yesterday (London: Weidenfeld & Nicolson, 1963), p. 408.

p. 177   "Subjective distortions": Horowitz, Radicalism and the Revolt Against Reason, p. 119.

p. 177   "collective hallucinations": A. James Gregor, Young Mussolini and the Intellectual Origins of Fascism (Berkeley: University of California Press, 1979), p. 23.

p. 178   "It is often the case": Ibid., p. 27.

p. 178   "my bedside book": Neil McInnes, "Sorel," in Paul Edwards, ed., Encyclopedia of Philosophy, Vol. 7 (New York: Macmillan Publishing Co., 1967), p. 497.

p. 178   a task *"grave, terrible, sublime"*: Gregor, *Young Mussolini*, p. 47.

p. 178   *"He is an Italian of the fifteenth century"*: Humphrey, *Georges Sorel*, p. 22.

p. 179   *"frightful inequality and suffering"*: Roth, *The Cult of Violence*, p. 45.

p. 179   *"a present morality stated in the future tense"*: McInnes, "Sorel," p. 498.

p. 179   *"would probably never abandon his inertia"*: Humphrey, *Georges Sorel*, p. 171.

p. 180   *"commercialized, jaunty, insolent"*: Berlin, *Against the Current*, p. 300.

p. 180   *"Ignorance is the condition"*: Anatole France quoted in Franklin L. Baumer, *Modern European Thought* (New York & London: Macmillan Publishing Co., 1977), p. 396.

p. 180   *"a community where political forms"*: Austin Wright, ed., *Victorian Literature* (New York: Oxford University Press, 1961), p. 6.

p. 180   *"not because of the quality of its faith"*: T. S. Eliot, "In Memoriam, " *Selected Essays*, new edition (New York: Harcourt, Brace, 1950), p. 294.

p. 181   *"bereft of Christianity's consolations"* . . . *"it is impossible not"*: Quoted in Annan, *Leslie Stephen, The Godless Victorian*, p. 188.

p. 181   *"Victorian society"*: Walter E. Houghton, *The Victorian Frame of Mind, 1830–1870* (New Haven & London: Yale University Press, 1957), p. 55.

p. 181   *"revealing his zoological conclusions"*: Ibid., p. 599.

p. 182   An age *"destitute of faith"*: Ibid., p. 155.

p. 182   *"with the air and spirit of a man"*: Ibid., p. 158.

p. 183   *"Oh, life would be all right"*: Henrik Ibsen, *The Wild Duck*, trans. R. Farquharson Sharp and Eleanor Marx-Aveling (New York & London: Dent, 1958), p. 164.

p. 183   *"Truth as a cloak"*: Breazeale, ed., *Philosophy and Truth*, p. 97.

p. 183   *"examines the status"*: Herman Wiegand, *The Modern Ibsen* (Salem, NH: Ayer, 1984), p. 166.

p. 183   could *"destroy civilization"*: Leon Edel, *Henry James the Master* (Philadelphia: J. B. Lippincott, 1972), p. 215.

p. 184   Niebuhr decided that the use of force: Steven C. Rockefeller, *John Dewey* (New York: Columbia University Press, 1991), pp. 451–62.

p. 184   *"The truest visions of religion"*: Quoted in Ibid., p. 462.

p. 184   *"People who are living"*: Quoted in Masur, *Prophets of Yesterday*, p. 407.

p. 185   *"the universal ethical will"*: Baumer, *Modern European Thought*, p. 484.

p. 185   *"Socialism is becoming a demagogy"*: Humphrey, *Georges Sorel*, p. 19.

p. 185   And the irony of that mutation: Horowitz, *Radicalism and the Revolt Against Reason*, p. 180.

p. 185   *"whether it would not be better"*: Thomas Mann, *Last Essays* (New York: Knopf, 1959), p. 155.

CHAPTER THIRTEEN

p. 186   *"We possess the truth"*: Sigmund Freud quoted in Ronald W. Clark, *Freud, the Man and the Cause* (New York: Random House, 1980), p. 189.

p. 186   *"Truth is unobtainable"*: *The Letters of Sigmund Freud*, ed. Ernst L. Fierd, trans. Elaine and William Robson-Scott. (New York: Basic Books, 1960), pp. 426, 430.

p. 186 *"Lies are an index of powerful propensities"*: Forrester, *Truth Games*, p. 86.

p. 187 *The masses "are lazy"*: Sigmund Freud, *The Future of an Illusion* (New York: Liveright, 1953), p. 6.

p. 188 *"is one that only a philosopher"*: *Ibid.*, p. 43.

p. 188 *"We call a belief an illusion"*: *Ibid.*, p. 49.

p. 188 *"We see that an appallingly large number"*: *Ibid.*, p. 61.

p. 188 *the concept of truth is not explored*: M. Guy Thomson, *The Truth About Freud's Technique* (New York: New York University Press, 1994), p. 2.

p. 188 *"Primitive and infantile man"*: Frederick J. Hacker in Benjamin Nelson, ed., *Freud and the Twentieth Century* (Gloucester, MA: Peter Smith, 1974), p. 130.

p. 189 *"Anyone turning biographer"*: Clark, *Freud, the Man and the Cause*, p. 64.

p. 189 *a "drive toward disenchantment"*: Philip Rieff, *Freud: The Mind of the Moralist* (Garden City, NY: Anchor Books, Doubleday & Co., 1961), p. 345.

p. 189 *People protect their well-being*: Sissela Bok, *Secrets* (New York: Vintage Books, 1983), p. 61.

p. 189 *suggesting a deep rift within the psyche*: *Ibid.*, p. 63.

p. 189 *a complete breakdown in treatment occurred*: Clark, *Freud, the Man and the Cause*, p. 348.

p. 190 *"Psychoanalysis sets up the conditions"*: Forrester, *Truth Games*, p. 67.

p. 190 *At a a conference of three dozen*: Sarah Boxer, "Analysts Get Together for a Synthesis," *New York Times*, March 14, 1998, p. B9.

p. 192 *"would have set off alarms in the mind"*: Frederick Crews, *New York Review of Books*, 18 (November 1993), p. 55.

p. 192 *a world "in which everything has a meaning"*: Steven Marcus, *Freud and the Culture of Psychoanalysis* (London: Allen & Unwin, 1984), p. 68.

p. 192 *the "source of the Nile"*: Clark, *Freud, the Man and the Cause*, p. 173.

p. 193 *his "first great error"*: *Ibid.*

p. 194 *the "shamefully moralized way of speaking"*: Nietzsche, *The Genealogy of Morals*, p. 137.

p. 194 *"civilization being necessarily hypocritical"*: Rieff, *Freud, the Mind of the Moralist*, p. 369.

p. 194 *"Let me tell you"*: Clark, *Freud, the Man and the Cause*, p. 191.

p. 194 *"a tough old humanist"*: Alfred Kazin, "The Freudian Revolution Analyzed," in Nelson, ed., *Freud and the Twentieth Century*, p. 14.

p. 194 *"based on a love of truth"*: "Analysis Terminabled and Interminable," in *Standard Edition of the Works of Freud*, ed. James Strachey, (London: Hogarth Press, 1954–76), Vol. 23, p. 247.

p. 195 *"If truthfulness about sexuality"*: Barry Allen, *Truth in Philosophy* (Cambridge, MA: Harvard University Press, 1995), pp. 54–55.

p. 195 *Freud wrote that there is no evidence*: Freud letter to Wilhelm Fliess in Jeffrey Masson, ed., *The Complete Letters of Sigmund Freud to Wilhelm Fliess 1887–1904* (Cambridge, MA: Harvard University Press, 1985), p. 264.

p. 196   *"follows closely this model relation"*: Rieff, *Freud, the Man and the Cause*, p. 136.

p. 196   *"suspicious of the obvious"*: Ibid., p. 119.

p. 196   *the ideal patient today*: Jeffrey Moussaieff Masson, *The Assault on Truth* (New York & Harmondsworth, UK: Penguin Books, 1985), p. 133.

p. 197   *"Though Freud loved to sermonize"*: Crews in *New York Review of Books*, pp. 55–56.

p. 197   *into the throes of an illusory, hysterical childbirth*: Frank J. Sulloway, *Freud, Biologist of the Mind* (Cambridge, MA: Harvard University Press, 1992), p. 77.

p. 198   *A sanitarium that did not exist*: Henri F. Ellenberger, *The Discovery of the Unconscious* (New York: Basic Books, 1970), p. 483.

p. 198   *"a double-edged sword"*: Sulloway, *Freud, Biologist of the Mind*, p. 57.

p. 198   *Two researchers friendly to Freud*: Seymour Fisher and Roger P. Greenberg, *The Scientific Credibility of Freud's Theories and Therapy* (New York: Basic Books, 1977), pp. 281–85.

p. 198   *"lay the recognition that fiction can cure"*: John Forrester, "Lying on the Couch," in Hilary Lawson and Lisa Appignanesi, eds., *Dismantling Truth* (New York: St. Martin's Press, 1989), p. 161.

p. 198   *"The doctor began to play"*: John Forrester, "Lying on the Couch," pp. 159–60.

p. 198   *the skeletons in the closets*: See Heinz Hartman in S. Hook, ed., *Psychoanalysis, Scientific Method and Philosophy* (New York: Grove Press, 1959).

p. 199   *Freud's work put truth into question*: Jacques Lacan, *Ecrits: A Selection*, trans. Alan Sheridan (New York: W. W. Norton, 1977), p. 118.

p. 200   *the "truth of the subject"*: Mikkel Borch-Jacobsen, *Lacan the Absolute Master* (Stanford, CA: Stanford University Press, 1991), p. 155.

p. 200   *"a sort of privileging of the lie"*: Ibid., p. 112.

p. 201   *the "cure by fiction"*: Ibid., p. 155.

p. 201   *clambered onto the bandwagon*: Jane Gallop, *Reading Lacan* (Ithaca, NY & London: Cornell University Press, 1996), p. 22.

p. 202   *The ambiguity of the hysterical* revelation": Borch-Jacobsen, *Lacan the Absolute Master*, p. 155.

p. 202   *"In this strange analytic universe"*: Ibid., p. 157.

CHAPTER FOURTEEN

p. 203   *"From the point of view of art"*: Pablo Picasso, in Herschel B. Chipp, ed., *Theories of Modern Art* (Berkeley, Los Angeles & London: University of California Press, 1968), p. 264.

p. 203   *"To try and approach truth"*: Matthew Arnold quoted in Houghton, *The Victorian Frame of Mind*, p. 177.

p. 203   *"If nature had been comfortable"*: Oscar Wilde in Ellman, ed., *The Artist as Critic*, p. 291.

p. 204   *"human character changed"*: Virginia Woolf, "Mr Bennett and Mrs Brown," in *Collected Essays* (London: Hogarth Press, 1966), Vol. 1, pp. 319–37.

p. 204   *modernism must now be seen as the core*: Norman Cantor, *The American Century* (New York: HarperCollins, 1997), p. 7.

p. 204   *one which looked to the future*: Matei Calinescu, *Five Faces of Modernity* (Durham, NC: Duke University Press, 1987), p. 101.

p. 204   *a society without privilege* : *Ibid.*, p. 104.

p. 205   *"it might possibly mislead"*: Graham Hough, *The Last Romantics* (London: Gerald Duckworth, 1949), p. 138.

p. 205   *"to the majority of acute people"*: Walter Pater, *Plato and Platonism: A Series of Lectures* (New York: Greenwood Press, 1969), p. 40.

p. 206   *the "weakness on the threshold"*: Peter Allan Dale, *The Victorian Critic and the Idea of History* (Cambridge, MA: Harvard University Press, 1977), pp. 177–78.

p. 206   *the "abnormal caution"*: R. M. Seiler, ed., *Walter Pater: A Life Remembered* (Calgary, Canada: University of Calgary Press, 1987), pp. 140–41.

p. 206   *"He liked the human race"*: Quoted in *ibid.*, p. 195.

p. 206   *"He never talks about"*: Richard Le Gallienne in Seiler, ed., *Walter Pater*, p. 159.

p. 206   *a new "faculty for truth"*: Carolyn Williams, *Transfigured World: Walter Pater's Aesthetic Historicism* (Ithaca, NY: Cornell University Press, 1989), p. 51.

p. 207   *"There is something interesting"*: Quoted in J. E. Chamberlin, *Ripe Was the Drowsy Hour* (New York: Seabury Press, 1977), p. 20.

p. 207   *"his hard-won heart"*: Houghton, *The Victorian Frame of Mind*, p. 80.

p. 207   *"Everything is changed"*: J. Hillis Miller, *The Disappearance of God* (Cambridge, MA: Harvard University Press, 1963), p. 5.

p. 208   *"Modern thought is distinguished"*: Walter Pater, *Appreciations, With an Essay on Style* (London: Macmillan & Company, 1910), p. 66.

p. 208   *"Father, give me this"*: Thomas Mann, *Essays of Three Decades* (New York: Knopf, 1947), p. 196.

p. 208   *"a many-sided but hesitant consciousness"*: F. C. McGrath, *The Sensible Spirit* (Tampa, FL: University Presses of Florida, 1986), p. 51.

p. 209   *a condition of "jaded intellect"*: Houghton, *The Victorian Frame of Mind*, p. 64.

p. 209   *"that inexhaustible discontent"*: *Ibid.*

p. 209   *the "great modern monster"*: Nicholls, *Modernisms: A Literary Guide*, p. 7.

p. 209   *"tedious and improving conversations"*: Oscar Wilde in Ellman, ed., *The Artist as Critic*, p. 305.

p. 209   *"clumsy Life again at her stupid work"*: Henry James, *The Spoils of Poynton* (London & New York: Penguin Books, 1987), p. 25.

p. 210   *depicts this dislocation*: Thomas Mann, *Doctor Faustus* (New York: Knopf, 1948), p. 260.

p. 210   *"instilled with the poison"*: *Ibid.*, p. 261.

p. 211   *He "needs no savior"*: Erich Heller, *The Ironic German* (Boston: Little, Brown, 1958), p. 260.

p. 211   *"What uplifts you"*: Mann, *Doctor Faustus*, p. 242.

p. 212   *"Truth" is a quarry*: Scruton, *Modern Philosophy*, p. 151.

p. 213 "*A Picasso studies an object*" . . . "*mocks the humanist fetish*": Nicholls, *Modernism*, p. 114.

p. 214 "*Yours is a hellish craft*": Richard Ellman and Charles Feidelson, Jr., eds., *The Modern Tradition* (New York: Oxford University Press, 1965), p. 77.

p. 214 *In the same vein, Auden*: Ibid., pp. 112–19.

p. 214 *Picasso . . . ridiculed the idea*: Ibid., p. 25.

p. 215 "*a sort of illegitimate Christ*": Scott Bates, *Guillaume Apollinaire* (New York: Twayne Publishers, 1967), p. 3.

p. 215 "*Though this art is not a god*": Ellman and Feidelson, Jr., eds., *The Modern Tradition*, p. 27.

p. 215 "*I affirm that it is not natural*": Allon White, *The Uses of Obscurity* (London: Routledge & Kegan Paul, 1981), p. 53.

p. 215 "*fascinated by liars*": Ibid., p. 49.

p. 216 *in part an expansion of this idea*: Ian Watt, *Conrad in the Nineteenth Century* (Berkeley: University of California Press, 1979), p. 247.

p. 217 "*The horror! The horror!*": Joseph Conrad, *Heart of Darkness* (New York: St. Martin's Press, 1989), p. 85.

p. 217 "*I hate, detest and cannot tell a lie*": Ibid., p. 41.

p. 217 "*Exterminate all the brutes!*": Ibid., p. 66.

p. 217 "*In the perspective of intellectual history*": Watt, *Conrad in the Nineteenth Century*, p. 247.

p. 218 "*is a monster-truth*": Ibid., p. 244.

p. 218 "*it appears likely that poets*": T. S. Eliot, *Selected Essays*, p. 248. Italics in original.

p. 218 "*I hate American simplicity*": Ross Posnock, *The Trial of Curiosity: Henry James, William James and the Challenge of Modernity* (New York: Oxford University Press, 1991), p. 54. There is a delicious story told by Edith Wharton in her memoirs of riding in England with Henry James, arriving in Windsor after nightfall, not knowing the way to the King's Road. James caught sight of an elderly, decrepit pedestrian who had stopped in the rain to look at them. "My friend, " said James, "to put it to you in two words, this lady and I have just arrived here from *Slough*; that is to say, to be strictly more accurate, we have recently *passed through* Slough, on our way here, having actually motored to Windsor from Rye, which was our point of departure; and the darkness having overtaken us, we should be much obliged if you would tell us where we now are in relation, say to the High Street, which, as you of course know, leads to the Castle, after leaving on the left hand the turn down to the railway station."

The pedestrian reacted to this with "silence and a dazed expression." James continued, "In short, my good man, what I want to put to you in a word is this: supposing we have already (as I have reason to think we have) driven past the turn down to the railway station (which in that case, by the way, would probably not have been on our left, but on our right), where are we know in relation to . . . "

"Oh, please," interrupted Mrs. Wharton, fearing another parenthesis. "Do ask him where the King's Road is. "

"Ah. " James veered toward the point. "Just so! Quite right! Can you, as a matter of fact, my good man, tell us where, in relation to our present position, the King's Road exactly *is*?"

"Ye're in it, " the elderly personage replied—Edith Wharton, *A Backward Glance* (New York: D. Appleton-Century Co., 1936), pp. 242–43.

p. 218   *"Man is the being"*: Jean-Paul Sartre, *Being and Nothingness*, trans. Hazel Barnes (New York: Citadel Press, 1965), p. 156.

p. 219   *"The obscurity of modernism"*: White, *The Uses of Obscurity*, p. 16.

p. 219   *"Innocence in the late James"*: *Ibid.*, p. 22.

CHAPTER FIFTEEN

p. 220   *"Language is the main instrument"*: Steiner, *After Babel*, p. 228.

p. 221   *"The whole of Japan is a pure invention"*: Oscar Wilde in Ellman, ed., *The Artist as Critic*, p. 315.

p. 221   *"Language, I suggest, is important"*: Richard Harland, *Beyond Superstructuralism* (London & New York: Routledge, 1993), p. 88.

p. 222   *"is true when it conforms to certain norms"*: Lee Paterson, "Literary History," in Frank Lettrichia and Thomas McLauglin, eds., *Critical Terms for Literary Study* (Chicago & London: University of Chicago Press, 1990), p. 257.

p. 222   *"Suddenly, all forms of writing"*: *Ibid.*, p. 257.

p. 223   *According to George Steiner, the problem*: Steiner, *After Babel*, p. 216.

p. 224   *"If they succeed in their office"*: Rockefeller, *John Dewey*, p. 405.

p. 224   *this falls afoul of the famous theorem*: See Steiner, *After Babel*, p. 220.

p. 224   *"None of the accounts"*: *Ibid.*, p. 224.

p. 225   *As a very young man living in Vienna*: Popper, *Unended Quest*, p. 33.

p. 227   *"nets in which we try to catch"*: *Ibid.*, p. 60.

p. 228   *"There are no facsimiles"*: Steiner, *After Babel*, p. 180.

p. 229   *The public properties vanquish the private ones*: Harland, *Beyond Superstructuralism*, pp. 15–23.

p. 230   *false beliefs . . . once had a social usefulness*: Peter Munz, *Our Knowledge of the Growth of Knowledge: Popper or Wittgenstein?* (London & Boston: Routledge & Kegan Paul, 1985), p. 74.

p. 230   *At a primary, prelinguistic level*: Derek Bickerton, *Language and Species* (Chicago & London: University of Chicago Press, 1990), pp. 100–06.

p. 232   *"A Semantic Theory of Truth"*: See *Philosophy and Phenomenological Research*, vol. 4, no. 3 (March 1944).

p. 232   *We set up the world to correspond*: Robert C. Solomon, *Introducing Philosophy* (New York: Harcourt Brace Jovanovich, 1981), p. 185.

p. 232   *Karl Popper praised Tarski*: Karl Popper, *Objective Knowledge: An Evolutionary Approach* (New York & Oxford: Clarendon Press, 1986), pp. 316–18.

p. 233   *"the loss of interest in the very concept of Truth"*: Solomon, *Introducing Philosophy*, p. 185.

p. 234   *"There is something glaringly wrong"*: Harland, *Beyond Superstructuralism*, p. 69.

CHAPTER SIXTEEN

p. 235   *"I am sitting with a philosopher"*: Ludwig Wittgenstein, *On Certainty*, ed. G. E. M. Anscombe and G. H. von Wright (New York: Harper & Row, 1972), p. 61e.

p. 235   *"I am willing to take life"*: W. Somerset Maugham, *A Writer's Notebook* (Harmondsworth, UK, & New York: Penguin Books, 1949), p. 73.

p. 236   *At the age of about eight*: Ray Monk, *Ludwig Wittgenstein: The Duty of Genius* (New York: Penguin Books, 1990), p. 3.

p. 236   *he decided that one might as well be untruthful*: Brian McGuiness, *Wittgenstein: A Life* (Berkeley: University of California Press, 1988), pp. 47–48.

p. 236   *"What is it?"*: Monk, *Ludwig Wittgenstein*, pp. 368–69.

p. 237   *"The event stood out"*: Rush Rhees, ed., *Recollections of Wittgenstein*, with an introduction by Norman Malcolm (New York & Oxford: Oxford University Press, 1984), p. 334.

p. 237   *"Lying to oneself"*: Quoted in Rush Rhees, ed., *Recollections of Wittgenstein*, (Oxford & New York: Oxford University Press, 1981), p. 174.

p. 237   *"a mighty, further elevation of culture"*: Quoted in Baumer, *Modern European Thought*, p. 369.

p. 239   *"you could see right through it"*: Allen, *Truth in Philosophy*, p. 113.

p. 240   *"but the requirement is now in danger"*: Ludwig Wittgenstein, *Philosophical Investigations* (Oxford: Basil Blackwell, 1997), p. 107.

p. 241   *"We prefer now to equate language"*: John Sturrock, ed., *Structuralism and Since* (Oxford & New York: Oxford University Press, 1990), p. 12.

p. 241   *"A child has much"*: Wittgenstein, *Philosophical Investigations*, pl. 249.

p. 242   *"If I make the same statement"*: Wittgenstein, *On Certainty*, p. 72e.

p. 242   *"The truth of certain empirical propositions"*: Ibid., p. 12e.

p. 243   *It is just "there, like our life"*: Wittgenstein, *Philosophical Investigations*, pl. 73.

p. 243   *"veneration for Wittgenstein"*: Monk, *Ludwig Wittgenstein*, p. 495.

p. 243   *the "numbing" effect*: Ibid., p. 263.

p. 244   *"seems to me one of the most important"*: Ernest Gellner, "Three Contemporary Styles of Philosophy," in S. G. Shanker, ed., *Philosophy in Britain Today* (Albany, NY: State University of New York Press, 1986), pp. 103–11.

p. 245   *"In the beginning was the deed"*: Ludwig Wittgenstein, *Culture and Value*, trans. Peter Winch (Chicago: University of Chicago Press, 1984), p. 31e.

p. 245   *"Now, believe!"*: Ibid., p. 32e.

p. 245   *"ugly nonsense"*: Ibid.

p. 245   *"Queer as it sounds"*: Ibid., p. 32e.

p. 245   *calls it "a disaster"*: Magee, ed., *The Great Philosophers*, p. 330.

p. 247 *"For the late Wittgenstein"*: Hilary Lawson, "Dismantling Truth," in Lawson and Appignanesi, eds., *Dismantling Truth*, p. xxiv.

p. 247 *"Often, it is only very slightly"*: Wittgenstein, *Culture and Value*, p. 37e.

p. 247 *"As long as there continues to be"*: Ibid., p. 15e.

p. 247 *"If people did not sometimes do silly things"*: Wittgenstein, *Culture and Value*, p. 50e.

p. 248 His business was to distinguish sense from nonsense: Monk, *Ludwig Wittgenstein*, p. 286.

p. 249 *"The Universe, for someone who was able"*: Quoted in P. N. Furbank, *Diderot: A Critical Biography* (New York: Knopf, 1992), p. 85.

p. 249 *"What a Copernicus or a Darwin"*: Wittgenstein, *Culture and Value*, p. 18e.

p. 249 *"lead to a sad underrating"*: Gellner, "Three Contemporary Styles of Philosophy," p. 111.

p. 250 There is a famous anecdote: Monk, *Ludwig Wittgenstein*, p. 261.

p. 250 *"I am a communist at heart"*: Ibid., p. 343.

p. 250 *"It was one more manifestation"*: Ibid., p. 354.

CHAPTER SEVENTEEN

p. 252 *"Lies are usually attempts"*: Adrienne Rich, *On Lies, Secrets and Silence*, pp. 187–88.

p. 252 *"The last time we had a president"*: Charles McCarry, "Candidates Can Be Too Candid," *New York Times*, December 13, 1999, p. A37.

p. 253 *"because he adores the truth"*: Quoted in Chamberlin, *Ripe Was the Drowsy Hour*, pp. 88–89.

p. 254 *"the refusal of the intensely feeling individual"*: Tanner *Jane Austen*, p. 91.

p. 255 *"Language design appears to be dysfunctional"*: Noam Chomsky, "Language and Mind," in D. H. Mellor, ed., *Ways of Communicating* (Cambridge & New York: Cambridge University Press, 1990), p. 78.

p. 256 *"beautiful but not usable"*: Ibid.

p. 256 maxims of conversation: See Paul Grice, *The Philosophical Review*, January 1957, pp. 58–67.

p. 256 *"as when I use language"*: Noam Chomsky, *Problems of Knowledge and Freedom* (New York: Pantheon Books, 1971), p. 19.

p. 256 vehemently opposed the aesthetic mode of writing: Jean-Paul Sartre, *What Is Literature?*, trans. Bernard Frechtman (New York: Philosophical Library, 1949) pp. 284–85.

p. 257 *"We can no longer take language"*: Irish Murdoch, *Sartre: Romantic Rationalist* (New Haven: Yale University Press, 1961), p. 27.

p. 258 *"By identifying himself with language"*: Roland Barthes, *Critical Essays*, trans. Richard Howard (Evanston, IL: Northwestern University Press, 1972), p. 146.

p. 258 as if *"truth were a material object"*: Ronald Hayman, *Proust: A Biography* (New York: Carroll & Graf, 1990), p. 214.

p. 258   *"We know now that a text is not"*: Quoted in Jonathan Culler, *Barthes* (London: Fontana Paperbacks, 1983), p. 11.

p. 258   *"unreadable" works that fly: Ibid.*, p. 10.

p. 259   *"struck silent"*: Richard J. Bernstein, ed., *Habermas and Modernity* (Cambridge, MA: MIT Press, 1985), p. 2.

p. 259   *"the cooperative search for truth"*: Jurgen Habermas, *Legitimation Crisis*, (Boston: Beacon Press, 1975), p. 107.

p. 260   an *"insistence on sameness"*: Helen Tager-Flusberg, Simon Baron-Cohen, and Donald Cohen, eds., *Understanding Other Minds* (Oxford & New York: Oxford University Press, 1994), p. 4.

p. 260   *A better test with humans: Ibid.*, p. 161.

p. 260   *a "cognitive watershed": Ibid.*

p. 261   *One mother, intensely concerned: Ibid.*, p. 167.

p. 261   *"all notion of the possible"*: Forrester, *Truth Games*, p. 23.

p. 262   *with a string of tall tales*: Henry James, "The Liar," in *The Short Stories of Henry James*, selected and edited Clifton Fadiman (New York: Random House, 1945), pp. 126–86.

p. 263   *The Age of Reason . . . looked askance*: See Marylin Gaul, *English Romantics: The Human Context* (New York: W. W. Norton, 1988).

p. 264   *"a gradual severance"*: Hough, *The Last Romantics*, pp. xvi–xvii.

p. 264   *how a context of meaning can subtly alter*: Vaclav Havel, *Disturbing the Peace: A Conversation with Karel Hvizdala*, trans. Paul Wilson (New York: Knopf, 1990), pp. 193–94.

p. 264   *pure truths asserted "which are pure lies": Ibid.*, p. 194.

p. 264   *"As practical intelligence has become"*: David Nyberg, *The Varnished Truth* (Chicago & London: University of Chicago Press, 1992), p. 1.

p. 265   *"In a sense, and in so far as this mask"*: Ervin Goffman, *The Presentation of Self in Everyday Life* (Garden City, NY: Doubleday & Co., 1959), p. 11.

p. 265   *"In our culture"*: Alasdair McIntyre, *After Virtue: A Study in Moral Theory* (Notre Dame, IN: University of Notre Dame Press, 1981), p. 179.

CHAPTER EIGHTEEN

p. 266   *"As a tactic of liberation"*: Leroy Searle in Hazard Adams and Leroy Searle, eds., *Critical Theory Since 1965* (Tallahassee, FL: Florida State University Press, 1968), p. 870.

p. 266   *"a scorn not only for reason"*: Alan Bullock, *The Humanist Tradition in the West* (New York: W. W. Norton, 1985), p. 153.

p. 266   *discovered "after many detours"*: Jonathan Culler, *Ferdinand de Saussure* (New York: Penguin Books, 1977), p. 29.

p. 266   *no proper concept for "pet": Ibid.*, p. 31.

p. 266   *Language has "no positive terms"*: Ferdinand de Saussure, *Course in General Linguistics*, trans. Wade Baskin (New York: Philosophical Library, 1959), p. 120.

p. 268   *only in respect of its size*: Culler, *Ferdinand de Saussure*, p. 34.

p. 268   *"Language is radically powerless"*: de Saussure, *Course in General Linguistics*, p. 75.

p. 269   *One critic claimed to detect*: Thomas Vargish and Delo E. Mook, *Inside Modernism* (New Haven & London: Yale University Press, 1999), p. 32.

p. 269   *"the visible world can become"*: Ibid., p. 33.

p. 270   *"If we achieve this realization"*: Ibid., p. 34.

p. 270   *The natural concepts that develop in us*: Elvee, ed., *The End of Science?*, p. 87.

p. 271   *Language acquires a life of its own*: Harland, *Superstructuralism*, p. 135.

p. 272   *"the right to say everything"*: John D. Caputo, ed., *Deconstruction in a Nutshell: A Conversation with Jacques Derrida* (New York: Fordham University Press, 1997), p. 58.

p. 273   *"terribly variable, deceptive"*: Ellman, *The Modern Tradition*, p. 83.

p. 273   *"the emergence of language itself"*: Jonathan Culler, *On Deconstruction* (Ithaca, NY: Cornell University Press, 1982), p. 185.

p. 273   *"truths are fictious"*: Ibid., p. 181.

p. 274   *Deconstruction "tries to keep alive"*: Ibid., p. 153

p. 274   *"The need for a theory of aesthetic autonomy"*: Hazard Adams, Introduction, in Adams and Searle, eds., *Critical Theory Since 1965*, p. 15.

p. 275   *Hesiod and Derrida have quite a bit*: David Roochnik, *The Tragedy of Reason* (New York & London: Routledge, 1990), p. 131.

p. 276   *"never stay upon the barren height"*: Wittgenstein, *Culture and Value*, p. 76e.

p. 276   *"because they are not able to converse"*: Plato, *Protagoras*, trans. Benjamin Jowett and Martin Ostwald (New York: Liberal Arts Press, 1956), p. 51.

p. 276   *"We would pour myrrh on his head"*: *The Republic of Plato*, 398a.

p. 277   *"That aestheticizing reality"*: Philip Rieff, *The Triumph of the Therapeutic* (New York: Harper & Row, 1966), p. 206.

p. 277   *"the rebel and the blasphemer"*: Rieff, *Freud: The Mind of the Moralist*, p. 379.

p. 277   *"Deconstruction must neither reframe"*: Jacques Derrida, *First Essay in Truth in Painting*, trans. Geoffrey Bennington and Ian McLeod (Chicago: Chicago University Press, 1987), p. 74.

p. 277   *a "certain practice of theoretical fiction"*: Ibid., p. 81.

p. 278   *"standing in the air"*: Jacques Derrida, *Dissemination*, trans. Barbara Johnson (Chicago: Chicago University Press, 1981), pp. 312, 280.

p. 278   *"Everything in the world tends"*: Quoted by James A. Winders, "Mallarmé, Stéphane and French Symbolism," in *The Johns Hopkins Guide to Literary Theory and Criticism* (Baltimore: Johns Hopkins University Press, 1994), p. 485.

p. 278   *"to make the words of a poem"*: Mallarmé, *Selected Prose Poems, Essays and Letters*, trans. Bradford Cook (Baltimore: Johns Hopkins University Press, 1956), p. 93.

p. 278   *"Nutshells enclose and encapsulate"*: Caputo, *Deconstruction in a Nutshell*, p. 31.

p. 279   *"for a democratic open-endedness"*: Ibid., p. 58.

p. 279   the *"Nietzschean affirmation"*: Jacques Derrida, "Structure, Sign and Play in the Discourse of the Human Sciences," in Adams and Searle, eds., *Critical Theory Since 1965*, p. 93.

p. 279   *"by the yet unnameable"*: Ibid., p. 91.

p. 280   *"Does not demand that Dogmas"*: Dale, *The Victorian Critic and the Idea of History*, p. 122.

p. 280   *craving for "intellectual deliverance"*: Ibid., p. 131.

p. 281   *"More and more, mankind will discover"*: Matthew Arnold, *Essays in Criticism, second series* (London: Macmillan, 1888), p. 2–3.

p. 281   *"My definition of language"*: de Saussure, *Course in General Linguistics*, p. 20.

p. 282   *"distance, absence, misunderstanding"*: Culler, *On Deconstruction*, p. 101.

p. 282   *"By a slow movement"*: Jacques Derrida, *Of Grammatology*, trans. Gayaatri Chakravorty Spivak (Baltimore: Johns Hopkins University Press, 1976), p. 6.

p. 283   *"truth" often means loyalty to a particular*: Richard Firth Green, *A Crisis of Truth* (Philadelphia: University of Pennsylvania Press, 1999), p. 33.

p. 283   *The parties "were not concerned"*: Ibid., p. 35.

CHAPTER NINETEEN

p. 285   *"I mistrust those hopes"*: Raymond Aron, *The Industrial Society* (New York: Simon & Schuster, 1968), p. 5.

p. 285   *"Man's foundation is mendacious"*: Nietzsche, *Philosophy and Truth*, p. 92.

p. 285   *"In the end, the Party"*: George Orwell, *1984* (New York: Signet Classics, 1981), p. 69.

p. 286   *"the truth is always mediated"*: Michael P. Zuckert, "Orwell's Hopes and Fears," in Robert L. Savage, James Combs, and Dan Nimmo, eds., *The Orwellian Moment* (Fayettsville, AR: University of Arkansas Press, 1989), p. 56.

p. 286   *"It is one of the most characteristic"*: Erich Fromm, "Afterword," in Orwell, *1984*, p. 263.

p. 287   *"If relativism signifies contempt"*: Quoted in Henry B. Veatch, *Rational Man* (Bloomington: Indiana University Press, 1962), p. 41. Cf. Helmut Kuhn, *Freedom Forgotten and Remembered* (Chapel Hill, NC: University of North Carolina Press, 1943), pp. 17–18.

p. 287   *"I had to be tricky"*: Galina Vishnevskaya, *Galina: A Russian Story* (New York: Harcourt Brace Jovanovich, 1984), p. 135.

p. 287   *"Lies, lies, lies"*: Ibid., pp. 138–39.

p. 288   *"The entrenched solidity of the government*: Luc Ferry and Alain Renaut, *French Philosophy of the Sixties*, trans. Mary H. S. Cattani (Amherst, MA: University of Massachusetts Press, 1990), p. 37.

p. 288   *"the very order of things"*: James Miller, *The Passion of Michel Foucault* (New York: Simon & Schuster, 1993), p. 167.

p. 289   *"language and the student movement"*: Louis-Jean Calvet, *Roland Barthes: A Biography* (Bloomington: Indiana University Press, 1994), p. 165.

p. 289   *"The truth is one"*: Ferry and Renaut, *French Philosophy of the Sixties*, p. xiii.

p. 289   a "contempt for the authenticity": John Ardagh, France in the 1980's (New York & London: Penguin Books in assoc. with Secker & Warburg, 1982), p. 534.

p. 290   "a practical person hatching intrigues": Nicholas Lobkowitz quoted in Spragens, The Irony of Liberal Reason, p. 144.

p. 291   the Marxian unity between theory and practice: Perry Anderson, Considerations on Western Marxism (London: NLB, 1976), p. 19.

p. 291   "Theory became": Ibid., p. 42.

p. 291   "the very process of failing": Thomas McLaughlin, Introduction, in Lentricchia and McLaughlin, eds., Critical Terms for Literary Study, p. 2.

p. 292   "was subject to a wider historical censor": Perry Anderson, Considerations on Western Marxism, p. 55.

p. 292   "The splinter in your eye": Martin Jay, Adorno (Cambridge, MA: Harvard University Press, 1984), pp. 11–12.

p. 293   "his refusal to compromise": Ibid., p. 16.

p. 293   also that is was a turning of the tables: Ibid., p. 38.

p. 293   He believed that true art: Ibid., p. 155.

p. 293   a "rupture with the established reality system": Herbert Marcuse in Bryan Magee, ed., Men of Ideas (New York: Viking Press, 1978), p. 70.

p. 294   when "reality loses" . . . "Ordinary language": Herbert Marcuse, Eros and Civilization (New York: Vintage Books, 1955), p. 89.

p. 294   "There is a sense that": Joel Kotkin, "Lying's Threat to the Left," The American Enterprise, vol. 10, no. 3 (May–June 1999), p. 55.

p. 294   "little more than a desperate holding operation": Christopher Norris, What's Wrong with Postmodernism? (Baltimore: Johns Hopkins University Press, 1990), p. 16.

p. 295   "truth isn't the reward of free spirits": Allen, Truth in Philosophy, p. 150.

p. 296   "The thought that there could be": Miller, The Passion of Michel Foucault, p. 336.

p. 296   The "games of truth" really ought: Ibid., p. 180.

p. 297   "no longer being, doing or thinking": Michel Foucault, "What Is Enlightenment?" in P. Rabinow, ed., The Foucault Reader (Harmondsworth, UK: Penguin Books, 1986), p. 46.

p. 297   Such a truth "does not belong": Miller, The Passion of Michel Foucault, p. 271.

p. 297   he "enjoyed one of the most important": Ibid., p. 306.

p. 297   "with a hint of desperation": C. G. Prado, Starting with Foucault (Boulder, CO, & Oxford: Westview Press, 1995), p. 137.

p. 298   "I would like and I hope": Miller, The Passion of Michel Foucault, p. 306.

p. 298   a "total transfiguration of this world": Ibid., p. 309.

p. 298   "accepting the new level of risk": Ibid., pp. 27–28.

p. 299   "the very concept of truth is fading": Ian Slater, Orwell: The Road to Airstrip One (New York: W. W. Norton, 1985), p. 161.

p. 299   the debauching of "every department of thought": Ibid., p. 246.

p. 299   was "completely sacrosanct": Ibid., p. 210.

p. 299   *And they were dealers in words, not deeds: Ibid.*, p. 160.

p. 299   *"murder is at most a word"*: *Ibid.*, p. 161.

p. 299   *"Lying becomes the norm"*: *Ibid.*, p. 210.

p. 300   *"without using the kind of words"*: *Ibid.*, p. 102.

p. 300   *"is crucial both to human liberty"*: Steiner, *After Babel*, p. 234.

p. 301   *the principle of "endlessly aiming"*: Ferry and Renaut, *French Philosophy of the Sixties*, p. 49.

p. 301   *"has too many meanings"*: Caputo, *Deconstruction in a Nutshell*, p. 59.

p. 301   *an antipathy to "stupid seriousness"*: Don Cupitt, *What Is a Story?* (London: SCM Press, 1991), p. 131.

p. 301   *"The concept of 'truth' "*: Russell, *A History of Western Philosophy*, p. 828.

CHAPTER TWENTY

p. 302   *" 'In the same novel,' said the Dean"*: Dorothy L. Sayers, *Gaudy Night* (New York & London: Harper & Row, 1986), p. 340.

p. 302   *"To pursue truth"*: Virginia Woolf, *To the Lighthouse* (New York: Harcourt, Brace & Co., 1989), p. 32.

p. 302   *In a biography of Liberace*: Darden Pyron, *Liberace: An American Boy* (Chicago: University of Chicago Press, 2000), reviewed in the *New York Times*, July 27, 2000, p. B7.

p. 303   *has now declared this ancient distinction*: Richard Rorty, *Philosophy and Social Hope* (New York & London: Penguin Books, 1999), p. xvi.

p. 304   *"doing their best to develop tools"*: *Ibid.*, p. xxiii.

p. 304   *"trimming the sails of our desires"* . . . *"Our conscious mind"*: Gellner, *Reason and Culture*, pp. 172, 173–74.

p. 304   *simply "to be good at being human"*: Quoted in Konstantin Kolenda, *Rorty's Humanistic Pragmatism* (Tampa, FL: University of South Florida Press, 1990), p. xii.

p. 305   *"compelled to look at a First Cause"*: Don Cupitt, *The Sea of Faith* (London: British Broadcasting Corporation, 1984), pp. 65–66.

p. 305   *"We will be wary"*: Julia Kristeva, *Language: The Unknown* (New York: Columbia University Press, 1989), p. 7.

p. 306   *"seems to us an unfortunate attempt"*: Richard Rorty, "Science as Solidarity," in Lawson and Appignanesi, eds., *Dismantling Truth*, p. 13.

p. 307   *"Syntactic behavior"*: Paul Heyer, *Nature, Human Nature and Society* (Westport, CT: Greenwood Press, 1982), p. 109.

p. 307   *"Literature must therefore"* . . . *the "recurrent anti-rational"*: Murdoch, *Metaphysics as a Guide to Morals*, pp. 206–8.

p. 308   *"to place before mankind"*: Carl Becker, *The Declaration of Independence: A Study in the History of Political Ideas* (New York: Knopf, 1942), p. 26.

p. 308   *"reason and fact, plain and unadorned"*: Terence Martin, *The Instructed Vision* (Bloomington: Indiana University Press, 1961), p. 156.

p. 309   *"As I have said so often"*: Herbert Schneider, *A History of American Philosophy* (New York: Columbia University Press, 1963), p. 481.

p. 309   *Jefferson read Kames*: Martin, *The Instructed Vision*, p. 6.

p. 310   *"What seems but common sense"*: Becker, *The Declaration of Independence*, p. 232.

p. 310   *"If common sense sometimes"*: Judith Butler, "A 'Bad Writer' Bites Back," *New York Times*, March 20, 1999, p. A27.

p. 311   *an intellectual catastrophe*: Bryan Magee, *Confessions of a Philosopher* (New York: Random House, 1997), pp. 42–43.

p. 312   *"transformed our culture"*: Shelby Steele, "A New Front in the Culture War," *Wall Street Journal*, August 2, 2000, p. A22.

p. 312   *it may all turn out to be a ghastly mistake*: Rorty, *Philosophy and Social Hope*, p. 87.

p. 313   *"the pi of Euclid and the G of Newton"*: Alan Sokal and Jean Bricmont, *Fashionable Nonsense* (New York: Picador USA, 1998), p. 2.

p. 313   *It may at first be an affectation*: Murdoch, *Metaphysics as a Guide to Morals*, p. 385.

p. 314   *"a curious, backhanded way"*: Pyron, *Liberace: An American Boy*.

Index

absolute truths, *see* universal (absolute) truths
abstractions, 63
Adam and Eve, 41–42
Adams, Hazard, 274
adaptation, 18–19, 26, 27, 33–34, 64, 172
Adorno, Theodor, 292–93, 294
Aeschylus, 70, 71
aestheticism, 13, 57, 205, 206, 207–8, 213, 215, 264, 277
Western Marxism and, 292–93
Aesthetic Theory (Adorno), 293
Agosin, Marjorie, 12
AIDS, 298, 302
Allen, Barry, 195
American Revolution, 309
Ames, William, 117
anatomical features:
intricate, 27
natural selection and, *see* natural selection, theory of
obsolete, 21–22, 28, 100, 138, 255
Anaximander, 47–48
Anaximenes, 48, 55
Anderson, Perry, 291, 292
Annan, Noel, 85, 113
Antisthenes, 75–76
apes, 41
aphasia, 92

Apollinaire, Guillaume, 213, 214, 215
Apology (Socrates), 276
Aquinas, Thomas, 81–82, 87, 114
arche (basic principle of the world):
of Anaximander, 47
of Anaximenes, 48
of Freud, 187
of Heraclitus, 50
of language for Husserl, 234
of mystery writers, 71
of Parmenides of Elea, 52
of Thales of Miletus, 46–47
Archelaus, 29
architecture, priority of surface over depth in, 166
Ardagh, John, 289–90
Arendt, Hannah, 135
arete, 66–67
Argiope spider, 21
Aristophanes, 66, 109
Aristotle, 43, 45, 47, 81–82, 118, 158–59, 276
Heraclitus and, 50–51, 56
Nicomachean Ethics, 159
nominalists and, 76
Parmenides and, 56–57
Poetics, 70–71
unity of God for, 113–14
view of nature, 65
"Aristotle on Detective Fiction," 71

arithmetic, 116
Arnold, Matthew, 203, 209, 280–81
artificial, the:
  modernism and triumph of,
    203–20
  as more "real" than the natural,
    166–67, 302–3
artificial languages, 268
arts, the, 15, 57, 264, 277, 280
  art for art's sake, 13, 205, 294
  the avante-garde, 204–5
  falsehoods of, 160, 168, 170, 172
  interpretation of, 196
  as mind-altering force, 204
  modernism and, 203–19
  perspective in, 269–70
  as a "play impulse," 293–94
  the sciences, relationship to, 13
  Western Marxists and, 292–93
  see also aestheticism
"As-if, philosophy of," 155–56
Athene, 44–45
Athens, 68–70
  the Assembly of, 68–69, 70
  Council of Five Hundred, 69
Auden, W. H., 214, 299
authoritarianism, 238
autism, 14, 260, 261
Avanguardia socialista, 178
avante-garde, 204–5
Averroës (Ibn Rushd), 81

Backes-Clement, Catherine, 289
Bacon, Sir Francis, 31, 72–73
Bantus, 265
Barnes, Jonathan, 56
Barth, Karl, 314
Barthes, Roland, 14, 257–58
Bates, Henry Walter, 18
Bateson, Geoffrey, 38
Baudelaire, Charles, 209
BBC, 299
Beauvoir, Simone de, 289
Beckett, Samuel, 79, 293
Beerbohm, Max, 205, 208

behaviorism, 123
belief as a virtue, 181
Bentham, Jeremy, 122
Bentley, Richard, 136
Berkeley, Bishop, 308, 309
Berlin, Isaiah, 128, 143, 174, 175
Beyond Good and Evil (Nietzsche),
    159, 160
Bickerton, Derek, 230–31
biology, language of, 307
birds, 22, 23, 38, 39
Birth of Tragedy, The (Nietzsche), 170
Blackwell, Thomas, 253
blenny (tropical fish), 19
Blunt, Anthony, 250
body language, 253
Borch-Jacobsen, Mikkel, 200, 202
boredom, 208–10
Borgmann, Albert, 67
Born, Max, 123
Boyle, Robert, 117, 120
Braithwaite, Richard, 119
Braque, Georges, 269
Breuer, Joseph, 197–98
British Association, 86
Bronowski, Jacob, 117
Brumbaugh, Robert, 67, 69
Buckland, Dean, 86
Burnyeat, Myles, 55
Butler, Judith, 310
Butler, Samuel, 33–34
butterflies, 18, 39

Canterbury Tales (Chaucer), 79
Cantor, Norman, 204
Caputo, John, 278–79
Carlyle, Thomas, 23, 182
Carpenter, Edward, 36
Carruthers, Mary, 78
categorical imperative of Kant,
    139–40
cause and effect, 107, 108, 109, 124
Cézanne, Paul, 269
chaos theory, 124, 125
Charles I, King of England, 117

Charles II, King of England,
117–18
Charron, Father Pierre, 94–95
Chaucer, Geoffrey, 78, 79, 148
chimpanzees, 39, 40–41, 260
Chomsky, Noam, 143, 254–56, 307
Christian gentleman, cult of the,
115, 119
Christianity:
absolutes of, 75, 86
language games and, 245
Machiavelli's view of, 25
myths of, 179
nominalism and, 75, 76, 78, 85
see also individual denominations
chromodynamics, theory of, 270
Cicero, 29, 118
city-state, 67, 68, 69
Civilization and Its Discontents
(Freud), 216
Clark, Ronald, 193
class struggle, 179
Clement of Alexandria, 49
Cleve, Felix, 55
Clinton, Bill, 11, 312
Clouds, The (Aristophanes), 66, 109
coherence theory of truth, 224
Coleridge, Samuel Taylor, 310
coloration of animals, 36, 38
commands (imperatives), 143
common sense, 106, 107, 226–27,
286, 291, 307, 308–11
communication, see language
communism, 299
attempts at simplification of theory, 112–13
failure of Soviet experiment, 289
see also Marxism; Soviet Union
complexity, 20
of language, 230
of the sciences, 119, 122, 124,
125–26, 307, 311
theories of, 124
"complicated simplicity," 124
conditional nature of truth, 207–8

Condorcet, Marquis de, 121–22
Conrad, Joseph, 215–18
conscience, Kant's good will and,
138
consciousness (reason, intelligence,
mind), 27, 28, 29, 30, 33,
224, 304
Darwin's view of, 28, 49, 163
Descartes' view of, 14, 90, 92,
94–101, 105, 163
Enlightenment view of, 25
faith and, see faith, reason and
Fichte's view of, 152
Freud's beliefs about, 188, 189,
193–94
Hamann's view of, 144, 146
Hume's view of, 106, 107, 108,
131
the idealists and, 238
Kant's view of, 131–38, 142–43,
146, 151, 242
Lamarck's view of, 26
meaning anchored in, 233
in nature, 33–39, 41
ability to understand the
world and, 43–57
Nietzsche on, 157, 163, 164–65
nominalism's distrust of, 79
Parmenides' view of, 52–53
Plato's view of, 74, 84
Pyrronists' view of, 92–96
Schopenhauer's view of, 152–53
Sorel's distrust of intellect, 174,
178–79
as unalterable truth, 52–53
contradiction, impossibility of, 62,
76, 81
Copernican system, 96, 97, 116,
142, 151
correspondence theory of truth,
142, 149, 184, 212–13, 224,
232, 233, 265, 306
Counter-Reformation, 87
Course in General Linguistics (Saussure), 222

Cratylus of Athens, 51
creation, divine, 22–23, 30, 86, 100,
113
Aquinas and, 82–83
"creeping," 38
Crews, Frederick, 191–92, 197
Crist, Eileen, 37–38
Critique of Pure Reason (Kant), 131,
133, 151–52
Cromer, Alan, 122
Cromwell, Oliver, 117
Cubism, 213, 214, 268, 269–70
cuckoos, 19
culture, 13, 220, 242–43, 278, 313,
314
of mistrust, 160–61
oral, 283
the Sophists and, 68
Cupitt, Don, 301
custom, 108
Hume and, 106, 107
Cycloptera (insect), 15

d'Alembert, Jean, 249
Dali, Salvador, 12
Danford, John, 109
Dante, 133
Danto, Arthur, 157–58
Darwin, Charles, 17, 21–30, 32,
34–35, 49, 65, 85, 133,
153–54, 162, 253–54, 303–4,
307, 313–14
Descent of Man, 18, 181–82
Hume's ideas and, 106, 108,
110
natural selection theory, *see* nat-
ural selection, theory of
Nietzsche and theories of,
163–64, 172
Origin of Species, 22, 26, 34, 100,
113, 153
David, Marie-Euphrasie, 174
"Decay of Lying, The," 166
deception, *see specific philosophers,
philosophies, and concepts*

Declaration of Independence, 308,
309
deconstruction, 14, 80, 201, 249,
271–84, 287–88, 289, 294,
300–301
deductive reasoning, 52, 72
Degas, Edward, 214
de Gaulle, Charles, 288
De la Sagesse (Charron), 94–95
democracy, 16, 80, 85, 304, 312
knowledge and, 121–22
rhetoric and, 68
Sorel's opinion of, 175, 176
truthfulness and, 16
Democritus, 92
Dennett, Daniel, 39–40
Denyer, Nicholas, 73
depth, priority of surface over,
166–67
de Quincey, Thomas, 129
Derrida, Jacques, 80, 271–84, 301
First Essay in Truth in Painting, 277
Glas, 274
Margins of Philosophy, 272
Descartes, René, 89–101, 102, 103,
105, 109, 114–16, 120, 234,
285, 304, 309
consciousness and, 14, 90, 92,
94–101, 105, 163
Discourse on Method, 94, 98, 99,
115
Le Monde, 96
Meditations, 90, 92
nature and, 97, 118
three dreams of, 91
view of God, 89–90, 91–92,
114–15, 163
Descent of Man (Darwin), 18, 181–82
Detienne, Marcel, 53, 54
de Waal, Frans, 39
Dewey, John, 223–24, 259
*Dialogue Concerning the Two Chief
World Systems* (Galileo), 96
Dialogues Concerning Natural Religion
(Hume), 105

Diogenes Laertius, 62, 63, 92–93
diplomacy, 26, 150
Discourse on Method (Descartes), 94, 98, 99, 115
Doctor Faustus (Mann), 210–11
Dodd, C. H., 50
dogs, 39
  instincts of, 28
Donatus, 148
Dostoevsky, Fyodor, 161
double standards, 311–12
"Double Truth," 86
double truth, doctrine of, 81–87
Draper, J. W., 85–86
dreams, Freud's interpretation of, 187
Duns Scotus, 82, 84
Dupré, Louis, 80–81

Ecce Homo (Nietzsche), 160
economic theory, Rational Man in, 156
Ego, 199, 200
Einstein, Albert, 124
  Hume's influence on, 110
  theory of gravitation, 123, 269, 282
  theory of relativity, 110, 123
  view of God, 31, 123
Elements of Newton's Philosophy Made Accessible to Everyone (Voltaire), 121
Eliot, T. S., 180, 218
Elkana, Yehuda, 123
England:
  Industrial Revolution in, 207
  Victorian era, *see* Victorian era
Enlightenment, 25, 80, 121, 127, 136, 143–44, 180, 280
  Hamann's opposition to, 144, 145
  Sorel's view of, 176–77
  speech and thought, separation of, 252–53
entropy, 176

Erasmus, 34, 118
Essays (Montaigne), 94
Etiology of Hysteria, The (Freud), 198
Euathlus, 63
Euclidean geometry, 86, 116
Europeans, The (James), 165–66
Euthydemus (Plato), 58–61, 62
Evangelicalism, 113
evolution, theory of, 17, 32, 100, 154, 172, 304, 313
  competition and, 17, 36–37, 163
  geographic isolation and, 33
  natural selection and, *see* natural selection, theory of
  sociobiology and, 37–38
evolutionary psychology, 15, 84, 153

facts, correspondence of truth and, *see* correspondence theory of truth
faith, 76, 280
  Evangelicalism and, 113
  language games and, 245–46
  reason and:
    Aquinas attempt to reconcile, 81, 82
    Ockham's views, 82
falsehood, *see specific philosophers, philosophies, and concepts*
Fascism, 185, 287, 293
Fates, the, 44
Fichte, Johann, 151–52, 224, 301
"fictions" of Vahinger, 155–56
figurative language, 272–73, 274, 275, 278–79
fireflies, 20, 23, 39
First Essay in Truth in Painting (Derrida), 277
Fitch, Robert, 294
Fontenelle, Bernard, 120
Forrester, John, 190, 198, 261
Forster, E. M., 166
Foucault, Michel, 295–98
  "limit experience" of, 297–98

"Fragment of an Analysis of a Case of Hysteria," 191
France:
    Fifth Republic, 288
    French Revolution, 120, 151, 152, 309
    moral temper in late nineteenth-century, 180
France, Anatole, 180
Franklin, Benjamin, 309
fraud, *see specific philosophers, philosophies, and concepts*
freedom of speech in Athens, 69
free will, 97, 151, 155–56
    Kant on, 138, 151
Frege, Gottlob, 238–39
French *moralistes,* seventeenth-century, 194
French Revolution, 120, 151, 152, 309
French *syndicats,* 179
Freud, Sigmund, 12, 13, 29, 186–202, 200, 203, 208, 304
    Civilization and Its Discontents, 216
    The Etiology of Hysteria, 198
    fantasies and illusions and, 177, 187, 188, 190, 193, 196–97
    hysteria and, 191–93
    the mind as liar, 188, 189, 193–94
    "overdetermination," 192
    the unconscious and, 193, 195
Freudian slip, 201
Fromm, Erich, 286
Furst, Lilian, 149

Galileo, 86, 96, 97, 116, 120
Gallop, Jane, 201
Garden of Eden, 41–42, 203
Gardner, John, 78–79
Garrison, W. L., 181
Gast, Peter, 164, 168
Gaudy Night (Sayers), 302
Gauguin, Paul, 269
Gaukroger, Stephen, 97

gay culture of San Francisco, Foucault and, 298
Gay Science, The (Nietzsche), 167
Gellner, Ernest, 98, 244, 249, 304
Genealogy of Morals (Nietzsche), 164
general strike, 179
genetics, 37
geometry, 86, 116
    non-Euclidean, 268–69
giraffes, 32–33, 36
Glas (Derrida), 274
God, 31, 137
    Aristotle's view of, 113–14
    creation, *see* creation, divine
    Descartes' view of, 89–90, 91–92, 97, 99, 105, 114–15, 163
    Einstein's view of, 31, 123
    Hamann's view of, 144–46
    incomprehensibility of, 83–84
        Duns Scotus and, 82, 83
        Ockham and, 77–78, 82, 83, 114
    intentionally deceptive, 22–23
    Kant's view of, 133
    Nietzche's view of, 164, 214
    unity and simplicity of, 113–15, 123
Gödel, Kurt, 224
    Incompleteness Theorem, 111
Goethe, Johann Wolfgang von, 43, 157
    Faust, 211, 245
Goffman, Ervin, 265
Golomb, Jacob, 141
good will, 138, 139, 141–42, 143
Gorbachev, Mikhail, 292
Gorgias, 69, 70, 71, 72
Gorgias (Plato), 72
Gorky, Maxim, 112
Gosse, Edmund, 206
Gosse, Philip, 22–23, 83
grammar, 255–56
    universal, 143, 228–29
Gramsci, Antonio, 250, 291, 292

Greece, ancient, 46, 47, 66–67, 174,
224, 303
invention of gods of Olympus,
170–71
myths of, 179
see also names of individual philosophies and philosophers
Green, Richard, 283
Gregor, James, 178
Gryllacris (grasshopper), 36
Guatemala, civil war in, 12

Habermas, Jurgen, 258–60, 301
habit, inheritance of, 26, 32–33
Hacking, Ian, 122–23
Haeckel, Ernst, 237
Hall, Robert, 70
Hamann, Johann, 144–47, 151–52
Hampson, Norman, 119
Harland, Richard, 221, 229, 234
Harré, Rom, 122
Hartman, Heinz, 199
Havel, Vaclav, 264
Heart of Darkness (Conrad), 216–18
Hegel, Georg Wilhelm Friedrich,
212, 224, 225, 272
Heidegger, Martin, 272
Heine, Heinrich, 127, 133, 152
Helen of Troy, 71
Helicondae (butterfly), 18
Heller, Erich, 211
Helvitius, Clause, 122
Henry, Granville, 50
Heraclitus, 48–52, 54–55
Herder, Gottfried von, 253
Hermes, 45
heroism, 178
Hesiod, 70, 275
Heyer, Paul, 307
history:
making your own, 296
modernism's attitude toward,
212, 213, 214
role of, 99, 100–101, 105
Sorel's view of, 177

Victorian era's view of, 211–12
Hobbes, Thomas, 109, 257
Hoffmannsthal, Hugo von, 253
Holmes, Oliver Wendell, 309
Homer, 44–45, 70–71
honeybees, 27–28
Hooke, Robert, 119
Hough, Graham, 264
Houghton, Walter, 181
House of Fame, The (Chaucer), 79
Human, All Too Human (Nietzsche),
161–62
humanism, 266, 297
Hume, David, 103–11, 124, 130,
131, 146, 309
breakdown of, 103
Dialogues Concerning Natural Religion (Hume), 105
personality of, 103–4
A Treatise on Human Nature, 103,
104, 110
Humphrey, Nicholas, 15, 41
Husserl, Edmund, 233–34, 272
Hutcheon, Linda, 141
Hutt, Rowland, 236
Huxley, T. H., 29, 214, 217
hypnotism, 198
hysteria, 191–93, 198

Ibn Rushd (Averroës), 81
Ibsen, Henrik, 161, 182–83
Id, 199
idealism, 237–38, 289, 305
Iliad (Homer), 70
illusions, Freud's views on, 187,
188, 190, 193, 196–97, 277
imagination, 94, 111, 263–64, 266,
303, 308, 309, 312–13
inclinations, 170
Kant on, 139–40, 142
Nietzsche on, 157
Incompleteness Theorem of Gödel,
111
Industrial Revolution, 161, 207
In Memoriam (Tennyson), 180

instinct:
   Darwin's view of, 26
   individual variance in, 27–28
   Lamarck's view of, 26
   for truth, 23–24, 25–26
insurance companies, health, 11
intelligence, *see* consciousness (reason, intelligence, mind)
"Invisible College," 117
Iran, 298
irony, 112, 146–50
Italy:
   Communist Party, 291
   intellectuals of twentieth-centu-
      ry, 178
   Mussolini, *see* Mussolini, Benito
   unification of, 179

James, Henry, 148–49, 165–66, 183,
   209–10, 215, 218, 219
   "The Liar," 262–63
   The Spoils of Poynton, 209–10
James, William, 223, 224
Jameson, Frederic, 166
Jardin d'Epicure, Le (France), 180
Jaspers, Karl, 57
Jefferson, Thomas, 308, 309, 310
jokes, 200–201
Jones, Ernest, 197
Jowett, Benjamin, 69–70, 205
Joyce, James, 196

Kafka, Franz, 196
Kaiser Family Foundation, 11
Kames, Lord, 308, 309
Kant, Immanuel, 86, 128–44, 265
   categorical imperative, 139–40
   Critique of Pure Reason, 131, 133,
      151–52
   good will and, 138, 139, 141–42,
      143
   Hamann and, 145–46
   on human desire for metaphysi-
      cal speculation, 133–35
   inclinations and, 139–40, 142

Logic, 134
   moral law of, 128–29, 137,
      138–40, 142, 143, 159
   on noumenon and phenome-
      non, 132–33, 137, 155
   *Prolegomena to Any Future Meta-
      physics,* 134–35
   servant Lampe, 129–30, 140
   three types of true assertion,
      131–32
   universal categories of the mind,
      132, 133, 139–40, 142–43,
      146, 151, 242
Kingsley, Charles, 182, 207
Kirk, G. S., 46
Knight's Tale (Chaucer), 79
Koyre, Alexandre, 89
Kracauer, Siegfried, 292
Kristeva, Julia, 291, 305
Kroner, Richard, 139
Küng, Hans, 87–88

Lacan, Jacques, 199–202, 223, 291,
   310
Lamarck, Jean-Baptiste, 26, 27, 28,
   32–33, 37
   defenders of, 34, 35
Lamb, Charles, 263
Langland, William, 78
language, 13–14, 65, 85, 200,
   220–34, 285, 314
   artificial languages, 268
   Chomsky's view of, 143, 254–56,
      307
   complexity of, 230
   deceit of, 42
   deconstructionist view of, 80,
      201, 271–84, 300
   as emotional expression, 253
   evolution from emotional cries
      of animals, theory of, 306
   Foucault's view of, 295
   as godlike, 235
   grammar, 255–56
      universal, 143, 228–29

Heraclitus' view of, 51–52, 54–55
irony and, 149
nominalists and, 78, 80–81
Parmenides' view of, 56
postmodernists and, 14, 29,
    252–65, 268
primitive, 230–31
purified form of, desire for, 239
redundancy in, lack of, 255
rhetoric, *see* rhetoric
Romantic view of, 253, 254
Saussure's theories of, 222–23,
    241, 266–67, 268, 270, 271,
    278, 289
the "signified" and the "signifi-
    er," 80, 223, 266–67, 268,
    270, 294
  deconstructionists and,
    271–84
the Sophists and, 68
speech and thought, relationship
    of, 252–53, 254
structure dependence of, 255–56
syntax, 225, 228, 229, 230, 231,
    255, 307
thought's relationship to,
    252–53, 254, 286, 305
transparency, end of, 257,
    295–96
universal form of, 241
Wittgenstein's evolving views of,
    77, 82, 235–51
  language games and, 77,
    235–36, 241–48
words, 71
  analytic philosophy and,
    224–25
  arbitrary nature of, 14, 51, 80,
    222, 228, 266–68, 270–71,
    307
  language games and, 245
  nominalist view of, 80–81
  Plato's view of, 74–75
  in Saussurian theory, 222,
    228–29, 266–67, 271

see also meaning
language games, 77, 235–36,
    241–48
larks, 36
La Rochefoucauld, 153
Lawson, Hilary, 247
Le Bon, Gustave, 177, 178
Lee, Desmond, 243
Leibniz, Gottfried Wilhelm, 122,
    212, 238, 254
Leigh, Vivien, 13
Lenin, Vladimir Ilich, 112, 113,
    173–74, 185, 204, 290
Leptalides (butterfly), 18
Lessing, Gotthold Ephraim, 208
Lewis, C. I., 102
Lewis, C. S., 102
Lewis, Wyndham, 167
"Liar, The," 262–63
Liar Paradox, 231–33
Liberace, 302–3
lie detector, 23–24
Life Force, Shavian, 35
Lifemanship (Potter), 67
"limit experience," 297–98
literacy, 283
literary criticism, 189, 196
literature:
  criticism, *see* literary criticism
  "death of the author," 258, 278
  Derrida's view of, 272, 274–75,
    277–79, 281
  obscurity of modernist, 13, 207,
    208, 215–19, 307
  of Victorian era, 182–83
  Western Marxism and, 292, 293
Lloyd, James, 20
Locke, John, 120–21, 122, 136, 253
logic, 13, 54, 57, 212, 225, 227
  truth and, 238–39
logical positivism, 225, 238, 240
Logic (Kant), 134
Logos, 65
  Heraclitus' view of, 49, 50, 51, 64
  as intelligible order, 49, 50, 127

Logos (*continued*)
  mathematical meaning of, 49–50
Louis of Bavaria, Emperor, 76, 77
Luck or Cunning? (Butler), 34–35
Luther, Martin, 78
Lutheran Pietists, 265
lying, *see specific philosophers, philosophies, and concepts*

McDonald, Kelly, 40
Machiavelli, Niccolo, 24–26, 85,
  128, 150–51
"Machiavellian intelligence," 24, 53
McIntyre, Alasdair, 265
macrocosm, inferences from the
  microcosm to the, 48
Magee, Bryan, 105, 246, 311
Mallarmé, Stéphane, 214, 257,
  277–78
Malraux, André, 215
Man and Superman (Shaw), 35
"man is the measure of all things,"
  62, 63
Mann, Thomas, 156, 173, 185,
  210–11
manners, good, 11–12
Marcuse, Herbert, 293–94
Margins of Philosophy (Derrida), 272
Marius the Epicurean (Pater), 206
Marsh, James, 310
Martin, Terence, 308
Marx, Karl, 29, 35, 86, 173–74, 250,
  290, 291
  doctrine of historical inevitability, 290
Marxism, 177, 204, 223, 225–26,
  288
  as philosophy of universal truth,
  290
  Western Marxists, 291–98
Masson, Jeffrey, 196
mathematics, 109, 120, 243, 257,
  280
Maugham, W. Somerset, 235
Mazzini, Giuseppe, 179

meadow pipit, 19
meaning, 221, 256
  context of, 264
  deconstructionists and, 271–74
  distinguished from truth,
  225–26
  Husserl's view of, 233
  language games and, 244
  in the Middle Ages, 136–37
  obscurity of modernist literature
  and its, 219
  public nature of, 242, 246
  quest for, 135
  truth as separate from, 195, 196,
  308
  Vahinger on, 154
Meditations (Descartes), 90, 92
  "Objections" to, 100–101
Megill, Alan, 172
Mellor, Anne, 147
memory, personal, 286
Menchu, Rigoberta, 12
Meredith, George, 215
Mersenne, Marin, 115
metabiography, 12–13
metaphors, 272–73, 275, 278–79
Metaphysical Society, 86
Method of Natural Philosophy (Newton), 116
Metis (Greek concept), 53–54, 57
Metis (Greek goddess), 53
Michaels, Robert, 190–91
middle class, 180
  modernists and, 205
  Sorel's distaste for, 174, 175, 176
Mill, John Stuart, 182
Miller, James, 298
Miller, Judith, 296
Miller, Perry, 116–17
mimicry in nature, 18–20
mind, the, *see* consciousness (reason, intelligence, mind)
Mitchell, Robert, 38, 39
modernism, 13, 57, 166–67,
  203–19, 292

aestheticism and, 57, 205, 206,
207–8, 213, 215
analytic philosophy of, 212
internal truth of works of art,
213–14
obscurity in writings of, 13, 207,
208, 215–19, 307
truth as a point of view in, 208
view of history, 212, 213, 214
Monboddo, Lord, 253
Monde, Le (Descartes), 96
Monk, Ray, 251
monkeys, 41
Montaigne, Michel de, 12, 93–96,
98, 115–16, 171, 252
Essays, 94
Mook, Delo, 270
Moore, G. E., 212, 310–11
morality, 309
Kant on, 128–29, 137, 138–40,
142, 143, 159
in late nineteenth-century
Europe, 180
Nietzche on, 157, 158
social, 312
Sorel on, 174, 175
Morley, John, 86, 182
Müller, Max, 235
Munz, Peter, 230
Murdoch, Iris, 58, 140, 257, 307,
313
Muses, the, 275, 276
Mussolini, Benito, 175, 178, 185,
287
myths, 15, 173, 181, 187, 275, 295
social, 175–79, 183, 184–85

Napoleon, 32, 179
*Natural Philosophy of Cause and
Chance* (Born), 123
natural selection, theory of, 18, 21,
23, 26–27, 39, 155
opponents of, 32, 33, 34–35
Natural Theology (Paley), 100
nature, 13, 65, 114, 203, 244

artifice and deceit in, 14–15,
17–30, 21, 23–29, 31, 32, 33,
37–42, 162
four levels of, 39
artificial as more "real" than the
natural, 166–67, 302–3
complexity of, 119
consciousness in, 33–39, 41, 49
ability to understand the
world and, 43–57
Descartes' view of, 97, 118
Hume's view of, 103–11
as ironical, 147
mimicry in, 18–20, 35–36, 37
nominalism's distrust of, 79
Parmenides as anti-naturalist, 52
as parsimonious, 114, 116
Nature, 29
Nature morte au panier (Cezanne),
269
Nazi Germany, 286
needs, 151
Fichte on, 152
Rousseau on, 130–31
Neiman, Susan, 135
neo-Darwinism, 37
Newman, Cardinal, 86
New Republic, The, 11
Newton, Sir Isaac, 31, 116, 117,
123, 126
Hume's ideas and, 110
laws of motion, 120, 128
Method of Natural Philosophy, 116
Opticks, 121
Principia, 121
Newtonianism for the Ladies, 121
*Newtonian System of Philosophy Adapt-
ed to the Capacity of Young
Gentlemen . . . ,* 121
New York Times, 310
Nicomachean Ethics (Aristotle), 159
Niebuhr, Reinhold, 183–84
Nietzsche, Friedrich, 15, 29, 86,
157–65, 167–72, 194, 195,
214, 241, 312

Nietzsche, Friedrich (*continued*)
  Beyond Good and Evil, 159, 160,
    169
  The Birth of Tragedy, 170
  breakdown, 164, 169
  on consciousness, 157, 163,
    164–65
  culture of mistrust and, 160–61,
    172
  Darwinian theories and, 163–64,
    172
  Ecce Homo, 160
  The Gay Science, 167
  The Genealogy of Morals, 164
  health of, 159–60
  Human, All Too Human, 161–62
  on irony, 149
  On the Pathos of Truth, 162
  personality of, 158
  The Philosopher, 162
  questioning the value of truth,
    159–60, 167–68, 169, 170,
    172
  suspiciousness of, 160–62
  On Truth and Lies in a Moral Sense,
    183
  Twilight of the Idols, 169
Nigger of the Narcissus, The (Conrad),
  216
1984 (Orwell), 16, 285–86, 299–300
Nobel Peace Prize, 12
nominalism, 75–84
nomos and *physis,* 65–67
Norris, Christopher, 294
noumenon:
  Kant on, 132–33, 137, 155
  Romanticist view of, 146
Novuum Organum (Bacon), 72–73
Nuremberg Trials, 259
Nyberg, David, 264–65

obscurity of modernist literature,
  13, 207, 208, 215–19, 307
Ockham, William of, 76–78, 80, 82,
  84

incomprehensibility of God,
  77–78, 82, 83, 114
  razor of, 77, 114, 116
Odysseus, 44–45, 54
Odyssey (Homer), 54, 168
Oedipus Complex, 193
"Of Liars," 115–16
Of Origin and Progress of Language
  (Monboddo), 253
Ohnsorg, Benno, 293
On the Gods (Protagoras), 62
*On the Harmony Between Religion and
  Philosophy* (Averroës), 81
On the Origin of Language (Herder),
  253
On the Pathos of Truth (Nietzsche),
  162
On Truth and Lies in a Moral Sense
  (Nietzsche), 183
Opticks (Newton), 121
orchids, 18–19
organs, useless, theory of evolution
  and, 21–22, 28, 100, 138,
  255
original, meanings of the word, 14
Origin of Species (Darwin), 22, 26, 34,
  100, 113, 153
Orwell, George, 16, 167, 285–86,
  291, 299–300
Overbeck, Franz, 164, 169

"Painter of Modern Life, The," 209
painting, *see* arts, the
Paley, William, 27, 100
Paris, student demonstrations of
  May 1968 in, 287–89, 293
Parmenides of Elea, 52–55, 56, 64,
  70
Pascal, Blaise, 136
Pascal, Fania, 236–37, 250
Pater, Walter Horatio, 13, 205–9
  Marius the Epicurean, 206
  Plato and Platonism, 208
  *Studies in the History of the Renais-
    sance,* 205

Perian Magi, 64
Pericles, 66, 70
perspective in art, 269–70
Pheidole bicornis (ant species), 19
phenomenology, 233
Pherosphus agnathus (beetle), 36
Philetas of Cos, 231
Philosopher, The (Nietzsche), 162
Philosophical Investigations (Wittgenstein), 241
Photuris (firefly), 20
Phyllobaenus (beetle), 19
physics, 122, 270, 307
physis and *nomos*, 65–67, 75
Picasso, Pablo, 13, 203, 214, 215, 269
pied flycatchers, 19
Piers Plowman (Langland), 78
pigmentation of animals, 36, 38
Pindar, 70
Piper tree, 19
Plato, 56, 58–59, 62, 68, 71, 73, 84, 272
  eternal truths and, 74–76, 208
  Euthydemus, 58–61, 62
  Forms of, 66, 75–76, 208, 238, 303
  Gorgias, 72
  Protagoras, 276
  Republic, 115, 128
  The Sophist, 67
  Symposium, 103, 148
  Timaeus, 83
Plato and Platonism (Pater), 208
pleasure, 306
plover, 41
Poetics (Aristotle), 70–71
poetry and poets, 70–71, 73, 172, 257, 275, 277–78, 281
  Derrida's view of, 274, 279
  the meaning of a poem, 276
  modernism and, 204, 207, 214, 218
  Romantic irony and, 149
  Valéry's view of, 272–73

Western Marxists and, 292
  see also arts, the
polis, 65, 68
politics, 16, 29, 85
  disillusionment with, 13
  fanaticism in, 238
  myths and, 173, 175–79
  truth as creature of political power, 286–87
  see also statesmanship
Pollock Sir Frederick, 309
polygraph, 23–24
Popkin, Richard, 96
Popper, Karl, 34, 225–26, 232
  "worlds" of knowledge, 226–27
positivism, 85, 113, 123
  logical positivists, 225, 238, 240
postmodernism, 57, 166, 167, 234, 248, 287, 295, 301
  language and, 14, 29, 252–65, 268
Potter, Stephen, 67
Poulton, Edward, 35–36
Pound, Ezra, 167
power to create the truth, 286
pragmatic theory of truth, 223–24
pragmatists, 273–74, 303, 305, 312
Premack, David, 41
Pre-Raphaelites, English, 161
Presentation of Self in Everyday Life, The (Goffman), 265
Prigogine, Ilya, 125
Prince, The (Machiavelli), 24, 150–51
Principia (Newton), 121
Problems of Philosophy (Russell), 45–46
progress, 306
  belief in, 121, 176
  material, 205
Prolegomena to Any Future Metaphysics (Kant), 134–35
Protagoras, 62–64, 66, 67, 70, 71, 159
Protagoras (Plato), 276

Protestantism, 85
Proust, Marcel, 127, 258
psychoanalysis, 13, 161, 189–202
  Freudian, see Freud, Sigmund
  historical truth and, 191
  secrecy in, 189–90
psychology, human, 108
  Hume and, 106, 107
  influence on history of, 177–78
Puritanism, 116–17, 308
pursuit of truth as preferable to its
    actual possession, 208
Pyron, Darden, 302
Pyrrho, 92–93
Pyrrhonism, 92–96
Pysgosteus pungitius (ten-spined
    stickleback), 38
Pythagoreans, 116

quantum mechanics, 270
quark doctrine of matter, 270
Queenan, Joe, 157

Randall, John Herman, 65, 68, 121,
    137
rationalists, 85–86, 306
  Sorel's distrust of, 174
Rational Man in economic theory,
    156
Reagan, Ronald, biography of, 12
reason, see consciousness (reason,
    intelligence, mind)
reductionism, 123
reed warbler, 19
Reflections on Violence (Sorel), 178,
    184
Reformation, 78, 96, 296
Reid, Thomas, 308, 309
relativism, 26, 72, 78, 92, 207–8,
    224, 286–87, 299
relativity, Einstein's theory of, 110,
    123
religion:
  as an illusion, 187
  Christianity, see Christianity
    collapse of trust in official doc-
      trines of, 181
    God, see God
    language games and, 245
    science and, relationship
      between, 85–86
    truth of, 50
    see also specific religions
Republic (Plato), 115, 128
revolution, 298, 309–10
  American, 309
  French, 120, 151, 152, 309
  against ideas, student demon-
    stration of May 1968,
    288–89
  Russian, 290
  as tool of social betterment, 177,
    184
rhetoric, 57, 68–73, 81
  "the Absolute Talker," 70
Rich, Adrienne, 112
Ricoeur, Paul, 29
Rieff, Philip, 194, 196, 277
Roman Catholic Church, 86, 96,
    120
  Counter-Reformation, 87
  double truth and, 86–87
  Galileo and, 96
  Inquisition, 96
  Reformation, 78, 96
  Second Vatican Council, 86–87
Romans, ancient, 179
Romanticism, 85, 128, 136, 146,
    161, 277, 279, 280, 290
  imagination and, 263
  irony and, 146–50
  language as expression of indi-
    vidual feeling, 253, 254
Roochnik, David, 275–76
Rorty, Richard, 303–6, 312–13
Rosaldo, Michelle, 283
Roscellinus, 75
Rousseau, Jean-Jacques, 128, 130,
    134, 138
Royal Society, 117–18, 119–20

Ruse, Michael, 28–29, 108–9
Ruskin, John, 209, 258, 263–64
Russell, Bertrand, 45–46, 150, 212, 301
Russian Revolution, 290
Ryle, Gilbert, 243

Saffra, Piero, 250
Sand, George, 112
Sanity of True Genius, The (Lamb), 263
Sartre, Jean-Paul, 218–19, 256–57, 258
   What Is Literature, 256–57
Saussure, Ferdinand de, 221–23, 228, 241, 266–67, 268, 270, 271, 278, 289
Savage-Rambaugh, Sue, 40
Savonarola, 25
Sayers, Dorothy L., 71, 129, 302
Schiller, Friedrich, 151, 293
Schlegel, Friedrich, 147
Scholasticism, 77
Schopenhauer, Arthur, 152–54
science(s), 85, 226, 238, 270–71
   the arts, relationship to, 13
   complexity of, 119, 122, 124, 125–26, 307, 311
   confidence in the possibilities of the, 237
   double truth and, 86
   experimental, rise of, 118–19, 120
   religion and, relationship of, 85–86
   Royal Society and, 117–18, 119–20
   simplicity and, 119–24
   Sturm und Drang movement's rebellion against, 144
Scottish School of Common Sense, 308, 309
Scruton, Roger, 89, 92
Searle, Leroy, 266
secularism, 85

self-deception, 15, 218
   Freud's view of, 186, 197
   psychoanalysis and, 189
   Schopenhauer on, 153
   Wittgenstein on, 236
self-preservation, Nietzsche's view of, 162–63, 169
self-restraint, 217
"Semantic Theory of Truth, A," 232
senses, the:
   Pyrrhonists and, 92–93
   simplicity and, 123–24
   see also consciousness (reason, intelligence, mind)
Sextus Empiricus, 92–93
Shattuck, Roger, 14
Shaw, George Bernard, 34–35
Sidney, Sir Philip, 149
Siger of Brabant, 81
simplicity and truth, 112–26, 203, 213
sincerety, 259, 264
singularities, 74–75, 85
skepticism, 92–93, 97
Sluga, Hans, 298
snakes, 22
socialism, 173, 177, 178, 185, 291, 292, 293, 295
social physics, 120–21
social policy, 311–12
Social Text, 313
sociobiology, 37–38
Socrates, 12, 29, 49, 60–61, 71, 75, 103, 109, 115
   Apology, 276
   irony of, 148
   Sorel's portrayal of, 174–75
Sokal, Alan, 313
Solomon, Robert, 109–10, 140, 150, 233
Sophist, The (Plato), 67
Sophists, 61–73, 75, 81, 118, 272, 276, 285
   Plato's opposing views, 68, 74
Sorbonne, Paris, 288–89, 293

Sorel, Georges, 173–79, 181
    collective will and, 174
    distrust of rationalism, 174
    Reflections on Violence, 178, 184
    social myths and, 175–79, 183,
        184–85
Soviet Union, 185, 250–51, 286,
        287, 289, 292
Spanish Civil War, 299
speech:
    Darwinian view of, 253–54
    Derrida's view of, 281–82
    Habermas' view of ideal, 259
    as separate from thought,
        252–53, 254
    see also language
Spencer, Herbert, 18
spiders, spinning skills of, 20–21
Spinoza, Baruch, 280
Spirituals (Franciscan group), 76
Spoils of Poynton, The (James),
        209–10
Sprat, Thomas, 118
Stalin, Joseph, 292, 299
statesmanship:
    in ancient Greece, rhetoric and,
        70
    Machiavelli's views on, 24–25
    see also politics
Steele, Shelby, 312
Steiner, George, 15, 42, 220, 223,
        224–25, 228, 300
Stent, Gunther, 270
Stephen, Leslie, 181
Stewart, Dugald, 308
Stoicism, 162
Stoll, David, 12
structuralism, *see* language, Saus-
        sure's theories of
Studies in the History of the Renaissance
        (Pater), 205
Sturm und Drang movement, 144,
        151
Sturrock, John, 241
Summa totius logicae (Ockham), 80

Superego, 187
surface, priority over depth of,
        166–67
surrealism, 199, 200, 266, 273
Symbolists, French, 161
Symons, Arthur, 215
Symposium (Plato), 103, 148
syndicats of France, 179
syntax, 225, 229, 230, 231, 255,
        307

Tanner, Tony, 165–66, 254
Tarski, Alfred, 231–32, 233
technology, rise of, 304
Tempier, Bishop Etienne, 83
Temps Modernes, Les, 289
Temptation (Havel), 264
Tennyson, Alfred, Lord, 180
Thales of Miletus, 46–47, 95, 275
"theater as metabiography," 12–13
Theory of Everything, 120, 124
"Theory of Everything," 45
"theory of mind," 260–61
Thomas, Lewis, 23–24
Tillich, Paul, 79–80
Timaeus (Plato), 83
totalitarianism, 175–76, 286,
        299–300
To the Lighthouse (Woolf), 302
Tractatus Logico-Philosophicus
        (Wittgenstein), 238, 240,
        246
tragedy, 71
transcendentalism, 309
transparency, 125, 126, 218,
        295–96, 310
Treatise on Human Nature, A
        (Hume), 103, 104, 110
Trilling, Lionel, 150
Trivers, Robert, 31, 38
Trollope, Anthony, 65, 68
truth, *see specific philosophers; philoso-
        phies, and concepts*
Truth (Protagoras), 62
Twilight of the Idols (Nietzsche), 169

unconscious, 201–2, 304
  Freudian analysis and, 193, 195
  Lacan's view of, 200, 202, 223, 310
  myths and, 176, 184–85
Unconscious Memory (Popper), 34
universal (absolute) truths, 74–75,
      79–80, 85, 86, 127, 144, 235,
      259, 297
  demise of, 286–87
  Descartes and, 90–91, 98
  desire for simplicity and, 122–23
  doctrine of double truth and,
      81–87
  Kant's beliefs of human ability
      to know, 132–33
  Marxism as philosophy of, 290
  modernism and, 206, 212, 215
  nominalism's threat to, *see* nomi-
      nalism
  Plato and, 74–76, 208
University of Paris, 81, 83, 288
  at Vincennes, 296
urban conditions, Industrial Revo-
      lution and, 207
Ussher, Archbishop, 22
Utopianism, 291, 293

Vahinger, Hans, 154–56
Valéry, Paul, 272–73, 278
Van Gogh, Vincent, 269
Vargish, Thomas, 270
Vernant, Jean-Pierre, 53, 54
Vico, 219
Victorian era, 13, 23, 30, 32, 85, 264
  artificiality of, 180
  boredom in, 209–10
  fear of social explosion in Eng-
      land, 181–82
  historical outlook of, 211–12
  literature of, 182–83
  simplification of truth in, 113
  state of urban areas in, 207
Vietnam War, 273
violence as tool of social better-
      ment, 177, 184

Vishnevskaya, Galina, 287
Vivante, Paolo, 45
Voltaire, 116, 121
Voluntarism, 83, 84, 89
von Helmholtz, Hermann, 27

Wagner, Cosima, 162
Wagner, Richard, 168, 170
Wallace, Alfred, 18
Wallis, John, 117
Watt, Ian, 216, 217
Waugh, Evelyn, 167
Welles, Orson, 12–13
Wenzel, Emil, 17
Wesleyanism, 113
Western Marxism, 291–98
What Is Literature (Sartre), 256–57
Wheelwright, Philip, 49
Whig revolution of 1689, English,
      120
White, Allon, 215, 219
Wild Duck, The (Ibsen), 182–83
Wilde, Alan, 166, 167
Wilde, Oscar, 166, 168, 173, 180,
      203, 205, 206, 207, 209, 221
will:
  bad, 150
  Fichte on, 152
  free will, *see* free will
  good, 138, 139, 141–42, 143
  myths and, 185
  Nietzche on, 157
  Schopenhauer's view of, 152–53
  Sorel's beliefs about the collec-
      tive, 174
Wings of the Dove, The (James), 219
Wittgenstein, Ludwig, 77, 82, 235,
      272, 276
  background of, 237
  critics of, 244
  dishonesty, feeling about,
      236–37, 249
  language games and, 77, 235–36,
      241–48
  Philosophical Investigations, 241

Wittgenstein, Ludwig (*continued*)
   Tractatus Logico-Philosophicus, 238,
     240, 246
Woolf, Virginia, 181, 203–4, 302
words, *see* language, words
World War I, 154, 175, 273

Wycliffe, John, 78

Xenephon, 67

Zeus, 44, 53–54

About the Author

Jeremy Campbell is the Washington correspondent for *The Evening Standard*. He is a graduate of Oxford University and lives in Washington, D.C., with his wife, Pandra.